Starting an Etsy® Business

FOR DUMMIES®
A Wiley Brand

2nd Edition

by Kate Gatski, Kate Shoup, and Allison Strine

FOR DUMMIES®
A Wiley Brand

Starting an Etsy® Business For Dummies®, 2nd Edition

Published by: John Wiley & Sons, Inc., 111 River Street, Hoboken, NJ 07030-5774, www.wiley.com

Copyright © 2013 by John Wiley & Sons, Inc., Hoboken, New Jersey

Published simultaneously in Canada

For general information on our other products and services, please contact our Customer Care Department within the U.S. at 877-762-2974, outside the U.S. at 317-572-3993, or fax 317-572-4002. For technical support, please visit www.wiley.com/techsupport.

Wiley publishes in a variety of print and electronic formats and by print-on-demand. Some material included with standard print versions of this book may not be included in e-books or in print-on-demand. If this book refers to media such as a CD or DVD that is not included in the version you purchased, you may download this material at http://booksupport.wiley.com. For more information about Wiley products, visit www.wiley.com.

Library of Congress Control Number: 2013942767

ISBN 978-1-118-59024-9 (pbk); ISBN 978-1-118-59009-6 (ebk); ISBN 978-1-118-59013-3 (ebk); ISBN 978-1-118-59021-8 (ebk)

Manufactured in the United States of America

10 9 8 7 6 5 4 3 2 1

Contents at a Glance

Introduction 1

Part I: Getting Started with Etsy 5

Chapter 1: Handmade for Each Other: Falling in Love with Etsy............................7
Chapter 2: Let's Get This Party Started: Signing Up 17
Chapter 3: There's No Place Like Home: Discovering Etsy's Home Page.................25
Chapter 4: Account Trackula: Navigating Your Etsy Account and Shop Settings...39
Chapter 5: Buy and Buy: Finding and Purchasing Items on Etsy.........................51
Chapter 6: Safe Word: Maintaining Privacy and Safety on Etsy.........................65

Part II: If You Build It, They Will Come: Setting Up Your Etsy Shop 77

Chapter 7: Sell Coverage: Understanding What You Can and Can't Sell on Etsy 79
Chapter 8: Come on In! Creating an Eye-Catching Storefront 85
Chapter 9: Policy Academy: Establishing Your Shop's Policies 115
Chapter 10: Come on Down, the Price Is Right! Pricing Your Work 127

Part III: She Sells Seashells (and More): Understanding the Etsy Selling Process 139

Chapter 11: Say Cheese! Photographing Your Wares 141
Chapter 12: Word Up: Composing Engaging Titles and Descriptions.....................165
Chapter 13: Selling Like (Burning Hot) Hotcakes: Listing Your Items 177
Chapter 14: Wrap It Up: Closing the Deal 199
Chapter 15: The Ship Hits the Fan: Shipping Your Items.................................209

Part IV: All Up in Your Bidness: Handling Business Matters 227

Chapter 16: High Exposure: Marketing Your Etsy Business.................................229
Chapter 17: You've Been Served: Providing Excellent Customer Service 247
Chapter 18: Business as Usual: Managing Your Etsy Store 269

Part V: Commune System: Exploring the Etsy Community 291

Chapter 19: Community Building: Joining the Etsy Community 293

Chapter 20: OMG, Did You Hear? Keeping Up with Etsy News 313

Chapter 21: A Love-Love Relationship: Showing
Your Love for Other Etsy Sellers 323

Chapter 22: Help! Getting It When You Need It 335

Part VI: The Part of Tens 343

Chapter 23: Ten Terrific Tips for Etsy Sellers 345

Chapter 24: Ten Strategies for Marketing Your Etsy Shop 349

Index 353

Table of Contents

Introduction 1

    About This Book 1
    Foolish Assumptions 2
    Icons Used in This Book 2
    Beyond the Book 3
    Where to Go from Here 3

Part 1: Getting Started with Etsy 5

    Chapter 1: Handmade for Each Other: Falling in Love with Etsy 7
        Handmade Crusade: Understanding Etsy's
        Purpose and Business Model 7
        World Up: Introducing the World of Etsy 9
            Upper register: Registering with Etsy 9
            Homeward bound: Navigating the Etsy home page 9
            Let us account the ways: Understanding
            Your Account and Your Shop 11
            For sale by artist: Discovering what's for sale on Etsy 13
            Safety first: Ensuring your safety on Etsy 13
        Storefront and Center: Setting Up Your Storefront 14
        Sell's Angels: Surveying the Etsy Selling Process 15
        Takin' Care of Business: Handling Business Matters 15
        Community Collage: Engaging in the Etsy Community 16

    Chapter 2: Let's Get This Party Started: Signing Up. 17
        Sign Me Up! Becoming a Registered User 17
            All about you: Submitting necessary info
            and confirming your account 18
            Signing away your firstborn: Reviewing the Terms of Use 21
        It's a Sign: Signing In 23

    Chapter 3: There's No Place Like Home:
    Discovering Etsy's Home Page 25
        Home Sweet Home: Viewing Etsy's Home Page 25
        Hitting the Links: Exploring the Links at the Top of the Page ... 27
        Tonight's Headerliner: Exploring the Header Bar 29
        Just Browsing: Browsing Etsy 31

Pick Me! Pick Me! Checking Out Handpicked Items 31
Finders, Keepers: Signing Up for Daily Finds 32
How Do I Love Thee? Let Me Count the Ways:
    Exploring More Ways to Shop.. 33
        Categories 33
        Gift Cards 33
        Colors 34
        Treasury 34
        Shop Local 35
        People Search 35
        Prototypes 35
Baby, You're a Star: Checking Out the Featured Shop 36
The Velvet Blog: Reading Recent Blog Posts 36
Ooh, I Want That! And That! And That! Viewing Recently Listed Items 37
Go Mobile: Exploring Etsy Mobile 37

**Chapter 4: Account Trackula: Navigating
Your Etsy Account and Shop Settings 39**

Total Access: Accessing Your Account 39
Final Accountdown: Checking Out Options under Your Account........... 40
    Buy crazy: Tracking your Etsy purchases 40
    Baby got feedback: Checking your feedback 41
    Public eye: Viewing your public profile 41
    Revision quest: Revising your account settings 42
    Appy ending: Tracking your Etsy apps 43
    Go proto: Exploring Etsy Prototypes 44
    Head case: Viewing reported cases 44
Shop Girl: Familiarizing Yourself with Your Etsy Shop Settings 44
    Listful thinking: Managing item listings 46
    Order up: Handling sold items 46
    I'm just a bill: Viewing your Etsy bill 47
    Bump, setting, spike: Changing shop settings 48
    Go through the promotions: Promoting your shop 49

Chapter 5: Buy and Buy: Finding and Purchasing Items on Etsy 51

Gimme One Reason: Understanding Why You Should Buy on Etsy........ 51
Go Fish: Using Etsy's Search Tool 52
Transactions Speak Louder Than Words:
    Delving into Transaction Details.................................... 54
        Affairs of the cart: Adding an item to your cart and checking out... 54
        Pays of our lives: Paying for your item 57
        Submissionary position: Submitting your order.................. 59
Feedback Is Forever: Leaving Feedback After You Buy........................ 60
Case in Point: Lodging a Case Against a Seller 62

Chapter 6: Safe Word: Maintaining Privacy and Safety on Etsy 65

Oh, Behave! Adhering to Etsy's Do's and Don'ts 65

Private Party: Guarding Your Privacy on Etsy 66

Privacy, please: Understanding Etsy's Privacy Policy 67

Leave me alone! Changing your privacy settings 67

Close sesame: Choosing a strong password 68

Safe Passage: Keeping Yourself Safe on Etsy 70

Scam I am: Avoiding scams on Etsy 70

Safety dance: Staying safe in Etsy's public places 71

Security guard: Making your account more secure 72

Always use protection! Using Etsy's Seller Protection program ... 73

Brooklyn, We Have a Problem: Reporting Issues to Etsy 75

**Part II: If You Build It, They Will Come:
Setting Up Your Etsy Shop 77**

**Chapter 7: Sell Coverage: Understanding
What You Can and Can't Sell on Etsy 79**

Yes, We Can! Figuring Out What You Can Sell on Etsy 80

The handmaid's tale: Selling handmade items 80

Oldies but goodies: Offering vintage items 81

Supplies and demand: Selling supplies 81

Just Say No! Understanding What's Not Allowed on Etsy 82

Achtung, baby: Knowing what items are prohibited 82

Service says: Selling only certain services 83

Off with Their Heads! Knowing What Happens If You Break a Rule 84

Chapter 8: Come on In! Creating an Eye-Catching Storefront 85

On Your Mark: Getting Started 86

Mind Your Banners: Adding a Banner to Your Shop Page 89

Title Wave: Adding a Shop Title and Announcement 92

Section Leader: Setting Up Sections 95

Money Talks: Setting Up Payment Options 96

Exam cram: Examining your options 97

Preferential treatment: Specifying your preferences 98

Bill Me: Setting Up Your Credit Card 101

High Profile: Setting Up Your Public Profile 102

All About Me: Adding an About Page 106

Biohazard: Writing a Winning Bio or Shop Story 112

Quiz show: Starting with a few essential questions 112

The tweak shall inherit the Earth: Tweaking your first draft 113

Extra! Extra! Adding a few extras 114

Team Edit-ward: Editing Your Shop Settings 114

Chapter 9: Policy Academy: Establishing Your Shop's Policies 115

Fair and Square: General Policy Tips 116
Financial Matters: Establishing Payment-Related Policies...................116
Ship Shape: Establishing Your Shipping Policies 118
Return to Sender: Handling Returns and Exchanges 119
Policy Wonk: Setting Up Your Shop Policies Page 120
    Introductory offer: Introducing the sections 120
    Population control: Populating the page.......................................123

Chapter 10: Come on Down, the Price Is Right! Pricing Your Work 127

Formulaic Plot: Breaking Down Your Pricing Formulas 128
    Material girl: Calculating the cost of materials 128
    Labor pains: Figuring labor costs 128
    Heads up: Adding up overhead...130
    Two-timer: Understanding the "times 2" 130
    Double or nothing: Pricing for wholesale and retail 131
    Some assembly required: Putting it all together 132
Eyes on the Price: Evaluating Your Prices 133
    Know thy enemy: Assessing your competition's pricing.............133
    Here's looking at you, kid: Studying your target market 135
    Floor it: Figuring out how to lower your prices 135
    Up the ante: Knowing when to raise your prices..........................136
Something Old: Special Considerations for Pricing Vintage Items 137
How Low Can You Go? Pricing for Sales..138

Part III: She Sells Seashells (and More): Understanding the Etsy Selling Process...................... 139

Chapter 11: Say Cheese! Photographing Your Wares 141

I'll Take That-a-One! Choosing a Camera with the Right Features 142
    Key club: Identifying key camera features....................................142
    Feature story: Considering extra features 143
In Style: Styling Your Photos..144
    Background check: Using backgrounds..145
    Prop it like it's hot: Working with props.......................................147
    Model citizens: Using live models...149
Lighting Bug: Lighting Your Shot...151
    She's a natural! Using natural light 151
    Dark matter: Avoiding the dark..151
    SPF 50: Avoiding direct sunlight 151
    Time to reflect: Using reflectors 153

Compose Yourself: Composing Your Shot 154
    For starters: Trying basic composition principles 155
    Third's-eye view: Applying the rule of thirds................................157
Focus, People! Focusing Your Image...158
Shoot, Shoot, and Shoot Some More: Taking Lots of Pictures 159
Clean-up on Image Five: Tidying Up Your
    Photos with Image-Editing Software.......................................160
    Expose yourself: Adjusting your photo's exposure and color.....161
    Crop circles: Cropping your photo..163

Chapter 12: Word Up: Composing Engaging Titles and Descriptions...165

Headline Muse: Writing Titillating Item Titles 165
Story Time: Telling a Story with Your Item Description.........................166
    Likely story: Uncovering your item's story 167
    Description prescription: Describing your item............................167
    Write away: Composing your item description 169
SEO Speedwagon: Using Search Engine Optimization to Drive Traffic ...170
    Keyword to your mother: Choosing the best keywords................170
    What you key is what you get: Using SEO with
        your item title and description......................................174
    Tag, you're it! Understanding tags..175
Proofread, Please! Proofreading Your Item Title and Listing 176

Chapter 13: Selling Like (Burning Hot) Hotcakes: Listing Your Items...177

Lister, Lister: Listing a New Item 177
    Ready, set, go! Starting the listing process...................................178
    About face: Filling in item information..180
    Vary cool: Adding listing variations 180
    Picture this: Uploading images of your item 181
    Description prescription: Describing your item............................182
    Getting specific: Adding the recipient, occasion, and style 183
    It's in the tag: Tagging your item 184
    Sales figures: Adding selling information for your item.................184
    The reviews are in! Reviewing your listing...................................185
Ch-Ch-Ch-Ch-Changes: Editing a Listing 188
Copycat: Copying a Listing...191
Renewable Resources: Renewing a Listing 191
    Don't be a sellout: Renewing a sold listing.................................192
    Stay active: Renewing an active listing 192
    Expiration mark: Renewing an expired listing 194
Pull the Plug: Deactivating a Listing..195
Rearrange Your Face: Rearranging Your Etsy Shop.................................196
    Be an enabler: Enabling the Rearrange Your Shop feature 196
    Get moving! Moving your listings 197
    Feature comforts: Featuring an item in your Etsy shop 198

Chapter 14: Wrap It Up: Closing the Deal 199

You've Got Sale: Finding Out You Have a Sale 199
Baby Got Track: Keeping Track of Sales in Your Account 201
Guided by Invoices: Handling Invoices 202
Show Me the Money: Receiving Payment 206

Chapter 15: The Ship Hits the Fan: Shipping Your Items 209

The Right (Packaging) Stuff: Obtaining Shipping Supplies 209
Package Deal: Showing Your Love and Care with Packaging.................210
Wrapper's delight: Wrapping any kind of item safely 211
Nice package! Using attractive, brand-friendly packaging 211
Goody-goody: Including extras in your parcel 212
Ship Shop: Choosing a Shipping Carrier 214
Stay First Classy: Surveying Shipping Options 214
Crafters without Borders: Shipping Internationally...............................216
Ship Happens: Creating a Shipping Profile 217
Insure Thing: Insuring Your Parcel 220
Print It to Win It: Printing Shipping Labels on Etsy..............................220
Deliverance: Sending Your Package on Its Merry Way 225
Marky Mark: Marking the Item As Shipped in Etsy 225

Part IV: All Up in Your Bidness: Handling Business Matters 227

Chapter 16: High Exposure: Marketing Your Etsy Business 229

Brandy, You're a Fine Girl: Building Your Brand....................................229
Tag lady: Composing a tagline 231
Loco for logos: Creating a logo 231
Integrate expectations: Working your brand into all you do 232
Poetry in Promotion: Using Etsy Tools to Promote Your Shop............232
Search party: Using Etsy Search Ads 232
Coupon d'état: Creating coupons 235
Badge to the bone: Creating an Etsy shop badge and hosting
an Etsy Mini..238
Save Facebook: Promoting your Etsy shop on social media..........242
Go Postal: Sending an E-mail Newsletter 245

Chapter 17: You've Been Served: Providing Excellent Customer Service 247

Let's Talk: Communicating with a Buyer Before, During,
and After a Transaction 247
Questionable behavior: Answering customer questions...............249
Mind your manners: Giving thanks..250
Ship happens: Double-checking the shipping address 252
Get a clue: Finding out how they found you....................................254

Lost in translation: Communicating with foreign buyers 254
Sample shout-out: Covering all the bases
    in one short, pleasant message 254
Speed Is of the Essence: Shipping It Quickly 255
Feedback Is Good: Leaving Feedback Promptly and Prompting for It 255
Bungle Fever: Handling a Bungled Transaction
    and Other Tough Issues 257
Hand it over: Prompting a buyer to pay up 257
Lost Etsy: Dealing with lost shipments 258
Case study: Dealing with a reported case 259
Refundsal, Refundsal, give back your fare: Issuing refunds 261
Tropic of cancel: Canceling an order 264
The customer is usually right(ish): Dealing
    with a difficult customer 266
No shirt, no shoes, no service: Refusing service to a buyer 266

Chapter 18: Business as Usual: Managing Your Etsy Store 269

I'm Just a Bill: Paying Your Etsy Bill 269
Taxing Matters: Appeasing Uncle Sam 273
To tax or not to tax: Collecting sales tax 273
Drawn and quartered: Paying quarterly income tax 274
Write this off: Determining tax deductions 275
Recording Artist: Keeping Accurate Records 276
Don't Be a Tool: Using Etsy Tools to Manage Your Shop 278
We need those numbers, stat! Viewing Shop Stats 278
Statistically speaking: Viewing Customer Service Stats 281
An app a day: Using Etsy apps to run your store 281
Too Legit to Quit: Making Your Business Legit 283
O sole mio: Understanding sole proprietorships 284
Grab your partner, do-sell-do! Getting a
    handle on partnerships 284
LLC Cool J: Looking at limited liability companies 285
Go corporate: Considering corporations 286
Sweet Charity: Handling Charitable Giving 286
The Artist Is Out: Switching to Vacation Mode 287
Hanging It Up: Closing Your Etsy Shop 288

**Part V: Commune System: Exploring
the Etsy Community 291**

Chapter 19: Community Building: Joining the Etsy Community 293

Talk amongst Yourselves: Using Etsy Forums 293
Forum letter: Accessing Etsy forums 294
Postess with the mostess: Viewing and
    responding to posts in a thread 295
Thread Zeppelin: Starting a new thread 299

Go Team! Exploring Etsy Teams 300
   Finders, keepers: Searching for an Etsy team 301
   Sign me up! Joining an Etsy team...303
   Start me up: Starting your own Etsy team.....................................304
Lab Partner: Exploring Etsy's Online Labs....................................308
Event Horizon: Staying Apprised of Etsy Events 309
Miss Manners: Respecting Community Etiquette 310

Chapter 20: OMG, Did You Hear? Keeping Up with Etsy News 313

All the News That's Fit to Print: Exploring Etsy Blogs...........................313
Mail Bonding: Signing Up for Etsy E-mail Newsletters...........................317
   Red-letter day: Sifting through different
     types of e-mail newsletters 318
   Subscription prescription: Subscribing to e-mail newsletters.....319
Social Skills: Staying in Touch Using Social Media.........................321
Proto Baggins: Joining Etsy Prototypes..322

Chapter 21: A Love-Love Relationship:
Showing Your Love for Other Etsy Sellers. .323

Heart and Sold: Hearting on Etsy..323
   A piece of my heart: Hearting items and shops...........................324
   Turn on your heart light: Viewing hearted items and shops 326
   A private matter: Being a secret admirer 327
Follow Me! Following Others on Etsy...328
   Where you lead, I will follow: Following another Etsy member...328
   Circle up: Viewing your Etsy "circle" 329
   Active ingredient: Checking your activity feed............................331
Treasure Island: Creating a Treasury 332

Chapter 22: Help! Getting It When You Need It 335

Search and Rescue: Searching for Help on Etsy 335
That's a FAQ Jack: Accessing Etsy FAQs 338
Getting Personalized Help from the People at Etsy 339
   Forum letter: Using the Etsy Help forum 339
   Life support: Contacting Etsy Support...340

Part VI: The Part of Tens *343*

Chapter 23: Ten Terrific Tips for Etsy Sellers 345

Have a Place for Everything 345
Save Time with Twosies 345
Organize Your Paperwork 346
Use What You Discover from Other Shops 346

Offer Service with a Smile...346
Network, Network, Network..346
Keep a Blog..347
Learn to Say No...347
Never Give In...347
Have Fun! 347

Chapter 24: Ten Strategies for Marketing Your Etsy Shop 349
Offer Tiered Pricing..349
Understand That Giving Begets Giving.......................................349
Provide a Guarantee...350
Consider a Loyalty Program..350
Impose a Deadline 350
Create a Great E-mail Signature 350
Connect with Social Media 351
Make Google Your Best Friend 351
Use Your Items in the Real World 351
Help Your Community 351

Index *353*

Introduction

● ●

Does this sound like you? You hate your day job. You trained as a teacher, but what you really want to do all day is knit. Or maybe you're busy waiting tables, but you dream of starting your own jewelry-making business. Or maybe your background is in law, but what you *really* love is constructing handbags out of gum wrappers. The problem? You've got bills to pay. It's not like people can just ditch their jobs to hand-craft Juicy Fruit purses all day, right?

Wrong. Thanks to Etsy (`www.etsy.com`), plenty of people have done just that: ditched their day jobs to start their own craft businesses, or supplemented their existing incomes by selling their own crafts. And armed with the information in *Starting an Etsy Business For Dummies,* 2nd Edition, you can become one of them!

What's Etsy? Etsy was created in 2005 to help artists and craftspeople sell their handmade wares online. (Since then, Etsy has evolved to allow the sale of vintage items and craft supplies.) Etsy's mission, in its own words, is "to reimagine commerce in ways that build a more fulfilling and lasting world." More precisely, Etsy allows creative types to channel their passion for their craft into their life's work. If your dream is to "make a living making things," then Etsy is for you!

About This Book

Above all, *Starting an Etsy Business For Dummies* is a reference tool. You don't have to read it from beginning to end; instead, you can turn to any part of the book that gives you the information you need when you need it. And you can keep coming back to the book over and over. If you prefer to read things in order, you'll find that the information is presented in a natural, logical progression.

Sometimes we have information that we want to share with you, but it relates only tangentially to the topic at hand. When that happens, we either mark that information with a Technical Stuff icon or place that information in a sidebar (a shaded gray box). Even though it may not be mission critical, we think you'll find it worth knowing. But you don't have to read it if you don't want to.

Within this book, you may note that some web addresses break across two lines of text. If you're reading this book in print and want to visit one of these web pages, simply key in the web address exactly as it's noted in the text, pretending as though the line break doesn't exist. If you're reading this as an e-book, you've got it easy — just click the web address to be taken directly to the web page.

Foolish Assumptions

When writing this book, we assumed that you want to run your Etsy shop as a proper business. Sure, it's possible to build and manage an Etsy shop with minimal effort, but that will yield only minimal results. We assume here that you're serious about making your Etsy shop a success and that you're willing to invest the time and energy to make that happen.

We also generally assume that you reside in the United States. Although most of the information discussed applies regardless of your geographic location, certain tidbits — such as matters related to taxation — are specific to U.S. residents.

Icons Used in This Book

Icons are those little pictures you see in the margins throughout this book, and they're meant to draw your attention to key points that can help you along the way. Here's a list of the icons we use and what they signify.

When you see this icon in the margin, the paragraph next to it contains valuable information on making your life as an Etsy seller easier.

Some information is so important that it needs to be set apart for emphasis. This icon — like a string tied around your finger — is a friendly reminder of info that you'll want to commit to memory and use over the long haul.

This icon highlights common mistakes that Etsy sellers make and pitfalls to avoid. An important part of achieving success is simply eliminating the mistakes; the information marked by this icon helps you do just that.

This icon highlights information that's interesting but not completely crucial to your life as an Etsy shop owner. If you're crunched for time, feel free to skip information marked with this icon.

Beyond the Book

In addition to the material in the print or e-book you're reading right now, this product comes with some access-anywhere goodies on the web. Check out the free Cheat Sheet at www.dummies.com/cheatsheet/ startinganetsybusiness for tips on creating an eye-catching Etsy storefront, pricing your work, taking beautiful product photos, and more.

Where to Go from Here

Glance through the Table of Contents and find the part, chapter, or section that flips your switch. That's the best place to begin. If you're just trying to get a sense of what's available on Etsy, turn straight to Chapter 5. If you're itching to launch your own Etsy shop, Chapter 8 steps you through the process of building it from scratch. If your shop is up and running but you're not sure how to handle business matters — say, paying taxes or choosing the right structure for your business — then you'll want to flip right to Chapter 18.

When you're finished reading this book, invest some time reading the Etsy Blog (www.etsy.com/blog), reading the Seller Handbook (www.etsy. com/sellerhandbook), and interacting with the larger Etsy community (get started at www.etsy.com/community). As your business grows, you'll undoubtedly encounter issues that this book doesn't discuss; when that happens, you're sure to appreciate these incredible resources.

Part I
Getting Started with Etsy

For Dummies can help you get started with lots of subjects. Visit www.dummies.com to learn more and do more with For Dummies.

In this part . . .

- ✔ Sign up for an Etsy account so you can get started buying and selling.

- ✔ Explore the Etsy home page, where everything starts.

- ✔ Discover the tools available to you for keeping track of your Etsy account and shop.

- ✔ Check out what Etsy has for sale so you can satisfy your inner shopaholic.

- ✔ Get the scoop on staying safe on Etsy and save yourself a whopper of a headache.

Chapter 1

Handmade for Each Other: Falling in Love with Etsy

• •

In This Chapter

▶ Understanding Etsy's purpose and how Etsy makes money

▶ Signing up for (and making your way around) Etsy

▶ Setting up your Etsy shop

▶ Understanding the selling process on Etsy

▶ Running your Etsy business with ease

▶ Exploring the Etsy community

• •

*I*f your goal is to "make a living making things," then Etsy is for you. Etsy was created specifically to enable artists and craftspeople to sell their wares online — "to reconnect makers with buyers." In short, Etsy enables creative types to channel their passion for their craft into their life's work!

In this chapter, we give you a bird's-eye view of Etsy — its purpose and business model, how to sign up for and navigate it, and all sorts of good stuff about opening and running your own shop.

Handmade Crusade: Understanding Etsy's Purpose and Business Model

Many people think of Etsy as a sort of eBay for arts and crafts. And you can see why: People use both Etsy and eBay to buy stuff from other individuals. Also, both sites charge listing fees and make a small commission on every sale. Plus, members use feedback to rate their transactions.

But the sites have big differences, too:

- ✔ Although Etsy is growing — in 2012, the site boasted 22 million registered users spanning the globe and facilitated more than $895 million in transactions — it's still the proverbial mouse to eBay's proverbial elephant.

- ✔ Etsy, which launched in 2005, doesn't use an auction format.

- ✔ Perhaps the biggest difference is that whereas (almost) anything goes on eBay, Etsy was created specifically to enable artists and craftspeople to sell their handmade wares online. (Over time, the site has evolved to also allow the sale of vintage items and craft supplies; find out more about what you can and can't sell on Etsy in Chapter 7.) Etsy itself puts it this way: "Our mission is to reimagine commerce in ways that build a more fulfilling and lasting world. We are a mindful, transparent, and humane business. We plan and build for the long term. We value craftsmanship in all we make. We believe fun should be part of everything we do. We keep it real, always."

So how does Etsy's business model work? Etsy stays afloat by charging sellers a fee for each item listed on the site. At this time, the listing is 20¢ per item. Etsy also collects a commission from the seller for each item sold — currently, 3.5 percent of the total price of the item, not counting shipping. In addition, Etsy collects fees (3 percent of the total price of the item plus an additional 25¢) from shopkeepers who use its handy-dandy Direct Checkout feature, which enables buyers to pay using a credit card or Etsy gift card. These fees, which you can pay using a credit card that you put on file with Etsy or using your PayPal account, are due monthly.

Moniker mystery tour: Probing the secret behind Etsy's name

The origins of Etsy's name are as murky as a drifter's past, but theories abound. Some say that the name Etsy is a play on the Latin phrase *et si,* meaning "and if." Others suggest that the name comes from the Greek *etsi,* meaning "so," "thus," or "in this way." Still others posit that Etsy derives from the Unix directory /etc, pronounced "et-C," or that it's meant to call to mind the word *itsy,* as in "itsy-bitsy," or "cute," which, of course, many items on Etsy are.

Any attempts for clarification by Etsy are met with playful — but misleading — answers by Etsy's staff, ranging from "Etsy is an acronym for Expanded Truncated Structural Y" to "It means 'horny person' in Japanese.'" And although Etsy founder Rob Kalin once insinuated that the answer to this riddle could be found in Fellini's film *8½,* no one has yet managed to solve it.

World Up: Introducing the World of Etsy

Just what can you do on Etsy? And how do you use it? This section scratches the surface.

Upper register: Registering with Etsy

You don't need to register with Etsy to scope out what goodies are for sale. But if you're in the market to buy any of said goodies — or to communicate with other Etsy members or participate in the site's community features, such as its forums, teams, and the like — you need to create an account with the site. Fortunately, creating an account is simple and free. All you need to do is enter your name and e-mail address, and choose a username and password. You don't even need to supply a credit card number!

If you plan to use Etsy to sell your own handmade, vintage, or supply items (and we assume you do, because you're reading this book!), you need to take a few more steps, as well as provide a major credit card (think MasterCard, Visa, Discover, or American Express) and other vitals, such as your address.

For step-by-step coverage of completing the registration process and signing in to your Etsy account, turn to Chapter 2. Chapter 8 covers the steps you need to take to become an Etsy seller.

Homeward bound: Navigating the Etsy home page

Whether you're buying or selling, exploring or researching, Etsy's home page is your home base. It's the page that appears when you go to www.etsy. com. You can also access Etsy's home page from anywhere on the Etsy site by clicking the Etsy logo in the upper-left corner of each page.

The Etsy home page, shown in Figure 1-1, includes several important sections:

- ✔ A set of links and a header bar along the top, which you can click to access various Etsy features

- ✔ Browse categories, Handpicked Items, Recently Listed Items, and More Ways to Shop, which make finding the perfect item a breeze

- ✔ The Featured Seller and Recent Blog Posts sections, which give access to information about exceptional Etsy sellers and other important topics, respectively

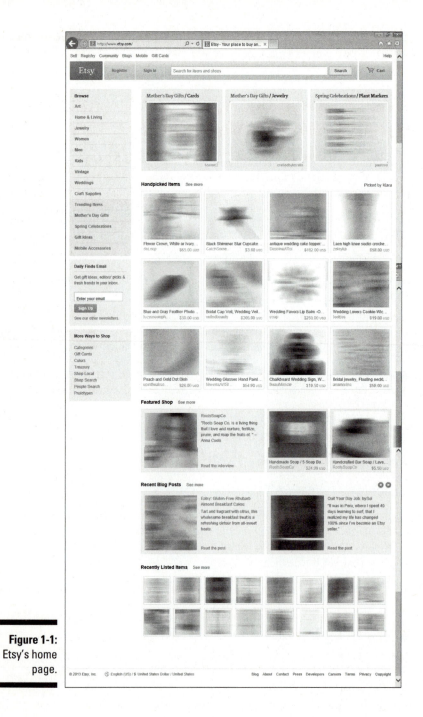

Figure 1-1:
Etsy's home
page.

For more information about these and other home page features, check out Chapter 3.

Let us account the ways: Understanding Your Account and Your Shop

On Etsy, managing your account is easy. Etsy has grouped all the key settings and info in two easy-to-reach places: Your Account (see Figure 1-2) and Your Shop (see Figure 1-3). Your Account and Your Shop, which you access by clicking the Your Account and Your Shop links, respectively, that appear along the top of every Etsy page when you're logged in to your Etsy account, act like instrument panels of sorts. They display all kinds of account-related info — items you've bought, feedback you've received, your public profile, your billing and shipping info, any Etsy-related apps you use, your Etsy bill, items you've listed, and various shop-related settings. For help with navigating Your Account and Your Shop, turn to Chapter 4.

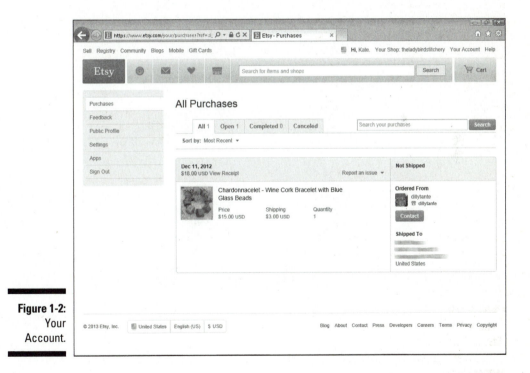

Figure 1-2: Your Account.

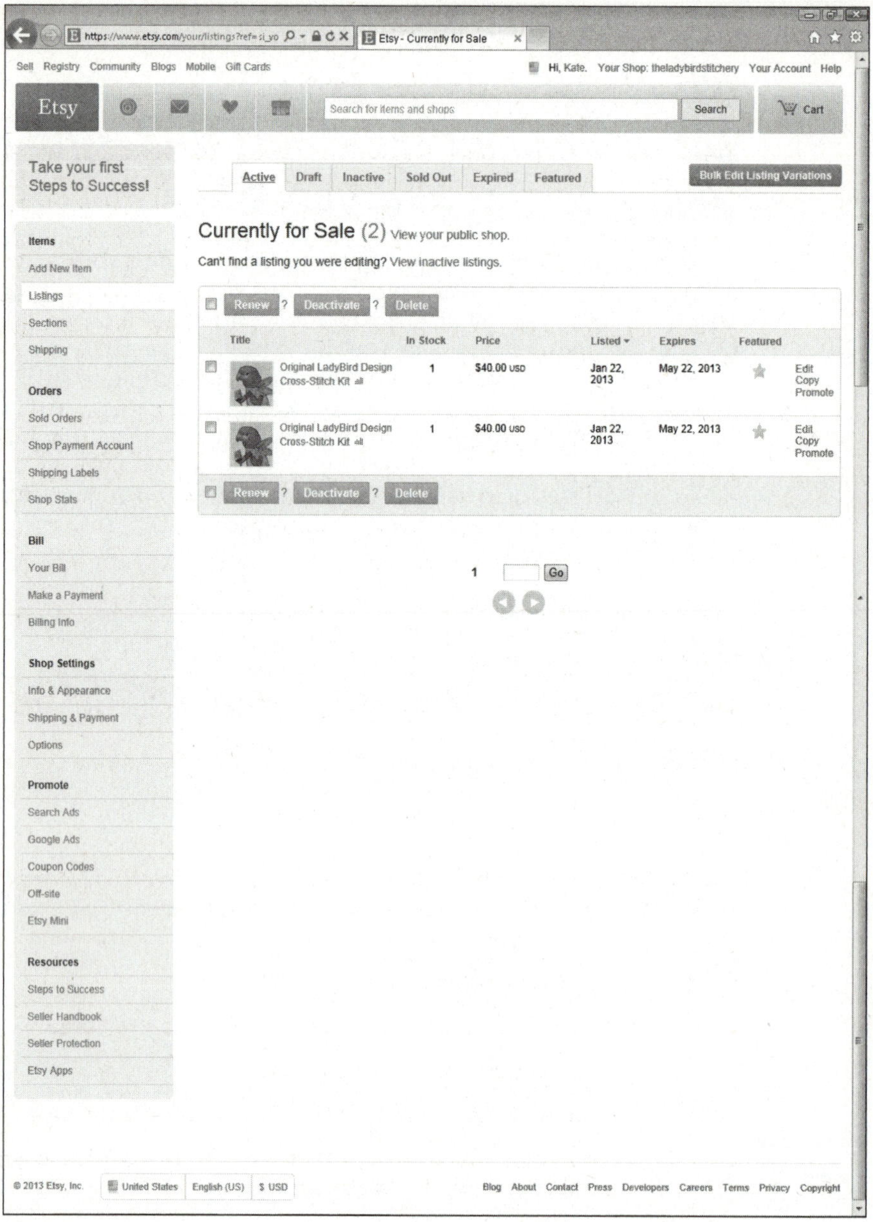

Figure 1-3:
Your Shop.

For sale by artist: Discovering what's for sale on Etsy

Etsy features unique, one-of-a-kind handmade and vintage items — goodies you simply can't find anywhere else — along with supplies for crafting your own pieces. In fact, Etsy offers an incredible breadth of items for sale, from accessories to ceramics, jewelry to quilts, and everything in between. And because there's no middleman — you buy directly from artists and craftspeople — prices on Etsy are generally very reasonable. At the same time, your purchase can enable these skilled artisans to earn a living wage. It's a total win-win!

To help you find a specific item, Etsy supports a robust Search tool. With it, you can search for handmade items, vintage items, and supplies. You can also use the Search tool to locate a particular shop. If you're just browsing, you'll appreciate Etsy's many browsing-related features, including Categories (although rumor has it Etsy will discontinue these), Handpicked Items, Recently Listed items, the Treasury, Shop Local, and more. You access these tools from Etsy's home page. For additional help, turn to Chapter 5.

Safety first: Ensuring your safety on Etsy

No doubt about it, one of the highlights of Etsy is its thriving community of interesting, arty folk. But you may still find an occasional bad apple on the site. Take a few key steps to ensure your safety:

✔ **To make sure that no one accesses your account without your authorization, you must choose a strong password.** Select one that meets all the following criteria:

- It's at least eight characters long.

- It doesn't contain your username or your real name.

- It doesn't contain a complete word.

- It differs from passwords that you've used in the past.

- It contains a mixture of uppercase letters, lowercase letters, numbers, symbols, and spaces.

For an added layer of protection, change your password every so often — say, every 30 to 90 days.

✔ **Be on the lookout for scams.** These often involve the use of money orders or cashier's checks, along with an offer to pay significantly more than is necessary to expedite shipping or to cover some other weird request. If you do get taken on Etsy, contact your financial institution on the double. Then report the situation to Etsy. You may also opt to alert your local law enforcement.

✔ **Before you jump into a forum or team discussion, monitor it for a while.** See whether the Etsians engaged in the discussion are people you really want to interact with. If a discussion goes south, simply disengage. Life's stressful enough — why embroil yourself in a conflict on a site that's supposed to be fun? Oh, and don't share your digits or other personal deets, such as where you live or work, on Etsy's forums or other public spaces. And if you decide to meet up with someone you've met on Etsy in person, pick a neutral, public place; let a friend or family member know about your plans; and be sure to bring a cellphone with you in case you need to call for help.

Chapter 6 covers important safety issues in more detail.

Storefront and Center: Setting Up Your Storefront

When you set up your Etsy storefront, you can personalize it in several ways (and doing so makes a huge difference!):

✔ Uploading a *banner* (a graphic that runs across the top of your shop's page)

✔ Including a shop title and shop announcement to describe your shop

✔ Using sections to organize your goods

✔ Populating your Etsy profile and your shop's About page, and choosing an avatar

As you set up your storefront, keep in mind that a major reason people shop on Etsy is to feel connected to the artists who make what they buy. If you want people to buy from *you,* make sure your Etsy shop reflects your personality! Are you serious? Then your shop should be, too. Ditto if you're whimsical, modern, traditional, edgy, or frilly. Let your personality shine through in your choice of banner, avatar, and other visual elements, as well as in your bio and other text-based elements. Not only will this increase your sales, but it may just help you make some friends along the way. (For more on setting up your Etsy shop, check out Chapter 8.)

Oh, one more pointer: As you set up your Etsy shop, you'll want to clearly lay out your shop policies — how much you charge for shipping, whether you accept returns, and so on. We cover smart policies in Chapter 9.

Sell's Angels: Surveying the Etsy Selling Process

Putting up an item for sale on Etsy is a simple process:

1. **Create the item you're selling and determine how much it costs (with the help of the pointers we provide in Chapter 10).**

2. **Photograph your piece.**

   You can include as many as five pictures of each piece in your Etsy shop. The photos you provide must convey the shape, size, color, and texture of your piece, and also be easy on the eye.

3. **Compose a snappy title and description for your item listing.**

4. **List your item on the site and wait for someone to snatch it up.**

5. **When the item sells, ship it to the buyer (after you receive your payment, of course)!**

Okay, that's a broad overview. Of course, the process has a little more to it, but trust us: It's nothing you can't handle. After you read Part III, you'll be up to speed.

Takin' Care of Business: Handling Business Matters

For some sellers, running an Etsy shop is merely a hobby — a way to make a little extra money on the side. For others, it's their day job, or "what they do." Regardless of which camp you're in, you need to treat your Etsy shop as a proper small business — building a brand, marketing your shop, and providing excellent customer service.

If you're in the latter category — someone who seeks to earn a living by selling on Etsy — you may choose to do even more. For example, you may opt to incorporate your business, obtain a business checking account, streamline your supply chain, use special tools to analyze your business, and so on.

Part IV covers all these topics and more, including how to handle tax matters and pair up with a friend to run an Etsy shop.

Community Collage: Engaging in the Etsy Community

Sure, Etsy is a great place to buy and sell handmade pieces, vintage items, and supplies. But it's more than that: It's a community of creative, crafty people that just begs for participation. Etsy offers several tools that help you jump right in, including these:

- ✔ Public message boards, called *forums*
- ✔ Teams, for connecting with likeminded Etsy members
- ✔ Online Labs, which are special events where Etsy staffers and members run online seminars, workshops, shop critiques, and other educational gatherings

You can also follow your favorite shops and sellers to keep up with their goings-on and more. And you can show your love on the site by "hearting" your beloved items and shops — that is, adding them to your favorites.

Other great resources for the Etsy community include the Etsy Blog (www. etsy.com/blog), which acts as a neighborhood newspaper of sorts. The Etsy Blog, which serves up fresh content daily, boasts material ranging from information to help you perfect various crafting techniques, to glimpses into the lives of other Etsy sellers, and more. In addition, Etsy maintains an Etsy Weddings Blog (www.etsy.com/blog/weddings), an Etsy News Blog (www. etsy.com/blog/news), and a Seller Handbook (www.etsy.com/blog/ en/category/seller-handbook), as well as blogs for members in France, Germany, the Netherlands, and the United Kingdom.

Etsy's e-mail newsletters are another great source of information and inspiration. And if you're among the more than eleventy-jillion people who maintain a Facebook account, you can connect with Etsy there, as well as on Twitter, Pinterest, Tumblr, YouTube, iTunes, and Flickr.

Etsy is super-easy to use, but you'll still need a little help sometimes. Fortunately, Etsy maintains copious resources to help members find answers to all their burning Etsy-related questions, from Help files to an interactive Help forum. Go to www.etsy.com/help for the scoop.

Ready to dive in? Flip to Part V for all the details on engaging in the Etsy community.

Chapter 2

Let's Get This Party Started: Signing Up

In This Chapter

▶ Registering for a basic Etsy account

▶ Signing in to your Etsy account

*F*ather of Taoism Lao Tzu once said, "A journey of a thousand miles begins with one step." (He also said, "Silence is a source of great strength" and "The sage does not hoard"; we're still working on digesting those.) On Etsy, that one first step is becoming a registered user by signing up with the site. After that, you're ready to embark on your own Etsy journey! This chapter gives you all the info you need to register with Etsy.

Sign Me Up! Becoming a Registered User

Anyone can browse Etsy to see what goodies are for sale. But if you're in the market to buy, or if you eventually want to open your own shop, you need to create an account with the site by becoming a registered user. It's easy and free! Just follow the guidelines in this section.

In addition to being able to purchase items on the site, registered users can keep track of their best-loved items or shops by "hearting" them, communicate with other Etsy members, and participate in the site's community features, such as the forums. Flip to Part V for more information about all these options.

All about you: Submitting necessary info and confirming your account

Assuming that you have a computer and an Internet connection, becoming a registered Etsy user is super-easy. Here's what you do:

1. **In your web browser's address bar, type** www.etsy.com **and press Enter or Return.**

   Etsy's main page appears (see Figure 2-1).

2. **Click the Register link in the header bar (refer to Figure 2-1).**

   The registration page appears (see Figure 2-2).

Register link

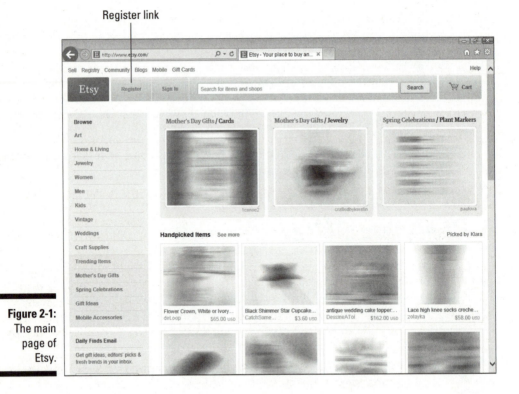

Figure 2-1:
The main page of Etsy.

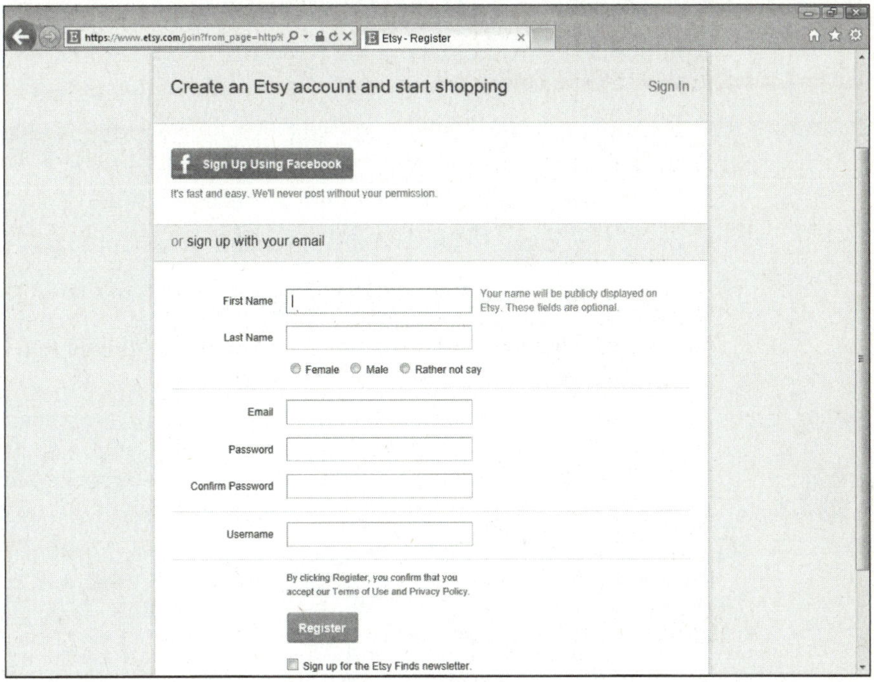

Figure 2-2:
The registration page.

3. **Type your first name in the First Name field and your last name in the Last Name field.**

   Note that filling out these fields is strictly optional. If you do fill them out, your name will be publicly displayed throughout the site. If you want, you can add simply your first name, or a nickname, or your initials — whatever. If you decide to leave both these fields blank, your username is the one that other Etsy users will see.

   If you prefer, you can save a few steps by clicking the Sign Up Using Facebook button to create your Etsy account. If you do, some of your activity on Etsy — for example, when you favorite an item — may be posted on your Facebook page. In the interest of being thorough, this section steps you through signing up for Etsy the old-fashioned way: by entering your info directly on Etsy's site.

4. **Click the Male, Female, or Rather Not Say option button to specify your gender (or not).**

5. **Type your e-mail address in the Email field.**

6. **In the Password field, type the password you want to use to access your Etsy account.**

   Create a password that's at least six characters — one that you can remember easily but that won't be too obvious to anyone else.

7. **Retype the password in the Confirm Password field.**

8. **In the Username field, type the username you want to use on Etsy.**

   This name must contain between 4 and 20 uppercase and/or lowercase letters or numbers (no spaces). Etsy notifies you if someone else has selected your username; if so, try another one until you find one that's available.

   You can't change your username, so make sure that the name you choose is something you can live with as long as you're on Etsy, and that you're cool with everyone you buy from and sell to seeing the username you choose. (In other words, "WinonaForever" might not be the way to go.)

9. **To read the terms of use, click the Terms of Use link, and to read Etsy's Privacy Policy, click the Privacy Policy link.**

   You can find out more about the Terms of Use in the next section. Flip to Chapter 6 for more on Etsy's Privacy Policy.

10. **If you want, select the Sign Up for the Etsy Finds Newsletter check box.**

    If you do, Etsy will send you a daily Etsy Finds newsletter full of fantastic finds on the site. This newsletter is one of several Etsy newsletters available to you; you can find out how to sign up for the rest in Chapter 20.

11. **Click the Register button.**

    Etsy creates your account and sends a confirmation e-mail to the address you supplied in Step 5 (see Figure 2-3).

    If you don't receive the confirmation e-mail right away, check your spam folder to make sure it wasn't intercepted.

12. **Open the e-mail from Etsy and click the link that it contains to confirm your account.**

    You're ready to go! Etsy sends you a second e-mail to officially welcome you to the site.

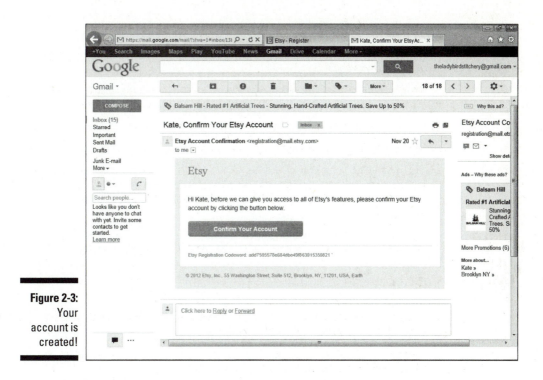

Figure 2-3:
Your
account is
created!

Signing away your firstborn: Reviewing the Terms of Use

Before registering with and using Etsy, take a moment to review the site's Terms of Use (Figure 2-4 shows them in part). To access the Terms of Use after you've already registered, follow these steps:

1. **Click the Help link in the upper-right corner of any Etsy page.**

   The Help page appears.

2. **Click Site Policies.**

   The Site Policies page appears.

3. **On the left side of the page, click Terms of Use.**

Figure 2-4:
Review
Etsy's Terms
of Use.

Etsy / Help Home   Search Help

Site Policies   **Terms of Use**

DOs & DONTs   PLEASE READ THESE TERMS OF USE ("AGREEMENT" OR "TERMS OF USE") CAREFULLY
                             BEFORE USING THE WEBSITE AND SERVICES OFFERED BY ETSY, INC. ("ETSY"). THIS
Terms of Use   AGREEMENT SETS FORTH THE LEGALLY BINDING TERMS AND CONDITIONS FOR YOUR USE
                             OF THE WEBSITE AT HTTP://WWW.ETSY.COM (THE "SITE") AND ALL SERVICES PROVIDED BY
Privacy   ETSY ON THE SITE.

Copyright & IP   By using the Site in any manner, including but not limited to visiting or browsing the Site, you (the "user"
                             or "you") agree to be bound by this Agreement, including those additional terms and conditions and
Fees   policies referenced herein and/or available by hyperlink. This Agreement applies to all users of the Site,
                             including without limitation users who are vendors, customers, merchants, contributors of content,
Direct Checkout   information and other materials or services on the Site.

Trademark Guidelines   If you have any questions, please refer to the Help section of the Site.

API Terms of Use   **1. Etsy is a Venue**
Gift Cards Terms of Use   Etsy acts as a venue to allow users who comply with Etsy's policies to offer, sell and buy certain goods
                             within a fixed-price format. Etsy is not directly involved in the transaction between buyers and sellers.
Billing Policy   As a result, Etsy has no control over the quality, safety, morality or legality of any aspect of the items
                             listed, the truth or accuracy of the listings, the ability of sellers to sell items or the ability of buyers to pay
                             for items. Etsy does not pre-screen users or the content or information provided by users. Etsy cannot
                             ensure that a buyer or seller will actually complete a transaction.

                             Consequently, Etsy does not transfer legal ownership of items from the seller to the buyer.

                             Etsy cannot guarantee the true identity, age, and nationality of a user. Etsy encourages you to
                             communicate directly with potential transaction partners through the tools available on the Site. You
                             may also wish to consider using a third-party escrow service or services that provide additional user
                             verification.

If you're like a lot of people, you're probably wondering why you need to read Etsy's Terms of Use. Here's our answer: Violating any of the policies spelled out in the Terms of Use is grounds for expulsion from the site. The "But I didn't know it was a policy!" defense doesn't fly.

In addition to its Terms of Use, Etsy maintains several other policy-related web pages that you need to read. You can access these web pages from the Site Policies page. These web pages include the following:

✔ **DOs & DON'Ts:** This web page outlines Etsy's expectations with respect to membership, conversations, transactions, feedback, shops and listings, flagging, and community.

✔ **Privacy:** This web page clarifies how Etsy treats personal information that it collects and receives.

✔ **Copyright & IP:** This web page spells out Etsy's policy with respect to copyright and intellectual property (IP) infringement.

✔ **Fees:** This web page gives you the lowdown on Etsy's fees — including listing fees, transaction fees, advertising fees, and payment-processing fees — as well as info on paying your bill and currency conversion.

✔ **Direct Checkout:** In this web page, Etsy spells out the legalese for its Direct Checkout feature. (Direct Checkout is an Etsy payment-processing service that enables sellers to accept credit-card payments directly through Etsy. We explain lots more about Direct Checkout later in this book.)

✔ **Trademark Guidelines:** This web page states Etsy's guidelines for protecting its trademark.

✔ **API Terms of Use:** This web page is probably outside your area of interest. But in case you're curious, it outlines Etsy's policies vis-à-vis its application programming interface (API). If you have some nifty programming skills, and you someday decide you'd like to put them to use by developing an app or tool to work in conjunction with Etsy, you'll want to check out this web page.

✔ **Gift Cards Terms of Use:** This web page spells out the ins and outs of using gift cards on Etsy.

✔ **Billing Policy:** For info about Etsy's billing policy, visit this web page, which covers auto billing and manual billing.

It's a Sign: Signing In

After you've created an account with Etsy, signing in is a snap. Simply go to www.etsy.com and click the Sign In link in the header bar (you can see this link in Figure 2-1 — it's just to the right of the Register link). Then, in the pop-up window that appears, type your e-mail address or username in the Email or Username field, type your password in the Password field, and click the Sign In button (see Figure 2-5).

When you sign in to Etsy, you have the option of selecting the Stay Signed In check box. If you do, you can navigate away from the site and return again without having to sign in.

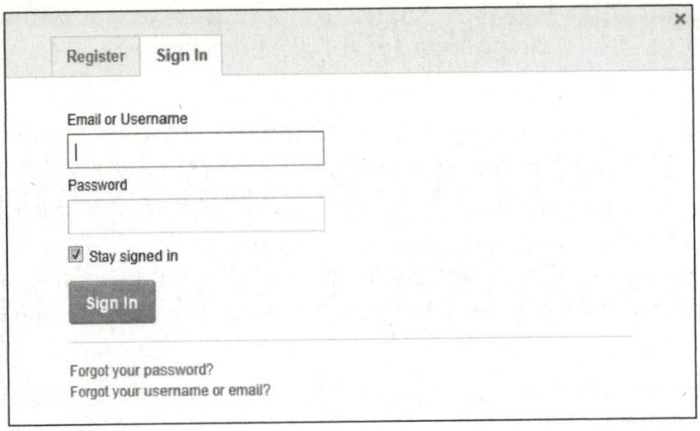

Figure 2-5:
Use your
username
or e-mail
address
and your
password
to sign in to
your Etsy
account.

WARNING!

Don't select this check box if you're on a public computer (for example, at a library or Internet cafe)!

Chapter 3

There's No Place Like Home: Discovering Etsy's Home Page

In This Chapter

▶ Getting an overview of Etsy's home page

▶ Checking out the links and the header bar

▶ Browsing items and viewing handpicked items

▶ Signing up for Daily Finds

▶ Exploring more ways to shop and checking out featured shops

▶ Perusing recent blog posts and recently listed items

*H*ome. It's a word with many meanings. It's where you live. It's where your heart is. It's where you hang your hat. It's where the cows finally come. Simply put, it's a place to which you always long to return.

Etsy's home page is no different. As you use the site, you'll find yourself always returning home — to the home page, that is. Whether you're buying or selling, exploring or researching, Etsy's home page is your home base. In this chapter, you explore the various features of the page and find out how to navigate from it.

Note: If your home page doesn't exactly match what we discuss here, don't freak out. Etsy regularly experiments with the layout of its home page.

Home Sweet Home: Viewing Etsy's Home Page

Etsy's home page is the page that appears when you type **www.etsy.com** into your web browser. You can also access the home page from anywhere on the Etsy site by clicking the Etsy logo in the upper-left corner of each page.

As you can see in Figure 3-1, the Etsy home page includes several important sections:

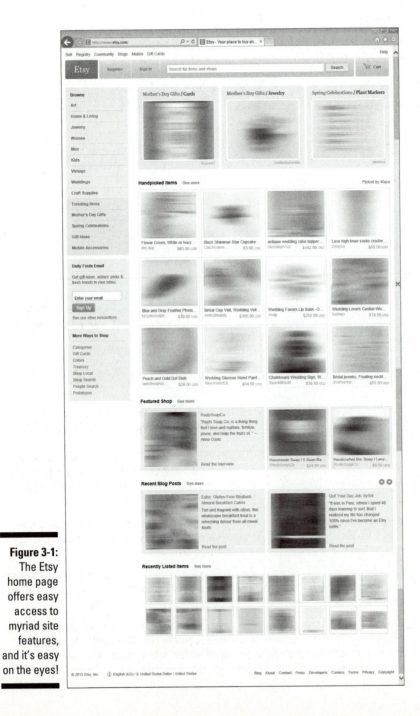

Figure 3-1:
The Etsy home page offers easy access to myriad site features, and it's easy on the eyes!

- ✔ Links
- ✔ Header bar
- ✔ Browse
- ✔ Handpicked Items
- ✔ Daily Finds Email
- ✔ More Ways to Shop
- ✔ Featured Shop
- ✔ Recent Blog Posts
- ✔ Recently Listed Items

We delve into each of these sections in this chapter.

Hitting the Links: Exploring the Links at the Top of the Page

As with many websites, Etsy includes a series of links along the top of its home page to help you navigate the site. Clicking one of these links directs you to the link's associated page on the site.

These links don't appear just on the Etsy home page; they appear on every page on the site. This feature helps make Etsy extremely easy to navigate.

The links that appear vary depending on whether you're signed in to your account. If you're not signed in, you get the following links (see Figure 3-2):

- ✔ **Sell:** For quick access to tools and resources for sellers — including a helpful guide to how fees work and info about what you can and cannot sell on Etsy — click the Sell link. (Parts II through IV of this book are devoted to selling on Etsy.)

- ✔ **Registry:** Planning on getting hitched? Then you'll be thrilled to know that Etsy enables you to create and maintain a wedding registry on the site, which you can access by clicking this link.

- ✔ **Community:** For quick access to Etsy's community features — the teams and forums, as well as a list of upcoming events — click the Community link. Chapter 19 covers the Etsy community in more detail.

- ✔ **Blogs:** The Etsy Blog is accessible from this link. This multifaceted blog plays host to any number of excellent posts relating to the handmade life, ranging from craft how-to's to tips for sellers and beyond.

While we're on the topic of the Etsy Blog, we should also mention a second blog, called the Etsy News Blog, accessible from the main Etsy Blog page. The Etsy News Blog is designed to keep Etsy users up to date on all the changes on the site, among other things.

✔ **Mobile:** If you have an iPhone, iPad, or Android device, you can enjoy Etsy on the go by downloading the Etsy mobile app, accessible from this link.

✔ **Gift Cards:** If you're in a giving mood, you'll love that Etsy offers gift cards, which can be redeemed in any U.S.-based shop that uses Etsy's Direct Checkout system. Available in denominations of $25, $50, $100, and $250, these can be e-mailed directly to the recipient or printed out for an in-person handoff. To purchase a gift card, start by clicking the Gift Card link along the top of any Etsy page.

✔ **Help:** For help with using the site, click the Help link. (We cover the details on getting help in Chapter 22.)

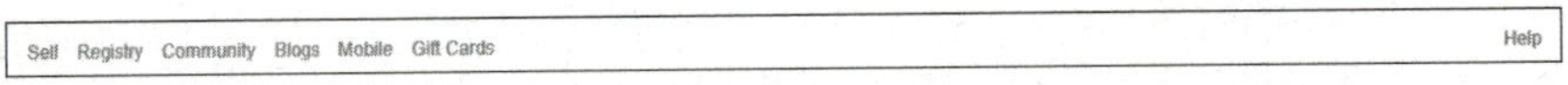

Figure 3-2:
If you aren't signed in to your Etsy account, just a few links are available.

Sell Registry Community Blogs Mobile Gift Cards   Help

If you *are* signed in to your account, you'll see the aforementioned links in addition to the following (see Figure 3-3):

✔ **Hi,** *Your Name:* To view and edit your Etsy user profile, click this link. (For more on editing your user profile, see Chapter 8.)

✔ **Your Shop:** *Your Shop Name:* After you set up your Etsy shop (see Chapter 8), this link offers you instant access to it and to tools that enable you to manage all aspects of it, from listing items to shipping them.

✔ **Your Account:** Access the Your Account page by clicking this link. (You get the scoop on Your Account in Chapter 4.)

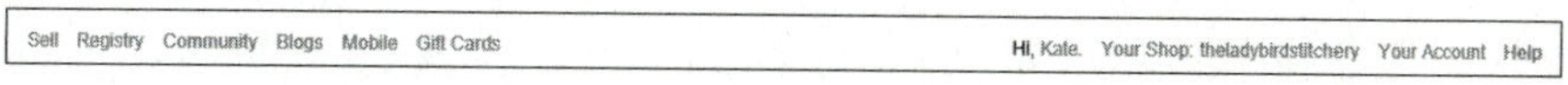

Figure 3-3:
Signing in
to your Etsy
account
gives you
access to
additional
links.

Sell Registry Community Blogs Mobile Gift Cards   Hi, Kate.   Your Shop: theladybirdstitchery   Your Account   Help

Tonight's Headerliner: Exploring the Header Bar

To help you easily and quickly access the tools you need, every Etsy page, including the home page, contains a header bar with several links. As with the links along the top of the page, the appearance of the header bar differs depending on whether you're signed in to your Etsy account. If you're not signed in, the header bar contains the following links (see Figure 3-4):

- ✔ **Etsy:** No matter where you are on the Etsy site, you can return to the home page by clicking the Etsy logo in the header bar.

- ✔ **Register:** Click this link to register with the site (refer to Chapter 2).

- ✔ **Sign In:** To sign in to your account, click this link (see Chapter 2 for more information).

- ✔ **Cart:** Click this link to view items in your shopping cart.

Figure 3-4:
Use the
header bar
to register
or sign in to
the site, as
well as view
items in
your shop-
ping cart.

Etsy   Register   Sign In   Search for items and shops   Search   🛒 Cart

When you sign in to the site, these links replace the Register and Sign In links (see Figure 3-5):

- ✔ **Activity:** If you opt to participate in the Etsy community — for example, by adding items or shops to your Favorites, creating Treasury lists, or following other Etsy members — you'll see evidence of that activity in your Activity Feed, which you access by clicking this button. For more information, see Chapter 21.

- ✔ **Conversations:** A conversation — or convo, if you don't have time for all those extra syllables — is a communication with another member using Etsy's internal messaging system. To view any active convos, click this link. (You find out more about convos in Chapter 17.)

- ✔ **Favorites:** Etsy enables you to bookmark your favorite items as shops by adding them to your Favorites. In Etsy-ese, this is also called *hearting*. To view your Favorites, click this link. For more on hearting, see Chapter 21.

- ✔ **Shop:** Clicking this icon offers quick access to the public-facing side of your Etsy shop, so you can get a quick idea of how the shop looks to your customers.

Figure 3-5:
Use the header bar to access your activity feed, your convos, your favorites, and your Etsy shop.

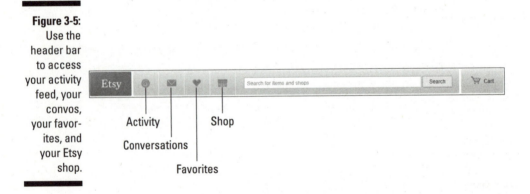

Regardless of whether you're signed in to your Etsy account, the header bar also displays Etsy's Search tool, which you can use to locate handmade items, vintage items, supplies, and shops. If you're signed in, you can also use the Search tool to search among your favorite items and your favorite shops. Simply type a keyword in the Search field and press Enter or Return or click the Search button. (Flip to Chapter 5 for more details on searching.)

Just Browsing: Browsing Etsy

At last count, Etsy featured roughly 850,000 shops. Don't worry, though: The items in these shops are displayed in browse pages, which are organized by broad themes — nine, to be exact, plus a few extra seasonal pages or trending items — so you can easily find what you're looking for. As shown in Figure 3-6, the themes include Art, Home & Living, Jewelry, Women, Men, Kids, Vintage, Weddings, and Craft Supplies. The extra pages in Figure 3-6 are Trending Items, Mother's Day Gifts, Spring Celebrations, Gift Ideas, and Mobile Accessories. Clicking a theme (on the left side of the home page) reveals a browse page featuring items in that theme, along with several clickable subcategories to help you narrow the field. Whether you're after a bit of jewelry or some vintage awesomeness, Etsy's browse pages can help you find the item that's just right.

Figure 3-6: Browse pages, which you access from these links, offer a great way to find goodies on Etsy.

Browse
Art
Home & Living
Jewelry
Women
Men
Kids
Vintage
Weddings
Craft Supplies
Trending Items
Mother's Day Gifts
Spring Celebrations
Gift Ideas
Mobile Accessories

Pick Me! Pick Me! Checking Out Handpicked Items

The Handpicked Items section of Etsy's home page, shown in Figure 3-7, features goodies assembled into a Treasury list by a fellow Etsy user. (You find out more about Treasury lists later in this chapter.) Etsy staffers then pluck this Treasury list from obscurity and plant it front and center on the site's home page. Often these items, which change several times a day, center on a particular color, style, holiday, or theme. If you're just browsing, the Handpicked Items section represents a great launching point.

Figure 3-7:
You'll find plenty to drool over in the Handpicked Items section of Etsy's home page.

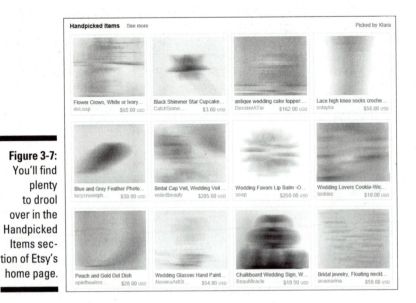

Finders, Keepers: Signing Up for Daily Finds

If you want to receive Etsy's daily e-mail that's chock-full of goodies for sale on the site, click the Sign Up button under Daily Finds Email (see Figure 3-8). Click the See Our Other Newsletters link to sign up for additional newsletters, such as Etsy Fashion, Etsy Weddings, Etsy Dudes — the list goes on. (Flip to Chapter 20 for full details on getting Etsy news.)

Figure 3-8:
Signing up for the Etsy Finds newsletter is a snap.

Daily Finds Email

Get gift ideas, editors' picks & fresh trends in your inbox.

Sign Up

See our other newsletters.

How Do I Love Thee? Let Me Count the Ways: Exploring More Ways to Shop

Remember in *When Harry Met Sally* . . . how Sally had her own unique way of ordering at a restaurant? "I just want it the way I want it," she explained. The same is true with shopping on Etsy. Not everyone wants to do it in the same way! Fortunately, Etsy offers several tools to enhance your shopping experience, located in the More Ways to Shop area of the site's home page (see Figure 3-9).

Figure 3-9:
There's
more than
one way
to shop on
Etsy.

More Ways to Shop

Categories
Gift Cards
Colors
Treasury
Shop Local
Shop Search
People Search
Prototypes

Categories

In addition to organizing items into browse pages, Etsy enables sellers to put them into categories — 31 in all (see Figure 3-10) — so you can easily find what you're looking for. To access these categories, click the Categories link under More Ways to Shop. Then, in the Categories page, click a category or subcategory to winnow your options. (Note that according to Etsy, Categories may soon go to the wayside. But as of this writing, they're a thing.)

Gift Cards

As mentioned earlier in this chapter, Etsy sells gift cards in a variety of denominations — $25, $50, $100, and $250. To buy one, you can click the Gift Cards link under More Ways to Shop, in the same way you can click the Gift Cards link above the Etsy header bar.

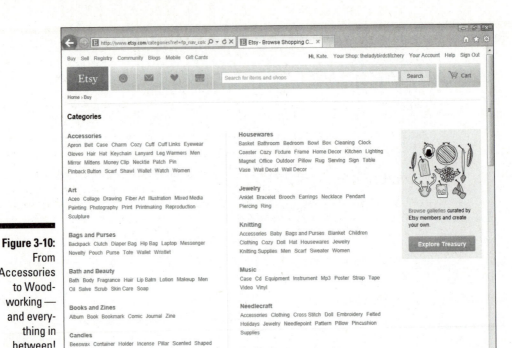

Colors

If you're looking to find the perfect bejeweled complement for your chartreuse-hued smoking jacket, check out Etsy's Color tool. With this tool, you simply click a color on the palette to view random items for sale in that color.

When you list an item in your Etsy shop, you can apply a "color" tag to it. So, if the item is predominately puce, you can add a "puce" tag. You find out more about tagging the items you list in Chapter 13.

Treasury

Etsy's vast community of members is a great resource for finding amazing items for sale on the site. To tap into this community, visit the Etsy Treasury. There, you'll find what Etsy describes as an "ever-changing, member-curated shopping gallery" composed of lists of items. These Treasury lists, which contain 16 items each, may focus on a particular color or theme — think pink!

Or Africa! Or *Battlestar Galactica!* — or they may simply contain that member's favorite Etsy finds. The Treasury, which is searchable, isn't meant for self-promotion. Instead, its purpose, according to Etsy's Help information, is to enable members to "acknowledge and share the many cool things for sale on Etsy." You discover how to create your own Treasury in Chapter 21.

Shop Local

Everyone knows how important shopping local is. For starters, it keeps money and jobs in your community. In addition, because the seller ships your item only across town instead of across the country, buying local blunts your impact on the planet.

It likely comes as no surprise that an organization like Etsy is hip to the whole "shop local" thing. Its Shop Local feature displays the most recently updated shops in your area. With Shop Local, you can find — and buy from — Etsy sellers right in your hometown. Just enter your town and state in the search field (if it's not pulled automatically from the info you supplied to Etsy when you signed up for an account) and what you're looking for. Easy!

To ensure that your shop appears in Shop Local, you must enter your hometown in your user profile. To find out how, turn to Chapter 8.

People Search

Suppose your neighbor just opened an Etsy shop, and you're dying to check it out. The only problem is, you forgot what she named her shop! Fortunately, Etsy enables you to search for other members on the site — shop owners and non–shop owners alike. Simply click the People Search link under Ways to Shop, type the name of the person you seek, and — *voilà!* — Etsy returns a list of members with matching names, with links to their profiles and shops (assuming they have one).

Prototypes

Your guess is as good as ours as to why Etsy included a link to its Prototypes program under Ways to Shop. But if you're interested in joining an Etsy Prototype, you can access them by clicking this link. For more on Prototypes, see Chapter 20.

Baby, You're a Star: Checking Out the Featured Shop

Every two days or so, Etsy staffers introduce a new featured shop — one that displays ingenuity, sells well-made items, and populates each listing with interesting descriptions and top-notch photos. The featured shop appears on Etsy's home page (see Figure 3-11), with a link to an interview with the proprietor of that shop and to item listings in it.

Figure 3-11: See who's making noise on Etsy with the Featured Shop feature.

 If you're just starting out on Etsy, reading up on the featured shop is a great way to ferret out tips and tricks for becoming a successful seller — not to mention be totally inspired!

The Velvet Blog: Reading Recent Blog Posts

To view new blog posts at a glance, scroll down to the Recent Blog Posts section of Etsy's home page (see Figure 3-12). There, you'll find headlines from newly posted content on the Etsy Blog. If you see a headline that looks interesting, click it to read the post. To view additional headlines, click the arrow buttons. Click the See More link to land on the main page for the Etsy Blog (which we describe in more detail in Chapter 20).

Figure 3-12:
Keep up with the Etsy Blog at a glance.

Ooh, I Want That! And That! And That! Viewing Recently Listed Items

As sellers list new items, some of those items appear in the Recently Listed Items section of the Etsy home page (see Figure 3-13). If you're looking to land the very latest goodies, or if you just want to get a sense of how active the site is, park your eyeballs here for a few minutes and prepare to be amazed. To see more recently listed items, click the See More link.

Figure 3-13:
Don't be surprised to find yourself mesmerized by the constantly updated, recently listed items.

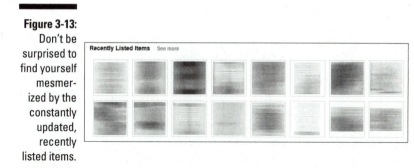

Go Mobile: Exploring Etsy Mobile

Of course, you don't want to be tied to your computer to get the latest on Etsy. That's where Etsy Mobile comes in. If you have an iPhone, iPad, or Android device, you can download Etsy Mobile from the Apple App Store (iPhone and iPad) or Google Play (Android), install the app on your device, and access Etsy while you're on the go. Although you can't use Etsy Mobile to view Etsy's blogs (or, if you're using an iPhone or iPad, to interact in Etsy's teams or forums), you can use it to browse the marketplace, find gifts, and more (see Figure 3-14). It's a great tool if you want to unshackle yourself from your desk and venture out into the wide world!

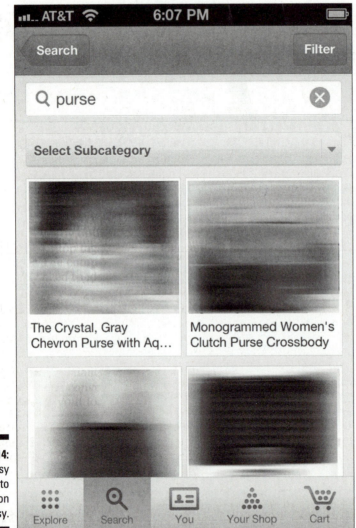

Figure 3-14:
Use Etsy
Mobile to
shop on
Etsy.

Chapter 4

Account Trackula: Navigating Your Etsy Account and Shop Settings

In This Chapter
▶ Opening the Your Account page
▶ Opening the Your Shop page
▶ Tracking purchases, dealing with feedback, and tackling other account-related tasks

Managing your Etsy account is super easy. Why? Because Etsy has gathered all the key settings and info in two easy-to-reach places: Your Account and Your Shop. Your Account and Your Shop act like dashboards, giving you access to all manner of account-related info. Your Account helps you keep track of items you've bought, feedback you've received, your public profile, your billing and shipping info, any Etsy-related apps you use, and any cases in which you're involved. In addition, if you've joined any Etsy prototype teams, those appear here. Your Shop is where you find all your shop-related stuff — current listings, sold orders, your Etsy bill, shop settings, tools for promoting your shop, and handy seller resources. In this chapter, you find out about the ins and outs of Your Account and Your Shop.

Total Access: Accessing Your Account

After you sign in (following the instructions in Chapter 2), you can access Your Account with one click of the mouse, on the Your Account link that appears on every Etsy page. When you click this link, you'll see a page like the one shown in Figure 4-1, listing any purchases you've made on the site (assuming you've made one). As you can see, various links run along the left side of the page; read on to find out where they lead.

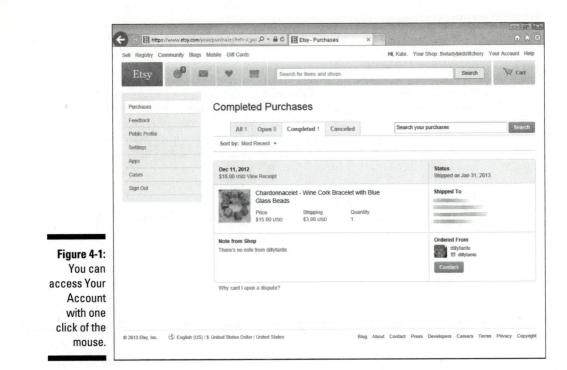

Figure 4-1:
You can
access Your
Account
with one
click of the
mouse.

Final Accountdown: Checking Out Options under Your Account

Etsy groups several account-related settings in one area in Your Account. These include options related to purchases, feedback, your public Etsy profile, settings, Etsy apps, prototypes, and cases. For more info, read on.

Buy crazy: Tracking your Etsy purchases

Anything that you buy on Etsy appears on the Purchases page (refer to Figure 4-1), which appears by default when you click the Your Account link along the top of any Etsy page. You may view your purchased items to review an item's receipt (by clicking the View Receipt link) or to reconnect with a seller (by clicking the Contact button or Shop link by her avatar). (Check out Chapters 14 and 18 for info on invoices, and see Chapter 17 for details on communicating with other folks on Etsy.)

Baby got feedback: Checking your feedback

To get a sense of your rep on Etsy, check out your feedback in Your Account. Simply click the Feedback link along the left side of the Your Account page; then select the Completed Feedback tab to see the scuttlebutt (see Figure 4-2). You can also leave feedback for other members and view appreciation photos in this area of Your Account. (For more on leaving and responding to feedback, check out Chapters 5 and 17.)

Public eye: Viewing your public profile

Your Etsy public profile is just what it sounds like: a page where other Etsians can go to learn all about you and your Etsy shop. Populating your public profile is a big part of running a successful Etsy shop; after all, a big reason people shop on Etsy is to forge a personal connection with the people who make what they buy. You populate your public profile from, well, the Your Public Profile page, shown in Figure 4-3. (You find out all about populating your public profile in Chapter 8.) To access this page, click the Public Profile link on the left side of the Your Account page.

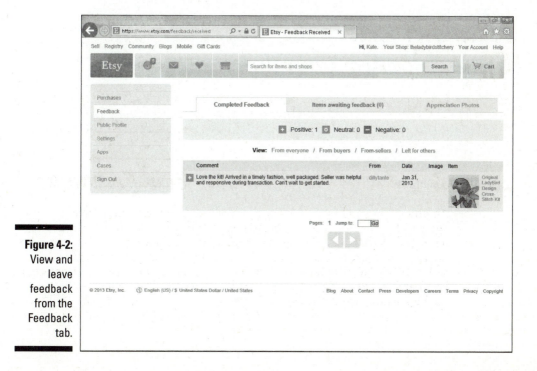

Figure 4-2:
View and leave feedback from the Feedback tab.

Revision quest: Revising your account settings

On Etsy, viewing and changing your account settings — such as your password; e-mail address; filtering, language, currency, and other preferences;

privacy settings; security settings; mailing and shipping addresses; credit-card settings; e-mail notification settings; and taxpayer ID — is a breeze. To access all these settings, click the Settings link on the left side of Your Account; then click the tab you need — Account (displayed by default, as shown in Figure 4-4), Preferences, Privacy, Security, Addresses, Credit Cards, Emails, or Taxpayer ID.

Appy ending: Tracking your Etsy apps

As you discover in Chapter 18, loads of apps are available for Etsians to enjoy. (An *app* is just a piece of software designed to help you perform a specific task.) For example, you can find apps to help you run your Etsy store, compile Etsy Treasuries, and more. You can access apps connected to your Etsy account on the Apps page, which you view by clicking the Apps link on the left side of Your Account. To see a list of available Etsy apps, click the App Gallery link on the Apps page.

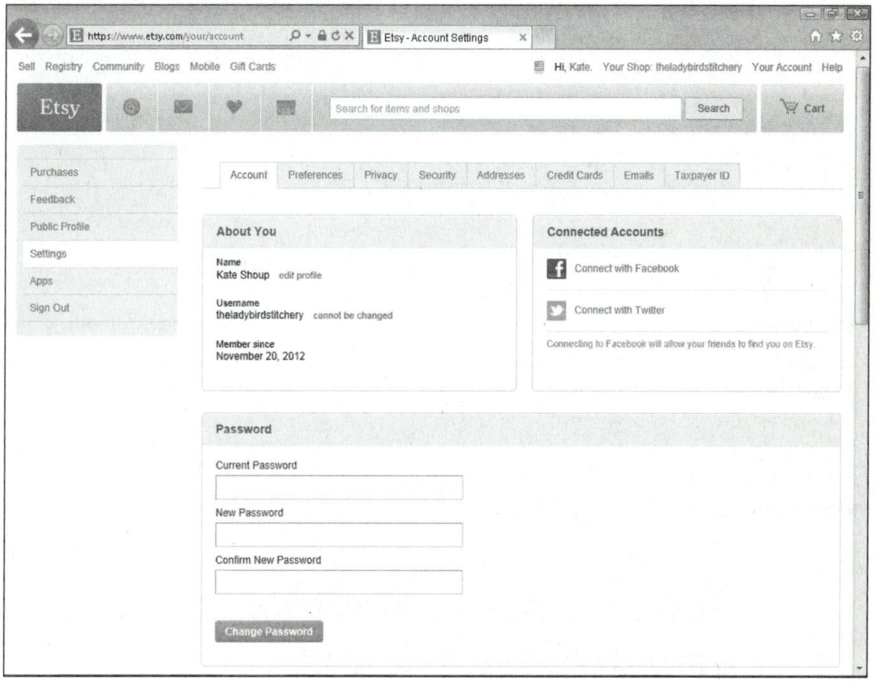

Figure 4-4:
Use this page to view and change your Etsy account settings.

Note that, for the most part, Etsy hasn't developed these apps; third-party vendors create them. If you have trouble with one, you need to contact the vendor, not Etsy.

Go proto: Exploring Etsy Prototypes

If you've opted to join any Etsy Prototypes, those will be accessible here. A Prototype is an experimental project that explores different ways of using Etsy. For more on Etsy Prototypes, see Chapter 20.

Head case: Viewing reported cases

If a buyer opens a case against your shop — which may happen if a buyer doesn't receive the item he ordered or if that item, in his view, was not up to snuff — you'll be able to view details about the case here. Note that you can also access this page by clicking the Cases link that appears in the Options section in Your Shop. In addition, an alert will appear at the top of your screen when you sign in to Etsy if your account has a new or open case. For more on cases, see Chapter 17.

Shop Girl: Familiarizing Yourself with Your Etsy Shop Settings

Your Account enables you to keep track of purchases, monitor your feedback, change your public profile, adjust your account settings, and keep track of Etsy apps (as we note earlier in this chapter). In contrast, Your Shop (see Figure 4-5), which you access by clicking the Your Shop link that appears along the top of every Etsy page, allows you to manage item listings, handle orders you've received, view your shop and customer service stats, view and pay your Etsy bill, change your shop settings, and promote your shop. This area also includes links to seller resources, including Etsy's handy Seller Handbook, which is a super-thorough compendium of articles about selling on Etsy, and the site's App Gallery (see the preceding section). Also available: access to info about Etsy's comforting Seller Protection program.

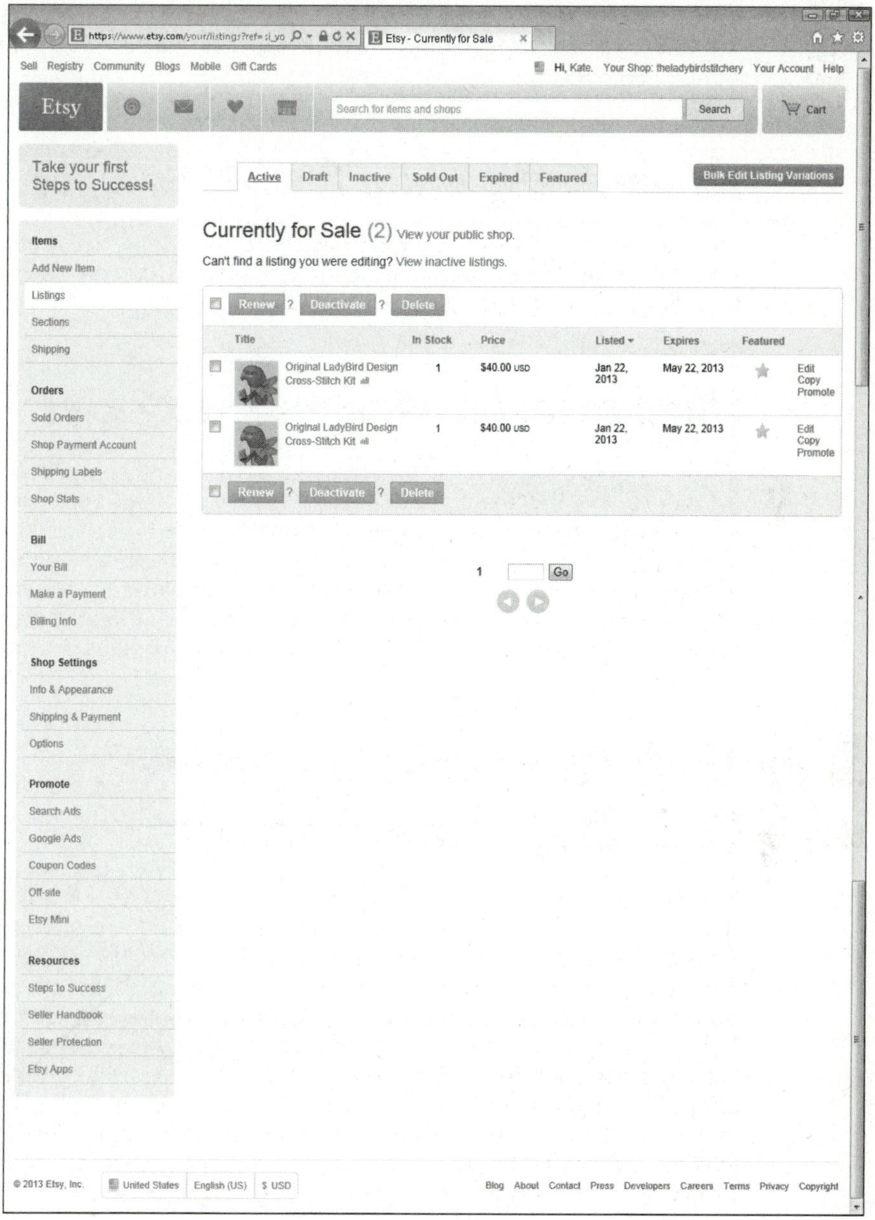

Figure 4-5:
Click the
Your Shop
link along
the top of
any Etsy
page to
access tools
for manag-
ing your
Etsy shop.

Listful thinking: Managing item listings

The Items links in the Your Shop area give you easy access to tools that enable you to do the following:

- ✔ Add new item listings.
- ✔ View, edit, renew, deactivate, and delete items currently for sale.
- ✔ Manage draft listings.
- ✔ View, edit, activate, and delete inactive item listings.
- ✔ View, edit, renew, and delete sold-out listings.
- ✔ View, edit, renew, and delete expired listings.
- ✔ View, edit, and rearrange featured listings.
- ✔ Create, edit, and reorder shop sections.
- ✔ Apply shipping profiles to multiple listings.

You find out how to do all these tasks (except for working with shop sections and applying shipping profiles to multiple listings) in Chapter 13. You find out about shop sections in Chapter 8 and shipping profiles in Chapter 15.

Order up: Handling sold items

With the Orders links in the Your Shop area, you can do the following:

- ✔ View and track sold items, as shown in Figure 4-6. (See Chapters 14 and 15 for more details.)
- ✔ Manage your Direct Checkout shop payment account (see Chapter 18 for more details).
- ✔ Print shipping labels (discussed further in Chapter 15).
- ✔ View shop stats and customer service stats (discussed further in Chapter 18).

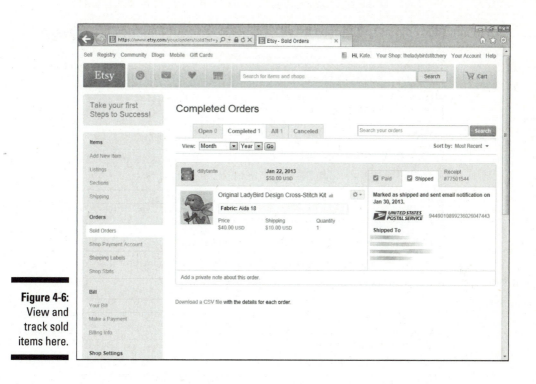

Figure 4-6:
View and
track sold
items here.

I'm just a bill: Viewing your Etsy bill

Although the best things in life really are free, there's no such thing as a free
lunch. If you opt to sell your handmade or vintage goodies on Etsy, you have
to pony up each month. To see how much you owe, click the Your Bill link
in Your Shop (see Figure 4-7). You can pay your bill by clicking the Make a
Payment Now button on the page that appears; alternatively, click the Make
a Payment link in the Bill section on the left side of any Your Shop screen. To
change your billing information, start by clicking the Billing Info link, found in
the same section. For more on paying your Etsy bill, as well as on how much
it costs to list an item on Etsy, turn to Chapter 18.

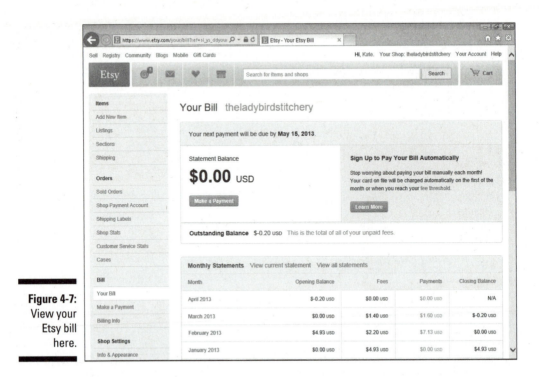

Bump, setting, spike: Changing shop settings

The Shop Settings links give you access to tools that enable you to do the following:

- Click the Info & Appearance link to access settings that enable you to establish the look of your shop and broadcast information about your shop and policies (covered in Chapters 8 and 9).

- Click the Shipping & Payments link to access settings that enable you to establish shipping profiles and accepted payment methods, accept sales tax, and set your preferred currency.

- Click the Options link to access shop options, vacation mode settings, and web analytics, as well as download shop data to a spreadsheet application (see Chapter 18 for additional details). You can also close your Etsy shop. (See Figure 4-8 for a look at the Shop Options screen.)

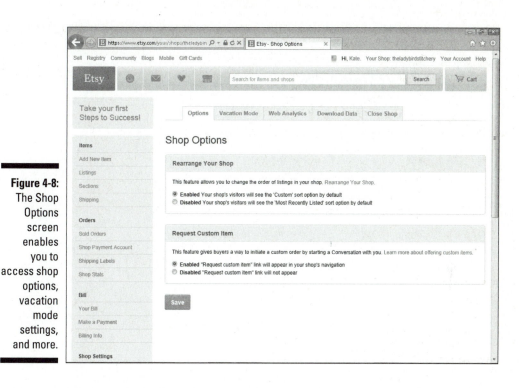

Figure 4-8:
The Shop Options screen enables you to access shop options, vacation mode settings, and more.

Go through the promotions: Promoting your shop

With literally millions of Etsy shops for buyers to choose among, making yours stand out is imperative. Your Shop provides easy access to several tools to help you achieve just that. For example, you can use these tools to do the following:

- ✔ Create Etsy search ads.
- ✔ Enable Google search ads.
- ✔ Generate promotional coupon codes and discounts.
- ✔ Create Etsy badges to embed in your own blog or website.
- ✔ Build your own Etsy Mini, for showing off your Etsy inventory on your own website.

These tools are major topics of conversation in Chapter 16.

Chapter 5

Buy and Buy: Finding and Purchasing Items on Etsy

In This Chapter

▶ Discovering Etsy's allure for buyers

▶ Searching for items on Etsy

▶ Understanding how transactions work

▶ Leaving feedback after a purchase

You've set up your Etsy account. You've gotten your bearings on the Etsy home page. You've explored the ins and outs of using the Your Account and Your Shop areas of the site. After all that work, you deserve a break! You know as well as we do that there's no better way to recharge than to engage in a little retail therapy. And there's no better way to engage in a little retail therapy than to shop — you guessed it — on Etsy. In this chapter, you discover how, and why, to buy on Etsy.

Gimme One Reason: Understanding Why You Should Buy on Etsy

Why buy on Etsy? Simple: Where else are you going to find a handmade bracelet featuring images of *The Golden Girls* cast in resin? Of course, even if you don't maintain a shrine to Rue McClanahan in your foyer, you can find plenty of compelling reasons to buy on Etsy. Consider just a few:

✔ Etsy features unique, one-of-a-kind handmade and vintage items — goodies you simply can't find anywhere else.

✔ Etsy offers an incredible breadth of items for sale, from accessories to ceramics, from jewelry to quilts, and everything in between.

✔ If you're in the market for craft supplies, Etsy is for you. At last count, Etsy's Supplies category listed more than 2.5 million items, including beads, buttons, fabric, yarn, paper, stamps, and more.

✔ Because there's no middleman — you buy directly from artists and craftspeople — prices on Etsy are generally very reasonable. At the same time, your purchase can help these skilled artisans earn a living wage.

✔ Buying on Etsy can make you a savvier seller. As a customer, you'll develop an eye for which selling practices work and which don't.

Go Fish: Using Etsy's Search Tool

If you've landed on Etsy with the idea of finding a specific item or certain items that relate to a particular theme — say, aardvarks — you'll be grateful for the site's robust Search tool. With the Search tool, you can search for handmade items, vintage items, and supplies. You can also use it to locate a particular shop, and to search among items and shops you've hearted.

To use the Search tool, follow these steps:

1. **From Etsy's home page, type a keyword or phrase in the Search field, located in the center of the header bar.**

   As you type your keyword or phrase, Etsy displays Search Suggestions — that is, links for items, sections, or shop names that may constitute a good match (see Figure 5-1). Etsy culls these suggestions from recent searches performed by other folks on the site. If one of these Search Suggestions matches what you're looking for, simply click it to view a list of relevant items.

Figure 5-1:
Type a keyword or phrase in the Search field.

Etsy					wine cork bracelet	Search
					wine cork bracelet	
Browse			Holidays / Ornaments		wine cork bracelet in **handmade**	For Him
					find shop names containing wine cork bracelet	

2. **Click the Search button or press the Enter or Return key on your keyboard.**

   Etsy returns a list of items that match your criteria (see Figure 5-2).

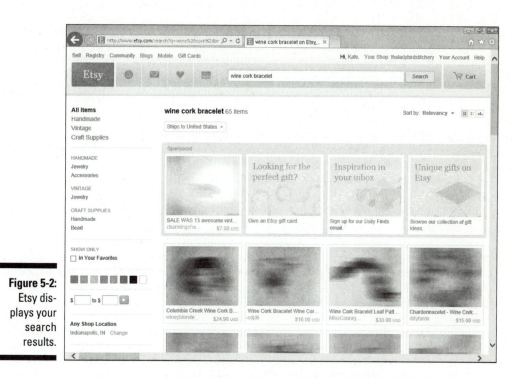

Figure 5-2: Etsy displays your search results.

3. **If you want, sort the search results by clicking the Sort By down arrow and choosing Most Recent, Relevancy, Highest Price, or Lowest Price.**

To narrow your search results to handmade items, vintage items, or craft supplies, click the appropriate option button on the left side of the screen. To view only results in a particular category (say, Jewelry), click the category link on the left side of the screen (refer to Figure 5-2).

4. **Click an item in the list to view the item's listing. Alternatively, click the shop name, listed below the item name (next to the price) to view other items in the seller's shop.**

If your search efforts fail to yield useful results — for example, Etsy returns too many matches — try these techniques:

✔ **To search for a specific phrase, surround it with quotation marks.**
For example, suppose that you want to find items related to the movie *Roman Holiday*. Searching for the phrase *Roman Holiday*, without quotation marks, returns pages that contain the phrase *Roman Holiday*. However, it also returns pages that simply contain the individual words *Roman* and *holiday*, which likely have nothing whatsoever to do with Audrey Hepburn's romp across Roma. Enclosing the phrase in quotation marks ("Roman Holiday") limits the results to pages that contain that phrase only.

✔ **To exclude pages with a certain word from your results, precede the word you want to exclude with a hyphen.** For example, suppose that you want to find listings that pertain to mustangs (as in, the horses). To omit listings that relate to the Ford Mustang automobile, you could add *-Ford* to the search string. (***Note:*** There is no space between the hyphen and the word.)

Searching is great when you have some idea of what you're looking for. But what if you just want to poke around the site? In that case, you'll enjoy Etsy's many browsing-related features. These include Browse Pages, Categories, Handpicked Items, Recently Listed items, Colors, Treasury, and Shop Local. You can access these tools from Etsy's home page. For help in using these tools, refer to Chapter 3.

Transactions Speak Louder Than Words: Delving into Transaction Details

As you browse or search the gazillion items available for sale on Etsy, you're bound to find a thing or two (or 7,968) that you simply can't live without. Fortunately, Etsy makes buying a breeze. As you find out in the following sections, all you do is add the item to your cart, check out, arrange for payment, and submit your order.

Before you buy, take a moment to view the seller's feedback score. To do so, click the Feedback link in the shop's home page or on the seller's public profile. If the seller boasts positive feedback, you can feel confident buying from him. If not, you may want to reconsider your purchase. (You find out more about feedback later in this chapter.)

Also, check the store's policies by clicking the Policies link that appears on the store's main page. To gain a little more confidence in the seller, you can find out more about her by viewing her shop's About page (you can access this page, assuming the seller has filled one out, by clicking the About link on the left side of the store's main page) and her public profile (click the seller's name, near her avatar, from any page in the seller's shop).

Affairs of the cart: Adding an item to your cart and checking out

To add an item to your cart and check out, follow these steps:

1. **Click the Add to Cart button found on the listing page for the item you want to buy (see Figure 5-3).**

   Etsy displays your shopping cart (see Figure 5-4).

2. **If you want to continue shopping, click the Keep Shopping button. (If you click Keep Shopping, you can return to your cart at any time by clicking the Cart link along the top of every Etsy page.)**

   Got cold feet? No worries. You can remove the item from your cart by clicking the Remove link. You can also click the Contact Shop Owner link to launch a convo with the shop owner. This option is helpful if you have questions about the item. (Flip to Chapter 17 for the scoop on convos.)

3. **Under How You'll Pay, indicate how you want to pay for the item.**

   Note that the options available here may differ by shop. Options include gift card or credit card (what Etsy refers to as "Direct Checkout"), PayPal, check, and money order.

Add to Cart button

Figure 5-3:
Click the
Add to Cart
button to
add an item
to your Etsy
shopping
cart.

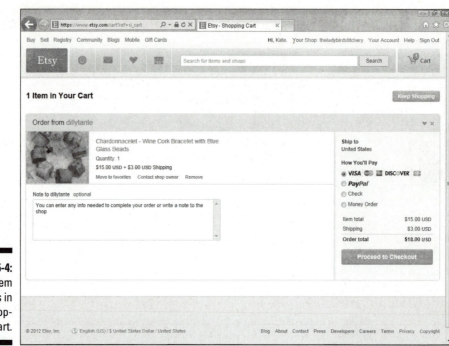

Some Etsy sellers issue coupon codes for their shops. When a seller issues a coupon code, a special Shop Coupon Code field appears on the page that's shown in Figure 5-4. If you have a coupon code for the shop you're buying from (maybe you grabbed a coupon code from a blog, or the seller posted it in his Etsy shop), you enter it in the Shop Coupon Code field and click the Apply button. Etsy updates your Order Total information.

4. **If you want, type a note to the seller in the Notes section.**

   Adding a note is important if you want to make a special request or you have a unique specification. In addition, in their item descriptions, some sellers request that you leave specifics about your order here — for example, personalization information.

   Note: When you purchase some items, you'll be prompted to supply additional information, such as size, quantity, or color.

5. **Click the Proceed to Checkout button.**

   Note that the exact verbiage on this button differs depending on which payment method you choose in Step 3.

Pays of our lives: Paying for your item

What happens after you add an item to your card and check out depends on which payment option you choose — credit card or gift card, PayPal, check, or money order. (As we mention earlier, not all sellers accept all the forms of payment covered here.) The following sections describe these options in more detail.

If your shopping cart contains items from multiple shops, you must pay each seller individually. You have to complete the checkout process for each shop separately.

Paying via credit card or gift card

Paying via credit card or gift card, or what Etsy calls "Direct Checkout," is a breeze. Just follow these steps:

1. **Choose a shipping address.**

   If the address you want to use is shown on the screen (see Figure 5-5), click the Ship to This Address button that appears above it. Otherwise, enter a new address in the fields provided and click the Ship to This Address button that appears underneath.

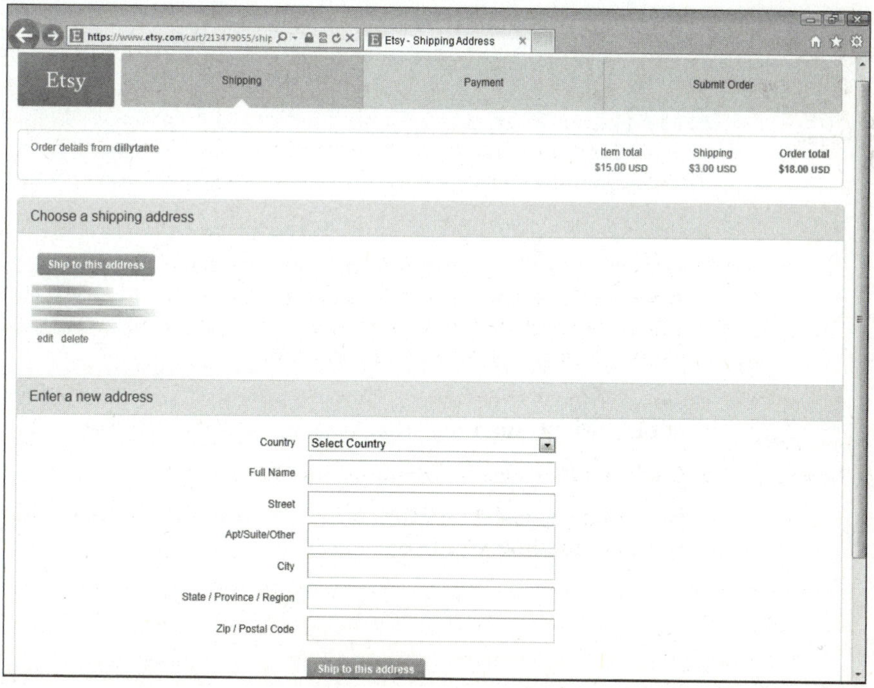

Figure 5-5:
Choose a shipping address.

2. **Select the credit card you want to use or, in the case of a gift card, enter the redemption code and click the Redeem Now button (see Figure 5-6); then click Continue.**

   If you haven't yet entered a credit card number for use on Etsy, you'll be prompted to do so.

A page that enables you to review and submit your order appears.

Paying with PayPal

If you choose to pay via PayPal, a PayPal window opens where you can log in to your PayPal account. Follow these steps:

1. **Verify your shipping address.**

   To change the address, click the Change link and choose from the list of alternate addresses that appears. To add a new address, click the Add a New Address link and follow the onscreen instructions.

2. **Choose your method of funding.**

3. **Review your information and click Continue.**

   PayPal returns you to the Etsy site. To find out how to submit your order, read on.

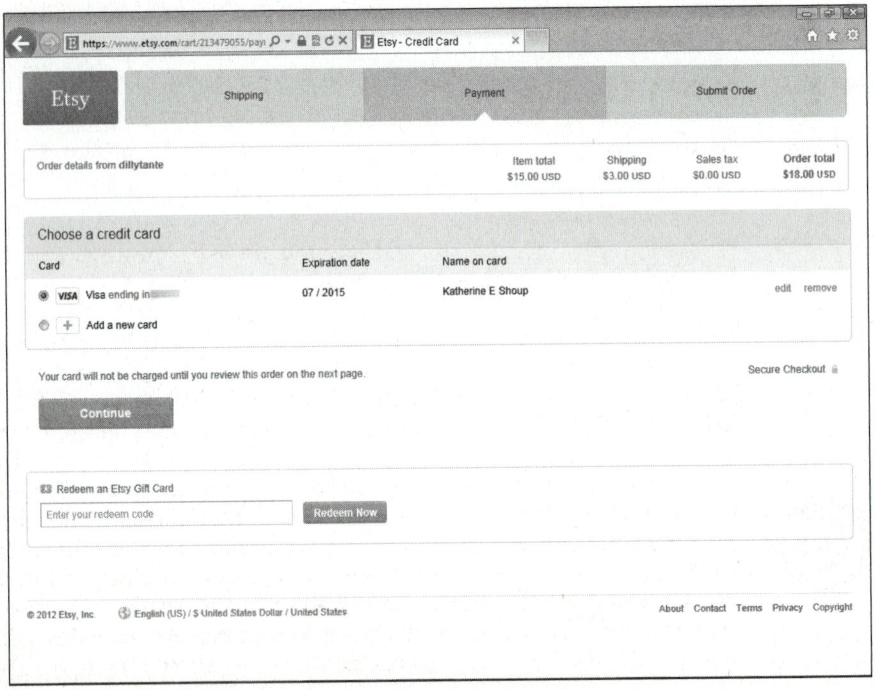

Figure 5-6:
Select a
credit card
or enter a
gift card
redemption
code.

Don't have a PayPal account? Don't worry. Setting one up is as easy as pie. You can even do it from Etsy during the checkout process. Simply choose PayPal as your payment method, and click the Check Out with PayPal button. Then, when you're prompted to pay, follow the onscreen instructions to register for a PayPal account.

Note that, in some cases, you may also be able to use PayPal to pay for your purchase with a credit card — for example, if the seller doesn't offer Direct Checkout. To do so, again choose PayPal as your payment method and click the Check Out with PayPal button. Then, when you're prompted to pay, click the Continue Checkout link on the left side of the page and follow the prompts.

Paying via check or money order

If you opted to pay via check or money order, you'll want to convo the seller to make the appropriate arrangements. (See Chapter 17 for the full scoop on convos.)

Submissionary position: Submitting your order

Before you submit your order, take a moment to review the order summary:

✔ If the shipping address shown isn't correct, click the Change Shipping Address link and click your preferred address in the list that appears. If the address you want doesn't appear in the list, enter the desired address in the fields provided and click the Ship to This Address button underneath.

✔ If something related to your payment details is out of order, click the How You'll Pay link and/or click the Back button in your browser window and choose the desired payment option.

If all the order details are error free, click the Submit Order button to submit your order (see Figure 5-7). In addition to displaying a special confirmation screen, Etsy e-mails you to confirm your order. All you have left to do is install yourself in the proximity of your mailbox until your item arrives.

As you wait for your purchase to arrive, you may need to review your order information. To do so, simply sign in to your Etsy account, click the Your Account link along the top of any Etsy page, and click Purchases. Your item will be listed among other purchases you've made, with helpful information about the status of the transaction — for example, whether it has been shipped. Note that the item's listing in the Purchases screen also includes a Contact button, which you can click to contact the seller should the need arise.

Requesting a custom item

Want a special, one-of-a-kind piece? Your favorite Etsy shopkeeper may be able to accommodate you. To find out, see if the shop features a Request Custom Item link, located in the Shop Info section on the left side of the shop's main page. If so, click it to launch a convo with the seller about the item you'd like to commission.

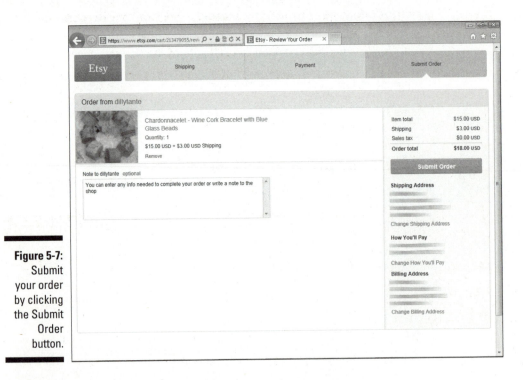

Figure 5-7: Submit your order by clicking the Submit Order button.

Feedback Is Forever: Leaving Feedback After You Buy

After you receive your item, take a moment to leave feedback about the transaction. When you leave feedback about a sale, you indicate whether the experience was positive, negative, or neutral. You also have the opportunity to share your comments about the transaction. Other Etsy users can then view this feedback to determine whether a particular seller is reliable.

Your feedback affects your seller's feedback score — and, by extension, her reputation on the site. It's super-important that you issue feedback consistently, fairly, and honestly.

Although leaving feedback is purely optional, doing so is a good idea; it helps ensure that everyone feels safe shopping on Etsy. Note that you have 120 days to leave feedback after the conclusion of a sale.

To leave feedback, follow these steps:

1. **While signed in to your Etsy account, click the Your Account link along the top of any Etsy page.**

2. **Click the Feedback link on the left side of the screen.**

   The Feedback page opens, with the Items Awaiting Feedback tab displayed (see Figure 5-8).

3. **Click the Positive, Neutral, or Negative option button under the transaction you want to rate.**

   If you've had a negative experience with a seller, first see if you can hammer out whatever issue is bothering you via e-mail or a convo. Often, conflicts on Etsy are simply the result of a misunderstanding.

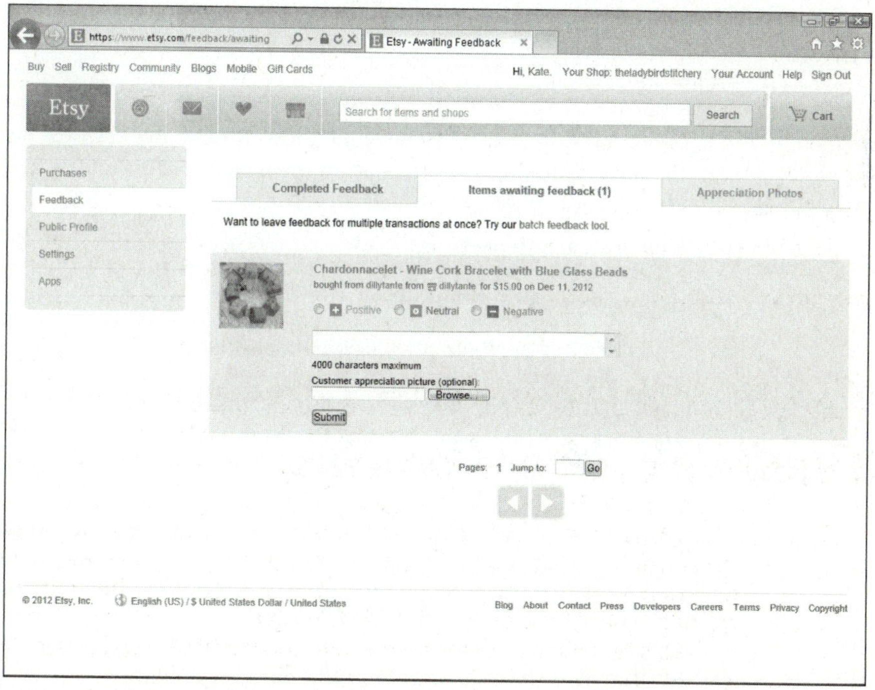

Figure 5-8: Leave feedback on this page.

4. **If you want, type a comment about the transaction or the seller.**

   If the transaction was fantastic, why not make the seller's day by saying something extra-nice in the comment field?

5. **If you want, upload an appreciation photo for the seller.**

   This photo may be an image of you wearing the item you bought, a photo of the item in its new home, or simply something silly to make your seller smile. Appreciation photos are a great way to share a little love on Etsy! To upload an appreciation photo, just click the Browse button; then locate and select the photo on your computer.

6. **Click Submit.**

   Etsy posts your feedback on the site.

Case in Point: Lodging a Case Against a Seller

If you have a problem with an Etsy seller — specifically, you didn't receive the item you ordered, or the item didn't match its description — you can report the problem by lodging a case against that seller (although Etsy urges you to attempt to work out the problem directly with the seller first).

To file a case, follow these steps:

1. **While logged in to your Etsy account, hover your mouse pointer over the Your Account link that appears along the top of any Etsy page and click the Purchases link that appears.**

2. **Hover your mouse pointer over the Report an Issue link; then choose I Did Not Receive an Item or An Item Does Not Match Its Description, depending on your situation.**

   Don't see a Report an Issue link? It could be that it's too early — or too late — to file a case. If the seller specified a processing time, you can file a case up to 45 days after the Ships On date or after the order is marked as shipped, whichever comes first. If no processing time was specified, you can file a case seven days after you placed the order, for up to 75 days.

3. **Indicate the item with which you're having a problem, describe the issue, and suggest a resolution — for example, "I would like a refund" or "I would like the item."**

   Etsy opens the case against the seller.

To view the case, click the Your Account link that appears along the top of every Etsy page and then click the Cases link on the left side of the page (see Figure 5-9). Click the link for the case to view details about the case (see Figure 5-10).

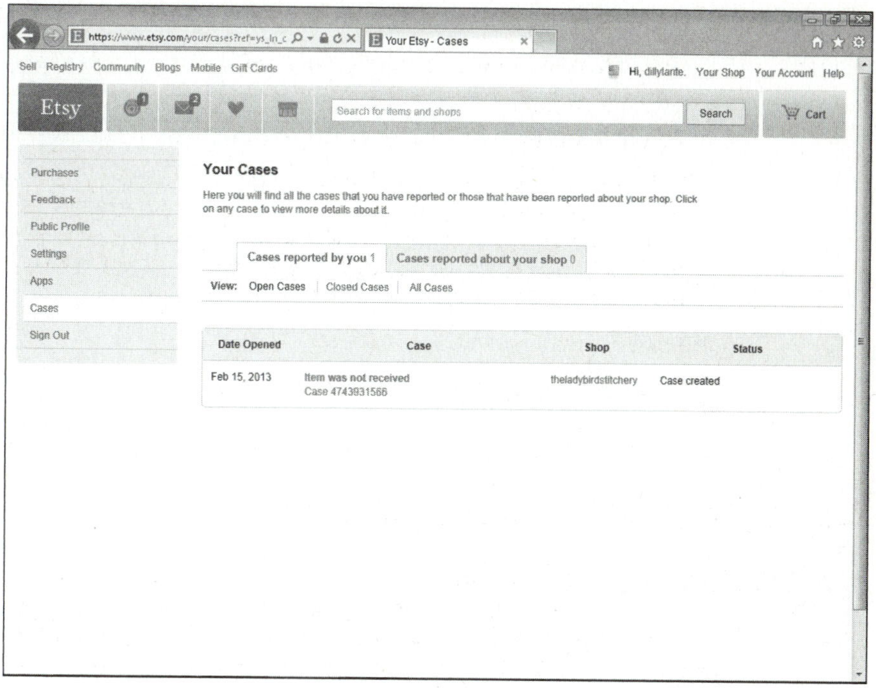

Figure 5-9:
View your
cases here.

You can use the Add Comment box to communicate directly with the seller about the case — something Etsy suggests you do. In addition, Etsy will communicate with the seller on your behalf by sending him a warning each week the case is open.

If you and the seller come to an agreement that is amenable to you, you can close your case. To do so, simply click the Close Case button on the case's page. Etsy asks you to confirm that you want to close the case; simply click the Submit button to proceed. When you do, both you and the seller will receive an e-mail confirming that the case is closed.

If, after a certain period of time (seven days if you purchased the item via Direct Checkout; two weeks if you paid via a different method), the case remains unresolved, you have the option to escalate the case. Alternatively, you can wait for Etsy to escalate it for you, which happens automatically after two weeks (if you purchased the item via Direct Checkout) or three weeks (if you paid via a different method). When a case is escalated, it means that it Etsy's Safety & Trust team will review it and take what actions it deems necessary.

Note: Although the Etsy Safety & Trust team can refund your money if you paid using Etsy's Direct Checkout system, it can't if you paid via, say, PayPal. In that case, you may want to contact PayPal directly for help.

Figure 5-10:
Click a
case's link
to view
details
about it.

Chapter 6

Safe Word: Maintaining Privacy and Safety on Etsy

In This Chapter

▶ Understanding Etsy etiquette

▶ Keeping your privacy intact on Etsy

▶ Outsmarting scammers and staying safe in the Etsy community

▶ Alerting Etsy to abuse

*O*n Etsy, as in life, safety is paramount. Just as you wear a seat belt when you drive, a helmet on your bike, and knee pads during roller derby, you must take the appropriate steps to remain safe on Etsy. In this chapter, you discover the precautions you must take to ensure your security and maintain your privacy on Etsy.

Oh, Behave! Adhering to Etsy's Do's and Don'ts

Every Etsy member must make it a point to peruse the site's DOs & DON'Ts. This page spells out everything you need to do to avoid committing a potentially embarrassing gaffe on the site. To view this page, click the Help link that appears in the upper-right corner of every Etsy page, click the Site Policies link, and click the DOs & DON'Ts link.

In brief, the DOs & DON'Ts page covers the following:

✔ **Membership:** This section of Etsy's DOs & DON'Ts outlines how members must behave on the site, specifies whether members can transfer ownership of an Etsy account to another party, clarifies the ins and outs of maintaining multiple accounts, specifies the scenarios under which collectives may be formed (see Chapter 18 for the scoop), and more.

✔ **Conversations:** This section pertains to the use of conversations, or convos (which we discuss more in Chapter 17). Although members may use convos to build friendly relationships with each other, they're intended primarily for communicating about transactions. Under no circumstances should you use convos to send spam, harass another member, or interfere with a transaction.

✔ **Transactions:** Here, Etsy defines what a transaction is, clarifies its own role in any transaction, and spells out policies relating to transactions for both buyers and sellers. This section also indicates what to do when the buyer doesn't pay up, what happens when a seller doesn't deliver, what recourse a buyer has when an item isn't up to snuff, and more. (Brush up on the basics of transactions in Chapter 5.)

✔ **Feedback:** As you find out in Chapter 5, Etsy members rely on feedback to gauge a buyer or seller's reputation. This section indicates the rules regarding leaving feedback and cites situations in which feedback may be removed or altered.

✔ **Marketplace Criteria:** To get the skinny on what is — and is not — acceptable for sale on Etsy, peruse this section.

✔ **Advertising on Etsy:** Many Etsy sellers advertise their items on the site to increase the number of eyeballs that see it. This section spells out a few of the rules with respect to this practice.

✔ **Flagging:** Members can use Etsy's flagging features to alert the site to potential problems. This section explains when flagging is appropriate and what happens when someone or something is flagged. You find out more about flagging later in this chapter.

✔ **Community:** In this section, members discover what Etsy deems appropriate behavior on the site's various community features, including its forums and teams (see Chapter 19 for more about these features). This section takes special care to remind members that these areas are public, meaning that people need to use common sense when sharing personal information on them. It also emphasizes the importance of treating everyone on the site with kindness and respect.

Private Party: Guarding Your Privacy on Etsy

Just because you're on Etsy doesn't mean you want everyone there all up in your business. Fortunately, Etsy takes your privacy seriously. You can take several steps to guard your privacy on Etsy.

If you're particularly concerned about maintaining your privacy, consider using a post office box as your address when conducting business on Etsy. That way, even if you buy or sell an item on the site, your home or work address remains private.

Privacy, please: Understanding Etsy's Privacy Policy

Like all reputable websites, Etsy maintains rigorous standards with respect to privacy. These standards relate to the following:

- ✔ How Etsy collects and treats personal information
- ✔ How Etsy handles service-related announcements and administrative messages
- ✔ What types of tracking technology Etsy uses
- ✔ How Etsy uses *cookies* (small bits of data from the site that are stored on your computer's hard drive)
- ✔ Measures Etsy takes to ensure that transactions on the site are secure

To view the highlights of the Privacy Policy, click the Help link that appears in the upper-right corner of every Etsy page, click the Site Policies link, and click the Privacy Policy link. To view the Privacy Policy in its entirety, click the Read Etsy's Full Privacy Policy link on the Private Policy Highlights page.

Leave me alone! Changing your privacy settings

By default, anyone who visits your Etsy page can view your favorites. However, you may prefer to keep this information private. Maybe you use Etsy to buy gifts for others, and you don't want them to be tipped off to gift ideas that you've hearted if they visit your page. Or maybe you don't want to alert your atheist boyfriend to your secret guilty pleasure: *Touched By an Angel*–themed soaps. Whatever your reason, you can easily change your privacy settings to keep your favorites on the down low.

You can also limit your "findability" by hiding your info from other Etsy members who use Etsy's Find Your Friends feature to find real-world friends on the site. (Chapter 21 has more on finding friends on Etsy by importing your contacts into the site.)

Here's how to do both these things after you log in to your Etsy account:

1. **Click the Your Account link along the top of any Etsy page.**

2. **Click the Settings link on the left side of the Your Account page.**

3. **Click the Privacy tab at the top of the page.**

4. **In the Favorites section of the Privacy tab, shown in Figure 6-1, click the Only You (Private) option button to select it.**

5. **In the Findability section, click the No option button to prevent other Etsy members from finding you when they use Etsy's Find Your Friends feature.**

6. **Depending on your settings, you may also see an option for preventing others from finding you via your Facebook account; if so, choose the desired setting.**

7. **Click the Update Privacy Settings button.**

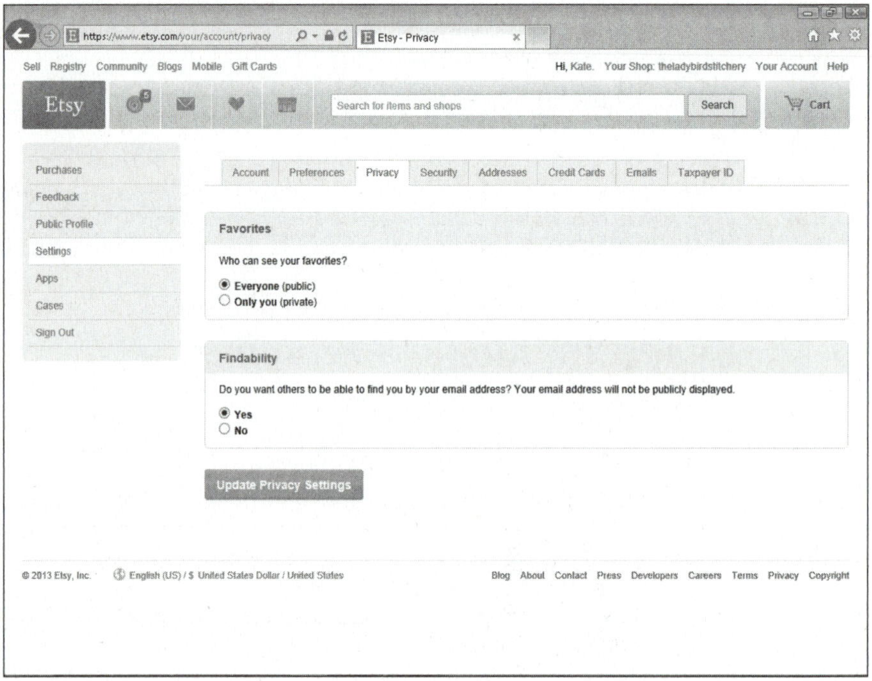

Figure 6-1:
Change your
privacy
settings.

Close sesame: Choosing a strong password

When you set up your Etsy account, you're prompted to select a password to prevent others from accessing your account (see Chapter 2 for details).

Unfortunately, many people opt for decidedly lame passwords — their birthdays, their kids' names, the word *password,* or something equally easy to guess.

To ensure that no one accesses your account without your authorization, you need to set a strong password. A strong password is at least eight characters long; doesn't contain your username or your real name; doesn't contain a complete word; differs from passwords you've used in the past; and contains a mixture of uppercase letters, lowercase letters, numbers, symbols, and spaces.

Don't use the same password on multiple sites. Otherwise, if someone figures out your password for one site, that person will have access to all your online accounts. For an added layer of protection, you need to periodically change your password — ideally, every 30 to 90 days.

To change your password, log in to your Etsy account and follow these steps:

1. **Click the Your Account link along the top of any Etsy page.**

2. **Click the Settings link on the left side of the Your Account page.**

    You should land automatically on the Account tab, but if you don't, click the Account tab at the top of the page.

3. **In the Password section of the Account tab, shown in Figure 6-2, type your current password in the Current Password field.**

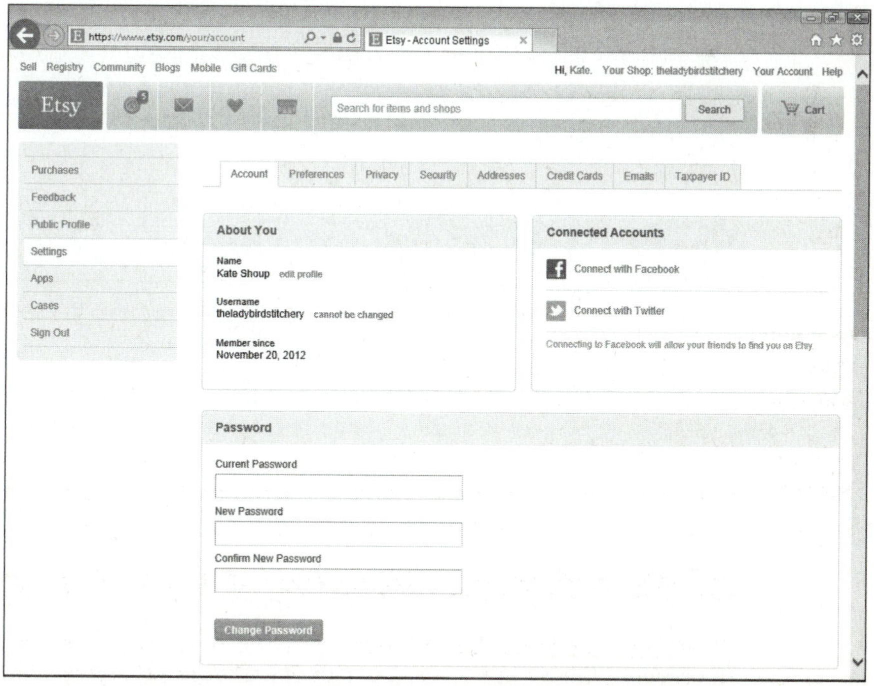

Figure 6-2: Change your Etsy password.

4. **In the New Password field, type your new password.**

5. **Retype your new password in the Confirm New Password field.**

6. **Click the Change Password button.**

If you're worried about forgetting your password, you can write it down — but make sure you store it somewhere safe and private. If you forget your password *and* where you wrote it down, you can enter the e-mail address you used to set up your account on this page: www.etsy.com/forgot_pass word.php. If you forget your password *and* where you wrote it down *and* the e-mail address you used to set up your account, you have to contact Etsy at support@etsy.com to ask for help (after upping your daily dose of *Ginkgo biloba,* of course). Ditto if you forget your username.

If you've signed on to your Etsy account using a public computer — for example, one at your local library or in an Internet cafe — be sure you log off when you're finished. Otherwise, the next person who uses that computer will be privy to your account information.

Safe Passage: Keeping Yourself Safe on Etsy

The good news is, since its inception in 2005, the Etsy community has grown like Shaquille O'Neal in the ninth grade — a lot. Unfortunately, that growth has made the site all the more attractive to scammers and other flimflammers, not to mention just plain jerks. In this section, you find out how to keep yourself safe on the site.

Scam I am: Avoiding scams on Etsy

Etsy isn't just home to artists and crafters; it's also a congregation of con artists and shafters. As you use Etsy, be on the lookout for scams.

On Etsy, most fraudulent activities involve the use of money orders or cashier's checks. For example, if someone contacts you with a vague offer to buy something in your Etsy shop via money order or cashier's check, but offers to pay more than is necessary to expedite the item or includes some other weird request or instructions, beware. This interaction is typically an attempt to relieve you of your merchandise.

Some of these scammers operate by purchasing an item — usually something expensive — and indicating that they'll pay by money order or cashier's check, but they tack on a substantial amount along with a request to, say, buy them a new notebook computer and ship it to them along with your valuable piece. The catch? The money order or cashier's check is really a forgery. The end result: Not only does the scammer effectively steal your item, but you reward her by buying her a computer!

If anyone asks you to front him some cash or some other expensive item, pronto, your answer should be a polite but firm "N to the O, no."

Sometimes people do have gift emergencies. They need one of your kitten-soft hand-knit scarves, like, yesterday. But sometimes people will foster a sense of urgency in an attempt to prey on your kindly nature — for example, begging you to ship an item right away, even though their cashier's check or money order hasn't cleared. Don't be reeled in by this tactic!

Given how many scams involve the use of cashier's checks and money orders, you may reasonably choose not to accept those forms of payment for items in your Etsy shop. (We discuss forms of payment in Chapter 9.)

Beyond these very obvious examples, how do you determine whether the person you're dealing with on Etsy is on the up-and-up? If she has engaged in countless transactions and received reviews as glowing as Kate Winslet's skin, then you can probably proceed without fear. (For help with checking a seller's reviews — or, in Etsy parlance, her feedback — refer to Chapter 5.) But trust your instincts. Assuming that you're not Billy Idol, those hairs on your neck are standing on end for a reason. Pay attention to them.

So, what do you do if you get taken on Etsy? First, contact your financial institution, on the double. Second, report the situation to Etsy. (See the next section for details.) You may also opt to alert your local law enforcement.

Safety dance: Staying safe in Etsy's public places

As any regular Etsy user will tell you, one of the great things about using the site is its robust community of interesting, arty folk. But as with any community — especially online — not everyone on Etsy is on the up-and-up. For this reason, it's critical to take steps to keep yourself safe on Etsy's public places, such as its forums and teams (which we describe in detail in Chapter 19). Keep a few points in mind:

- ✔ **Lurk before you leap.** Before jumping into a forum or team discussion, monitor it for a while. See whether the Etsians engaged in the discussion are people you want to interact with.

- ✔ **Don't hesitate to exit left.** If a discussion goes south, simply disengage. Life's stressful enough — why embroil yourself in a conflict on a site that's supposed to be fun?

- ✔ **Limit personal information.** Don't share your digits or other personal details, such as where you live or work, on Etsy's forums, teams, or other public spaces.

- ✔ **Avoid oversharing.** Although participating in the Etsy community can foster a sense of closeness among members, avoid the temptation to over-share. If you wouldn't be comfortable sharing something with, say, your boyfriend's grandmother, then it probably doesn't belong on Etsy, either.

- ✔ **Think before you connect in real life.** Although using Etsy is certainly a great way to pick up a new BFF and even fall in love (for proof, search for the Etsy Love Stories series on the Etsy Blog at `www.etsy.com/blog`), take care before you agree to connect with other Etsy users in real life. If you do decide to meet in person, pick a neutral public place — somewhere you'll feel comfortable. Make sure a friend or family member is hip to your plans, and be sure to bring a cellphone.

- ✔ **Be nice.** If you're kind to others online, chances are, others will be kind back. Not only is it bad karma to knowingly insult or harass another Etsy member, but it's against the site's rules. Abusive behavior can get you kicked off the site for good.

Buyers — as well as fellow sellers — read the forums. Not being on your best behavior can cast a shadow on your shop and your business!

Security guard: Making your account more secure

In case you're extra concerned about security, Etsy offers a few optional features to make your account more secure:

- ✔ **Full-Site SSL:** Secure Sockets Layer (SSL) adds a layer of security on the Internet. Certain pages on Etsy — ones that contain sensitive information, such as your credit card number or your actual weight (kidding) — are already SSL enabled. If you want to apply SSL to all the pages you view on Etsy, simply enable this feature. (You can tell when pages are encrypted with SSL by their URL, which starts with `https` instead of `http`.)

- ✔ **Two-Factor Authentication:** This security feature adds a layer of protection above and beyond your password. Here's how it works: You receive a text message or phone call with a super-secret code, which you must enter in addition to your password to log on to Etsy. You'll receive a new code every 30 days or when you attempt to log in using a different browser.

- ✔ **Login History:** Enable this feature to track when and where you sign in to your Etsy account. This is handy if you're concerned that someone else may be logging on to your account. As an added bonus, it enables you to sign out of any open sessions — for example, if you signed on to Etsy using a public computer (say, at the library or at an Internet cafe) and you forgot to log off when you were finished.

To access these features, follow these steps:

1. **Click the Your Account link along the top of any Etsy page.**
2. **Click the Settings link on the left side of the Your Account page.**
3. **Click the Security tab along the top of the page.**

   The Security Settings page, shown in Figure 6-3, opens.
4. **To enable Full-Site SSL, click the top Enable button.**
5. **To enable Two-Factor Authentication, click the middle Enable button.**

   Etsy prompts you to enter a mobile phone number and to indicate whether you want to receive your two-factor code via text or phone call. Do so, and click the Confirm Phone Number button. Then obtain your code from your phone and enter it in the field that appears.
6. **To enable Login History, click the bottom Enable button.**

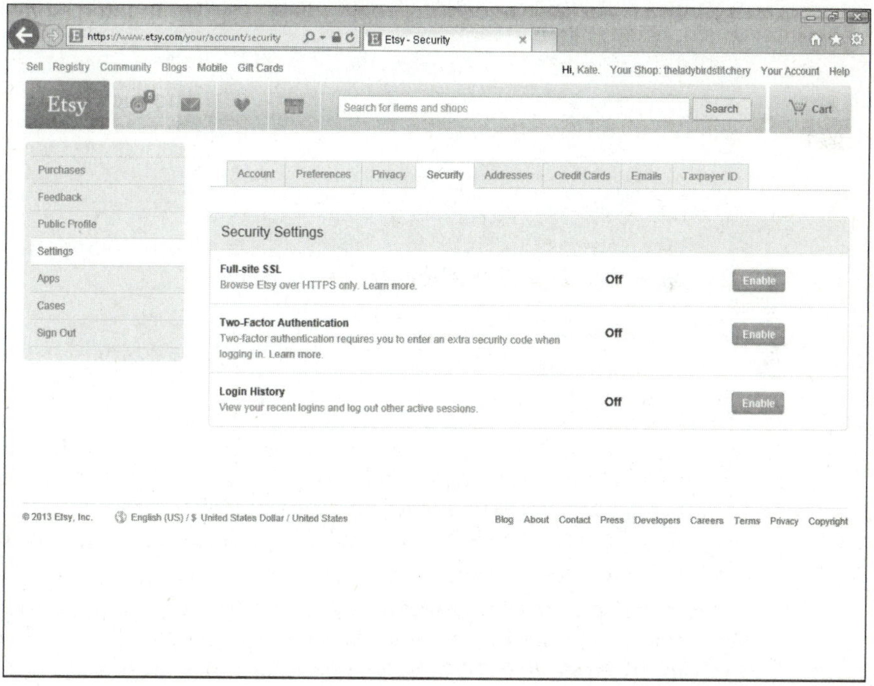

Figure 6-3:
The Security
Settings
page.

Always use protection! Using Etsy's Seller Protection program

Try as you might, not every transaction will be as smooth as Mick Jagger with the ladies. Fortunately, Etsy offers Seller Protection. Seller Protection guarantees that your account status will remain unaffected if a buyer reports a problem with a transaction with your shop.

To be eligible for Seller Protection, you'll need to do the following:

- ✔ Publish your policies with regard to returns, exchanges, and custom orders on your shop's Policies page.

- ✔ Communicate with buyers via convos (rather than, say, e-mail or carrier pigeon).

- ✔ Accurately photograph and describe the items you list. Descriptions should include such details as color, size, materials, conditions, and the like. In the case of custom orders, it's critical that you confirm the details of the order via convos. (You'll learn about photographing your wares and writing good descriptions in Part III.)

- ✔ Using the tools supplied by Etsy, provide buyers with a "ships-by" date — that is, the date by which the item(s) will ship, or the amount of time you need to process the order — and ship the item(s) as promised.

- ✔ Ship your item to the address listed on the Etsy receipt (or to a different address, as agreed upon with the buyer via convos).

- ✔ After the item is sent, mark it as such on Etsy.

- ✔ Provide proof of shipping and, for items shipped within the United States, proof of delivery.

- ✔ If your item is priced above $250, use a trackable shipping method that allows for signature confirmation at delivery.

- ✔ Respond to dispute cases and to correspondence from the buyer involved in the case within seven calendar days. In addition, you must respond to requests from Etsy for more information about the case within seven calendar days.

As an added bonus, Etsy's Seller Protection program fully covers items purchased via Etsy's Direct Checkout tool (that is, via credit card or gift card), up to $1,000. So, if a good transaction goes bad, you'll be in the clear.

Note that Seller Protection doesn't apply across the board. For example, it isn't available for transactions that involve digital goods or other items delivered electronically. The same goes for items that aren't shipped — for example, items delivered in person or workshops or classes.

Brooklyn, We Have a Problem: Reporting Issues to Etsy

Suppose you run across a problem while using Etsy. For example, perhaps you've stumbled across an item that shouldn't be sold on the site (in other words, it isn't handmade, vintage, or a craft supply). If so, you can report it.

To report an item listing or shop that appears to be in violation of Etsy's policies, click the Report This Item to Etsy link (at the bottom of the listing page) or the Report This Shop to Etsy link (on the left side of the page, under the Actions heading). A dialog box appears, asking you to specify why you're reporting the listing or shop; click the appropriate option button, add any pertinent comments, and click Submit Report.

To report something else — say, a sketchy or harassing convo — contact Etsy Support. To do so, follow these steps:

1. **While logged in to your Etsy account, click the Help link that appears along the top of any Etsy page.**

   The How Can We Help You? page opens.

2. **Scroll to the bottom of the page and click the Email Us link.**

   The Email Etsy Support page opens (see Figure 6-4).

3. **Click the Select a Topic drop-down arrow.**

   The Select a Topic drop-down list opens.

4. **Choose the option that relates most closely to the issue you want to report.**

5. **Type a subject for your message.**

6. **Type your message.**

7. **Click Submit.**

   Etsy notifies you that your report has been submitted; it also sends you a confirmation e-mail.

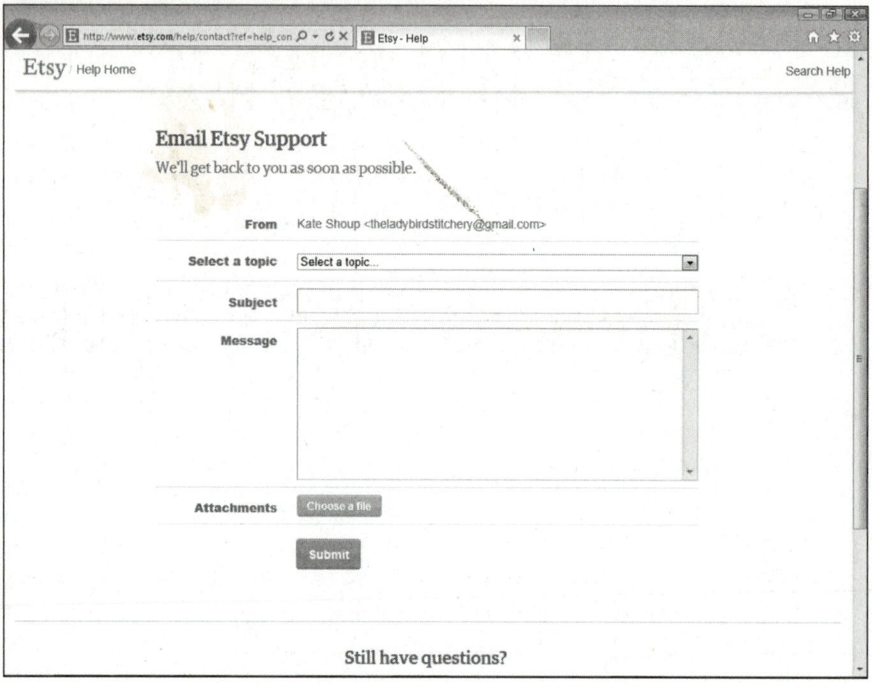

Figure 6-4:
Reporting a
problem on
Etsy is easy.

Part II

If You Build It, They Will Come: Setting Up Your Etsy Shop

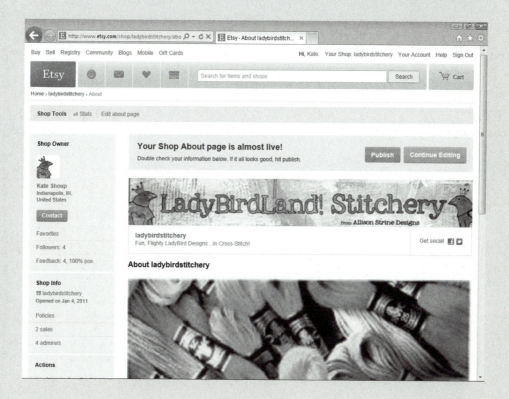

web extras

Find out more about creating an eye-catching banner in an article at www.dummies.com/extras/startinganetsybusiness.

In this part . . .

- ✔ Discover what you can — and can't — sell on Etsy so you can plan which wares you'll sell.

- ✔ Make your Etsy shop stand out from the crowd so you can rack up the sales.

- ✔ Explore the important, yet oft-overlooked, subject of shop policies to let buyers know what you will and won't accept.

- ✔ Price your work so it sells at a fair price.

Chapter 7

Sell Coverage: Understanding What You Can and Can't Sell on Etsy

· ·

In This Chapter

▶ Figuring out what you can sell on Etsy

▶ Determining what items Etsy doesn't allow

▶ Understanding the consequences of selling prohibited items

· ·

Many people think of Etsy as a sort of eBay for arts and crafts. Indeed, Etsy and eBay *are* similar — people use both sites to buy stuff from other individuals; the sites' business models, which involve charging listing fees and taking a small commission on every sale, are clearly related; and members use feedback to rate sellers.

But the differences are hard to ignore. For starters, unlike eBay, Etsy doesn't use an auction format. Furthermore, although Etsy is certainly growing, it's significantly smaller than eBehemoth. But the biggest and most obvious difference is that, unlike eBay, where sellers can list pretty much anything (anyone need a ghost in a jar?), sellers on Etsy are limited to selling items that meet Etsy's strict criteria. In this chapter, we fill you in on what you can — and can't — sell on Etsy.

For more information about what you can and can't sell on Etsy, see the site's DO's & DON'Ts page (www.etsy.com/policy/dosdonts). Specifics appear in the Marketplace Criteria section of this page. If you don't find your answer there, check Etsy's Site Help forum. (You find out more about forums in Chapter 19.)

Yes, We Can! Figuring Out What You Can Sell on Etsy

In a nutshell, you can sell three types of items on Etsy:

- ✔ Handmade items
- ✔ Vintage goods (20 years or older)
- ✔ Supplies for crafting

The following sections describe these three categories in detail and address questions you may have about them.

Some items transcend these categories. For example, you may have vintage or handmade items that also qualify as supplies. If your inventory includes items like these, you need to decide which category applies best.

The handmaid's tale: Selling handmade items

Etsy's primary raison d'être is to serve as a marketplace for handmade goods, with no mass-produced items allowed. But the site isn't for selling just *any* handmade goods. Etsy sellers must offer handmade goods *made by them* (or by members of their Etsy collective — flip to Chapter 18 for more about collectives). Selling an item that someone else made, even if it was painstakingly crafted by hand, isn't permitted.

Naturally, this requirement raises a few key questions:

- ✔ **What if you upcycle or otherwise alter an existing item?** Up-whatting? *Upcycling* is the process of fashioning new, higher-quality items out of materials or products that you might otherwise throw away. So, maybe you specialize in making purses out of old license plates. Or perhaps you screen-print your own designs onto mass-produced T-shirts. In both cases, you're covered. In Etsy's view, items that are altered by hand in this manner can still be considered "handmade." Note, however, that Etsy doesn't feel that way about items that you've simply tailored, restored, or repaired.

- ✔ **What if you craft an item yourself from a kit?** Etsy doesn't view items that you've created using a "ready to assemble" kit as being handmade, unless you substantially alter the design as you work. So, if you were planning to profit from your passion for paint-by-number, you may need to rethink your position.

✔ **What if someone helps you make your item?** For example, maybe you have an assistant who, under your supervision, assists with a portion of the creative process. Or perhaps you've enlisted a third-party vendor to handle some aspects of your workflow, such as printing your artwork onto greeting cards. Either way, you're golden. Etsy understands that more than one pair of hands may need to touch your item. It's also okay by Etsy if you have an assistant help you with such shop-related tasks as listing items in your Etsy shop, shipping items, communicating with buyers, keeping records, and so on. But you cross a line if that assistant or vendor handles most of the work involved in the item's creation.

On a quasi-related note, drop shipping is not allowed. That is, you can't work at one location but ship from another. All items must be shipped under the direct supervision of the seller.

✔ **What if you creatively repackage a commercial item?** Nope. No matter how great the finished product is, you can't list a gift basket stuffed with non-handmade items and try to pass off the package as a handmade good.

The whole point of Etsy is to enable artisans and craftspeople to connect with buyers. Etsy is more than an online craft fair; it's an attempt to build an alternative, artisanal economy of sorts — one that eschews mass production. If your inventory isn't in line with this philosophy, Etsy may not be the marketplace for you.

Oldies but goodies: Offering vintage items

Although Etsy was originally conceived as a marketplace for handmade goods, it also serves as an excellent venue for vintage goods and collectibles. Items can include bags, books, clothing, electronics, furniture, jewelry, toys, and more.

So, how old does something have to be in order to be considered vintage? It depends on who you ask. But if you ask Etsy, the answer is 20 years old. Unless your item was manufactured during Kurt Cobain's lifetime (or before), you need to find another venue for it.

Supplies and demand: Selling supplies

In an effort to support its crafty community, Etsy allows the sale of commercial crafting supplies on the site: beads, buttons, fabric, findings, paper, patterns, tools, trim, wire, wool, and whatnot. Shipping and packaging supplies are also acceptable.

What's not allowed: items that, although perhaps considered commercial crafting supplies, are ready for use as is — think mass-produced dollhouse furniture and the like. Ditto mass-produced goods that may be used in conjunction with handmade items but aren't crafting supplies themselves. In other words, although your handmade eye shadow is a totally legitimate item on Etsy, selling the mass-produced brush you use to apply it as a separate item isn't kosher.

Do you have a closet full of crafting supplies? If so, consider culling your collection and listing your leftovers on Etsy. Not only will you pull in a little extra cash, but you'll give those goodies a new lease on life.

Just Say No! Understanding What's Not Allowed on Etsy

You know what you can sell (thanks to the previous section): handmade items (when you've made them), vintage goods, and supplies. You may assume, then, that as long as your item fits into one of those categories, it's acceptable for sale on Etsy. But you know what happens when you assume! In the following sections, we describe the items and services that Etsy doesn't allow.

Achtung, baby: Knowing what items are prohibited

Any number of items may meet the aforementioned criteria but aren't permitted on Etsy. One obvious example is items that are illegal; every Etsy seller is responsible for following all local laws. Other prohibited items include the following:

- Alcohol
- Drugs, druglike substances, and drug paraphernalia
- Firearms and weapons
- Hazardous materials (materials that are flammable, explosive, corrosive, poisonous, and so on)
- Live animals and illegal animal products
- Human remains or body parts (excluding hair and teeth)
- Motor vehicles (automobiles, motorcycles, boats, and so on)
- Pornography
- Real estate
- Recalled items
- Tobacco and other smokeable products

Risqué business: Selling mature items on Etsy

Although Etsy prohibits the sale of pornography, it permits the sale of NC-17 items — think goods that involve a depiction of male or female genitalia or sexual activity, a depiction of graphic violence, or profane language. However, sellers who list such items must comply with certain policies to ensure that Etsy remains appropriate for a G-rated audience. Specifically, items of this sort must be tagged with the word *mature* and must contain the word *mature* in their titles. That way, users can restrict searches to omit these listings by including the exclusionary term *-mature* in their searches. Furthermore, the first thumbnail image of the item must be appropriate for general audiences, although additional images may show the item in all its mature splendor.

Finally, although you can sell items that contain mature content or profane language, you may not use this type of content or language in your username, profile, item titles, item tags, avatar, banner, shop announcement, shop section titles, or About page.

In addition, Etsy prohibits the sale of items that

- ✔ Promote hatred toward people or demean them based on race or ethnicity, gender or gender identity, disability, or sexual orientation
- ✔ Promote or glorify illegal activity
- ✔ Promote or glorify harmful acts

Service says: Selling only certain services

In general, you can't sell your services on Etsy. The site is designed as a marketplace for goods. So, even if you're the best dog-walking, house-sitting masseuse this side of the Mississippi, you can't advertise your business on Etsy. You're not even allowed to avail yourself to members seeking your skills in the realm of tailoring, restoring antiques, retouching old photos, and the like.

If, however, your service results in a new, tangible item, you may offer it for sale on the site. For example, you may sell your services as a graphic designer, offering custom logos for clients, delivered via a digital file. Or maybe you give workshops; in that case, as long as participants leave your class with an actual physical object — an instructional booklet, a finished project, or what have you — it counts.

Off with Their Heads! Knowing What Happens If You Break a Rule

If you list a prohibited item or service on Etsy, vigilant staffers or other site members may flag it for review by Etsy's Marketplace Integrity Trust & Safety Team. (Note that you're not privy to information about who flagged your item.)

In extreme cases, Etsy may delist your item immediately. More typically, however, Etsy will contact you to attempt to remedy the problem. In some cases, you may be asked to remove the prohibited item from your shop. If you fail to do so, Etsy will remove it for you. In other cases, Etsy will send you a questionnaire, asking you to

- Name each person and detail his or her role in your shop.
- Describe the materials and equipment you use to make your items.
- Outline in detail how you make your items
- Show photographs of the raw materials used, as well as step-by-step photographs of your handmade process. (This is part of an effort to thwart so-called "resellers," or people who sell things that they did not, in fact, make and that are not considered "vintage" or "supplies.")

In egregious cases, Etsy may opt to suspend or even terminate your selling privileges. Note that, as a seller, you'll still be responsible for any outstanding fees if Etsy removes an item or suspends or terminates your account.

Chapter 8

Come on In! Creating an Eye-Catching Storefront

....

In This Chapter

▶ Setting up your shop

▶ Hoisting a banner on your shop page

▶ Composing your shop title and announcement

▶ Organizing your Etsy store into sections

▶ Entering your payment and billing info

▶ Sharing personal info on your About page and profile

....

*I*f you want to join the ranks of people who supplement their income or earn their living on Etsy, you need to take one more step: Set up your Etsy shop. Fortunately, doing so is a snap, as you discover in this chapter.

You can personalize your Etsy shop in any number of ways: by adding a banner, by including a shop title and a shop announcement to describe your shop, and by using sections to organize your goods. You can also personalize your shop by populating your Etsy profile and your About page. Certain items that you add, such as your profile picture, or *avatar,* will appear on your shop page, too.

We've said it before and we'll say it again: A major reason people shop on Etsy is to feel connected to the artists who make what they buy. To make sure people buy from *you,* you want your Etsy shop — and the items you list there — to reflect your personality. Whether you're serious or whimsical, modern or traditional, edgy or frilly, let your individuality shine through in your choice of banner, colors, and fonts, as well as your avatar and other visual elements. Your choice of words in your bio and other text-based elements also needs to reflect your personality. By revealing your true self in your Etsy shop, not only are you likely to increase your sales, but you may just make some friends along the way!

Don't forget to proofread all the text in your Etsy shop — your shop title, shop announcement, section titles, bio, and so on. Running a shop that's riddled with spelling and grammatical errors sends shoppers the wrong message — namely, that you're sloppy, lazy, and/or incompetent. That image isn't likely to win you any buyers!

One more thing: This chapter steps you through the process of setting up your shop. Your shop won't officially go live, however, until you've added your first listing — which you learn how to do in Chapter 13.

On Your Mark: Getting Started

Becoming an Etsy seller is a simple matter of setting up a shop on the site and listing your first item. (The former is covered here; the latter, in Chapter 13.)

1. **Click the Sell link in the upper-left corner of the main page.**

    The Sell page (shown in Figure 8-1) appears. This page reminds you what you can and can't sell on Etsy. (For a more thorough review, refer to Chapter 7.)

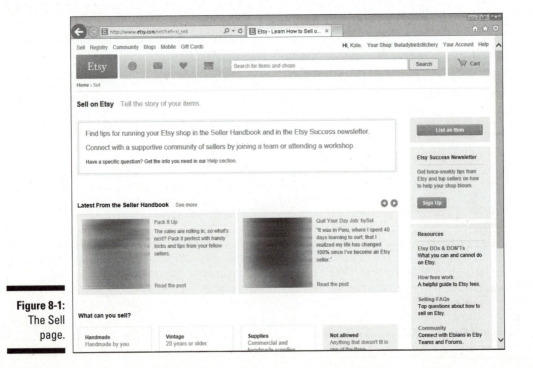

Figure 8-1:
The Sell
page.

2. **Click the Open an Etsy Shop button.**

   Etsy prompts you to choose a language, currency, and country for your shop.

   Although most Etsy sellers hail from the ol' U. S. of A. — which is one reason the site's default currency is the U.S. dollar — plenty of Etsy sellers call other countries home. If you're in that latter group, or if you find that your buyers tend to be clustered in a particular region abroad, you can list items and receive payments in a different currency (assuming that it's one of the other 20-plus currencies supported, including those of Australia, Canada, the European Union, Great Britain, Hong Kong, Israel, Japan, Mexico, New Zealand, Singapore, Thailand, and more).

3. **If your shop language is English, your shop currency is the U.S. dollar, and your shop country is United States, simply click Yes. If not, click the No, I Want to Choose link; choose the desired language, currency, and shop country; and click Save.**

   Etsy saves your changes and prompts you to select a shop name, as shown in Figure 8-2.

4. **Click the Enter Your Shop Name link.**

   The Shop Name screen appears, as shown in Figure 8-3.

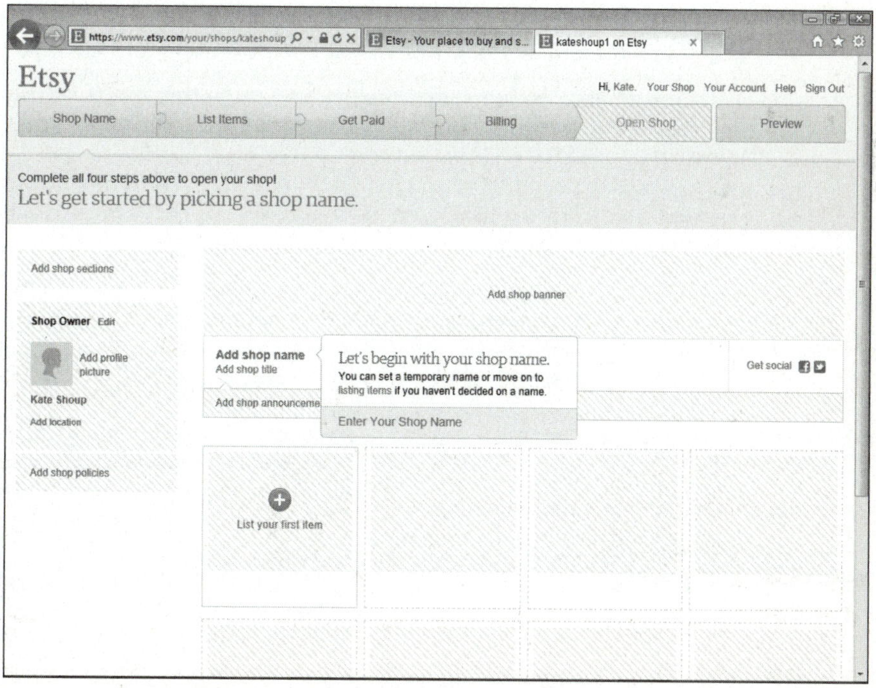

Figure 8-2: Etsy prompts you to enter your shop name.

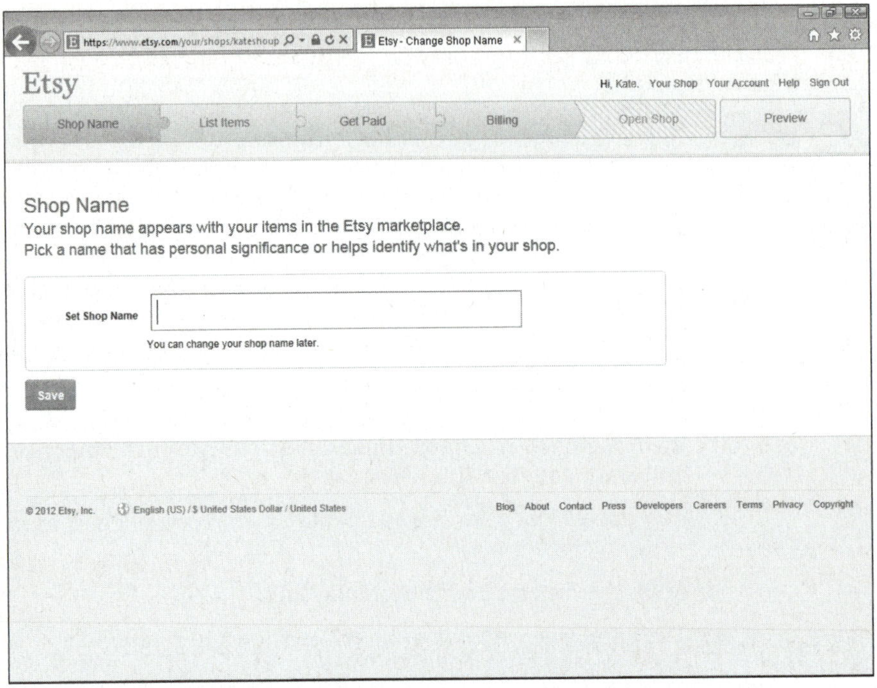

Figure 8-3:
The Shop
Name
screen.

5. **Type the name you'd like to use for your shop and click Save.**

Assuming no other seller has beaten you to the punch and selected your shop name already, Etsy assigns to your shop the name you typed.

Although Etsy prompts you to list an item next, we skip that step for now. You find out all about listing items in Chapter 13. For now, we focus on gussying up your shop.

Choosing a solid shop name

When choosing your shop name, keep these points in mind:

✔ Opt for a name that's easy to remember, that's easy to spell, and that contains no more than a few words that flow well together.

✔ If you already have a following elsewhere — for example, at craft fairs, in art galleries, or somewhere else — consider using your own name as your shop. Using your own name may make it more difficult to maintain your privacy on the site, but it can help you capitalize on your real-world successes.

✔ **Consider choosing a name that reflects what you sell.** For example, if you specialize in selling refrigerator magnets, you may want to include the word *magnet* in your shop. Keep in mind, though, that this leaves little room for growth if you decide to expand your selection beyond the magnetic.

Note that you can create multiple accounts to run more than one Etsy storefront — say, one for your thriving refrigerator magnet business and another for your hand-knit fingerless gloves enterprise. Doing so creates its own set of problems, though, most stemming from the challenges of keeping up with more than one shop.

✔ **Select a name that reflects your style.** You don't want to select an elegant, refined name if you plan to sell wacky hand-knit balaclavas.

✔ **For legal reasons, steer clear of trademarked words (including the word** *Etsy***).**

✔ **Don't be a copycat.** Do some research across the Internet, not just on Etsy, to make sure you aren't infringing on another brand name or shop name that exists elsewhere.

Note: You can change your shop name, but if you do so more than once, you may have to run it by Etsy first.

Mind Your Banners: Adding a Banner to Your Shop Page

To personalize your Etsy shop, you can add a *banner* (a graphic that runs across the top of the page). Your banner should incorporate your shop name and can include photos of your work, a shop slogan (assuming you have one), or even a special announcement.

Don't just create a banner willy-nilly. The banner you create needs to give viewers some idea of what they'll find in your shop and has to reflect the aesthetic of the items you make in some way. It also must tie in with your overall branding. (You find out more about branding in Chapter 16.)

If you have commitment issues, fear not. You can change your banner any time you want. For example, you can change your banner to reflect promotions that you're running or update it seasonally to keep your shop looking fresh.

You can create your banner from scratch using just about any image-editing software you like — even free stuff online. Here are just a couple image-editing tools to choose from:

✔ **Photoshop (**www.photoshop.com**):** Like Tylenol and Kleenex, Photoshop is so ubiquitous, it has crossed over into the general vernacular. It's by far the most respected and full featured image-editing program available today. It's also among the most expensive and complicated to use (although Adobe, the maker of Photoshop, does offer a cheaper, scaled-down version called Photoshop Elements, which has more than enough bells and whistles to do the job, as well as a more affordable "subscription" option for its beefier software).

✔ **GIMP (**www.gimp.org**):** This free, downloadable image-editing tool is nearly as powerful as its costly counterpart, Photoshop — albeit somewhat clumsier in design. It's great for performing essential image-editing tasks like resizing, editing, and cropping. You can even use it for more advanced purposes, such as adjusting levels and the like.

✔ **Picasa (**www.picasa.com**):** Offered free from Google and available for download for both Mac and Windows, Picasa supports basic photo-editing functionality, including color enhancement and cropping.

If you use a Windows PC, you can also use the Paint program, which was included free with your computer. Yet another option is to use the software that came with your digital camera.

Unfortunately, we can't cover the ins and outs of actually creating a banner. If you're new to image-editing software, you'll have to delve into your program's Help info for guidance. But we can give you this pointer: Whatever program you use, the key to creating a banner for your Etsy shop is ensuring that it's cropped to fit properly on your Etsy shop page. Specifically, all banners must be 760 pixels wide and 100 pixels high.

If you're no Rembrandt, why not let the pros take over and invest in a professionally designed custom banner? Many talented designers offer this service from their own Etsy shops. Try searching Etsy for "Etsy shop banner" and see what comes up. Just be sure you go the "custom" route rather than opting for a ready-made version. Otherwise, buyers may well stumble upon other shops using the same banner as yours. Not the best way to build your unique brand!

When you have your banner in hand, it's time to upload it to your Etsy shop. Here's how:

1. **If it's not open already, open the Shop Name page by clicking the Your Shop link along the top of any Etsy page.**

   The Shop Name page (shown in Figure 8-4) opens.

2. **Click the Add Shop Banner link.**

   The Info & Appearance page opens.

3. **In the Shop Banner Image section, click the Browse button (see Figure 8-5).**

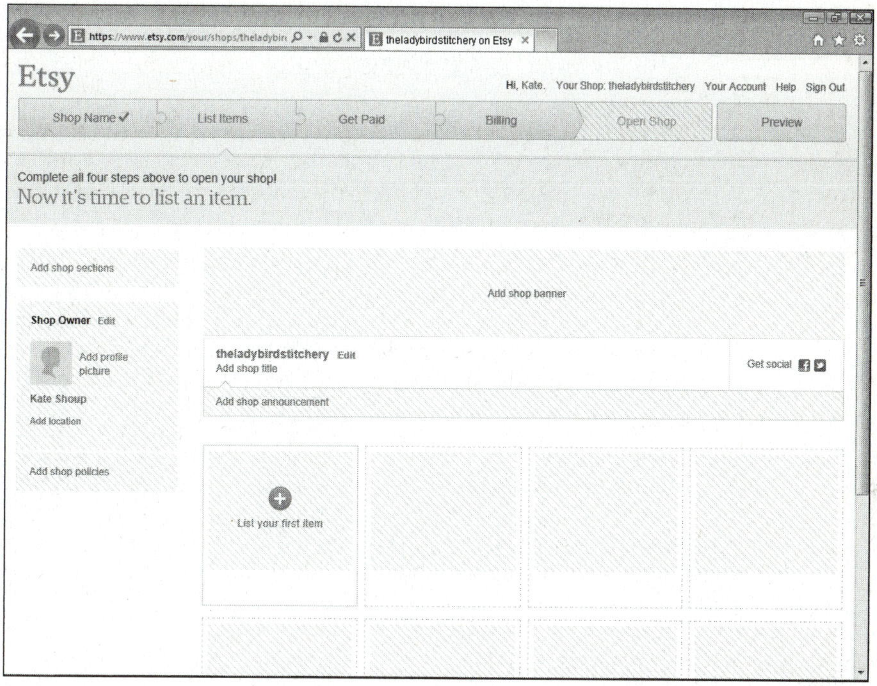

Figure 8-4:
The Shop
Name page.

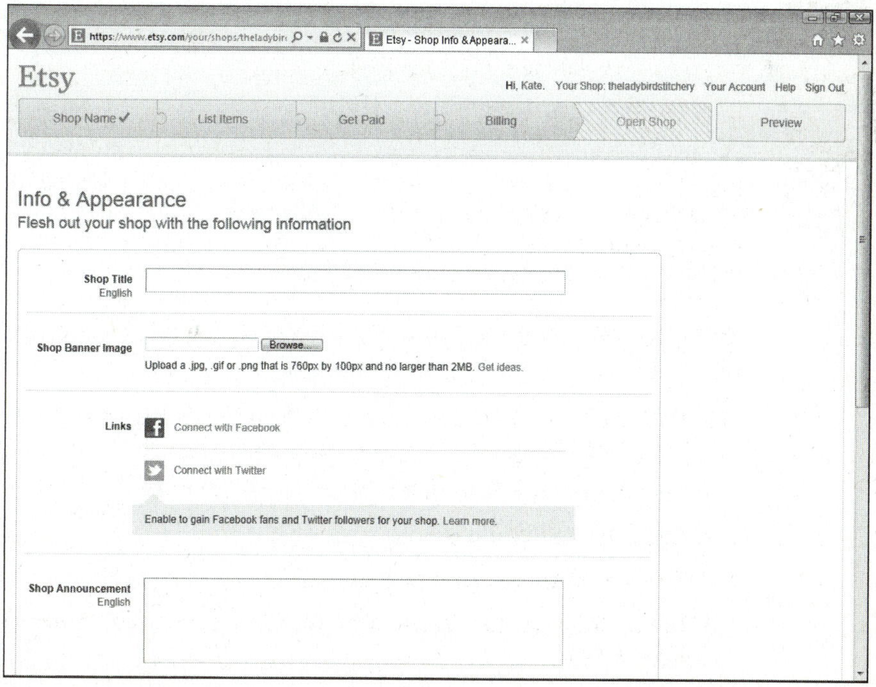

Figure 8-5:
Click
Browse
to begin
uploading
your banner.

    4. **Locate and select your banner file; then click the Open button.**

    5. **Click the Save Changes button.**

       Etsy uploads your banner to your shop (see Figure 8-6).

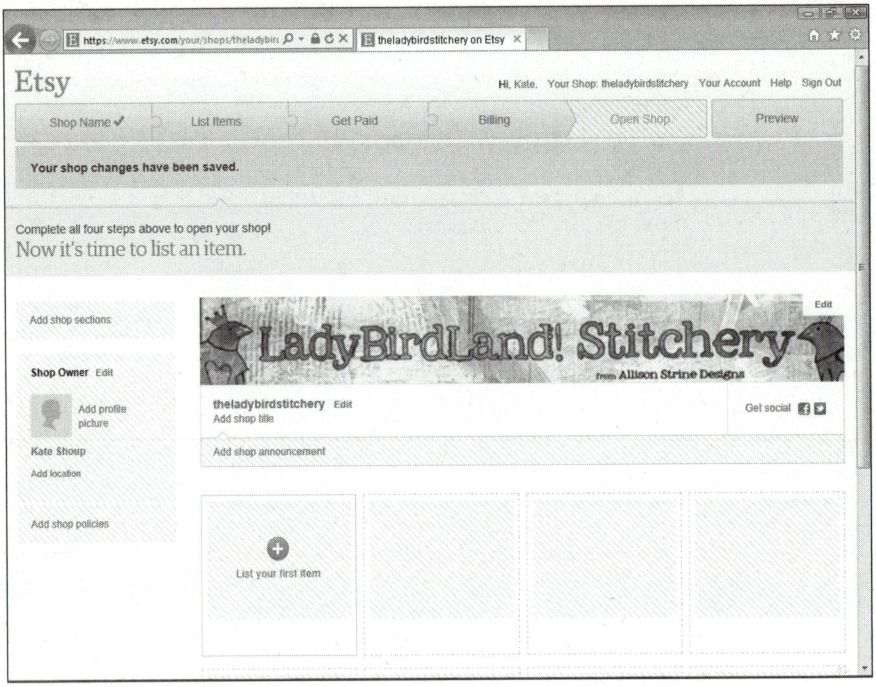

Figure 8-6:
What a difference a banner makes!

Title Wave: Adding a Shop Title and Announcement

Looking for a way to tell visitors what your shop's about? Look no further. Etsy enables you to include a shop title and shop announcement on your shop's main page.

Think of your shop title as a tagline of sorts. It needs to briefly sum up what your shop is about. For example, if you sell belt buckles, your shop title — which appears just below your username on your Etsy shop page — may be "Keep Your Pants On . . . With Becky's Belt Buckles." If customers are likely to search for you by your full name or your business name, consider including that in your shop title.

The shop announcement, in contrast, is a great way to, well, announce things about your shop. For example, you may use it to trumpet the types of items you sell, the variety of materials or ingredients you use, or your artistic philosophy. Alternatively, your shop announcement may broadcast when your next sale will be or share a summary of your shop policies.

 If your shop focuses on high-end, pricier items, you can use your shop announcement to indicate why. Maybe you use only the finest materials, or perhaps you employ a particularly difficult technique to craft your pieces. Either way, you can share this information with prospective buyers in your shop announcement.

To add a shop title and announcement to your shop, follow these steps:

1. **If it's not open already, open the Shop Name page. To do so, click the Your Shop link along the top of any Etsy page.**

   The Shop Name page opens.

2. **Click the Add Shop Title link, under your banner and shop name.**

   The Info & Appearance page opens.

3. **Type your shop title in the Shop Title field.**

4. **Type your shop announcement in the Shop Announcement text box (see Figure 8-7).**

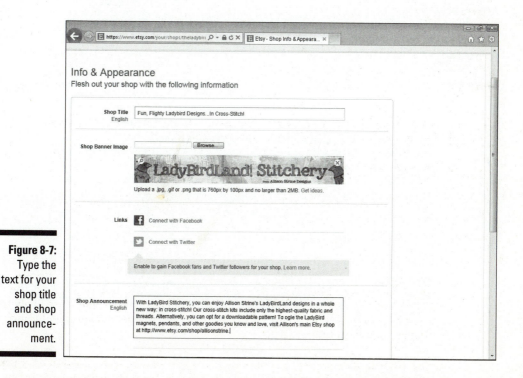

Figure 8-7:
Type the text for your shop title and shop announcement.

5. **Click the Save Changes button.**

Etsy adds your shop title and shop announcement to your shop (see Figure 8-8).

Figure 8-8: Your shop announcement appears under your banner; the shop title is under your username.

Note: Your shop announcement can be as short or as long as you want. Just be aware that if it's more *Anna Karenina* than haiku, not all of it will be visible by default. To read it in its entirety, click the Read More link that appears after the first few lines.

The first 160 characters of your shop announcement, along with your shop title, are used as the meta description for your shop. In English, that means if someone uses a search engine to search for keywords that appear in your shop title or announcement, as well as section names and your bio (see the following section), your Etsy shop will appear in his search results. So, you want to make sure that you include the really important stuff — what you sell, what it's made of, and so on — right up front. You find out more about using search engine optimization (SEO) to boost traffic to your Etsy shop in Chapters 12 and 16.

Section Leader: Setting Up Sections

What if, when you went to your grocery store, everything was set out haphazardly — with the milk alongside the charcoal briquettes, the kitty litter next to the radishes, the cheese by the sardines? You'd never be able to find everything you needed to buy! That's why grocery stores are organized into sections and aisles: so you can find what you're looking for.

Why should your Etsy shop be any different? Fortunately, Etsy enables you to organize your items by section. For example, if you sell different types of items — say, magnets, notebooks, and picture frames — you can use sections to organize your shop by item. Even if you don't sell different types of items — maybe you're all about knit caps — you can use sections to organize your goods by, say, yarn type, size, or price. You're allowed ten sections in all, as well as the default All Items section that's available in every shop.

To create a section, follow these steps:

1. **If it's not open already, open the Shop Name page by clicking the Your Shop link along the top of any Etsy page.**

   The Shop Name page opens.

2. **Click the Add Shop Sections link on the left side of the page.**

   The Shop Sections page opens (see Figure 8-9).

3. **Type a name for the new section in the Create a Section field.**

   The name can contain as many as 24 characters.

   In addition to using your shop title and shop announcement, Google uses your section titles as keywords for search. Opt for section titles that double as likely keywords. (Check out Chapters 12 and 16 for more about SEO.)

4. **Click the Save button.**

   Etsy creates a section, using the name you typed.

5. **To add another section, click the Create New Section link and repeat steps 3 and 4.**

6. **To change the order in which sections appear, click the icon to the left of the section and drag it to the desired spot in the order.**

To change a section's name, click its Edit link (it looks like a pencil), type a new name for the section, and click the Save button. To delete a section, click the Delete link (it looks like a trash can). Etsy prompts you to confirm the deletion; click OK. (Note that deleting a section doesn't delete the listings in that section.)

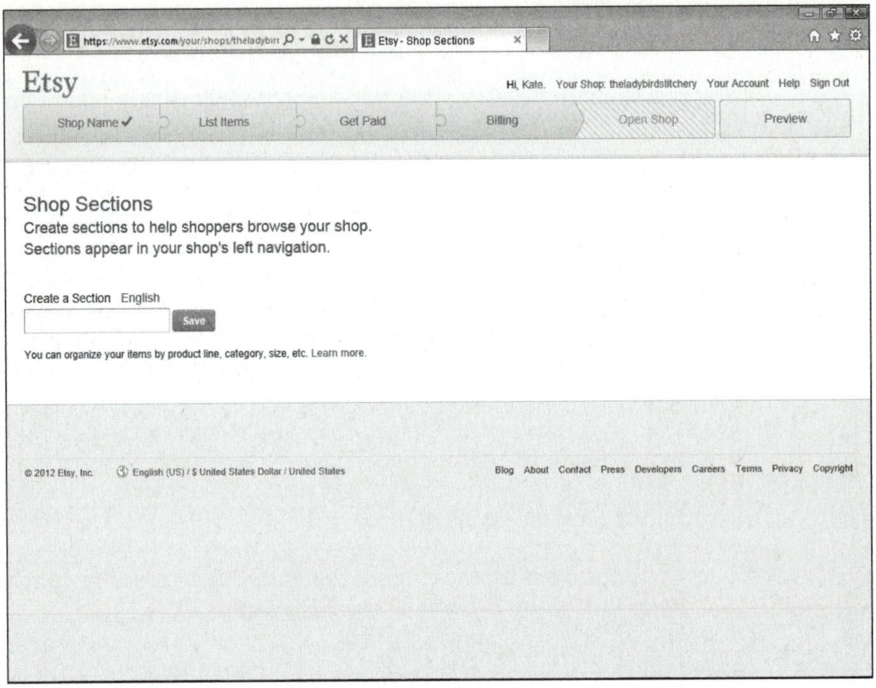

Figure 8-9:
Create sec-
tions for
your Etsy
shop.

If you haven't created any shop listings yet, you can't view sections on your shop's main page. After you create a listing, however — and assign it to a section — that section gets listed along the left side of your Etsy shop page. You find out how to create a shop listing and assign that listing to a section in Chapter 13.

Money Talks: Setting Up Payment Options

At the risk of sounding crass, odds are that you've set up your Etsy shop in the hopes of pulling in some coinage. Before you can do that, however, you have to indicate to Etsy what forms of payment you want to receive.

Exam cram: Examining your options

You can set up your Etsy shop to accept the following forms of payment:

✔ **Credit card (Visa, MasterCard, American Express, and Discover):** Etsy's Direct Checkout feature enables you to accept payment via credit card — namely, Visa, MasterCard, American Express, and Discover. Although it's currently available only in the United States (look for expansion to international sellers in 2013), this payment method is easily the most popular on the site. But wait, there's more: Direct Checkout offers protection from fraud and enables you to purchase and print U.S. Postal Service shipping labels directly from your Etsy shop.

Note: If you go the Direct Checkout route, be aware that Etsy charges a processing fee for each Direct Checkout order: 3 percent of the total sale (including shipping and sales tax), plus 25¢.

✔ **PayPal:** PayPal is another popular method of payment among Etsy users. Electronic payments are instantly deposited into your PayPal account, and transferring money from your PayPal account to a bank account is easy and free.

✔ **Money order:** Some people are simply old school. They prefer the time-honored system of paying by money order over using newfangled digital solutions like Direct Checkout or PayPal. Fortunately, Etsy allows you to accommodate these buyers. The downside? Unlike with Direct Checkout and PayPal, payment isn't rendered immediately. You have to wait for the buyer to snail-mail you the money order (or send it via some other type of delivery service).

✔ **Personal check:** Allowing payment by personal check offers the same basic advantages and disadvantages as permitting payment via money order: You indulge the Luddites, but you have to wait for delivery of payment.

✔ **Other:** If you want, you can accept additional payment methods — say, cashier's checks, gold doubloons, shiny beads, or what have you. If you opt to accept other forms of payment, be sure to indicate on your Shop Policies page what types you accept. (You find out how in the next chapter.)

If you choose to accept personal checks, money orders, or cashier's checks as payment, do so with care. These forms offer less protection from fraud. Never, never, ever ship an item to a buyer until her personal check, money order, or cashier's check clears, no matter how nicely she asks!

Preferential treatment: Specifying your preferences

When you've decided what forms of payment to accept, you need to indicate your preferences on Etsy. Here's how:

1. **If necessary, click the Your Shop link along the top of any Etsy page.**

   The Shop Name page opens.

2. **Click the Get Paid tab.**

   The Get Paid page opens, as shown in Figure 8-10.

   If you want to accept credit cards and gift cards as forms of payment, you must enable Etsy's Direct Checkout feature. (To confuse matters, Etsy sometimes refers to this as a "Shop Payment account.")

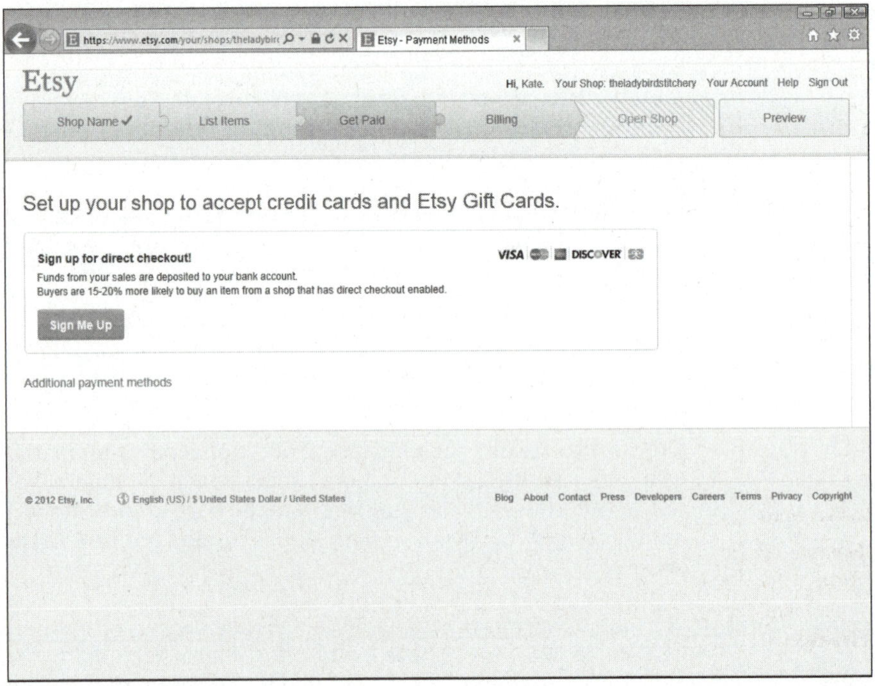

Figure 8-10: The Get Paid page.

3. **To enable Direct Checkout, click the Sign Me Up button.**

   Etsy displays the Terms of Service.

4. **Read the Terms of Service, and then click the Continue button to accept them.**

   As shown in Figure 8-11, Etsy prompts you to enter your personal information — your name, your date of birth, the last four digits of your Social Security number or federal tax ID number, your home address, your phone number, and your business name (optional). (Note that none of this information will be displayed publicly on Etsy. Pinkie swear.)

5. **Enter the requested information and click the Continue button.**

   Next, enter your bank info — the type of account you use, the name of the account owner, your bank's routing number, and your account number (see Figure 8-12).

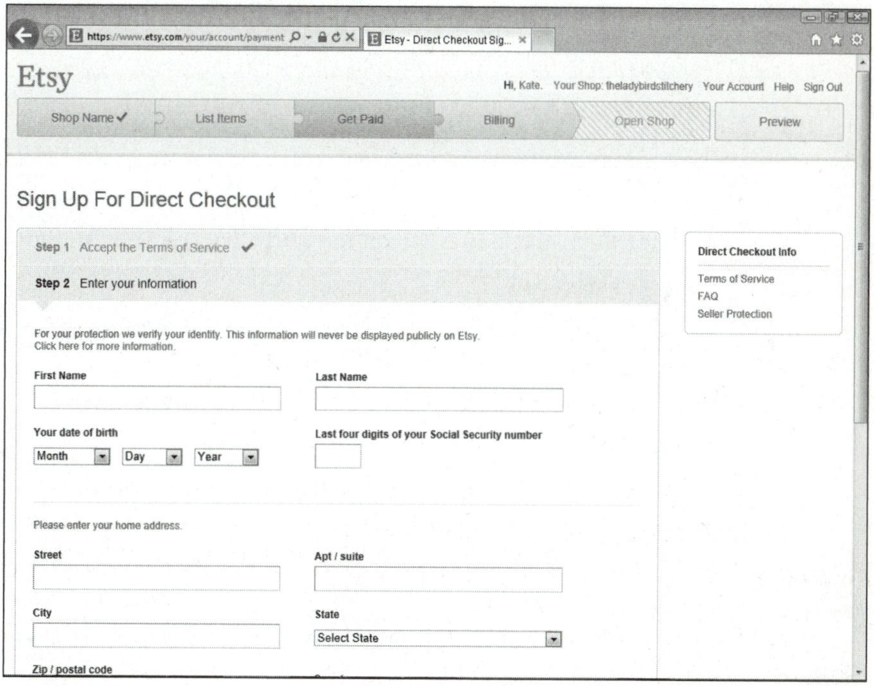

Figure 8-11: Time to get personal!

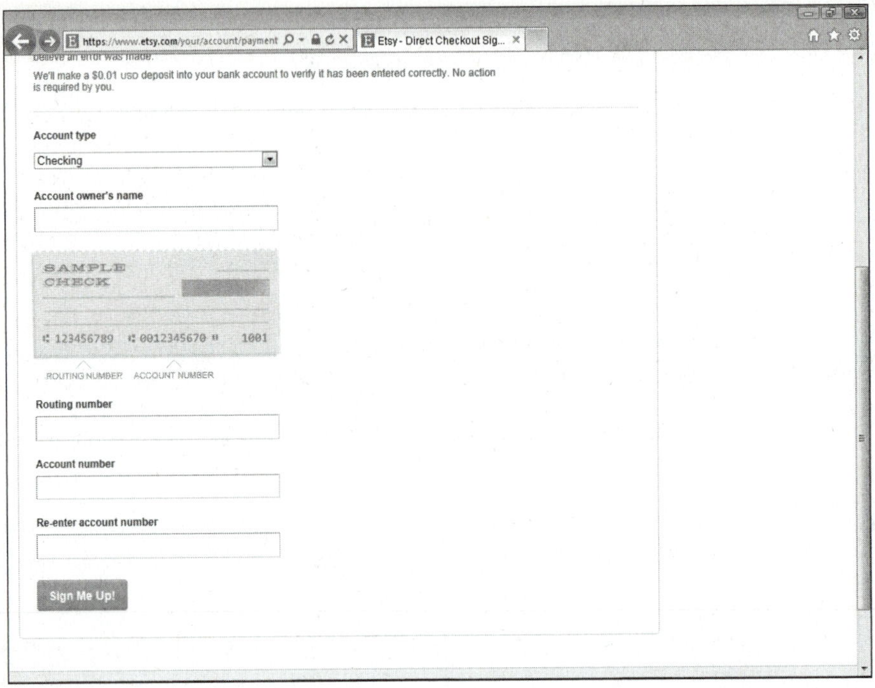

We'll make a $0.01 USD deposit into your bank account to verify it has been entered correctly. No action is required by you.

Account type

Checking ▾

Account owner's name

SAMPLE
CHECK

⑆ 123456789 ⑆ 0012345670 ⑈ 1001

ROUTING NUMBER   ACCOUNT NUMBER

Routing number

Account number

Re-enter account number

Sign Me Up!

Figure 8-12:
Enter your
bank info
here.

6. **Enter the requested information and click the Sign Me Up! button.**

   Etsy enrolls you in Direct Checkout.

7. **To accept other forms of payment — PayPal, money order, personal check, other — click the Get Paid tab.**

8. **If necessary, click the Additional Payment Methods link.**

   Etsy reveals additional payment options.

9. **Click the check box next to each type of payment you want to accept.**

10. **Click the Save button.**

    Etsy saves your changes.

Note that this is a global shop setting. Any items that you list in your shop will offer these payment options.

Bill Me: Setting Up Your Credit Card

Of course, you're not the only person here trying to make a buck. Etsy deserves a bit of compensation for helping you to sell your item, wouldn't you agree? As mentioned in Chapter 1, Etsy stays afloat by charging sellers a listing fee (currently, 20¢) for each item listed on the site. In addition, Etsy collects a commission from the seller for each item sold — currently, 3.5 percent of the total price of the item (not counting shipping or tax).

To pay these fees, a credit card is required. That means you must supply Etsy with one before your shop can go live. To enter your credit card info, follow these steps:

1. **If necessary, click the Your Shop link along the top of any Etsy page.**

   The Shop Name page opens.

2. **Click the Billing tab.**

   The Billing page opens, as shown in Figure 8-13.

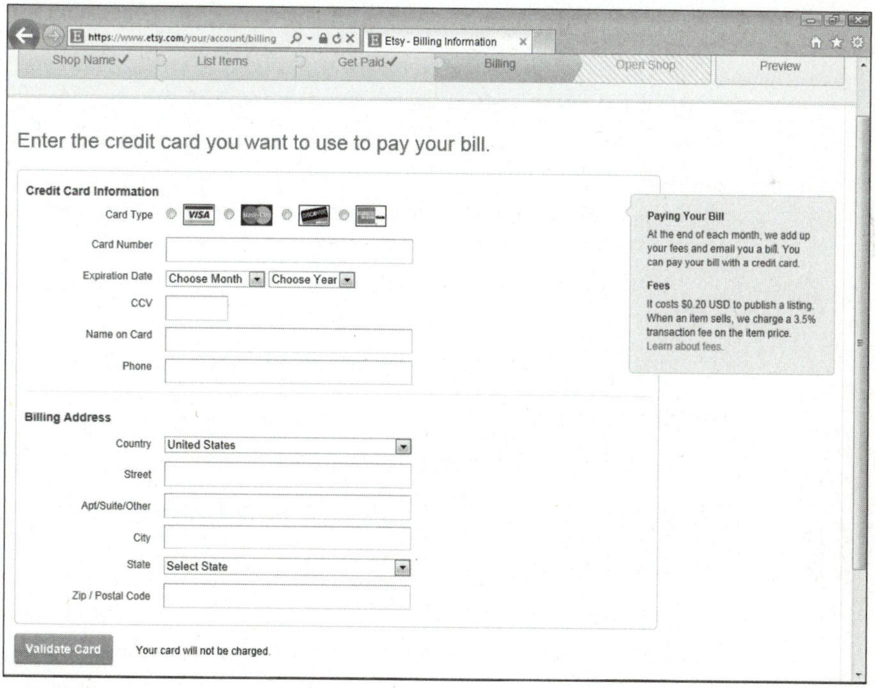

Figure 8-13: The Billing page.

3. **Enter your credit-card information in the fields provided.**

4. **Enter your billing address in the fields provided.**

5. **Click the Validate Card button.**

   Etsy validates the card.

Note: You can set up your account to pay your Etsy bill automatically. For more information, see Chapter 18.

High Profile: Setting Up Your Public Profile

Everyone on Etsy has a public profile page. Why? A couple reasons. For one, being able to check out other Etsy members helps to inspire confidence in the site. That is, it's not populated by a bunch of faceless buyers and sellers; it's populated by actual *people!* For another, it's fun to see who else is on the site.

An Etsy profile can include the following tidbits:

✔ Your profile picture (also known as your avatar)

✔ Your name

✔ Your gender

✔ Your city

✔ Your birthday

✔ Your bio

✔ A list of your favorite materials

Anyone who visits your Etsy shop can access your public profile by clicking your name or avatar on any page in your Etsy shop.

To populate your Etsy public profile, follow these steps:

1. **Click the Your Account link along the top of any Etsy page.**

   The Your Account page opens.

2. **Click the Public Profile link on the left side of the screen.**

   The Your Public Profile page appears (see Figure 8-14).

3. **To add a profile picture, or avatar, to your profile, click the Browse button; then, in the dialog box that appears, locate and select the image you want to use.**

4. **If you want, indicate your gender.**

   If you prefer to keep that information private, select the Rather Not Say option button.

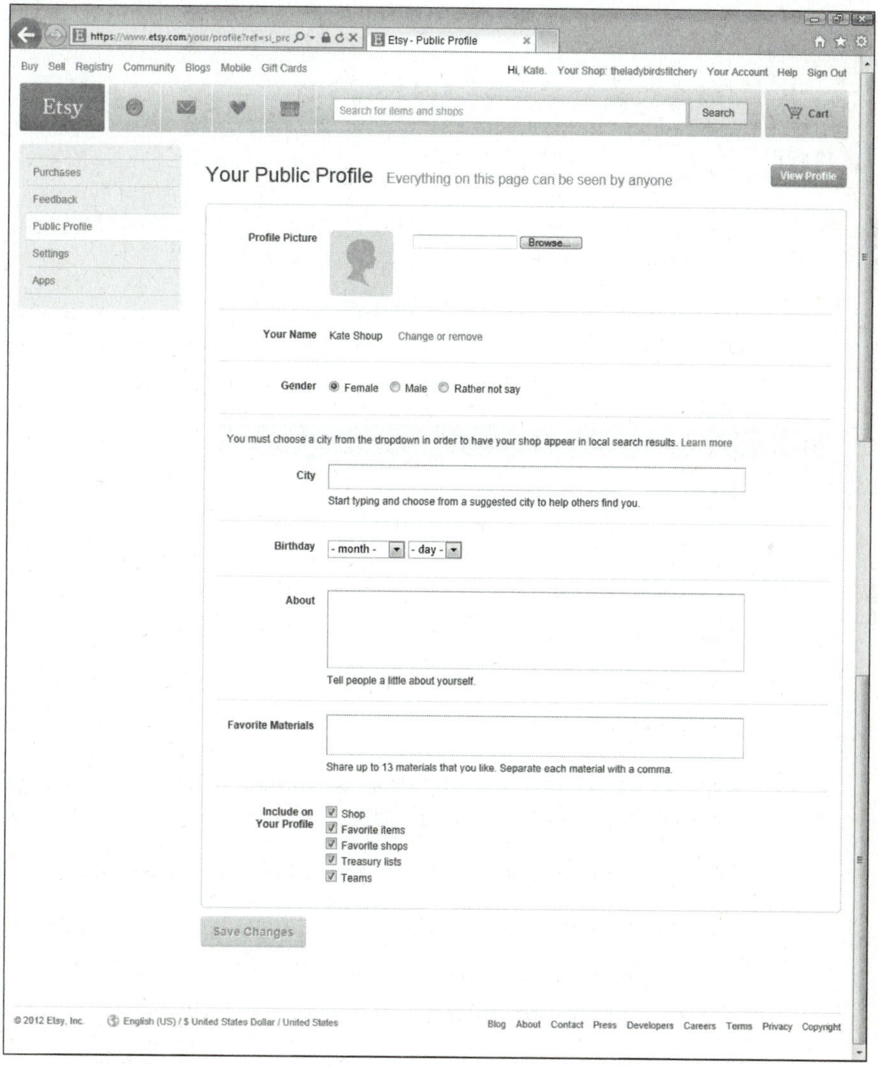

Figure 8-14:
To populate your profile, click the Public Profile link on the Your Account page.

Avatar hero: Choosing an avatar

Your profile picture, or *avatar,* isn't just something people see when they peruse your profile page or visit your shop. It's the image that represents both you and your store across the site. When you post on a forum, your avatar appears next to it. Ditto when you comment on the Etsy Blog or participate in teams or online workshops. You want to select an avatar that reflects well on you and your shop.

So, what type of image do you want to choose? Consider a few ideas:

✔ **Your store logo:** If you've developed a logo for your Etsy store, consider using it as your avatar. It's a great way to reinforce your brand on the site. (Flip to Chapter 16 for details on developing a logo.)

✔ **A product shot:** Using a product shot as your avatar is an excellent way to convey what you sell in your store. It's like having a little window right into your shop. (Chapter 11 has the scoop on taking great product shots.)

✔ **An emblematic image:** Suppose that you make lavender sachets. In that case, an image of, say, a field of lavender may serve as your avatar. It's not exactly a product shot (that is, you're not selling the field), but it's emblematic of your product.

✔ **A picture of you:** You may consider using a photo of yourself for your avatar — particularly if it reflects the overall aesthetic of your shop or if you're wearing or holding an item you sell.

Be aware that avatar images are quite small — 75 by 75 pixels, to be exact. You can't use that panoramic shot you took of the Sistine Chapel ceiling (or, at the very least, you'll need to crop it).

5. **Type your city in the City field.**

   As you type, Etsy displays a list of matching locales; click your town in the list to select it.

   By entering your location, you enable Etsy buyers to find your shop using the Shop Local tool. Chapter 3 has more information about this feature.

6. **Use the Month and Day drop-down lists to enter your birthday.**

7. **Type your bio in the About box.**

   For tips on writing your bio, see the section "Biohazard: Writing a Winning Bio or Shop Story" later in this chapter.

   Note: You should also disclose any other usernames you use on Etsy in the About box of your public profile. For example, you might write, "I'm also on Etsy under these usernames. . . ."

8. **In the Favorite Materials box, indicate which materials you like to use, separating entries with a comma and a space.**

   You can add as many as 13.

9. **If you want your profile to include your shop, any favorite items or shops, any Treasury lists you've compiled, and any teams you've joined, leave the check boxes at the bottom of the screen checked.**

   Just remember: If you choose to share your favorite items, Treasury lists, or teams with the public, buyers visiting your shop can see them, too. Make sure that you keep things on the appropriate side and that these items are a good reflection of who you are as a brand.

10. **Click the Save Changes button.**

    Etsy saves the changes you made to your profile.

11. **To preview your profile, click the View Profile button.**

    Etsy shows you how your profile will appear to others (see Figure 8-15).

Figure 8-15:
Preview your profile.

All About Me: Adding an About Page

Part of the reason people shop on Etsy is that they want to feel a personal connection with the living, breathing artists and craftspeople who make what they buy. Enter the About page. This page is a bit like the bio on your public profile, only expanded.

You won't be able to create your About page until after you've created your first listing. (For info on how to create listings, turn to Chapter 13.) After you've done that, you'll want to flip back to this section to get the lowdown on creating your About page.

To create your About page, follow these steps:

1. **Click the Your Shop link along the top of any Etsy page.**

   Notice that the page that appears is different, now that your shop is completely set up. Links along the left side of the page offer immediate access to tools for adding and managing listings, handling orders, dealing with bills, changing shop settings, promoting your shop, and more.

2. **Under Shop Settings, click the Info & Appearance link.**

   The Info & Appearance page opens.

3. **Click the About tab.**

   An editable About page opens.

   The first step in creating an About page is to add info about the shop owner, as shown in Figure 8-16.

4. **In the Portrait section, click the Add Photo link; then, in the dialog box that appears, locate and select the image you want to use.**

5. **In the Name field, type your name.**

6. **In the Role section, select any check boxes that apply: Maker, Designer, and/or Curator. (Owner is selected automatically.)**

   If your role is best described in some other way, type it in the field provided.

7. **Enter a short bio.**

   You're limited to 250 characters here, so keep it short. You'll find out where your more full-featured bio goes in a moment.

8. **Click the Add Shop Member button.**

   Etsy saves your info and clears the fields in the Shop Members section, enabling you to add more members as needed. It also reveals additional editable sections: Shop Story, Shop Photos, and Shop Links.

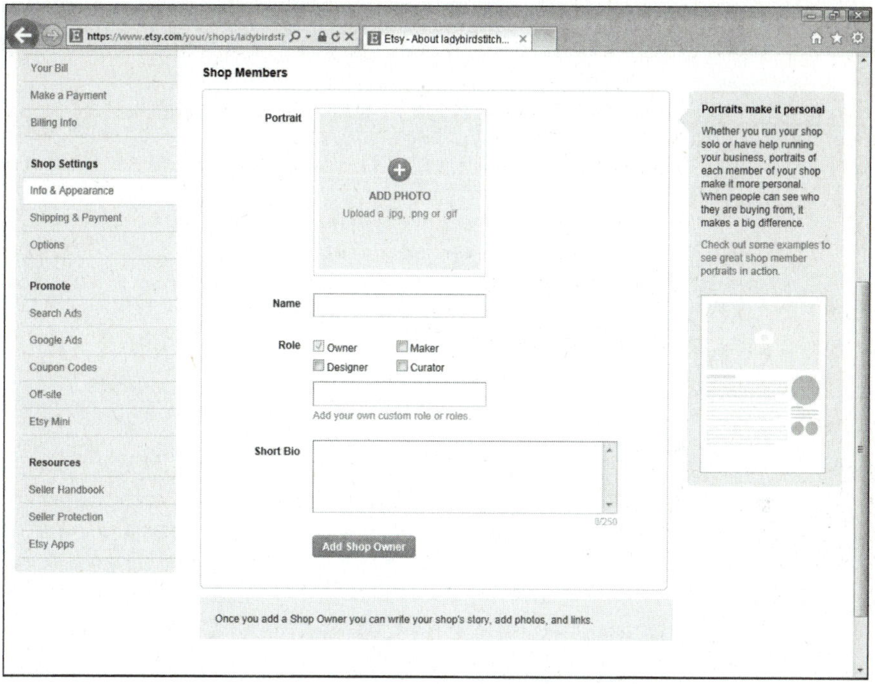

Figure 8-16:
The editable
About page.

9. **If you share the responsibilities of running your shop with others, repeat steps 4–8 as many times as needed to add their info.**

Absolutely nothing can stop you from opening an Etsy shop with, say, your grandma, your best friend, or the guy whose welding studio is across the hall from yours. (Etsy refers to shops run by or including goods crafted by more than one person as collectives.) But be aware that you can't attach multiple names to an Etsy account. That is, if you're the one who creates the account for the collective, your name — and your name only — is associated with that account, even though you can (actually, you're *required* to, per Etsy) add other shop members to your shop's About page. In other words, Etsy holds you responsible for all account-related activities. So, even if you had nothing to do with that flame war Grandma launched on the Etsy Ideas forum while using the collective's account, you're the one who'll be blamed for it. To find out more about running an Etsy collective, see Chapter 18.

The next step in creating an About page is to tell your story, or the story of the shop.

10. **In the Shop Story section (see Figure 8-17), type a headline in Story Headline field.**

This may or may not be similar to your shop title.

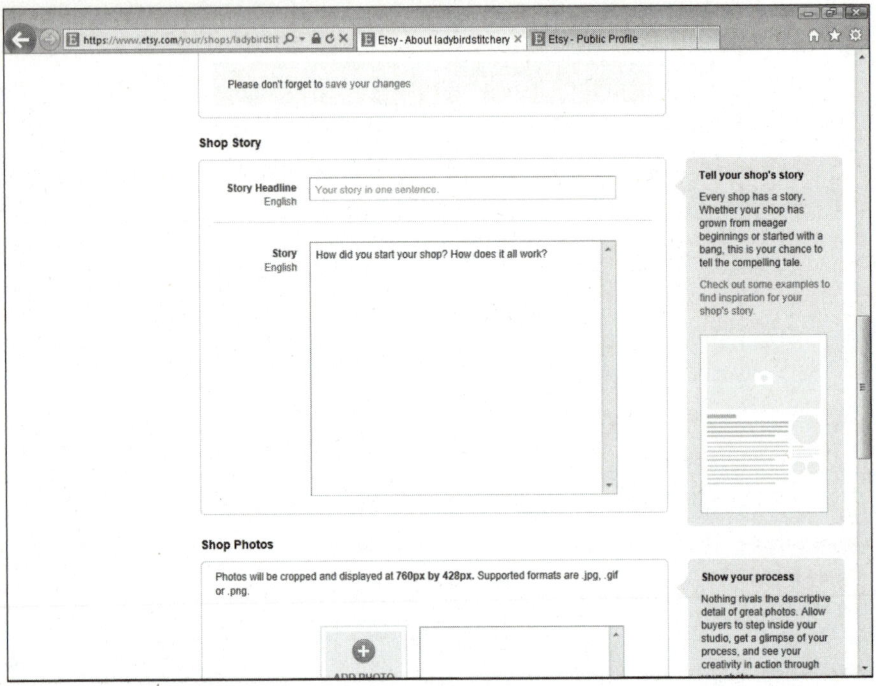

Figure 8-17:
The Shop
Story
section.

11. **In the Story field, type up your bio, or your shop's story.**

This might be similar to the bio you wrote for your public profile, but it doesn't have to be. Lots of Etsy sellers use the Story section to get into the nitty-gritty of what they do and why. Alternatively, it might discuss who the seller is on a more personal level, what their studio is like, or how a normal day is for them.

The next step in creating an About page is to add photos. Opt for images that show you, your process, your shop, or maybe a partly finished product. The idea is to give viewers an idea of who you are and how you work.

12. **In the Shop Photos section (see Figure 8-18), click an Add Photo link; then, in the dialog box that appears, locate and select the image you want to use.**

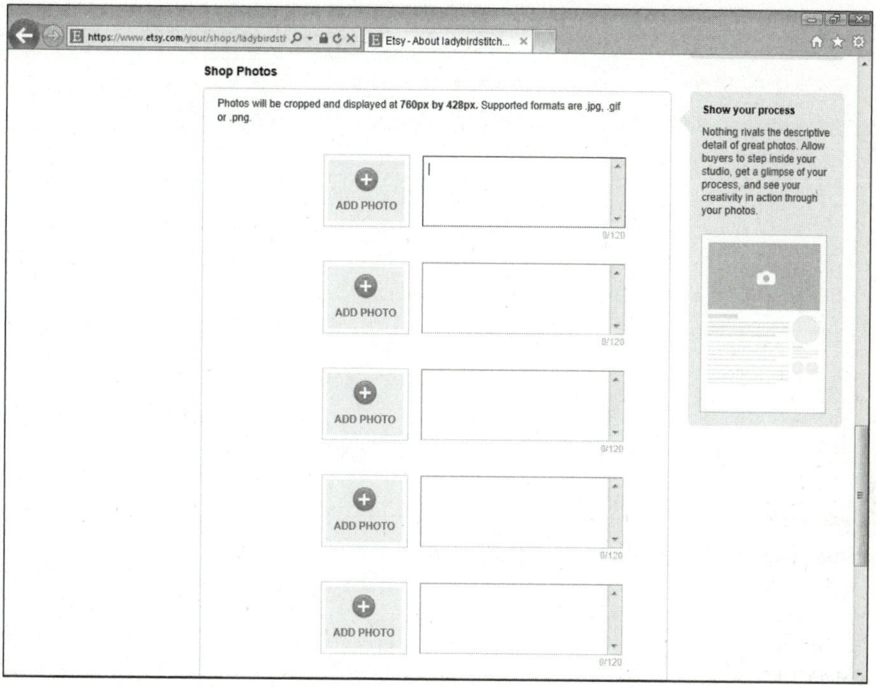

Figure 8-18:
The Shop
Photos
section.

13. **Repeat Step 12 to add as many images as you'd like.**

    These images will be presented in slideshow form on your About page.

    The next step in creating an About page is to add links to other sites you maintain for your craft business. This might be a Facebook page, a Twitter feed, a blog, or a separate website. (Note that this separate website can't be one where you sell the same items listed in your Etsy shop.)

14. **In the Shop Links section (see Figure 8-19), click the Link Type drop-down list and choose Facebook, Twitter, Shop Blog, or Shop Website.**

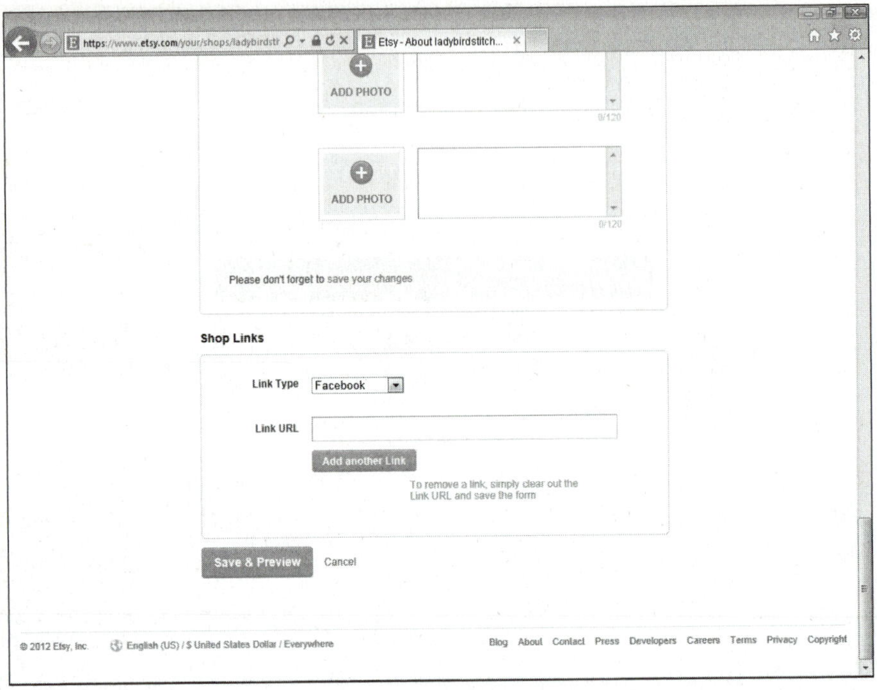

Figure 8-19:
The Shop
Links
section.

15. **Enter the page's URL in the Link URL field.**

16. **Optionally, repeat Step 15 to add more links.**

17. **Click Save & Preview.**

    Etsy displays a preview of the About page, as shown in Figure 8-20.

18. **If you don't love the page, click the Continue Editing button to make changes; otherwise, click the Publish button.**

    Etsy publishes the page.

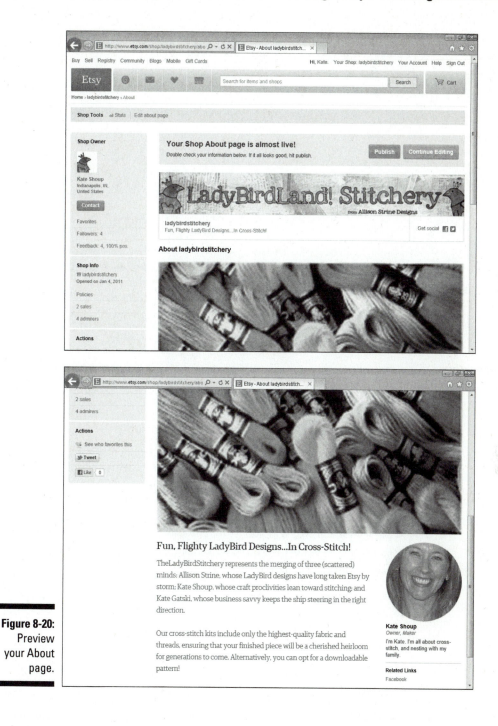

Figure 8-20:
Preview your About page.

Biohazard: Writing a Winning Bio or Shop Story

For many crafty types, the idea of writing anything — let alone a piece about themselves — is about as enticing as spelunking in Yucca Mountain. But a succinct, clever, well-written bio, or shop story — both the one that appears in your public profile and the one on your About page (which may be similar, but don't have to be) — is essential to the success of your Etsy shop. Why? Lots of reasons. Here are just two:

✔ **Your bio enables buyers to see who they're buying from.** Through your bio, you become a bona-fide human being in your buyers' eyes.

✔ **Your bio lets you toot your own horn a bit.** Maybe your work has been recognized in some way. Or maybe you studied your craft at the most prestigious school around. If so, you want to make sure that everyone who visits your shop knows about it!

In the following sections, we explain how to write a first draft of your bio, edit it effectively, and polish it with a few extra details.

Quiz show: Starting with a few essential questions

If writing your bio seems a bit daunting, don't freak out. Writing your bio is a process, just like anything else. It starts with writing down answers to a few key questions:

✔ Who are you?

✔ What's your educational and/or artistic background?

✔ What do you make? Do you have a signature product? If so, what's the story behind that product?

✔ What do you enjoy most about making the things you sell?

✔ What are your hobbies?

✔ What are you passionate about?

✔ Who or what inspires you?

Armed with your answers, you're ready to write the first draft of your bio. Notice that we said "first draft." That's code for "Don't try to be perfect right out of the gate." For now, just put your pen to paper (or your fingers to keyboard) and see what comes out. The idea is to tell buyers a little bit about yourself, your business, and the products you sell.

Some people write their bios in first person, while others opt for third person. Our view? Unless you're the queen or you play in the NBA, stick with first person.

The tweak shall inherit the Earth: Tweaking your first draft

With your first draft complete, it's time to tinker and tweak. As you do, try incorporating some or all of these tips:

✔ **Say hello.** If you were the proprietor of a real-world boutique, you'd certainly greet customers as they entered your store. Do the same for folks visiting your Etsy shop. While you're at it, thank them for stopping by. It's just good manners.

✔ **Start strong.** The first few pages of a novel need to grab readers by the throat and shake them until their lunch money falls out of their pockets (figuratively speaking). Likewise, the first paragraph of your Etsy bio needs to seize buyers by the eyeballs to convince them to read on. (Again, we're talking figuratively; *actually* seizing someone by the eyeballs would probably subject you to litigation.)

✔ **Be friendly and approachable.** This strategy will yield substantially better results than taking the opposite tack — being rude and inaccessible. Also, a little bit of humor can go a long way.

✔ **Tell a story.** An anecdote about how your business started or a story about the spark behind your store name may be just the thing to pull a buyer in.

✔ **Go the fictional route.** If it's true that all fiction is autobiographical, why not opt for a clever fictional "bio"?

✔ **Keep it short.** It's your Etsy bio, not *War and Peace.* A few short paragraphs will do.

✔ **Break your information into sections.** For most people, reading large blocks of text is about as appealing as chewing gum pried off the floor of a subway car. If your bio is running a little long, people perusing it will appreciate your use of sections, with titles, to break up your information.

✔ **Proofread.** Before you post your bio, triple-check it to make sure that it doesn't contain any spelling or grammatical errors. Better yet, ask your English-major friend to check it for you.

✔ **Be professional . . . sort of.** No, you don't have to wear pin-striped suits and practical pumps and drive a no-nonsense four-door sedan. But you do need to project an air of competence — even if your shop is all about fun. You want to be taken seriously as a seller, right? That being said, the tone of your bio needs to match the tone of your shop and products. If your business is about whimsy, a stuffy bio just won't do!

Extra! Extra! Adding a few extras

In addition to sharing your story with readers, you can use your bio to include the following information:

✔ **Press clippings:** If you or your business has garnered a nod in the media, don't hesitate to provide a link to the story in your bio. Just don't go too crazy with the clippings. Having links to more than a few may make your shop seem more corporate than co-op.

✔ **Product info:** If you find yourself answering the same question about one of your products over and over again ("Yes, the sweaters are knit from hair shed by my hamster"), consider spelling out the information in your bio.

✔ **Disclaimer:** If your product merits a disclaimer, you can include it in your bio. For example, if you sell vintage items, you may want to include a disclaimer indicating that your goodies are old and used. If you sell, say, copper jewelry, you can mention in your disclaimer that your pieces may turn people's skin green. Or if you craft toys, but they aren't meant for babies, you can include a disclaimer to that effect.

✔ **Charitable giving:** Many Etsy sellers donate a portion of their take to charity. If you're one such seller, you can indicate that in your bio. (Note that charitable listings and shops are subject to a few rules, outlined here: www.etsy.com/help/article/483#charity.)

Team Edit-ward: Editing Your Shop Settings

Inspiration may strike after you set up your shop. Maybe you'll want to update your banner, revise your shop announcement, or change some other aspect of your storefront. Fortunately, doing so is easy. You access the vast majority of settings discussed in this chapter by clicking the Your Shop link along the top of every Etsy page and then clicking the Info & Appearance link on the left side of the page that appears. Additional settings — namely, those pertaining to your payment and billing info — are also accessible via Your Shop; this time, though, you choose from the links in the Bill section on the left side of the screen.

Chapter 9

Policy Academy: Establishing Your Shop's Policies

· ·

In This Chapter

▶ Understanding policy basics

▶ Setting payment-related policies

▶ Setting shipping policies

▶ Establishing your policy for returns and exchanges

▶ Setting up your Shop Policies page

· ·

Rules. Who needs 'em? In a word, you. Or, to be more precise, your Etsy shop. As you set up your Etsy shop, it's critical that you lay some ground rules for buyers. You want to establish clear store policies, especially with respect to payment, shipping, and returns and exchanges. That way, your customers know what to expect if they buy from you and they'll feel more confident and at ease. Setting clear policies, and spelling them out on your Shop Policies page, also enables you to head off problems down the road.

Although developing your shop policies will likely be an ongoing process — and one that will probably result in a set of policies that's as unique as the items you sell — this chapter can help you get started.

Keep in mind that although you can avert a lot of crises by establishing clear store policies, you'll still face the occasional conflict with customers. When that happens, you need to take three actions: Communicate, communicate, and communicate. Oh, and one more thing: Communicate. For more on dealing with disagreements and other customer service issues, see Chapter 17.

Fair and Square: General Policy Tips

Before we get into policy specifics in the rest of this chapter, we want to talk in general terms about what, apart from honesty, constitutes a good policy. A good policy has two key characteristics:

- ✔ **It's fair.** Yes, you put policies in place to protect your business. But a good policy also protects your customers. Your shop policy needs to be one for which you would be grateful if, through some amazing breach in the space–time continuum, *you* were your customer.

- ✔ **It's simple.** Although it's important to use your words, you don't want to use too many of them when crafting your shop policies. Keep your policies simple, clear, and concise.

One more thing: When it comes to setting your shop's policies, you have a lot of leeway. Shops' policies are often as unique as the items they sell. That being said, you do need to adhere to Etsy's terms of use (www.etsy.com/policy/terms) and respect the site's DOs & DON'Ts (www.etsy.com/policy/dosdonts). And of course, you must comply with all local and federal laws.

Financial Matters: Establishing Payment-Related Policies

Perhaps the most important policies you need to consider relate to payment. After all, you started your Etsy shop in the hopes of pulling in a few Benjamins, right? In Chapter 8, you see how to specify what forms of payment you'll accept, as well as your preferred currency. You'll want to be sure to be sure to convey both to your buyers on your Shop Policies page. As you craft your payment-related shop policies, you'll also want to cover sales tax.

If, after checking the local laws in your area and consulting a smarty-pants accountant, you've determined that you must collect sales tax, you can easily do so. In fact, with Etsy's tax calculator, you can collect sales tax during the checkout process. When you do, Etsy automatically assesses a sales tax for buyers in the region that you specify. (Not sure whether you need to collect sales tax? See Chapter 18 for more info.)

Before you can set up Etsy's tax calculator, you'll need to have finalized the setup of your shop — which means you'll have to have added at least one item listing. (You find out how to add item listings in Chapter 13.) After you've done that, you'll want to flip back to this section to get the skinny on getting set up to collect sales tax.

Follow these steps:

1. **Click the Your Shop link along the top of any Etsy page.**

2. **Click the Shipping & Payment link, under Shop Settings, on the left side of the page.**

   The Shipping & Payment page opens.

3. **Click the Sales Tax tab.**

   The Sales Tax Settings page opens (see Figure 9-1).

4. **If you live in the United States, click the State drop-down list and choose your state.**

   If you live in Canada, choose a province from the drop-down list in the Canada section. If you live in another country, select it from the drop-down list under Other Countries.

5. **Click the Add Tax Rate button.**

6. **Enter the appropriate tax rate in the Tax Rate box.**

7. **If the laws in your area require you to charge sales tax on shipping fees, select the Apply Rate to Shipping check box.**

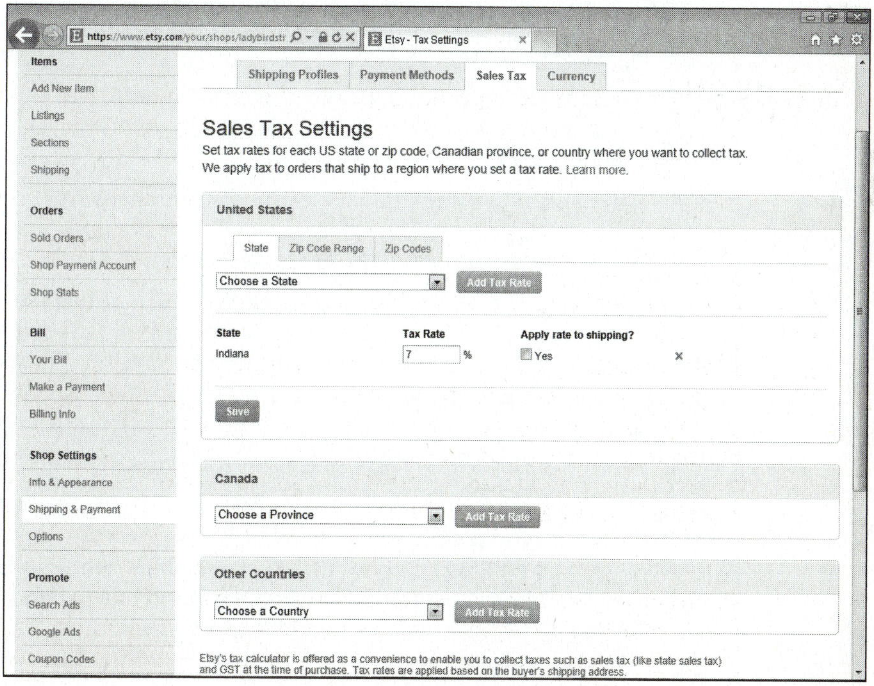

Figure 9-1:
Set up the Etsy tax calculator to automatically collect taxes.

8. **If local laws require you to assess a sales tax on buyers from specific zip codes, click the Zip Code Range or Zip Codes tab, enter the applicable zip code range or zip code, and repeat steps 5 and 6.**

9. **Click the Save button.**

   Etsy saves your settings.

You find out more about collecting sales tax in Chapter 18.

Ship Shape: Establishing Your Shipping Policies

Unless you enjoy keeping customers in the dark about how and when they can expect to receive their items, you'll want to outline a clear policy with respect to shipping.

As you develop your shipping policy, consider these areas:

- ✔ **What shipping carrier you'll use:** Do you plan to ship via the U.S. Postal Service (USPS)? FedEx? UPS? DHL? Pony Express? Delivery owl? (For help in choosing a shipping provider and making other shipping-related decisions, see Chapter 15.)

- ✔ **Which delivery option you'll select from your shipping carrier:** Say that you've opted to ship via USPS. Will you choose First Class? Priority Mail? Media Mail?

- ✔ **Whether you'll include delivery confirmation or insurance:** Smart money has you providing both — especially for higher-priced items. That way, if a package gets lost en route, you're covered.

- ✔ **Whether you're willing to ship internationally:** If you are, decide whether you or the buyer will be responsible for any Customs fees incurred.

- ✔ **How you'll handle combined shipping:** Many sellers discount shipping when buyers purchase multiple items from their Etsy shop at once. Although you're certainly not obligated to do so, adopting this practice can be a good way to increase sales.

- ✔ **How quickly you'll ship the item:** Some sellers promise to ship items within one business day. Other sellers need a little more time. Be sure to let your buyers know what they can expect from you in this regard.

   If you make custom items, you want to account for the time it takes to make the item when estimating how quickly you'll ship it.

✔ **Your willingness to upgrade:** Sometimes buyers need their items quickly. To accommodate those buyers, consider offering expedited shipping — for example, overnighting the item.

✔ **How you'll package items you ship:** Will you send your piece in a padded envelope or a box? Do you recycle packaging materials? Is gift wrapping available?

After you decide on your basic policies, you can add them to your shop's Shop Policies page, as we describe later in this chapter.

Return to Sender: Handling Returns and Exchanges

Obviously, you want all your customers to love your items. But — no disrespect — sometimes they won't. (What? We said "no disrespect"!) When that happens, you need to refer buyers to your policy on returns and exchanges.

Your policy for returns and exchanges needs to cover the following:

✔ **Whether you accept returns or exchanges:** Some sellers do; other sellers don't. Be sure to spell out your policy on both regularly listed items and custom pieces.

Some items just aren't conducive to being returned — think panties, swimsuits, bath and beauty products, personalized items, and the like.

✔ **Under what circumstances returns or exchanges are permitted:** Some sellers accept returns or exchanges for any reason, the theory being that they want their customers to be happy, no matter what. Other sellers allow returns or exchanges only in certain circumstances — for example, if the item doesn't fit correctly or if it was damaged en route.

✔ **How long customers have to return or exchange an item:** If you do allow returns and exchanges, you want to lay down the law on how long customers have to contact you with their concerns and send their item back to you — for example, 1 week, 2 weeks, or 30 days.

✔ **Who pays to ship the item back to you:** Do you cover shipping costs, or does the buyer?

After you select your return and exchange policies, it's time to add them to your Shop Policies page, as we describe in the next section.

Policy Wonk: Setting Up Your Shop Policies Page

With your policies established, all that's left is to share them with your buyers. Fortunately, your Etsy shop includes a special Shop Policies page, where you can do just that. In the following sections, we list the page's sections and explain how to populate the page with your shop's specific information.

Your Shop Policies page doesn't have to be all business. Although it includes information of a serious nature, there's nothing to stop you from letting your quirky personality creep in.

It's a good idea to read other shops' policies. You're almost certain to run across great policies that you never thought of implementing. To view a shop's Shop Policies page, go to the shop's main page and then click the Policies link on the left side of the screen, under Shop Info.

Introductory offer: Introducing the sections

The Etsy Shop Policies page includes the following sections (see Figure 9-2).

Welcome

The Welcome area is a great place to, well, welcome customers to your shop. You can also talk a bit about your shop, the pieces you sell, and your overarching philosophy as an artist or craftsperson. Here's an example of a solid Welcome statement:

> Welcome to LadyBird Stitchery! Thank you so much for visiting. Our cross-stitch kits include only the highest-quality fabrics and threads. Alternatively, you can opt for a downloadable pattern! We hope you find something here to love. Please check back often, as we regularly add new kits and patterns!

This section is also a great place to reiterate important announcements — for example, if you're away on vacation for a week and you won't be shipping items during that time.

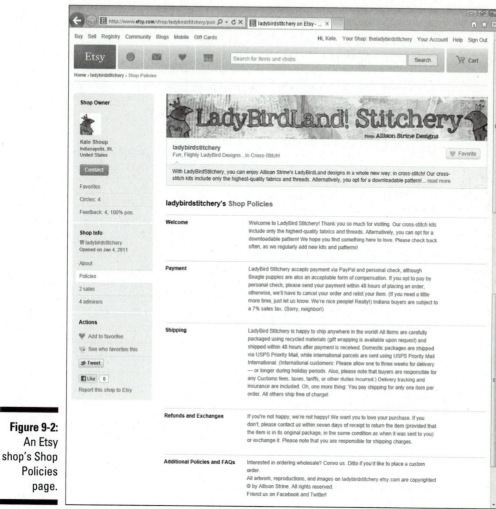

Payment

This area is where you spell out any policies that relate to payment: forms of payment you accept, whether (and for whom) you charge sales tax, your preferred currency (assuming that it's not the default, U.S. dollars), how long buyers using methods of payment other than PayPal have to pay for their goodies, and so on. Check out this example of a strong Payment statement:

LadyBird Stitchery accepts payment via Direct Checkout and personal check. Beagle puppies are also an acceptable form of compensation. (Kidding!) If you opt to pay by personal check, please send your payment within 48 hours of placing an order; otherwise, we'll have to cancel your order and relist your item. (If you need a little more time, just let us know. We're nice people! Really!) Indiana buyers are subject to a 7 percent sales tax. (Sorry, neighbor!)

Shipping

Indicate your shipping policies here — how you ship items (and how quickly), whether you ship internationally, whether buyers can upgrade shipping to expedite delivery, how items are packaged, and so on. Here's an example of a thorough Shipping statement:

LadyBird Stitchery is happy to ship anywhere in the world! All items are carefully packaged using recycled materials (gift wrapping is available upon request) and shipped within one to two business days after payment is received. Domestic packages are shipped via USPS Priority Mail, while international parcels are sent using USPS Priority Mail International. (International customers: Please allow one to three weeks for delivery — or longer during holiday periods. Also, please note that buyers are responsible for any Customs fees, taxes, tariffs, or other duties incurred.) Delivery tracking and insurance are included. Oh, one more thing: You pay shipping for only one item per order. All others ship free of charge!

Refunds and Exchanges

Here's where you say whether you accept returns or exchanges, and under what circumstances. You can also indicate how long customers have to contact you about an item they want to return or exchange, and who pays to ship the item back to you. Here's an example of a good Refunds and Exchanges statement:

If you're not happy, we're not happy! We want you to love your purchase. If you don't, please contact us within seven days of receipt to return the item (provided that the item is in its original package, in the same condition as when it was sent to you) or exchange it. Please note that you are responsible for shipping charges.

Additional Policies and FAQs

You guessed it: This area is where you include any additional information that you want to share about you, your shop, or your products. For example, you can use this space to indicate that you welcome wholesale inquiries or accept custom orders. You can also include a copyright statement to scare off design poachers, as well as provide your contact information. Here's an example:

Interested in ordering wholesale? Convo us. Ditto if you'd like to place a custom order.

All artwork, reproductions, and images on ladybirdstitchery.etsy.com are copyrighted © by Allison Strine. All rights reserved.

You might also use this space as an FAQ of sorts, so you don't have to respond over and over again to the same question from potential buyers. Finally, this is a great place to include care instructions, sizing information for wearables, and/or other details pertaining to personalization.

Population control: Populating the page

To populate your Etsy Shop Policies page, follow these steps:

1. **Click the Your Shop link along the top of any Etsy page.**

   The Shop Name page opens.

2. **Click the Add Shop Policies link on the left side of the page.**

   The Shop Policies page opens (see Figure 9-3).

   Note: If your shop is already open (that is, you've created your first listing), you can access this page by clicking the Your Shop link, clicking the Info & Appearance link on the left side of the page, and clicking the Policies tab.

3. **In the Welcome Message text box, type a welcome message for your customers, share your philosophy, and enter any other bits you want to share.**

4. **In the Payment Policy text box, indicate which payment methods you accept, along with your payment terms, deadline requirements, tax policy, cancellation policy, and the like.**

5. **In the Shipping Policy text box, enter what shipping method you use, whether you're willing to upgrade shipping, whether you ship internationally, and so on.**

6. **In the Refund Policy text box, indicate whether you issue refunds and under what circumstances.**

7. **In the Additional Info text box, add any other policies you've established.**

8. **Do you live in the European Union? Or are you specifically targeting customers in that region? If so, then you should fill in the Seller Information field to include your name, the physical address from which you run your shop, an e-mail address that buyers can use to contact you, and, where applicable, your tax ID number.**

   Click the FAQ link under the Seller Information box for more information on this subject.

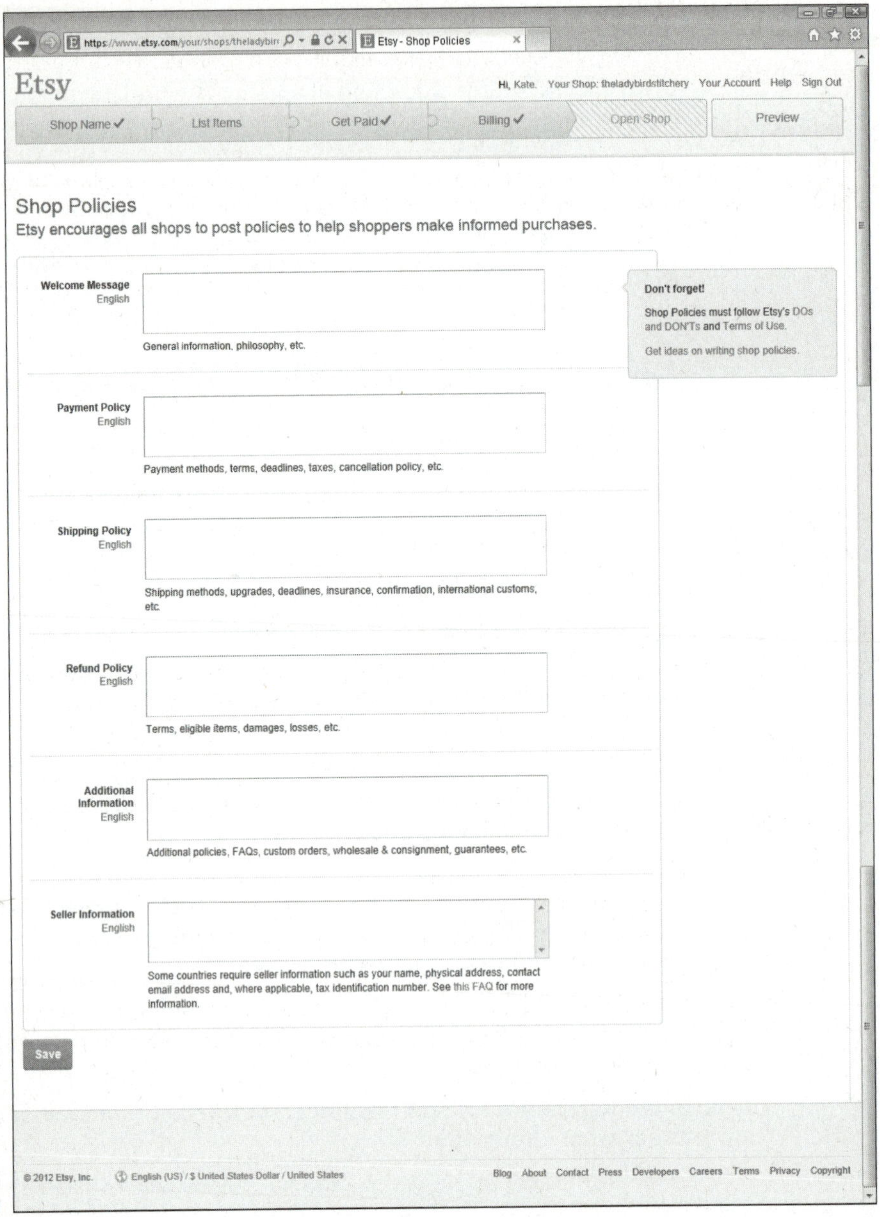

Figure 9-3: Spell out your shop policies.

9. Click the Save button.

Etsy saves the changes you made to your Shop Policies page.

Be sure to proofread your policies before you post them in your Etsy shop. You don't want any grammatical errors or misspellings making you look like an idiot! That being said, you can always go back and edit your shop policies, as well as many other store settings. (For more on that, see Chapter 18.)

Chapter 10

Come on Down, the Price Is Right! Pricing Your Work

In This Chapter

▶ Understanding pricing formulas

▶ Making sure your prices make sense

▶ Assessing the value of vintage items

▶ Pricing items to move during sales

Years ago, a close friend developed a keen business idea: the million-dollar hot dog. The million-dollar hot dog would be just like any other hot dog, except that it would cost a million dollars. Yes, demand for the million-dollar hot dog may be low. But as our friend rightly points out, "You really only ever need to sell *one!*"

Ironically, most Etsy sellers err on the other end of the spectrum, underpricing the pieces they sell. Often they're so thrilled that someone wants to buy something they made, it doesn't occur to them that they could've sold it for more. But just as overpricing your pieces has its problems (you never sell anything), so does underpricing them. Specifically, underpricing results in lost profits and, worse, the perception that your pieces are "cheap" — that is, products of low quality. Particularly with one-of-a-kind items like yours, customers use the piece's price to assess its value.

The trick, then, is to strike a balance with your pricing. You want to price your pieces high enough to cover your costs and turn a healthy profit. (After all, you're running a business.) But you need to price your items low enough that you can sell a reasonable volume of goods. Finding that sweet spot is the focus of this chapter.

As you become more adept and efficient at crafting your pieces and running your business, your profit margin will naturally improve.

Formulaic Plot: Breaking Down Your Pricing Formulas

Hands down, one of our favorite *Saturday Night Live* sketches was the one with Chevy Chase as President Gerald R. Ford, taking part in a presidential debate. After being asked an extremely complicated question involving numerous dollar figures and percentages, Chase, sweating profusely, stammered, "It was my understanding that there would be no math during the debates. . . ."

No doubt, many Etsy sellers feel exactly the same way. After all, don't most of us become artists or crafters specifically to avoid ever having to do arithmetic? Unfortunately, if you hope to run a profitable Etsy shop, you need to get comfortable with doing a little math, especially when it comes to pricing your pieces. But don't freak out! We're not talking calculus here or even trigonometry. All you have to learn are two very simple formulas:

$$\text{Wholesale Price} = (\text{Materials} + \text{Labor} + \text{Overhead}) \times 2$$

$$\text{Retail Price} = \text{Wholesale Price} \times 2$$

In the following sections, we break down each item in the preceding formulas and show you how to put the formulas to work.

Material girl: Calculating the cost of materials

When calculating your cost for materials, include the price of every little component in your piece. For example, suppose you sell handmade puppy plush toys for babies. Your material cost for each pup may include the cost of fabric, a label, rickrack, stuffing, and thread.

When you calculate the costs of your materials, you need to consider only the price of what you used to produce one piece. For example, if you bought 3 yards of fabric when purchasing your supplies, for a total of $12, but you used only a third of that fabric to produce a single pup, you want to divide what you paid for the fabric by 3, to calculate your material cost for the fabric — here, $4.

Labor pains: Figuring labor costs

While perusing the want ads in your local newspaper, suppose that you happened upon this listing:

> **Wanted:** A skilled professional to expertly fabricate our product by hand. Must also run every aspect of our business, including sourcing supplies, maintaining and marketing our shop, interacting with customers, and ensuring that items sold are artfully packaged and shipped to buyers. Pay: Nil.

Odds are, that's a job you'd pass up. Why, then, do so many Etsy sellers seem to pay themselves *nada* to run their shops? Don't fall into this trap! Your time is valuable. Like anyone, you deserve to be compensated for your work. Your pricing formula needs to include the cost of your labor.

Calculating your labor costs requires you to first set an hourly rate for your time. Be sure to pay yourself a fair wage — one that accounts for the skill required to craft your piece. Also, think about how much you want or need to make for your time. (This consideration is especially important if you're looking to quit your day job.)

If you're just starting out, you may opt for a lower hourly rate. You can give yourself periodic raises as your skills improve.

Another approach to figuring your hourly rate is to work backward. That is, figure out how much you need to be able to "bill" for each day and divide that by the number of hours you intend to work. For example, if you need to earn $100 a day to survive, and you plan to work five hours per day crafting the items you plan to sell, then you can simply divide $100 by 5, for an hourly rate of $20.

Armed with your hourly rate, you're ready to work out your labor costs. These costs must take into account the time it takes to design a piece, shop for supplies for the piece, construct the piece, photograph the piece, create the item listing for the piece (including composing the item title and description), correspond with the buyer, and package and ship the item.

As with materials costs (described in the previous section), you can *amortize* some of the labor costs — that is, you can spread them out. For example, if it took you four hours to develop the design for a piece, but you plan to make 50 of them, you have to amortize those four hours over the 50 finished pieces. Similarly, you likely shop for supplies for several pieces at once, meaning that you can spread the time that you spend shopping across all the projects that you plan to craft using those supplies. Oh, and if you're collaborating with others, you'll want to make sure you include the cost of *their* labor as well!

Let's use our plush toy pups as an example. Suppose you spend four hours designing your toy, and another hour shopping for enough supplies to construct 50 units. Your labor cost — assuming that your hourly rate is $20 — is $100, or, spread out over 50 toys, $2 per toy. Suppose further that each toy takes 30 minutes to make, photograph, and package ($10 in labor). Your labor cost per toy is then $12.

If you clear more than $400 per year with your Etsy shop, you probably need to pay taxes on it (although you should always consult an accountant or tax professional before making any assumptions). Especially if you plan to quit your day job and devote yourself exclusively to running your Etsy shop, you want to inflate your hourly wage to account for that. For more information about taxes, see Chapter 18.

Heads up: Adding up overhead

In addition to calculating your costs for materials and labor, you want to account for your overhead. Your overhead may encompass tools and equipment used in the manufacture of your products, office supplies, packaging supplies, utilities (for example, your Internet connection, electricity used to power your sewing machine, and so on), and Etsy fees. (*Note:* These costs don't include shipping. Be sure to calculate those costs separately and pass them along to the buyer. Chapter 15 has more details on calculating shipping costs.)

As with your labor costs, you need to amortize your overhead costs. That is, you total your overhead and then spread out that cost over all the items you make. As a simple example, if you calculate your monthly overhead at $100, and you produce 100 pieces a month, your overhead is $1 per piece. Of course, this calculation gets tricky when your overhead involves purchases of such things as tools and equipment used in the manufacture of your products. In those cases, you want to amortize the items over their life span. For example, suppose that you buy a $250 sewing machine that you plan to use for five years. In that time, you anticipate that you'll sew 500 pieces. Your overhead for the machine is then 50¢ per piece.

If you simply can't face calculating all these overhead costs, try adding together your materials cost and your labor cost for each piece you make; then multiply the sum by 10 percent or 15 percent and call that your overhead. It won't exactly reflect your actual overhead, but it'll probably be in the ballpark.

Two-timer: Understanding the "times 2"

In the formula we provide earlier in this chapter, you may have noticed that after adding together your costs for materials, labor, and overhead, you multiply the sum by 2. What's up with that? Simple. That "times 2" is your profit. It's what you invest back in your business. If your sewing machine breaks, the "times 2" is what you use to buy a new one. If you decide to expand your product line, that "times 2" is where you find the capital you need to grow.

Or you may just use your "times 2" revenue to build a nice nest egg for your business or a fund to fall back on if times get tough.

Although some sellers may feel uncomfortable with all this two-timing, thinking that their labor costs are their "profit," don't make the mistake of omitting this part of the formula. Yes, you may be paying yourself to make your products, but if your business grows, that may not always be the case. Multiplying your costs by 2 enables you to ensure that your business is profitable, regardless of how it's structured.

Double or nothing: Pricing for wholesale and retail

As the proprietor of your own small manufacturing business, you need to establish two prices for your goods: the wholesale price and the retail price. The wholesale price is for customers who buy large quantities of your item to resell it. That customer then sells your piece to someone else at the retail price, which is usually double the wholesale price. You obtain your wholesale price by using the following formula:

$$\text{Wholesale Price} = (\text{Materials} + \text{Labor} + \text{Overhead}) \times 2$$

To determine the retail price, we typically multiply the wholesale price by 2. Some sellers, however, may choose a higher number, multiplying the wholesale price by 2.5 or even 3 to determine the retail price, assuming that the market will bear that. Basically, the multiplier you choose is up to you.

Wait, don't say it. We know what you're thinking: "I'm going to sell my stuff only through my Etsy store, so I'll just charge everyone my wholesale price." Wrong! Even if you plan to sell your items exclusively through your Etsy shop, you need to establish both a wholesale price and a retail price, and you need to sell your pieces on Etsy at the retail rate. Why? A couple reasons:

✔ Even if you have no plans to expand beyond your Etsy shop, you don't want to cheat yourself of the opportunity to offer wholesale prices to bulk buyers if the opportunity arises.

✔ You'll almost certainly want to run the occasional sale in your Etsy shop. By pricing your goods for retail, you'll have some leeway to discount them as needed and still turn a profit.

If you do develop a wholesale business, it's especially important that you sell the pieces in your Etsy shop at the retail price. Otherwise, you're undercutting your wholesale customers! Unless it's your stated goal to alienate these customers, avoid this practice.

Although it's not yet available for public consumption, Etsy is in the process of developing Etsy Wholesale, a special marketplace for connecting sellers like you with wholesale buyers. If you're looking to take your business to the next level by selling wholesale to bricks-and-mortar outlets, then you'll want to keep an eye out for developments on the Etsy Wholesale front!

Some assembly required: Putting it all together

To help you get comfortable with pricing your pieces, we run through a couple examples here. Let's start with the puppy plush toys mentioned earlier. Suppose the following:

- ✔ The cost of materials for each toy is $2.50.
- ✔ Your hourly rate is $20. Your amortized labor costs for designing the toy and shopping for supplies is $2 per toy. It takes you 30 minutes to create, photograph, and package each toy, or $10 per toy. So, your total labor rate is $12 per toy.
- ✔ Your overhead for each piece is $1.10.

Your pricing equation then looks something like this:

Wholesale Price = (Materials + Labor + Overhead) × 2 = ($2.50 + $12 + $1.10) × 2 = $31.20

Retail Price = Wholesale Price × 2 = $31.20 × 2 = $62.40

Consider another example: Suppose you've designed a new bracelet for your jewelry line, and you need to determine how much to charge for it. The beads, findings, and thread you used to construct the bracelet put you back $12. Your labor rate is $14 per hour, and it takes you 45 minutes to make each bracelet (including amortized values for time spent on other business-related activities), which means that your labor cost is $14 × 0.75 = $10.50. Finally, suppose that your overhead for each bracelet is $1.75. Here's what your pricing equation looks like:

Wholesale Price = (Materials + Labor + Overhead) × 2 = ($12 + $10.50 + $1.75) × 2 = $48.50

Retail Price = Wholesale Price × 2 = $48.50 × 2 = $97

Offering products at different price points is a great way to increase your customer base. For example, say you specialize in ceramics. In that case, you may make ceramic mugs to sell at a lower price point; simple, medium-size bowls to sell at a slightly higher price point; and ornate platters to sell at a premium price point. This structure enables you to reach a larger range of potential buyers, which may help you increase your overall sales. As a bonus, if you're just starting out on Etsy, this strategy is a great way to nose out your niche in the market. You'll soon see which products your buyers respond to best.

Eyes on the Price: Evaluating Your Prices

You've done it: You've used the pricing formulas in the preceding section to determine your wholesale and retail prices. You're finished, right? Wrong. These formulas simply deliver the price you need to charge for your piece to turn a healthy profit. To ensure that the price you've hit on is, in the immortal words of Goldilocks, "just right," you need to do a little research, as we explain in the following sections.

Many artists and craftspeople underestimate their worth. They lack confidence in their work and their vision. As a result, they inevitably underprice their pieces. Underestimating the value of your work doesn't just hurt you; it hurts everyone who's trying to earn a living by selling their handmade goods. Deflated prices are bad all the way around! If you suffer from this malaise, channel your inner Stuart Smalley: You're good enough, you're smart enough, and, gosh darn it, people like you!

Know thy enemy: Assessing your competition's pricing

Your first order of business is to scope out your competition, both on and off Etsy. What are they charging? If their prices are roughly in line with yours, you're probably in good shape. But what if they're significantly higher or, more likely, lower? In that case, put yourself in your prospective buyer's shoes and ask yourself the following questions:

✔ Would I buy my product or a competitor's product? Why?

✔ Is my product made of better materials than my competitors' products?

✔ Did crafting my product or my competitors' products require more skill?

✔ Is my product different or special in any way?

✔ What do I think my product is worth?

Your answers to these questions help you determine whether you need to adjust your price upward or downward. For example, if your product is better made than your competitor's, you may be able to adjust your price upward. Ditto if it required more skill to build. Of course, if the opposite is true, you may need to lower your price.

As you research the price of items sold on Etsy, you'll appreciate Etsy's Market Research Tool. This tool enables you to see the price points of items sold on Etsy in general terms. To use the tool, log in to your Etsy account and conduct a search for an item you want to research — for example, cross-stitch kits. Then, on the search results page, click the Research View button next to the Sort By options. Etsy displays a graph depicting the prices of these items and the top tags used (see Figure 10-1).

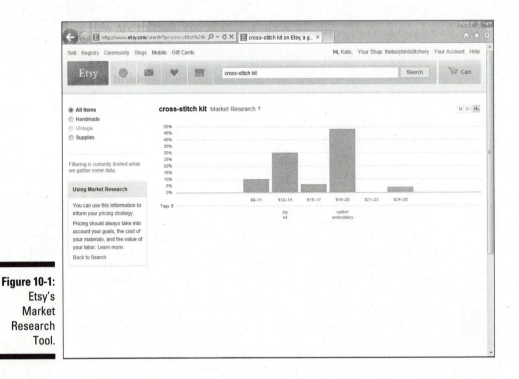

Figure 10-1:
Etsy's
Market
Research
Tool.

Your competition doesn't consist just of people who make an item similar to yours; it's anyone who's targeting the same market you are. Using the puppy plush toy example, your competition wouldn't be limited to shops that sell puppy plush toys; it would be any shop that makes toys or gifts for babies.

Here's looking at you, kid: Studying your target market

In gauging your price, you need to consider your target market. Who, in your estimation, will buy your piece? How much disposable income does that person have? If your target market is 20-something hipsters, chances are, they're not quite as flush as, say, your 40-something set, so you may need to keep your prices lower. On the flip side, if that 40-something set is the market you're after, you may be able to command a higher price.

Has this ever happened to you? You're shopping for a gift — say, earrings for your sister — but the pair you've found is priced far below what you want to spend, so you don't buy the set, even though the earrings are gorgeous and you know she'd love them. People often shop for gifts with a certain price point in mind — say, $25 for a friend or $50 for a family member. If your product is aimed at this market, ask yourself, who's the ultimate recipient for this gift? A best friend? An acquaintance? Someone's nephew? Then think about what most people would spend on a gift for that person, and price your piece accordingly.

Floor it: Figuring out how to lower your prices

If your research has revealed that your prices will likely give your market sticker shock, you may need to lower them. The best way to make this work is to attempt to lower your own costs. Can you purchase your materials more cheaply from a different supplier? Can you spend less time making each piece? Or can you redesign your product to require less in the way of supplies or labor time — for example, omitting the decorative rickrack piping on your plush pup? After you've managed to lower your costs, apply the formulas we talk about earlier in the chapter to determine the new price.

Don't lower your prices to compete with machine-made or imported items. Handmade items have more value and need to be priced accordingly.

Bundle up: Bundling your items

You may be able to increase sales by *bundling* your items — that is, selling multiple items together, as a package deal. For example, suppose you specialize in making jewelry. Instead of selling a $20 pair of earrings and a $30 necklace separately, you may bundle them into a single listing for, say, $45. Offering value bundles — say, buy two, get one free — is another tactic. Yes, you'll make less than you would if you sold them separately, but you'll move more merchandise, you'll save on shipping, and your customer will feel like she's gotten a super deal.

Up the ante: Knowing when to raise your prices

True, you need to lower your price in some circumstances, but other times you can charge — wait for it — *more*. See, people perceive some products to be more valuable than others. For example, consider the fact that some painters can command stratospherically high prices for their paintings. It's not because their raw materials were substantially more expensive — paint and canvas cost pretty much the same amount for everybody. And it's not that their paintings took longer to create. No, these paintings are insanely expensive because the public perceives their paintings to be valuable.

When pricing your items, see if you can take advantage of this perceived value and position your pieces as "premium" products. Maybe you use exceptional materials in crafting your piece. Or maybe you've developed a unique technique that makes your piece especially beautiful or durable. Note that buyers will also perceive your work as more valuable if you've developed a reputation as an artist — perhaps by showing your pieces at galleries or gaining publicity in some other way.

Be sure to talk up your work in your shop announcement and item descriptions. Share why your pieces are valuable. For example, if you not only craft necklaces, but also make your own beads, be sure to say so. If you use only the best organic cotton to sew your baby clothes, include words to that effect. If you use a particularly difficult technique that only a few other people have mastered, spell that out, too. (Flip to Chapter 8 for details on creating a profile page, and see Chapter 12 for details on writing item descriptions.)

Sometimes the very act of tagging your piece with a higher price can make buyers perceive it as more valuable. Of course, that doesn't mean you should offer some useless doodad or otherwise unremarkable item at an outrageous price. (Remember the million-dollar hot dog we mention earlier in this chapter?) People will see right through that ploy. But if you offer an item that's beautifully crafted and truly unique, you may be able to capitalize on this phenomenon.

If demand for an item that you sell is so high that you simply can't keep up, it may be an indication that you've priced it too low. On the flip side, when items don't sell, many shop owners assume that it's because they're priced too high. However, your price may be too *low*. Before you start slashing prices in your store, try raising them. You may be pleasantly surprised by the result!

Evaluate and raise your prices on an annual basis. The beginning of the new year is a good time to bump up prices.

Something Old: Special Considerations for Pricing Vintage Items

If your Etsy shop specializes in the sale of vintage goodies rather than hand-made items, you can forget about everything that we discuss earlier in this chapter. No "formula" exists for pricing these types of items. Instead, you have to rely on your knowledge of the piece. Specifically, you want to be armed with the following information:

- ✔ **What is the piece?** Obviously, you want to know what, exactly, you have for sale.

- ✔ **How old is the piece?** Older pieces tend to be more valuable than newer ones.

- ✔ **What company manufactured the piece?** Certain manufacturers are held in higher esteem than others. That's why a Tiffany lamp is a lot more valuable than one made by another company and can command a much higher price.

- ✔ **What condition is the piece in?** Obviously, an item in good condition can command a higher price than one that appears to have passed through a farm thresher.

- ✔ **How desirable is the piece?** Items that are rare or highly collectible generate much more interest than run-of-the-mill pieces.

When pricing a vintage item, also consider how much time you've invested in the piece, both in researching it and in finding it in the first place. Finally, assuming that you bought the item (instead of, say, unearthing it in your Aunt Mildred's attic), you must take into account how much you paid for it, as well as any costs you incurred to clean it up, fix any broken bits, and so on.

Still not sure where to start? Try scoping out the competition. Search Etsy or, dare we say it, eBay to see if any other sellers have listed something similar. If so, how much are they charging? Assuming that your piece is in the same condition as theirs, it can give you a good starting point.

How Low Can You Go? Pricing for Sales

Many businesses use any excuse to run a sale. ("It's Arbor Day! Take 20 Percent Off!") The idea is, they'll draw in loads of customers and move more merchandise. Although this may be an effective strategy for large, mass-market stores, it's not the best model for your Etsy shop. Running frequent sales not only devalues your work, but it trains your customers to buy from you only when you're running some type of promotion.

That's not to say, however, that you should never run a sale. For example, you may run a once-a-year sale to celebrate your store's anniversary. Or you may run a twice-a-year sale to let go of seasonal inventory. Another idea is to create a permanent "sale" section in your Etsy shop for discontinued, seasonal, or experimental pieces.

When you do run a sale, you want to ensure that you still turn a profit on your items — or at least break even. Fortunately, you can easily do so if you use the formula outlined earlier in this chapter to price your goods and you list them at the retail price. You can then discount them by as much as 50 percent and still make money. (Of course, how much you actually discount your items depends on how desperate you are to get rid of them.)

If you do decide to run a sale, make sure you spread the word. For more information, see Chapter 16.

Part III
She Sells Seashells (and More): Understanding the Etsy Selling Process

Photo courtesy of Angela Mahoney (www.swede13.etsy.com)

Find out how to offer custom items in your Etsy shop in a free article at www.dummies.com/extras/startinganetsybusiness.

In this part . . .

- Photograph your wares so they'll grab shoppers' attention.
- Write an engaging title and description that'll draw people to your item and make them want to buy.
- Discover how to list your item so you can get it out the door.
- Get tips on making the final sale.
- Ship your wares to your buyers quickly and efficiently.

Chapter 11

Say Cheese! Photographing Your Wares

In This Chapter

▶ Picking a camera

▶ Setting up your shoot

▶ Exploring lighting options

▶ Composing your shots

▶ Focusing on your items

▶ Working some magic with photo-editing software

*E*ver heard the saying "It's a vision thing"? Nowhere is this more true than on Etsy. Because shoppers on Etsy can't touch, smell, lick, or otherwise handle the goodies in your Etsy shop, they must evaluate each item based on sight. If you plan to sell on Etsy, it's up to you to supply potential buyers with excellent images of your products — beautiful photos that not only convey the shape, size, color, and texture of your pieces, but also reflect you and your broader brand identity.

Your photos must elicit in potential buyers a deep, abiding thirst for your items that they can satisfy only with their purchase. Unfortunately, we can't teach you everything you need to know about photography to make that happen; after all, you can find entire libraries of books on the topic of becoming an expert photographer (like the latest edition of *Digital Photography For Dummies,* by Julie Adair King [Wiley]). But this chapter *does* at least enable you to get your feet wet!

You can find lots of photography resources on Etsy. A good place to start is here: www.etsy.com/blog/en/2010/etsys-guide-to-photography.

If taking pictures just really isn't your thing, there's nothing to stop you from hiring a professional photographer to do it for you.

I'll Take That-a-One! Choosing a Camera with the Right Features

Although you *can* use a film camera to take photos of your pieces and then use a scanner to digitize those images, we don't recommend it. All that film is expensive, and scanning your photos takes time. Truth be told, if you plan to use Etsy to sell your handmade pieces, you need a digital camera. And, no, the one on your phone doesn't count — it simply can't deliver the level of quality you need to pique buyers' interest.

In the following sections, we describe some essential features that your digital camera needs to have, as well as a few extras that you may find helpful.

Read your camera's manual! Yes, we know, it's boring. But if you want to get the most out of your camera, you need to know what it can and can't do. If you've lost your manual, don't fret — chances are, you can download a copy from your camera manufacturer's website.

If you're in the market for a new camera, get the best model you can afford. And don't be turned off by gently used models — they can be just the ticket for an Etsy seller, at a much lower price!

Key club: Identifying key camera features

You don't need some fancy camera that can do everything for you *and* draw you a bubble bath afterward. A trusty digital point-and-shoot in the 4-megapixel range will serve you well, especially if it offers a few key features:

- ✔ **A macro setting:** This setting, typically represented by a flower icon, enables you to shoot extreme close-ups — critical when photographing smaller pieces, such as jewelry, or when you want to reveal the texture of an item.

- ✔ **Autofocus:** These days, pretty much all cameras offer autofocus. In most cases, you use it by pointing your camera at your subject and pressing the camera's shutter button halfway down; the camera automatically focuses on the subject. To capture the image, simply press the shutter button the rest of the way.

If you want the area of focus to be off center, just move your camera to the left or right while keeping the shutter button pressed halfway down; then, when you've achieved the desired composition, press the shutter button the rest of the way. (We talk about focusing your photos later in this chapter.)

✔ **A white balance setting:** With this setting, usually represented with a light bulb icon, you can help your camera identify pure white. The idea here is that if the camera can capture pure white correctly, it can correctly capture (and render) all other colors as well. Setting your camera's white balance before you shoot can save you a bushel of time later trying to correct the color in image-editing programs. (You find out more about image-editing programs later in this chapter.)

Feature story: Considering extra features

A few other camera features may serve you well (see the upcoming sidebar "Say what? Defining a few camera terms" if you need to brush up on technical camera talk):

✔ **An aperture-priority mode:** Although this feature is less "must have" and more "nice to have," aperture-priority mode helps you achieve the photography equivalent of a mullet: an image that's sharp in the front, blurry in the back. Simply engage aperture-priority mode, set your camera's f-stop as low as it goes, press the shutter button halfway down to autofocus on your item, and then snap your photo. (You can read more about the benefits of blurry backgrounds later in this chapter, in the section "Focus, People! Focusing Your Image.")

✔ **A manual mode:** Although you can certainly use the automatic settings on your digital camera, switching to manual mode gives you scads more control over your image's exposure. With manual mode, you can set the camera's aperture size, shutter speed, and ISO. In this way, you prevent the image from being underexposed (too dark) or overexposed (like Justin Bieber).

If your camera doesn't offer a manual mode, see if it supports a feature called exposure compensation. This feature enables you to instruct the camera to expose more or less than it normally would, given the lighting conditions.

Say what? Defining a few camera terms

We throw a few new terms at you in the previous section — most notably, *exposure, aperture, shutter speed,* and *ISO.*

✔ *Exposure* refers to the amount of light that strikes a digital camera's sensor (which replaced the film in old-school cameras). Achieving proper exposure involves selecting the appropriate aperture size, shutter speed, and ISO.

✔ *Aperture* is the hole through which light passes en route from your camera's lens to the sensor. The size of the aperture affects the image's *depth of field,* which you read about in the later section "Focus, People! Focusing Your Image." You change the size of the aperture by changing the camera's f-stop setting. (Somewhat counterintuitively, a smaller f-stop value indicates a larger aperture.)

✔ *Shutter speed* refers to the amount of time the aperture is open, allowing light to pass through.

✔ *ISO* measures the sensor's sensitivity to light.

Note that changing one of the last three settings — the aperture size, the shutter speed, or the ISO — requires adjustments to the other two settings. For example, if you make the aperture larger, you need to increase the shutter speed and/or choose a less sensitive ISO to ensure that the resulting image isn't overexposed. The key is to strike a balance. (If all this information is freaking you out, simmer down. Just use your camera's automatic setting.)

In Style: Styling Your Photos

Photographers who specialize in product shoots are no strangers to *stylists* — people who work closely with the photographer and other professionals to ensure that the shot contains all the necessary elements. Indeed, high-profile shoots — for example, shoots for magazine advertisements, brochures, and the like — may well have multiple stylists on set, including prop stylists, food stylists, and wardrobe stylists, not to mention full-blown set designers.

Chances are, the shoots you conduct for your Etsy shop won't look anything like these affairs. But you can still adopt some of the style pros' practices when you're setting up your shoot. These extras include backgrounds, props, and live models to both complement and emphasize the pieces you photograph.

Your item listing can feature as many as five photo slots, and you should use them all. If you like, you can show your item with a prop and without, with a model and without, and so on.

Background check: Using backgrounds

Although white is the background color of choice for many Etsy sellers — it's crisp, simple, and neutral — it's not your only option. When choosing a background for your photo shoot, keep these points in mind:

✔ **Scout your environment for "everyday" backgrounds.** Do you have a garden? If so, consider using a plant or flower as your background (see Figure 11-1 for an example). Or maybe your living-room wall is exposed brick, another excellent background. Really, just about anything works — wooden tables, tile floors, stone walkways, wicker baskets, wooden crates, whitewashed fences . . . the list goes on. These natural backgrounds can serve as excellent complements to your piece.

Figure 11-1: Sometimes everyday backgrounds are best.

Photo courtesy of Angela Mahoney (www.etsy.com/shop/swede13)

✔ **Reflective surfaces can really shine.** This advice is especially true if your items are delicate or finely made. Placing them on a mildly reflective surface, such as a sterling platter or a white ceramic plate, enables you to add interest, as well as improve lighting.

✔ **Avoid basic black.** Although black is indisputably the color of choice if you're attempting to hide those ten extra pounds, it's not so great as a background color when you're photographing goodies destined for your Etsy shop. Why? Because darker pieces get lost. Instead, opt for an almost-black background — charcoal works well — preferably with a bit of texture to add visual interest.

✔ **Add pop with color.** Pieces can really pop with a contrasting-color paper or fabric background. Subtle patterns that complement your piece also work well as backgrounds.

For inexpensive colorful backgrounds, check out your local craft store's scrapbook section. There, you'll find 12-by-12-inch sheets of paper in more colors and patterns than you ever dreamed possible. These papers make perfect backgrounds for smaller pieces. Just steer clear of patterns that are super-busy.

✔ **Create a seamless background.** Tape one end of a long sheet of thick paper — the kind you cut from a roll — to your wall, letting it drape down onto a table, where you can clamp the other end. You'll get a seamless "runway" effect that's especially useful for extreme close-ups or times when you don't want anything distracting from your piece (see Figure 11-2).

Figure 11-2:
Call attention to your item with a seamless background.

Photo courtesy of Mark Poulin

✔ **Avoid the "accidental" background.** Heavens to Etsy! The last thing you want potential buyers to see is all your dirty dishes or that pile of newspapers you keep forgetting to recycle! Don't taint your item by photographing it amid all your daily detritus. Make sure that any background you include in your product shots is there *on purpose* and complements your piece.

✔ **Don't give your background star billing.** If your background is more noticeable than the piece you slaved over for days, don't use it.

Prop it like it's hot: Working with props

REMEMBER

Props are a great way to add interest to your shot or convey something about the item you're selling. The trick to using them is making sure they don't detract from the piece you want to sell or otherwise confuse potential buyers. A prop must enhance your piece, conveying to buyers its possibilities. Props also must reflect your brand (see Chapter 16). That is, if your brand is elegant, you want to steer clear of props that scream "Behold my quirkiness!" (and vice versa).

The swell thing about props is that they're everywhere! You can find potential props in your garden shed, your craft closet, your grandmother's attic, your nephew's toy chest, or your uncle's garage. Experiment with lots of different props to see what works best. For example, you can use props as follows:

✔ **To convey the scale of your piece:** Using a universal prop — something everyone recognizes, like a coin, a book, a pencil, a chair, a toy, food, or whatnot — is a great way to show potential buyers the size of your piece. (Figure 11-3 shows a necklace on a pile of beans.)

Figure 11-3:
Using a universal prop can convey the scale of your piece.

Photo courtesy of Jonathan Wilson

✔ **To show how your piece can be used:** By putting your piece in its "natural environment," you give potential buyers an idea of how they can use it. For example, if you make USB drives shaped like R2-D2, you may insert one into your laptop's USB port. Or maybe you craft gorgeous place cards; in that case, you may position one atop a lovely vintage plate, to reinforce what your item is and does. (Figure 11-4 shows a colorful handmade pillow on a little girl's bed.)

Figure 11-4: You can feature a prop that suggests how to use your piece.

Photo courtesy of Elizabeth Wallberg, e photography

- ✔ **To reflect how your piece was made:** Do you use special tools to construct your item? If so, consider using those implements as props. Knitting needles, embroidery hoops, pliers, cutters, paintbrushes, pencils, scissors, blowtorches — all these constitute excellent props; they add interest by conveying how the piece was made.

- ✔ **To suggest what inspired your piece:** Did the idea for your piece come to you while you were walking in the woods? Then a leaf, branch, or pine cone may make an excellent prop. Or if you had the epiphany for your piece while strolling along the seashore, a bit of sand or a seashell may serve as a prop. As another example, Figure 11-5 shows an orange soap set with a group of oranges.

- ✔ **To complement your piece:** A great way to create interest in your product shots is to place your piece alongside an object that complements it visually. Maybe the object you use as a prop is a complementary color — for example, the object is violet, and your piece is yellow. Or maybe the object reflects the genre of your piece in some way — say, the object is a vintage bowling pin, and your piece is a hand-sewn bowling shirt.

Photo courtesy of Whispering Willow (www.etsy.com/shop/WhisperingWillowSoap)

Model citizens: Using live models

Yes, models can be terrible divas. But the fact is, when they're not busy fling-
ing cellphones at your head, models — whether they're babies, kids, adults,
or your pet hamster — can do wonders for your product photos. Why? For
two reasons:

- **Using a live model helps you convey the scale or fit of your piece.**
  If you shoot your gorgeous necklace with a simple white background,
  potential buyers may not be able to get a handle on its length.
  Photographing that same necklace on a model, however, enables buyers
  to deduce at a glance how long it is, as well as how it rests on the décol-
  letage (see Figure 11-6). Likewise, if you sell hand-sewn clothes in your
  Etsy shop, photographing your pieces on a live model shows potential
  buyers how they'll fit.

- **Using a live model makes your piece more relatable.** Models human-
  ize your piece. When potential buyers see a model wearing your item,
  they inevitably imagine it looking just as fantastic on themselves or their
  loved ones. The same is true when you show a model using your item:
  Potential buyers naturally imagine themselves or their loved ones using
  it in the same way.

Figure 11-6:
Using a live
model can
really bring
your piece
to, er, life.

Photo courtesy of Rae Aldrich-Keisling

If your pieces are of an intimate nature — think panties or earrings — be sure to note that the ones worn by the model are samples. You'll send an unworn pair to the buyer.

Of course, you can't use just any model. You want to choose models who enhance, not detract from, your piece. Be sure to select models who reflect your brand and your target audience. For example, if your brand and your target audience are on the edgy or punk end of the spectrum, your models need to be, too (think tattoos, piercings, mohawks, and so on). However, if your aesthetic is more romantic, your models need to look that way as well.

Who should you enlist to model your pieces? Friends and family are obvious (and inexpensive) choices — assuming that they're appropriate for your brand and aesthetic. If you're selling a premium item, consider investing in a pro.

Lighting Bug: Lighting Your Shot

If you've ever seen Cybill Shepherd in *Moonlighting,* you know the importance of flattering lighting! No doubt about it, whether you're photographing an aging actress or a tea towel on which you've embroidered the periodic table, good lighting is essential. Without it, your camera simply can't capture the color and texture of your piece. The following sections note a few lighting-related points to keep in mind when photographing your pieces.

She's a natural! Using natural light

You don't need to start selling your plasma to afford to buy an expensive lighting rig. The fact is, when it comes to photographing the goodies you've made for your Etsy shop, natural lighting — say, from a north-facing window or even when outside on an overcast day — is best. It's by far the most flattering light source. In addition, it enables you to capture the colors and texture of your piece.

Dark matter: Avoiding the dark

Unless you live with the Inuits and it's that season when the sun never sets, shooting at night is a bad idea — most notably because simply not much natural light is available.

Instead, you want to photograph during the "golden hours." No, we're not recommending that you shoot during reruns of *The Golden Girls.* We're encouraging you to use the natural light available in the early morning, right after the sun rises, or near sunset, when the sun is low in the sky. You'll find the natural light during these periods to be as flattering as 4-inch heels.

SPF 50: Avoiding direct sunlight

Direct sunlight can overexpose your photo, washing it out. If you can't avoid direct sunlight (people in Nevada, we're talking to you), try diffusing the light — for example, positioning a sheer curtain between the sun and the piece you're photographing.

Figures 11-7 and 11-8 show the difference between an object photographed in full sun and one photographed in diffused light. Notice how the diffused light in the second image softens the whole shot.

Figure 11-7:
Notice how
shooting
in full sun
washes out
an image.

Photo courtesy of Angela at Teeny Bunny (www.etsy.com/shop/teenybunny)

Figure 11-8:
Diffused
light softens
an image,
making it
much more
appealing.

Photo courtesy of Rebecca Lang

Another option you can try when you can't avoid direct sunlight is positioning your piece so that the sun is behind it. This technique creates a warm glow around the edges. In this scenario, you may need to use reflectors or, as a last resort, your flash. If you must use your flash, diffuse it to avoid casting harsh shadows on your piece. See the next section for more information.

Time to reflect: Using reflectors

For the love of all that's holy, if you can avoid it, don't use your flash when photographing items for your Etsy shop — unless harsh shadows, glare, reflections, and a generally flat appearance will somehow enhance your item's salability.

If you simply cannot achieve the necessary exposure without using your flash, consider covering the flash with tracing paper, white facial tissue, or some other sheer material to diffuse it (we introduce the idea of diffused light in the previous section).

Even better, instead of using your flash, you can put reflectors to work. Use white walls or other home-grown reflective items (think white poster board, a hanging bed sheet, or, for a brighter reflection, a mirror) to "bounce" light onto your piece. Figures 11-9 and 11-10 show the difference between a shoot that didn't use reflectors and a shoot that did. Notice that the first image, for which a reflector wasn't used, is darker and a wee bit muddy; its colors just don't stand out. In contrast, the face of the angel in the second image pops a bit more, for an overall brighter, happier look.

Figure 11-9: The photographer didn't use a reflector for this shot.

Photograph courtesy of Allison Strine

Figure 11-10:
Notice how using a reflector really lights up the piece.

Photograph courtesy of Allison Strine

Especially if you craft wee things — jewelry, personalized guitar picks, pet portraits on grains of rice — you may want to consider using a light tent. A *light tent,* sometimes called a *light box,* is a small structure made of transparent white fabric or plastic in which you place your item to photograph it. Light tents, which can be used with natural light or a simple lighting kit, come in a variety of shapes and sizes. Alternatively, you can build your own for a song. For help, visit `www.etsy.com/blog/en/2007/fortys-foto-tips-2-make-a-light-box`.

Compose Yourself: Composing Your Shot

Suppose you found yourself at the Statue of Liberty with Annie Leibovitz. And suppose further that both of you were photographing Lady Liberty. No offense, but her pictures would probably be way better than yours — more captivating, more vital, more powerful, more interesting. Why? Well, lots of reasons. One, Leibovitz probably has a camera that's so good, it practically has super powers. But more than that, Leibovitz has a keen eye for *composition* — the arrangement of visual elements in an image.

Just because you're no Annie Leibovitz doesn't mean you can't compose some really swell photos of your own for your Etsy shop. The pointers in the following sections can help.

For starters: Trying basic composition principles

As you shoot your pieces, keep these basic compositional points in mind:

- **Angle the camera.** Angling, or tilting, the camera puts the subject slightly off center and creates movement and flow. The result: a more dynamic, intriguing image, as you can see in Figure 11-11.

- **Shoot tight.** Filling the frame with your subject not only adds visual impact, but also enables potential buyers to see how well made your piece is (see for yourself in Figure 11-12).

Figure 11-11:
Angling the camera produces interesting results.

Photo courtesy of Colette Urquhart

Figure 11-12:
Shoot tight, for added impact.

Photo courtesy of Kristen Timmers

✔ **Blur the background.** Remember that photographic mullet we mention earlier, in the section "Feature story: Considering extra features"? It's such a good idea, we're bringing it up again. By using a shallow depth of field (read: a low f-stop setting), you can blur the background to dramatically highlight your piece, as shown in Figure 11-13.

Figure 11-13:
Blur the background to emphasize your item.

Photo courtesy of Betsy and Bess (Christopher and Adrienne Scott; www.etsy.com/shop/betsyandbess)

When the background is blurred, you can shoot in almost any setting; just make sure that the background colors don't clash with your subject. (For more on depth of field, see the later section "Focus, People! Focusing Your Image.")

✔ **Remember that less is more.** Don't crowd the scene with extraneous objects. Otherwise, potential buyers may not understand exactly which item in your photo is for sale.

✔ **Frame your subject.** One way to draw the viewer's eye to your piece is to frame it — that is, place some darker element in the perimeter. This technique helps prevent the viewer's eye from straying from your item.

✔ **Group pieces.** Especially if you make itsy-bitsy goodies, you can try grouping them to catch a buyer's eye. Not only does this strategy make for a more eye-catching photograph, but it also shows potential buyers how pieces in your collection work together. Just be sure to note in your listing description which one of the items in the group is actually up for grabs. Also, avoid groups that are too large; using three to five pieces does the trick.

Third's-eye view: Applying the rule of thirds

To be perfectly honest, we're not big on rules. (This fact may explain why we're self-employed.) But one rule we can absolutely get behind is the rule of thirds. In addition to conveying a sense of tension and energy, the rule of thirds helps pique the viewer's interest. According to this rule, you should use two horizontal lines and two vertical lines to divide the scene you're photographing into nine equal parts (think of a tic-tac-toe grid, as shown in Figure 11-14). Then place key elements at any of the four points where the vertical and horizontal lines intersect (see Figure 11-15), or use the lines themselves as guides as you compose your image.

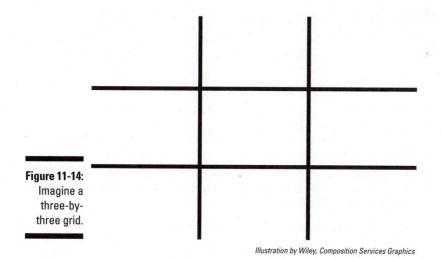

Figure 11-14: Imagine a three-by-three grid.

Illustration by Wiley, Composition Services Graphics

Photo courtesy of Heather Torre (www.etsy.com/shop/myselvagedlife)

Figure 11-15:
Use the grid
to compose
your image.

Note: With some digital cameras, you can display a grid on the LCD view-finder, enabling you to organize your image around the lines and cross points.

Focus, People! Focusing Your Image

It probably goes without saying, but in the interest of being thorough, we'll say it anyway: A surefire way to turn off buyers is to include blurry images in your Etsy shop, especially if they're close-ups. How's a potential buyer supposed to view your piece in all its detailed splendor if your photos are as hazy as a Lindsay Lohan alibi? It's imperative that your product photos be crisp and clear, as in Figure 11-16.

To ensure excellent focus if you're shooting a close-up, use your camera's macro setting. This setting (which, as mentioned in the earlier section "Key club: Identifying key camera features," is usually indicated with a flower icon) ensures that your focus is sharp.

If you're using a slower shutter speed or you just drank a quadruple espresso, you need to take special care to keep your camera still as you photograph your piece. Using a tripod is one way to go; alternatively, you can rest your camera on a table or a stack of books.

Figure 11-16:
Notice how crisp and clear this in-focus photo is.

Photo courtesy of Becca Balistreri

We mention it a few times in this chapter: the so-called "photographic mullet," in which you keep your item in focus while blurring other parts of the scene. The way to achieve that look is to use a low f-stop setting to yield a shallow depth of field. However, this tip begs the question: What is depth of field? *Depth of field* refers to how much of the area in front of and behind the subject will appear in focus. In an image with a shallow depth of field, you get that blurred background we talk so much about, and the subject is in focus. You achieve a shallow depth of field by using a low f-stop setting. Images with a deep depth of field have the background, the subject, and the foreground in focus. A high f-stop setting yields a deep depth of field.

Shoot, Shoot, and Shoot Some More: Taking Lots of Pictures

Back when film — not to mention the cost of developing it — put you back a pretty penny, you may have been justified in being stingy with your shots.

But these days, it's digital, dawg! You can — and should — shoot lots of shots. And by lots, we mean *lots*. Like, a whole bunch. A gazillion should do the trick.

The point is, your product photos have to be *great* — like, Muhammad Ali, Audrey Hepburn, Paul Newman great. As we say earlier in this chapter, they need to convey the shape, size, color, and texture of your piece, as well as reflect you and your broader brand identity. On top of all that, they need to be easy on the eyes. Unless you're Helmut Newton (which would be amazing, given that he's dead), you're just not going to capture all that with a single click of the shutter button.

One more tip: As you shoot, make it a point to experiment. Swap out props and backgrounds. Try different angles, lighting, and depths of field. It's the only way to ensure that you wind up with a winning picture.

Before you start, make sure your camera's batteries are charged. The only problem worse than setting up your shoot and then discovering that you're out of juice is having to entertain your live model while you recharge.

Whatever your approach, you should try to designate a place for taking pictures and establish a routine. At the very least, write down your methods. All sellers, but particularly vintage sellers, will find themselves spending a lot of time taking pictures. Developing a specific method to follow each time will help keep labor costs down.

Clean-up on Image Five: Tidying Up Your Photos with Image-Editing Software

Even the best photos can use a little tidying up. For example, you may want to adjust the image's brightness or contrast, tweak the color in an image to make it really pop, or crop the image to make your subject stand out.

Please, we beg you: Don't use image-editing software to try to "fix" a bad photo. Some photos — photos that are dark, blurry, or otherwise foul — are simply beyond repair. Image-editing programs are for enhancement purposes only.

Fortunately, any number of image-editing programs are available to you, ranging in price from free to the cost of your arm and your leg. If you use a Windows PC, you can also use the Paint program, which came free with your computer. Yet another option is to use the software that came with your digital camera.

Unfortunately, we can't cover the ins and outs of using all these programs. But to give you a basic idea of how it's done, in the following sections, we step you through the process using Picasa, a free online photo-editing service, to fix your photos. (Note that the steps outlined here pertain specifically to Windows 7. If you use a different version of Windows, or a Mac, the steps may be slightly different.) To download and install Picasa, go to `http://picasa.google.com`. (Note that you must have an account with Google to download and install Picasa.)

Before you install Picasa, be sure to copy the images you want to clean up from your camera to your computer. Picasa will automatically detect all images on your hard drive.

Expose yourself: Adjusting your photo's exposure and color

Suppose that your photo is a little bit dark. Or maybe your subject is slightly washed out. In either case, you can adjust its exposure. In addition, you can tweak the color. Here's how:

1. **Launch Picasa as you would any other program.**

   Picasa opens in Library view, displaying thumbnail versions of images on your hard drive.

2. **Navigate the folders on the left side of the screen to locate the image you want to clean up (see Figure 11-17).**

   Alternatively, you can search for the image by typing its name in the Search field in the upper-right corner of the screen.

3. **Double-click the image you want to open.**

   Picasa displays the image in an editing window, as shown in Figure 11-18.

   The Commonly Needed Fixes tab (the one featuring a wrench) offers several tools for adjusting your image's exposure and color.

4. **For a quick fix, click the I'm Feeling Lucky button. Alternatively, click the Auto Contrast and Auto Color buttons individually. To adjust the fill light, drag the Fill Light slider.**

   If you don't like how the image looks with the new settings applied, simply click the Undo button.

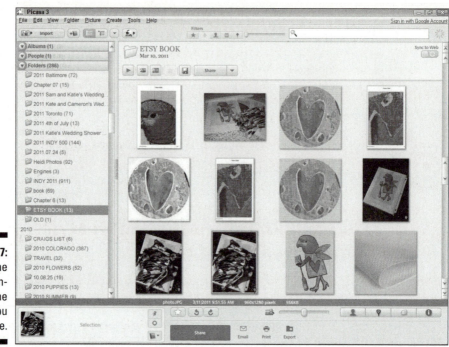

Figure 11-17:
Open the folder containing the image you want to use.

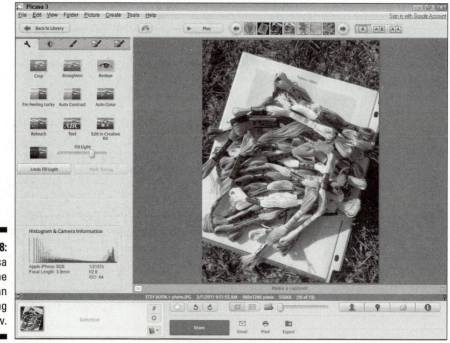

Figure 11-18:
Picasa opens the image in an editing window.

Crop circles: Cropping your photo

If you've captured some extraneous items in your image, or you simply want to focus it more tightly on your piece, you can crop it. Here's the drill:

1. **Click the Crop button.**

   Picasa assumes you want to set the dimensions of the crop manually. To choose another option — for example, 4×6, 4×3, square, or what have you — choose it from the drop-down list that appears.

2. **Click in the image and drag to create a box.**

   This indicates where the cropping should occur. The area of the image outside the box will be cropped from the image (see Figure 11-19).

3. **To move the box, click inside it and drag it until it covers the part of the image you want to keep. To resize the box, click any of its four edges and drag inward or outward. To resize the box but keep its proportions intact, click any of its four corners and drag inward or outward.**

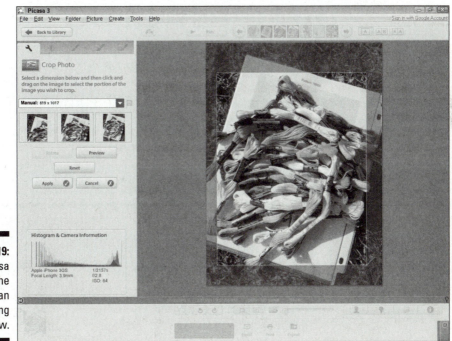

Figure 11-19:
Picasa opens the image in an editing window.

4. Click the Apply button.

Picasa crops the image. If you don't like how the image looks with the crop applied, click the Undo button.

Product images bound for your Etsy shop must be at least 570 pixels wide. Note that we said *at least* 570 pixels wide; for best results, opt for an image that's between 800 and 1,000 pixels wide. That being said, if your image file is too large, you'll have a hard time uploading it to Etsy when you create the item listing in which the photo will appear (see Chapter 13 for details). For this reason, when you save your image in Picasa, you must ensure that it's no larger than 250KB and doesn't exceed 1,000 by 1,000 pixels.

To ensure that all your hard work doesn't go to waste, you must save your edited photo. To do so, simply choose File⇨Save As, and save the file in the desired folder. Note that the file must be a JPEG, GIF, or PNG; Etsy doesn't support other file types.

Watermark, watermark everywhere: Watermarking your photos

If you want, you can apply a *watermark* to your photos — that is, you can superimpose text over your image to prevent others from using it without your permission. Watermarks are especially useful if you're a photographer, painter, or some other type of graphic artist, and you sell prints of your images. If you do watermark your image, keep it subtle; otherwise, the watermark may overpower your image. Be aware, too, that Etsy will usually avoid using watermarked images in any promotional way — for example, watermarked images rarely appear on Etsy's front page.

To apply a watermark using Picasa, follow these steps:

1. **Click the Text button in the Commonly Needed Fixes tab (the one with a wrench on it).**

2. **Choose a font, choose a size, and set a level of transparency.**

3. **Click in the image and type the text you want to add.**

4. **Click and drag the text to move it as needed.**

5. **Click the Apply button.**

Chapter 12

Word Up: Composing Engaging Titles and Descriptions

In This Chapter

▶ Composing strong item titles

▶ Making your item descriptions stand out

▶ Driving traffic to your listing with search engine optimization

▶ Proofreading your listing

*T*rue, a gorgeous photo of your piece may catch a buyer's eye. But the way you write about your piece in your item title and description can keep your buyer's attention. With these textual elements, you have an opportunity to engage buyers with a story about you and your piece. You can also answer questions about your piece, such as what it's made of, what it does, and why someone should buy it. Indeed, well-written and interesting titles and descriptions may just persuade a buyer to add your piece to her cart.

If your talents lie more in crafting and less in writing ("I'm a candy-wrapper handbag maker, not a writer!"), don't freak out. As you discover in this chapter, writing engaging item titles and descriptions is plenty doable. You also find out how to optimize your item titles, descriptions, and tags for searching, making it easier for prospective buyers to find your piece.

Headline Muse: Writing Titillating Item Titles

Any newspaper writer will tell you that a first-rate headline is critical in grabbing readers' attention. A strong headline both hints at what the following story contains and coaxes the audience to read on. Superlative headlines — which, almost by definition, are brief — may use humor, puns, alliteration, rhymes, or other types of wordplay and often include clever double-entendres. "Headless Body in Topless Bar," the headline of a *New York Post* piece on a local murder, is one example of an excellent (albeit disturbing) headline; another is "Super Cagey Go Ballistic Celtics Are Atrocious," the headline for a piece in *The Sun* (the United Kingdom's biggest-selling newspaper) about the Inverness Caledonian Thistle football club trouncing its Celtic rivals in the Scottish Cup.

As you've probably guessed, your item title acts a lot like a good headline. It's designed to grab a buyer's attention and entice him to read more about you and your item. But your Etsy item title also serves another important purpose in that it factors into Etsy's search system. So, although you want to come up with a title that will pique a buyer's interest, you also want to make sure it's optimized for search. Otherwise, that buyer may not ever find your item! (You find out more about search engine optimization later in this chapter.)

Here are some things to keep in mind when composing item titles:

- ✔ **Keep it short.** Your item title must be brief — no more than 155 characters (including spaces).

- ✔ **Clearly describe your item at the beginning of the item title.** This helps improve the chances that others will find your item when searching on Etsy.

- ✔ **Be clever.** Use humor, puns, alliteration, rhymes, or other types of wordplay.

- ✔ **Use strong, concise words.** Avoid vague verbiage! Some words and phrases are just better than others. For example, don't just call your piece "small"; also call it "miniature."

- ✔ **Use a mix of uppercase and lowercase letters.** Too many all-uppercase words, and it seems like you're shouting. Too many lowercase words, and it seems like you're e. e. cummings.

Your item title needs to broadcast key information about your piece — most notably, what it is, what it's made of, and perhaps a few choice details about the piece, such as its color, size, or other personal touches.

Story Time: Telling a Story with Your Item Description

People who buy on Etsy aren't interested in meaningless, mass-produced goods. They want pieces with a past — something that has a story. Etsy allows sellers to enter an item description so they can tell the story behind their product. In the following sections, we explain how to uncover an item's story, answer questions about the item, and compose a thoughtful description.

Likely story: Uncovering your item's story

Not sure what your piece's story is — or whether it even has one? Fear not. Start spinning your yarn (figuratively speaking) by answering a few questions:

- ✔ **What inspired you to create the piece?** Mentioning your source of inspiration is a great way to get the ball rolling. If you're a candy-wrapper handbag maker, maybe you got the idea to make candy-wrapper handbags while traveling in Mexico, where artisans craft all manner of items out of candy wrappers, including clutches, totes, and placemats.

- ✔ **How was the piece made?** Indicating the skills involved in making an item can be an excellent way to forge a connection with buyers. Was it woven? Sewn? Assembled by magical hamsters?

- ✔ **Who taught you the skills you use to create your piece?** Sharing how you learned the techniques you use to craft your pieces can be a great way to bond with prospective buyers. Maybe your great-grandmother learned the fine art of candy-wrapper handbag making and passed her skills down to you. Or maybe your uncle was a Mayan studies scholar and taught you their paper-weaving techniques — techniques that you then put to use making candy-wrapper handbags to justify your prodigious candy-eating habit.

 Even if you choose not to focus on the story behind your item, don't hesitate to let your own personality and the "personality" of your brand shine through in your item description. If you and your brand tend toward quirky, then your item descriptions should, too. Ditto if you and your brand have a darker bent.

Description prescription: Describing your item

It probably goes without saying that, in addition to including the "story" behind you and your piece, your item description must contain, well, a description of your item. But we believe in being thorough, so we're saying it. Think about what questions buyers are likely to have about your piece. Then answer all those questions in your item description. The description may cover the following points:

- ✔ **What is your piece?** Although it may seem obvious to you that your item is a handbag made of Snickers wrappers, to others, it may be less apparent.

- ✔ **What does your piece do?** Does your piece have a function? Or is it for decoration only? Be sure to note this info in your item description.

✔ **Who is your piece for?** Dogs? Babies? Men? On the flip side, who is it *not* for? For example, if it contains pieces on which an infant may choke, you should definitely note that in your item description.

✔ **How does your piece work?** Does it have a clasp? Or buttons? Or a zipper? Do you tie it? Does it need batteries, or do you power it by driving a DeLorean equipped with a lightning rod past the town clock tower during a thunderstorm?

✔ **What color is your piece?** Colors may translate differently on different computer monitors. Including detailed color information in your item description is a good way to bridge that gap.

Be specific here. Don't say that your piece is red when it's actually scarlet, brick, ruby, cherry, crimson, or burgundy.

✔ **How big is your piece?** Remember in *This Is Spinal Tap* when Nigel Tufnel sketches out specs for a Stonehenge stage set but accidentally uses a double-prime mark (for inches) instead of a prime mark (for feet)? The result is an 18-inch Stonehenge monument that is, as David St. Hubbins observes, "in danger of being crushed by a dwarf." To save your buyer from experiencing similar disappointment, include detailed and accurate sizing information about your piece. Avoid vague terms like *small* or *large,* and instead opt for precise measurements, especially if you sell clothing. By the way, it doesn't hurt to include both systems of measurement — metric and old-school — in your item descriptions.

✔ **What materials did you use?** Do you use organic cotton? Hand-dyed wool? Swarovski crystals? Wrappers from Reese's Peanut Butter Cups? Whatever materials you use, they need to appear in your item description.

✔ **What techniques did you use to construct your piece?** Did you knit it? Weave it? Sew it? This info helps tell the story of your piece and reinforces to buyers that you made it by hand. It also helps attract buyers who are partial to a particular crafting technique.

Especially if you've priced your item on the higher side, be sure to indicate why in your item description. Whether it's because you used high-end materials or because you crafted it using a particularly difficult technique, you need to share this info with your buyer. What is it that makes it special or valuable or unique? (Flip to Chapter 10 for more information on pricing your items.)

✔ **What does your piece feel like?** Is it soft? Smooth? Slick? Rough? Nubby? Scaly? Prickly? Stubbly? Indicate your item's tactile qualities in your item description.

✔ **What does your piece smell like?** Does it have a scent, such as lavender or ylang-ylang? If it's a vintage piece, does it have a musty odor? Does it come from a smoker's home?

Having a sale in your shop? Be sure to mention it in your item description and your shop announcement.

Write away: Composing your item description

You have a handle on the story behind your item, and you know what information your item listing needs to contain. Now it's time to put the proverbial pen to paper and write your item description.

To make your item description as effective as possible, put the most important information about your item first. Putting important items first not only makes it easier for shoppers to quickly get the information they need about your piece, but also enables you to optimize your shop for search. (We talk more about search engine optimization later in this chapter.) Of course, what constitutes "the most important information" may differ from piece to piece; in general, however, this info likely includes what your item is, what it does, what it looks like, and what it's made of. From there, you can get into more "nice to know" information, such as what your item smells like (unless, of course, the whole point of your item is its smell, as is the case with soap, perfume, and the like), as well as the story behind your item or your work.

To keep your prospective buyer reading, use short paragraphs and bullet points. That construction is easier on the eyes than a gigantic block of text. Another way to break things up is to use subtitles — for example, one above the item description, one on top of any measurements information, and so on. You can set these subtitles apart from regular text by using all caps or boldface font.

Consider this example of an item description that falls short:

> Bag made of candy wrappers.
>
> Size: Medium

We don't know about you, but nothing in this description makes us want to buy the bag. Yes, the seller was brief — score one for her. But this description almost completely lacks any useful information! Worse, it's as though the seller just can't be bothered to tell anyone about her item.

Following is an example of a much more effective item description:

> Bonkers for bonbons? Then this candy-wrapper handbag is for you. This colorful, eco-friendly handbag, carefully hand-woven using Kit Kat, Nestlé Crunch, and Snickers candy wrappers, is just the right size to carry a phone, wallet, and candy bar (of course).
>
> I crafted this handbag, which can double as a makeup bag, using a technique I learned from my candy-crazy aunt. The handbag, which measures 22 centimeters (8.7 inches) across and 14 centimeters (5.5 inches) high, features a zipper along the top, as well as a color-coordinated wristlet for easy carrying. The use of candy wrappers gives the handbag a slightly shiny, reflective quality and a mild, chocolaty aroma.

This candy-wrapper handbag is perfect for anyone with a sweet tooth!

Now, *this* description makes us want to buy this handbag, pronto. (And also to pound a Kit Kat.)

SEO Speedwagon: Using Search Engine Optimization to Drive Traffic

Remember *Field of Dreams?* The whole "If you build it, they will come" thing, when Kevin Costner's DIY baseball diamond attracted the 1919 roster for the Chicago Black Sox and, subsequently, a large enough crowd to save his family farm? Don't get us wrong — it's a nice story and all. But unless you specialize in hand-crafting redemption for disgraced baseball players from another dimension, the odds of the same thing happening with your Etsy shop are as slim as Kate Moss.

You have to do more than just build your Etsy shop to entice people to visit it. As you find out in this book, you need to supply gorgeous photos and intriguing descriptions of your wares. In addition, you need to engage in a little something called *search engine optimization* (SEO). By using SEO, you can increase the likelihood that people who use search engines such as Google, Yahoo!, or Bing to search for certain keywords will see — and click on — a link to your Etsy shop in their list of results. SEO is also critical to ensuring that shoppers already on Etsy's site can find your items.

How can you harness the power of SEO for your Etsy shop? One way is to plant relevant keywords in your shop title, shop announcement, shop sections, and user profile (see Chapter 8 for details on these items). That way, people searching for those keywords will see your Etsy shop in their search results. Another way is to include these keywords in your shop item titles, descriptions, and tags, which is the focus of this section.

Keyword to your mother: Choosing the best keywords

All this talk of keywords and SEO begs one obvious question: What keywords do you want to use?

In-bound and determined: Garnering in-bound links

In addition to the keywords and phrases you plant in your item title and item description (as well as in your shop title, shop announcement, and other Etsy areas), you can optimize your Etsy shop or item for search through in-bound links. An *in-bound link* is a link from another page to your Etsy shop or item. Google and other search engines rate pages on how interesting they are, which they gauge in part by determining how many in-bound links a page has, as well as how credible the pages containing those links are. So, the more pages link to your Etsy shop or item listing, and the more credible those pages are, the higher your shop or listing appears in search results.

How can you garner more in-bound links? One way is to ask friends and family members who maintain blogs or social media accounts (for example, on Facebook or Twitter) to link to your shop. (You can also use your own blog and social media accounts for the same purpose.) In addition, you can build in-bound links by participating in the Etsy forums (see Chapter 19) and commenting on Etsy Blog articles (see Chapter 20). You can even include links to pages in your shop *within your shop* to build in-bound links, even though that may seem kind of like cheating. And, of course, you can encourage others to link to your Etsy shop and items by linking to their Etsy shops and items. What goes around comes around!

Suppose you hand-craft bracelets out of bottle caps. Sure, you can use keywords like *bracelet* or even *jewelry* in your item listings — in fact, you should. The problem is, you're not the only one using those terms. A recent search for the term *jewelry* yielded roughly 336,000,000 matches. Adding *bracelet* to the search string narrowed the list somewhat, but it still yielded almost 80,000,000 hits. Including *bottle cap* got us down to about half a million.

No doubt about it, 500,000 is better than 336,000,000 — but not if your shop is buried in the bottom 499,999 matches. Why? Because when most people use a search engine, they don't dig deeper than the first few pages of search results (if they even go that far) to find what they're looking for. To increase traffic to your Etsy storefront, you must ensure that links to your items or shop appear in those first few pages — preferably on page one.

Short of purchasing Google or Yahoo! outright, how can you improve your search results? By doing a little research to determine whether the keywords you're using are appropriate or whether other keywords may serve you better. To aid you, Google offers its handy, dandy Keyword Tool. You use it like so:

1. **Launch your web browser and type** https://adwords.google.com/select/ KeywordToolExternal **in its address bar.**

   The page for the Google AdWords Keyword Tool opens (see Figure 12-1).

2. **Type any keywords or phrases that you use in the Word or Phrase box.**

   Include one keyword or phrase per line.

3. **Fill out the CAPTCHA form — that is, type the characters that appear in the picture.**

4. **Click the Search button.**

   The Keyword Tool shows how often the keywords you typed are searched, as well as other keywords you may want to consider. In Figure 12-2, more than 700 local searches focused on the phrase *bottle cap bracelet*. That is, over a one-month period, 700+ people in the United States searched for the phrase *bottle cap bracelet*. A second search reveals that, in the same period, more than 9,000,000 people searched for the term *jewelry*.

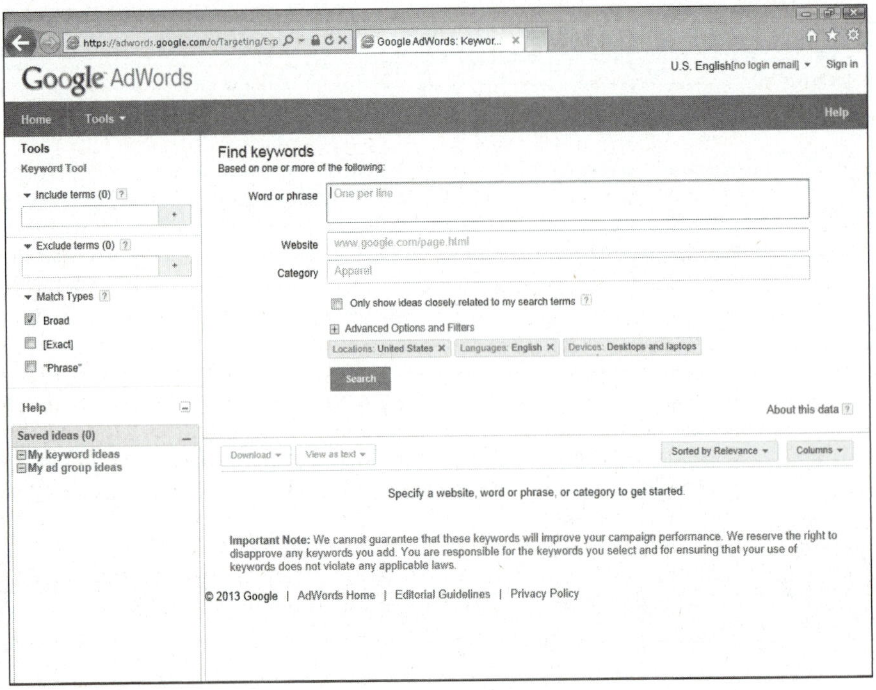

Figure 12-1: The Google AdWords Keyword Tool.

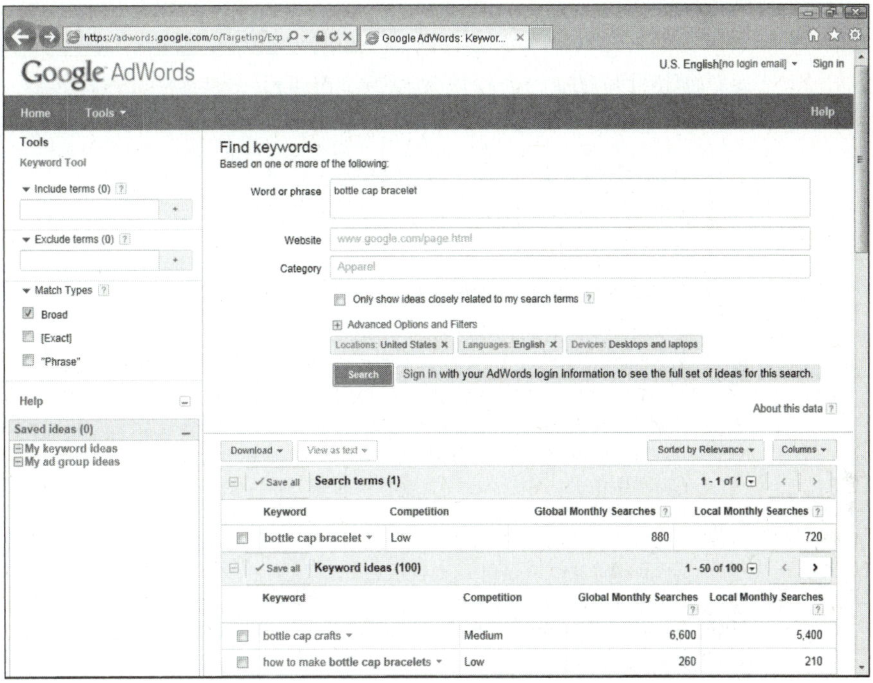

Figure 12-2:
Note how
often
your key-
words are
searched.

Now, you may think that you need to focus on the higher-volume keywords or phrases — that is, keywords like *jewelry* rather than phrases such as *bottle cap bracelet.* After all, more people are searching for those. But given how many matches are in that category, the chances of your shop or item ranking near the top are essentially nil. You have a much better chance of appearing near the top of the results for a narrow search, like *bottle cap bracelet.*

What about finding keywords that may work better than the ones you're using? Simple. Just read through the list of keywords that the Keyword Tool spits out to find ideas for keywords or phrases you can use. This list contains actual search terms that people have entered into search engines to find items like yours. In this example, you may add *bottle cap jewelry* or *bottle cap crafts* as keywords.

You can use Etsy Shop Stats to see which keywords visitors used to find you on Etsy. For more on Etsy Shop Stats, flip to Chapter 18.

What you key is what you get: Using SEO with your item title and description

It's not enough to write catchy item titles. You also need to ensure that those titles are optimized for search. Keep a few points in mind:

✔ **Include keywords, but not too many.** Every item title that you write needs to contain at least one keyword or phrase (more, if possible). You want to make sure that your title contains as many keywords as possible. But stuffing your title with too many keywords for the sake of SEO may render it terribly boring, if not completely unreadable. The idea is to write titles that are catchy for both people *and* PCs.

✔ **Put keywords first.** Place keywords at or near the beginning of your item title. Although search engines search your entire title for keyword matches, they display only the first 66 characters (including spaces) of it in the list of results. To increase the chances that anyone searching for that keyword will visit your shop, you want to make sure that the keyword shows up in that results list.

The same points apply to your item description — except one: Search engines display more characters from your item description in search results (160 in all, including spaces). But again, even though you have a little more wiggle room, you want to make sure that your keywords appear toward the beginning. You also want to repeat any keywords at least once (but preferably two or three times) in your item description, to boost your Etsy shop in the search rankings.

Here's an example of an item listing that makes good use of keywords:

Nehi Grape Bottle Cap Bracelet: Grape Expectations

Quench your thirst for handmade jewelry with this bottle cap bracelet! This eco-friendly bracelet represents the finest in bottle cap crafts. Constructed from vintage Nehi Grape bottle caps from my grandfather's attic, sterling silver findings, and purple Swarovski crystal beads, the bracelet measures 7 inches (17.7 centimeters) across but can be adjusted to accommodate a more diminutive wrist.

As you type your item title and description in Etsy, you can view how it will appear in Google search results, as shown in Figure 12-3. Simply click the Show Preview link under the Description text box. (For more on entering titles and descriptions as you list items, see Chapter 13.)

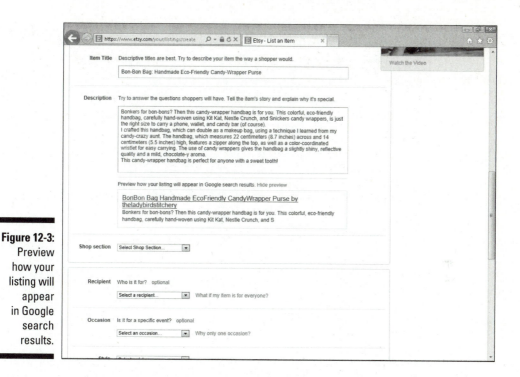

Figure 12-3:
Preview
how your
listing will
appear
in Google
search
results.

Tag, you're it! Understanding tags

In addition to incorporating keywords into your Etsy item listings, you must add tags. A *tag* is a word or short phrase, called *metadata,* that is attached to your item. Etsy uses these tags to help shoppers locate your item. Think of a tag as being the yin to a keyword's yang. For example, suppose that you've tagged your item with the term *bottle cap.* If someone types *bottle cap* when performing an Etsy search, your item will be among the results.

Because tagging is so critical to Etsy's search functionality, it's crucial for you to apply strong tags to your listing. When deciding what tags to apply, ask yourself what keywords you would enter if you were searching for your item. Also, keep an eye on your Shop Stats to find out what search terms people are using to find your items. Start with the most obvious terms first. For example, suppose that you're selling a hand-sewn handbag. You may apply tags such as *purse* and *handbag.* Next, you may apply tags that indicate the style of the handbag — say, *formal, casual, Goth, hippie, frilly,* or whatever. Then you may add tags to convey the bag's size (for example, *large*), texture (such as *quilted, shiny, matte,* or what have you), and color (*ochre, navy,* and so on). You may also add tags to indicate any motifs used in the purse (think *Betty Boop, owls,* or *race car*). Finally, you may apply tags that reflect materials used (*twill, satin, wool, leather,* and so on) and who the item is for (*women, men, children,* and so on). If your piece is for a mature audience, you must tag it with the word *mature.* One more thing: It doesn't hurt to use some of the keywords from the item title and description, as well as the attributes you've set as tags.

Proofread, Please! Proofreading Your Item Title and Listing

Years ago, a neighborhood nursery posted a lovely yellow sign. It had been painted with care, its green letters tidy and even. The problem? Those green letters spelled out the following word: SHURBS. Presumably, the nursery, known for its fine selection of plants, had intended to advertise its lovely collection of shrubs. Instead, it broadcast its carelessness and lack of attention to detail.

As an Etsy shop owner, it's imperative that you (or someone you trust) proofread everything you post in your shop — item titles and descriptions included. Failing to do so may well lead potential buyers to conclude that you're sloppy, that you don't take pride in your work, or that you're incompetent. And *that* conclusion will likely prompt them to shop elsewhere!

Use a word-processing program (like Microsoft Word) to compose your item titles and descriptions instead of composing them while you're creating your listing on Etsy (see Chapter 13). That way, you can take advantage of word-processing tools like spell check. You can then copy and paste the item title and description from your word-processing document to Etsy. As a bonus, this approach makes it easier to reuse item descriptions either in part or in full for new items down the road.

In addition to proofreading for spelling and grammatical errors, peruse your posts for other problems, such as redundant information. Big, pretentious words and fancy, genre-specific terms are other no-nos. For best results, stick with the common vernacular.

Also keep in mind that not everyone on Etsy speaks English as a first language. Don't include words or phrases in your listings that are likely to cause problems for these shoppers.

Chapter 13

Selling Like (Burning Hot) Hotcakes: Listing Your Items

. . . .

In This Chapter

▶ Listing an item

▶ Modifying a listing

▶ Duplicating a listing

▶ Relisting an item

▶ Removing a listing

▶ Tidying up your Etsy shop

. . . .

Fish gotta swim. Birds gotta fly. Camels gotta spit. And an Etsy seller . . . well, she's gotta sell. The first step to selling on Etsy — after setting up your Etsy store (and crafting the piece you want to sell) — is to create an item listing.

Simply put, an item listing is a page in your Etsy store that contains information about an item you have for sale. This item listing contains an item title and description, a list of materials you used to create your piece, a category and tags to help buyers find your item, images of your piece (you can include as many as five), pricing information, shipping details, and more.

In Chapter 11, you discover how to photograph your items. Chapter 12 is devoted to the ins and outs of composing item titles and descriptions. In this chapter, you put it all together and create your first Etsy listing!

Lister, Lister: Listing a New Item

Listing a piece in your Etsy shop is surprisingly painless — provided you've done all the necessary legwork first. (You've composed your item title and description, captured a few gorgeous pictures of your piece, set its price, established your shop policies, and so on.) Etsy steps you through the whole process, which we cover in the following sections.

Ready, set, go! Starting the listing process

After you log in to your Etsy account, follow these steps to begin the listing process:

1. **Hover your mouse pointer over the Your Shop link along the top of any Etsy page.**

   As shown in Figure 13-1, a list of options appears.

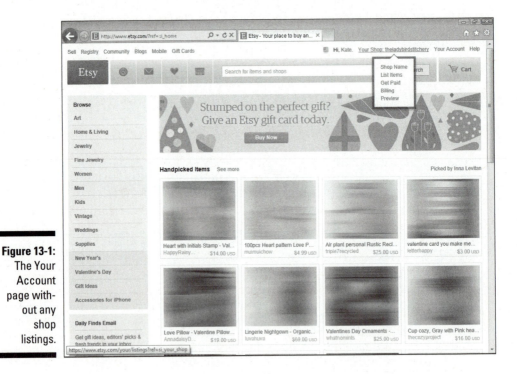

Figure 13-1:
The Your Account page without any shop listings.

2. **If this is the first listing you've created for your Etsy shop, click the List Items option. If you've created listings before, click Add New Item.**

   The List an Item page opens (see Figure 13-2). (Note that this page may look a little different depending on whether this is the first listing created for your shop, as shown here. Nevertheless, the options will be the same.)

Figure 13-2:
Use this page to create a listing.

About face: Filling in item information

Your first step is to enter some basic info about the item — who made it, what it is, when it was made, and under which category it should appear (see Figure 13-3). Follow these steps:

1. **In the About This Item section, click the Who Made It? drop-down list and select the option that best reflects who made the item.**

2. **Click the What Is It? drop-down list that appears and indicate whether the item is a finished product or a supply or tool to make things.**

3. **Click the When Was It Made? drop-down list that appears and choose the option that best describes when the item was made.**

4. **In the Categories section, click the What Is It? drop-down list and choose a category for your item.**

5. **Click the What Type? drop-down list that appears and choose a subcategory.**

6. **Choose as many subcategories in the What Type? drop-down lists as necessary to categorize your item.**

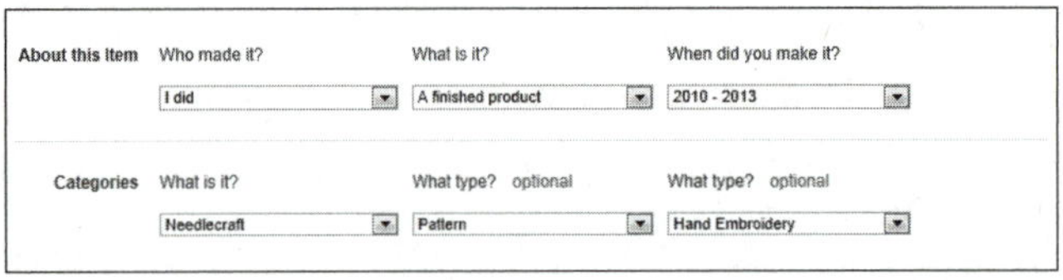

Figure 13-3:
Add basic
item info
here.

About this item	Who made it?		What is it?		When did you make it?	
	I did	▾	A finished product	▾	2010 - 2013	▾
Categories	What is it?		What type? *optional*		What type? *optional*	
	Needlecraft	▾	Pattern	▾	Hand Embroidery	▾

Vary cool: Adding listing variations

If your item comes in different sizes, materials, colors, finishes, or what have you, you can indicate this in the Variations section (see Figure 13-4). You can choose up to two variations per item. When buyers purchase your item, they'll need to choose from the options you set here. Follow these steps:

1. **In the Add Variations section, click the Select a Property drop-down list and choose the correct property.**

   Examples include Size, Color, Finish, and more.

2. **Add more information about the variation.**

   For example, choose the color from the drop-down list that appears; alternatively, type the relevant info when prompted and click the Add button. Repeat as needed.

Figure 13-4:
If you want,
you can add
variations.

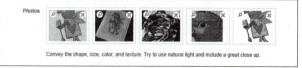

Don't see the property you need? No worries. You can add a custom one. To do so, click the Select a Property drop-down list, choose Add a New Property, type the name of the property, type the options you offer in the text box that appears, and click the Add button. Repeat as needed.

Picture this: Uploading images of your item

Next up is adding photos to your listing. Here's the drill:

1. **In the Photos section, click the Add Photos button.**

   The Choose File to Upload (PC) or File Upload (Mac) dialog box opens.

2. **Locate and select the first image you want to upload, and click the Open button.**

   Any images that you upload must be at least 570 pixels wide (the height can vary) and no more than 1,000 pixels wide or high. Note, too, that image files must be of the JPG, GIF, or PNG variety.

3. **Repeat steps 1 and 2 to add more images to your listing (see Figure 13-5).**

Figure 13-5:
Upload your
product
photos.

Convey the shape, size, color, and texture. Try to use natural light and include a great close up.

Your listing can feature as many as five images — and that's how many you want to include!

4. **To change the order in which the images appear in your listing, click the image that you want to move and drag it either left to move it up in the order or right to move it down in the order.**

The first image in the list will be the thumbnail image that appears in search results and as the main, featured image in the item listing. Make it a good one!

Description prescription: Describing your item

To help convey your item's fabulousness, you must include an item title and description, as shown in Figure 13-6. (Refer to Chapter 12 for help with composing your item title and description.) And if you've created sections for your shop, as discussed in Chapter 8, you can specify the section in which this item should appear. Here's how:

1. **In the Item Title field, type a title for your item.**

2. **In the Description field, enter a description of your item.**

   Notice that a preview of how your listing will show up in Google search results appears below the Description field (see Chapter 12 for details).

3. **If you've created sections for your shop, click the Shop Section drop-down list and choose the section in which you want the listing to appear. (If you haven't entered sections for your shop yet, you can do so later, and assign each of your listings to a section you create.)**

Figure 13-6:
Enter a title and description for your item.

As you toodle around Etsy, you may notice the occasional listing whose title contains the word *reserved*. A *reserved listing* is simply a listing that a seller has posted for a specific buyer — someone with whom she's communicated previously. For example, if a buyer contacts a seller to create a custom piece, the seller posts the piece as a reserved listing.

Getting specific: Adding the recipient, occasion, and style

Is your item made for a specific audience — say, babies or dogs? If so, you can indicate this in your listing. You can also specify an occasion for which your item is made (think wedding or birthday or Chinese New Year), as well as a style for your item (examples range from Goth to kitsch to tribal). Here's how (see Figure 13-7):

1. **Click the Recipient drop-down list and choose a recipient.**

   If your item is for everyone, it's better to leave this option blank.

2. **Click the Occasion drop-down list and choose an occasion.**

   As with the Recipient option, if your item is for all occasions, leave this option blank.

3. **Click the Style drop-down list and choose a style.**

   If you want to add a second style, repeat this step.

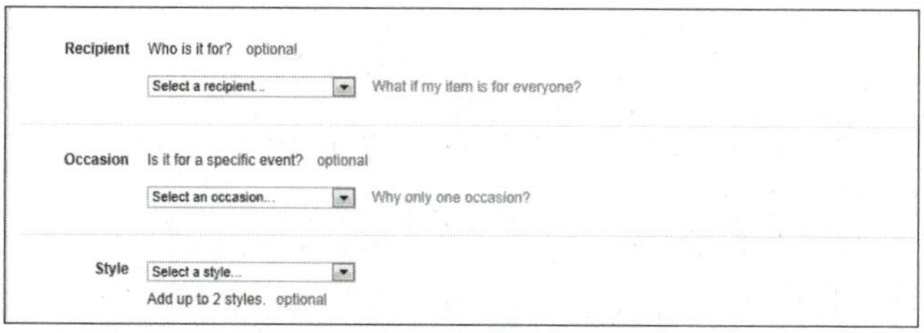

Figure 13-7:
Optionally, add the recipient, occasion, and style.

If you don't see the style you need, you can add a custom one. To do so, click the Select a Style drop-down list, choose Add a Style, type the name of the style in the text box that appears, and click the Add button.

It's in the tag: Tagging your item

As you know, tagging is critical to Etsy's search functionality. To tag your listing, follow these steps (see Figure 13-8):

1. **Type a tag for your item in the Tags field and click the Add button.**

2. **Repeat Step 1 until you've added all appropriate tags.**

   You can apply as many as 13 tags to your listing. To maximize the chances of buyers finding your item, you want to use as many tags as you're allowed. If you run out of ideas for tags, turn to your trusty thesaurus for help. Also, it's okay to use phrases. (Chapter 12 has the full scoop on tagging.)

3. **To indicate the materials used in your piece, type a material in the Materials field and click the Add button.**

4. **Repeat Step 3 until you've added all appropriate materials.**

   You can apply as many as 13 materials to your listing. Enter as many materials as you can.

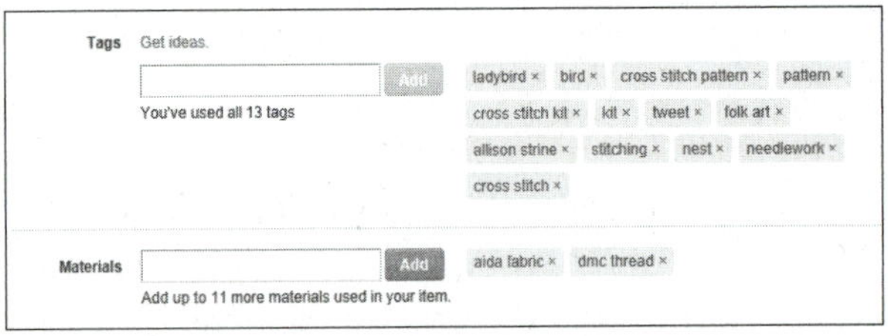

Figure 13-8:
You tag your item in this section.

Sales figures: Adding selling information for your item

Follow these steps to enter the item's price and quantity, as well as a few tidbits on shipping (see Figure 13-9):

1. **Enter the item's price in the Price field.**

2. **Type the item's quantity in — you guessed it — the Quantity field.**

   Note that you will be charged 20¢ total for your item listing, regardless of quantity.

3. **Optionally, in the Shipping section, click the Ready to Ship In drop-down list and choose the option that reflects how much time you'll need to prepare the order for shipping.**

4. **Click the Ships From drop-down list and choose your geographic location.**

   Etsy updates the Shipping section to enable you to indicate how much shipping will cost when the item is sent within the United States and elsewhere. Enter the appropriate info.

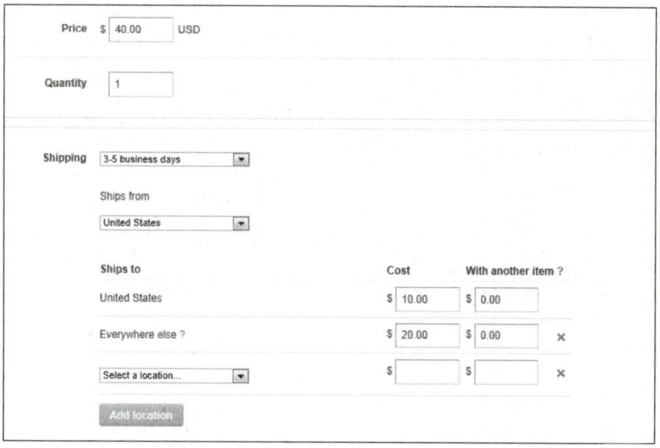

Figure 13-9:
Enter the item's price, quantity, and other details here.

Price	$ 40.00	USD		
Quantity	1			
Shipping	3-5 business days ▼			
	Ships from			
	United States ▼			
	Ships to	Cost	With another item ?	
	United States	$ 10.00	$ 0.00	
	Everywhere else ?	$ 20.00	$ 0.00	✕
	Select a location... ▼	$	$	✕
	Add location			

To expedite this step, you can create shipping profiles for your items. A *shipping profile* is simply a collection of shipping-related settings that you can apply to an item listing in one fell swoop instead of entering them one by one. If you have a lot of listings to upload, you'll find that using shipping profiles makes your work go a lot faster! Once you've created a shipping profile, Etsy enables you to select it in the Shipping section shown in Figure 13-9. You see how to create shipping profiles in Chapter 15.

The reviews are in! Reviewing your listing

You're almost done! Follow these steps to review your listing one last time:

1. **Click the Preview Listing button at the bottom of the List an Item page.**

   Etsy displays a preview of your listing (see Figure 13-10).

Figure 13-10:
Review your
listing.

2. **Review your listing; if you notice something that you need to change, click the Edit button at the top of the page, make your change, and click the Preview Listing button again.**

   As you review your listing, note whether the listing's thumbnail photo needs adjusting. If it does, click the Adjust Photo button and fix it as needed.

3. **To submit your listing, click the Publish button at the top of the page.**

   The listing is submitted to Etsy and appears in the Currently for Sale page in Your Shop (see Figure 13-11).

Figure 13-11: Your listing is posted.

If this is the first listing to be created in your shop, you won't see a Publish button. Instead, you'll see a Save as Draft button. Click that button instead. Then click the Open Shop button in the screen that appears. Finally, ensure the check box next to the listing is selected in the window that opens, and click the Publish Listings and Open Shop button (see Figure 13-12). Etsy opens your shop and publishes this as your first listing.

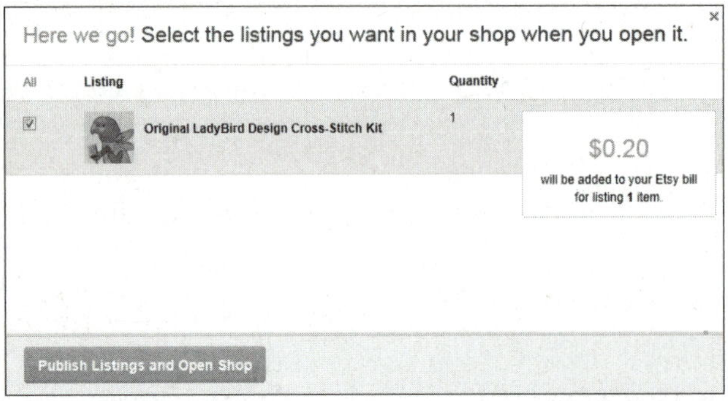

Figure 13-12:
Click the
Publish
Listings and
Open Shop
button to
publish your
first listing
and open
your Etsy
shop.

Here we go! Select the listings you want in your shop when you open it.

All	Listing	Quantity
☑	Original LadyBird Design Cross-Stitch Kit	1

$0.20
will be added to your Etsy bill
for listing 1 item.

Publish Listings and Open Shop

One more thing: Notice the message in Figure 13-12 that reads: "$0.20 will be added to your Etsy bill for listing 1 item." This fee is your one-time listing fee, for which Etsy will bill you. (Note that this fee is nonrefundable, even if you unlist your item.) In addition to this listing fee, you're charged a transaction fee when your item sells (not *if* — let's be optimistic!). This transaction fee amounts to 3.5 percent of your total sale price (not including shipping). These fees are assessed at the end of each month. For more info on paying your Etsy bill, see Chapter 18.

Ch-Ch-Ch-Ch-Changes: Editing a Listing

Look, nobody's perfect (although, obviously, you're pretty close). You may make a mistake when creating your listing and need to change it. Or maybe a potential buyer asks a question about the item you have for sale, and you want to update the item's listing to reflect your answer. Or you may want to add or change a listing photo.

Fortunately, regardless of why you need to change a listing, editing Etsy listings is a breeze (and free). You can edit any part of your item listing — the item title, item description, price, images, tags, materials, shipping information, you name it. To edit a listing, log in to your Etsy account and follow these steps:

1. **Click the Shop icon in your Etsy header bar.**

   Your Etsy shop opens (refer to Figure 13-11).

2. **Click the listing that you want to edit.**

   The listing opens (see Figure 13-13).

Figure 13-13:
Your listing
opens.

3. **Click the Edit link in the Listing Tools toolbar along the top of the listing.**

   The Edit Listing page opens (see Figure 13-14). This page is nearly identical to the List an Item page shown earlier in this chapter (refer to Figure 13-2).

   You can also launch the edit operation from the Currently for Sale page (see Figure 13-15). To begin, hover your mouse pointer over the Your Shop link along the top of any Etsy page; then click the Listings link to open the Currently for Sale page. Next, click the Edit link on the right side of the listing that you want to edit.

4. **Edit the listing using the same techniques you employed to create it.**

5. **Click the Preview Listing button to preview the listing.**

6. **Click the Publish button to publish the edited listing.**

To ensure that no one can view the listing while you edit it, click the Deactivate This Listing link at the top of the Edit Listing page. Etsy deactivates the listing, displaying it in the Inactive Listings page. To edit the listing, click its Edit link; then complete steps 4 through 6 as normal.

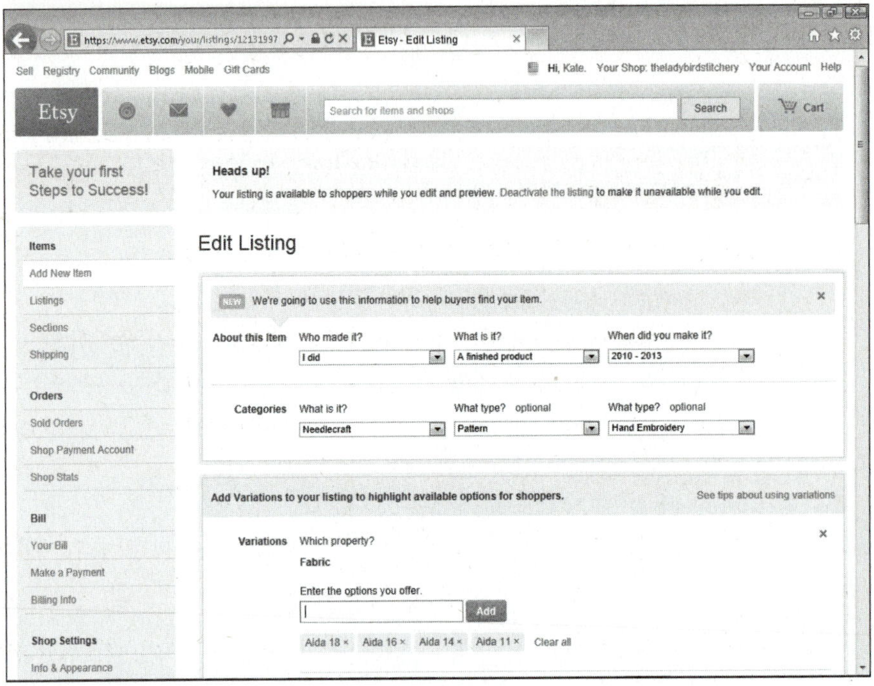

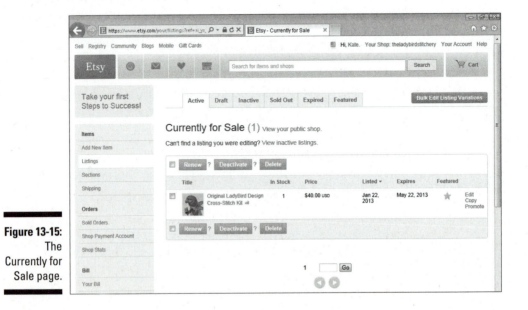

Figure 13-14:
Edit your
listing.

Figure 13-15:
The
Currently for
Sale page.

Copycat: Copying a Listing

Suppose that you've created multiple items that are the same. In this case, instead of building a new listing for each item from scratch, you can create one listing and then copy it. Here's how you do so (after you log in to your Etsy account):

1. **Click the Shop icon in your Etsy header bar.**

   Your Etsy shop opens (refer to Figure 13-11).

2. **Click the listing that you want to copy in your Etsy shop.**

   The listing opens (refer to Figure 13-13).

3. **Click the Copy link in the Listing Tools toolbar along the top of the listing.**

   The List an Item page opens.

   Another way to launch the copy operation is to open the Currently for Sale page in Your Shop and click the Copy link on the right side of the listing that you want to copy.

4. **Step through the listing-creation process, as described earlier in this chapter.**

   As you do, notice that the information in each section is entered for you, based on the listing you copied. You can change this information as needed.

5. **Click the Preview Listing button to review your listing.**

6. **To post the listing, click the Publish button.**

   A new listing based on the one you copied is posted.

Renewable Resources: Renewing a Listing

In addition to copying listings, you can renew them. For example, you may renew a listing if it has expired, or if the item has sold and you want to restock your shop by offering a new, identical item.

You can also renew an active listing. When you do, the listing gets a new listing date and a new expiration date (four months from the date of renewal). A renewal can breathe new life into the listing, placing it closer to the top of item searches and briefly in the Recently Listed Items section.

When you renew a listing, even an active listing, you're assessed a 20¢ listing fee, regardless of the quantity entered.

Don't be a sellout: Renewing a sold listing

To restock your shop by renewing a listing for a sold item, log in to your Etsy account and follow these steps:

1. **Hover your mouse pointer over the Your Shop link along the top of any Etsy page.**

   A list of options appears.

2. **Click the Sold Orders link.**

   The Open Orders page opens, as shown in Figure 13-16.

3. **If the listing you want to renew appears in the Open Orders page, click it; if not, click the All tab and click the listing there.**

   A page for the listing opens, as shown in Figure 13-17.

4. **Click the Renew Sold link.**

   A preview of the listing appears, much like the one shown in Figure 13-10.

5. **Click the Renew button to renew your listing.**

   Etsy posts a new listing.

An even faster way to renew the listing is to click the little gear icon to the right of the listing in the Open Orders or All tab and choose Renew from the menu that appears.

Stay active: Renewing an active listing

Here's how you renew an active listing while you're logged in to your Etsy account (it's a cinch!):

1. **Hover your mouse pointer over the Your Shop link along the top of any Etsy page.**

   A list of options appears.

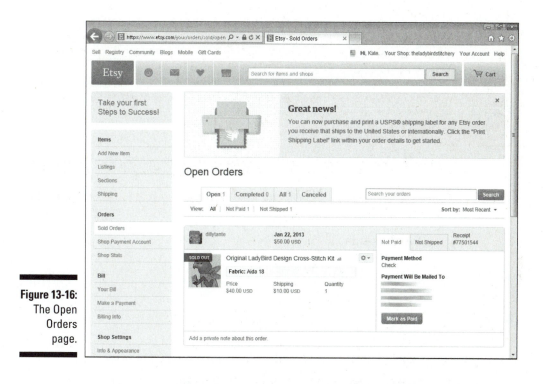

Figure 13-16:
The Open
Orders
page.

Figure 13-17:
A page
opens, indi-
cating when
the item
was sold.

2. **Click the Listings link.**

   The Currently for Sale page opens (refer to Figure 13-15).

3. **Click the check box next to the listing you want to renew.**

   To renew more than one active item at a time, click the check box next to each active listing that you want to renew. To select all your listings, click the check box just above or below the list. This same trick applies when you renew expired listings, covered in the next section.

4. **Click the Renew button (there's one at the top of the list of active listings and another one at the bottom of the list).**

   Etsy prompts you to confirm the renewal.

5. **Click Renew again.**

   Etsy renews the listing.

You can also renew an active item from within your Etsy shop. To do so, log in to your account, click the link to your shop in the Etsy header bar, open the listing that you want to renew, and click the Renew link in the Listing Tools toolbar along the top of the listing (refer to Figure 13-13 to see this link). When prompted to confirm the renewal, click the Renew button.

Expiration mark: Renewing an expired listing

Renewing an expired listing is a lot like renewing an active listing:

1. **Hover your mouse pointer over the Your Shop link along the top of any Etsy page and click the Listings link.**

   The Currently for Sale page opens (refer to Figure 13-15).

2. **Click the Expired tab.**

   The Expired Listings page opens. This page looks a lot like the Currently for Sale page.

3. **Click the check box next to the expired listing you want to renew.**

4. **Click the Renew button (there's one at the top of the list of expired listings and another one at the bottom of the list).**

   Etsy prompts you to confirm the renewal.

5. **Click Renew again.**

   Etsy renews the listing and directs you to the Expired tab.

Pull the Plug: Deactivating a Listing

Suppose that, after you crafted an item and listed it in your Etsy shop, your dog ate it. While you construct a replacement, you can deactivate the listing. You can deactivate listings in your Etsy shop for any reason, free of charge. When you deactivate a listing, it disappears from your Etsy shop. Note, however, that deactivating a listing doesn't change its expiration date.

To deactivate a listing, log in to your Etsy account and follow these steps:

1. **Hover your mouse pointer over the Your Shop link along the top of any Etsy page and click the Listings link.**

   The Currently for Sale page opens (refer to Figure 13-15).

2. **Click the check box next to the listing that you want to deactivate.**

   To deactivate more than one active item at a time, click the check box next to each active listing that you want to deactivate. To select all your listings, click the check box just above or below the list.

3. **Click the Deactivate button (there's one at the top of the list of active listings and another one at the bottom of the list).**

   Etsy deactivates the listing.

When you're ready to reactivate the listing, again making it visible to people who visit your Etsy shop, here's what you do:

1. **Hover your mouse pointer over the Your Shop link along the top of any Etsy page and click the Listings link.**

   The Currently for Sale page opens (refer to Figure 13-15).

2. **Click the Inactive tab.**

   The Inactive Listings page opens (see Figure 13-18).

3. **Click the check box next to the listing that you want to reactivate.**

   To reactivate more than one deactivated item at a time, click the check box next to each listing that you want to reactivate. To select all your listings, click the check box just above or below the list.

4. **Click the Activate button (there's one at the top of the list of deactivated listings and another one at the bottom of the list).**

   Etsy reactivates the listing, removing it from the Inactive Listings page.

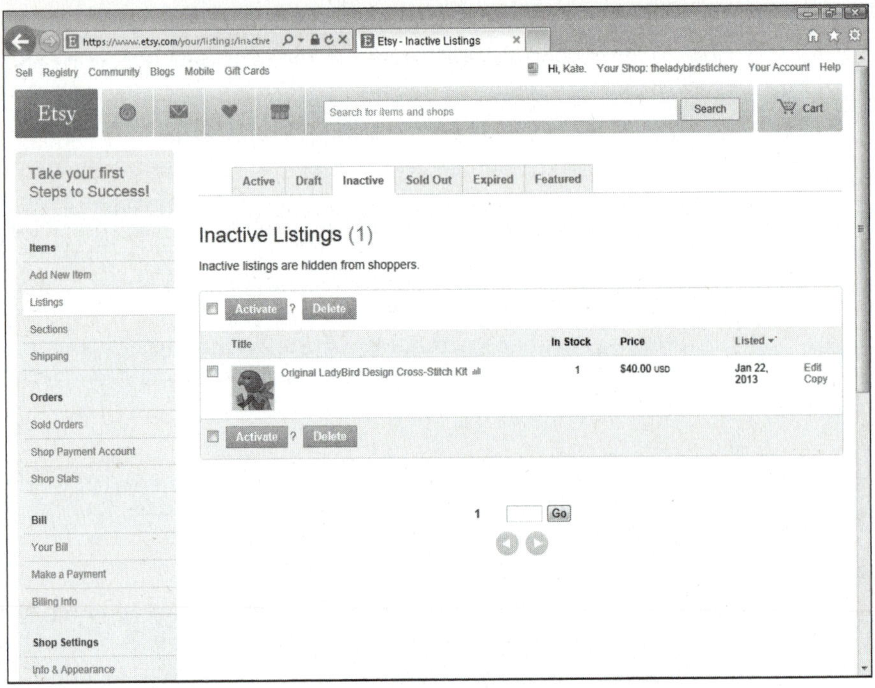

Figure 13-18:
Renew an
active
listing.

Rearrange Your Face: Rearranging Your Etsy Shop

As you add more listings to your Etsy shop, you may decide that you want to rearrange the order in which they appear. For example, instead of having your items listed in the order you added them to your shop, with older items appearing farther down in the list (the default), maybe you want to group together all items of a certain color. Or put all items of a single type on one page. Or move all the most expensive items to the top of your store's main page. Or move an older listing to the top of your list. Lucky you — rearranging your shop is simple, as you find out in the following sections.

Be an enabler: Enabling the Rearrange Your Shop feature

Before you make a move, you have to log in to your Etsy account and enable Etsy's Rearrange Your Shop feature. Here's how:

1. **Click the Your Shop link along the top of any Etsy page.**

2. **Click the Options link on the left side of the page, under Shop Settings.**

   The Shop Options page opens (see Figure 13-19).

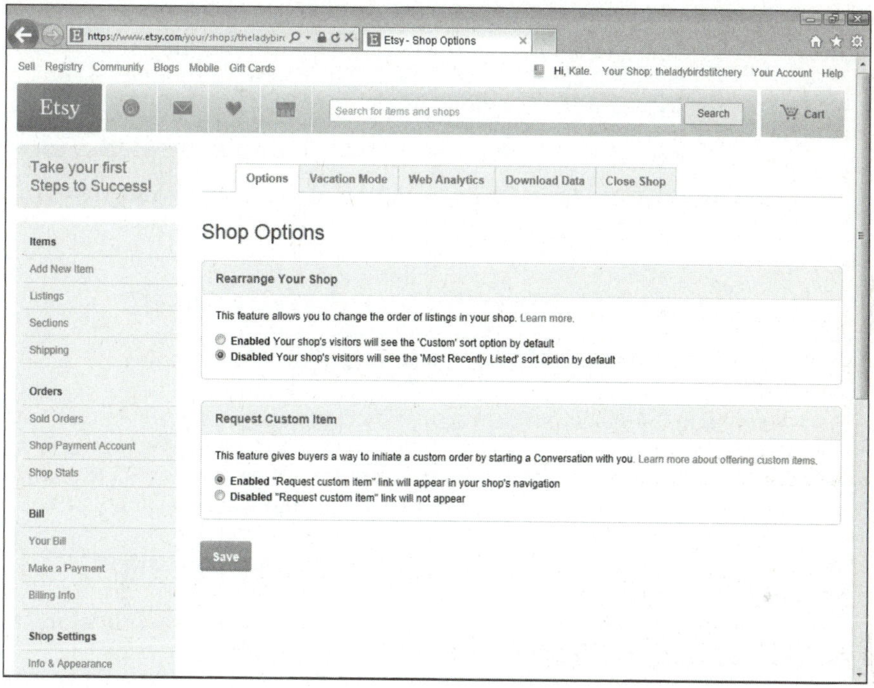

Figure 13-19: The Shop Options page.

3. **Under Rearrange Your Shop, click the Enabled option button.**

4. **Click the Save button.**

   Etsy saves your changes.

Get moving! Moving your listings

Now you're ready to get down to business rearranging your goodies. Here's what you do:

1. **Click the Shop icon in your Etsy header bar.**

   Your Etsy shop opens.

2. **Click the Rearrange Your Shop link, under Your Shop, on the left side of the page.**

   Your shop changes to Rearrange mode.

3. **To change the order of a listing, click the listing, drag it to the desired spot in the order, and release your mouse button.**

   The listing is moved.

   To move a listing to a different page in your Etsy shop, hover your mouse pointer over the item that you want to move. Then click the page you want to move it to.

4. **Repeat Step 3 until the items in your shop are in the order you want.**

5. **Click the Save Changes button to save your arrangement.**

Feature comforts: Featuring an item in your Etsy shop

When it comes to rearranging your Etsy shop, another option is to feature certain item listings. When you do, those listings appear in a special "Featured" section on your shop's main page and across the bottom of your shop's About page. You can feature as many as four item listings at a time.

To feature an item listing in your shop, follow these steps:

1. **Hover your mouse pointer over the Your Shop link along the top of any Etsy page and click the Listings link.**

   The Currently for Sale page opens (refer to Figure 13-15).

2. **Click the star in an item listing's Featured column to feature that listing in your shop.**

   Voilà! The item listings that you selected appear at the top of your shop's main page.

To change the order in which featured items appear on your shop page, follow these steps:

1. **Hover your mouse pointer over the Your Shop link along the top of any Etsy page and click the Listings link.**

   The Currently for Sale page opens (refer to Figure 13-15).

2. **In the Currently for Sale page, click the Featured tab.**

   The Featured Listings page opens.

3. **To move an item up in the order, click its Up button; to move it down, click its down button.**

Chapter 14

Wrap It Up: Closing the Deal

. . . .

In This Chapter

▶ Finding out when you've sold something

▶ Tracking sales in Your Account

▶ Viewing invoices

▶ Receiving payments

. . . .

Hallelujah! You've made a sale! It's time for some rejoicing — and possibly some invoicing. In this chapter, you get the scoop on how to deal with such end-of-sale matters as finding out when you've sold something, tracking your sales, invoicing, and receiving payments.

You've Got Sale: Finding Out You Have a Sale

When you sell an item in your Etsy shop, Etsy notifies you via e-mail straight away. As you can see in Figure 14-1, this e-mail contains loads of important information, including the following:

✔ Which item sold

✔ The price and quantity of the item that sold

✔ The payment method used

✔ The buyer's details, including his shipping address and e-mail address

✔ Any notes the buyer left

✔ A link to the sales invoice (we discuss invoices in more detail later in this chapter)

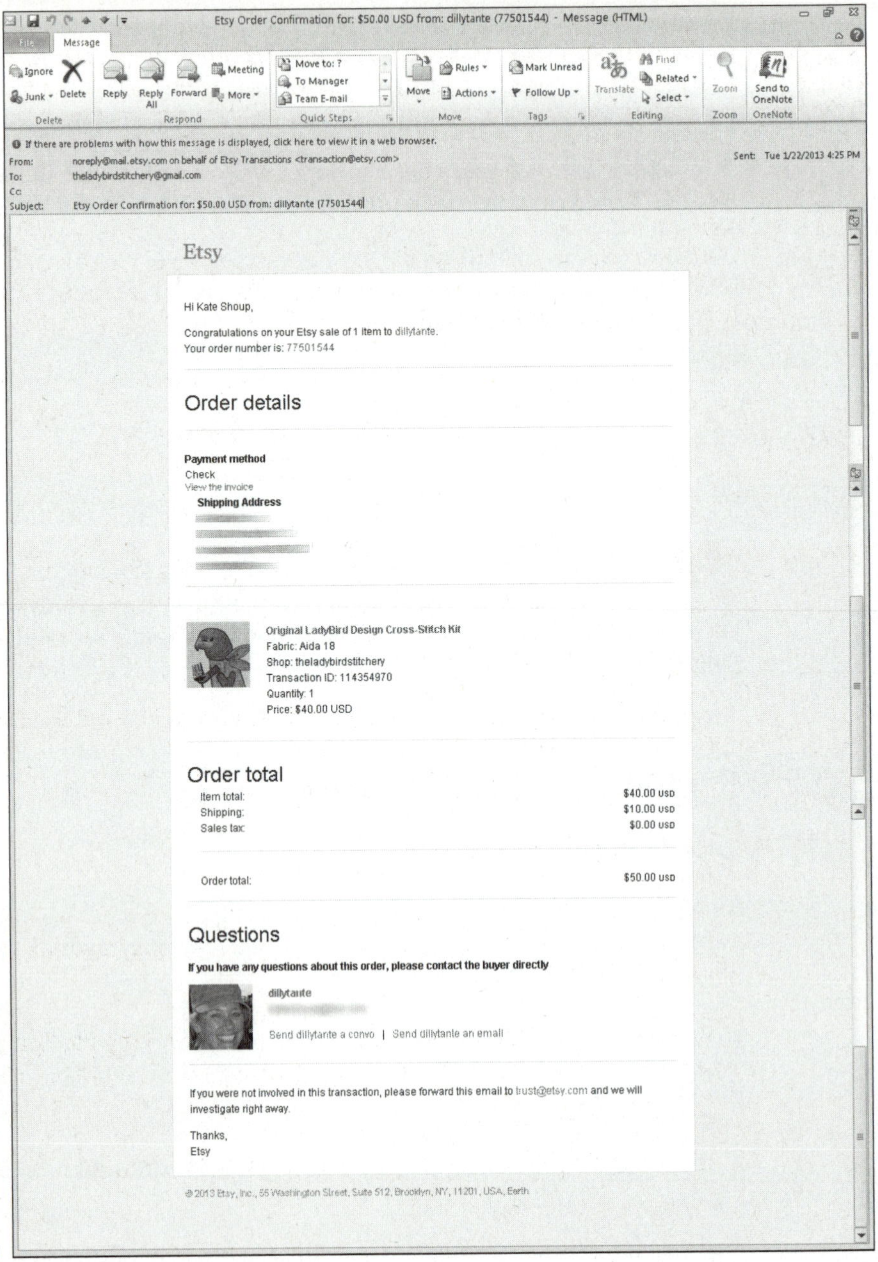

Figure 14-1:
Etsy e-mails you whenever you sell an item in your Etsy shop.

To make sure that your e-mail program's spam filter doesn't come between you and these notification e-mails, consider adding the e-mail address `transactions@etsy.com` to your list of safe senders. For details on how to perform this task, see your e-mail program's help information.

One way to stay on top of sales is to set up your e-mail program to send a text message to your phone whenever you receive e-mails with the word *Etsy* in the subject line. For details on taking care of this task, see your e-mail program's Help information. Alternatively, you can use EtsyText, a free Etsy app that sends you a text message any time something in your shop sells (standard text-messaging rates apply). For more info, visit `www.etsytext.com`.

Baby Got Track: Keeping Track of Sales in Your Account

When you know you've sold an item, you can view it in Your Shop. You can keep track of what sales you've made, which items the buyers have paid for, and whether you've shipped the items. To view a sale in Your Shop, log in to your Etsy account and follow these steps:

1. **Hover your mouse pointer over the Your Shop link along the top of any Etsy page.**

   A list of options appears.

2. **Click the Sold Orders option.**

3. **If necessary, click the Open tab.**

   The Open Orders page opens, displaying a list of items that you've sold but not yet shipped (see Figure 14-2). We talk about shipping in detail in Chapter 15.

Note that you can view orders you've shipped by clicking the Completed tab. To see all orders — ones that are open and ones that have shipped — click the All tab.

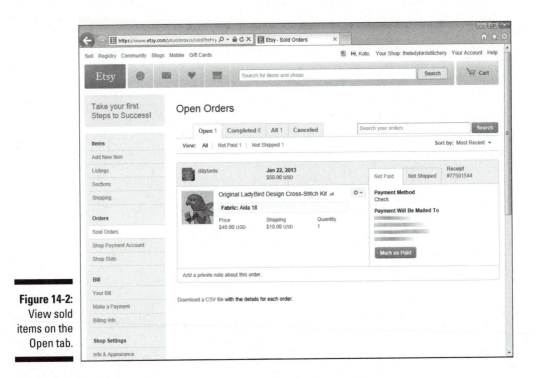

Figure 14-2:
View sold
items on the
Open tab.

Guided by Invoices: Handling Invoices

When someone buys something from your Etsy shop, that person will receive an e-mail from Etsy (see Figure 14-3). It's a receipt of sorts and contains all the details of the order. Buyers can click the order number (if purchased via Direct Checkout) or View the Invoice (if a different payment was used — say, personal check, money order, frankincense, or myrrh) link found in the e-mail to view the order online. In addition, if the buyer paid for the item via PayPal, PayPal will send her an additional receipt for the payment transaction via e-mail.

Even though Etsy handles receipts and invoicing for you, you should still reach out to your buyer to express your thanks. This is an important part of customer service — and it's essential to the success of your shop (see Chapter 17).

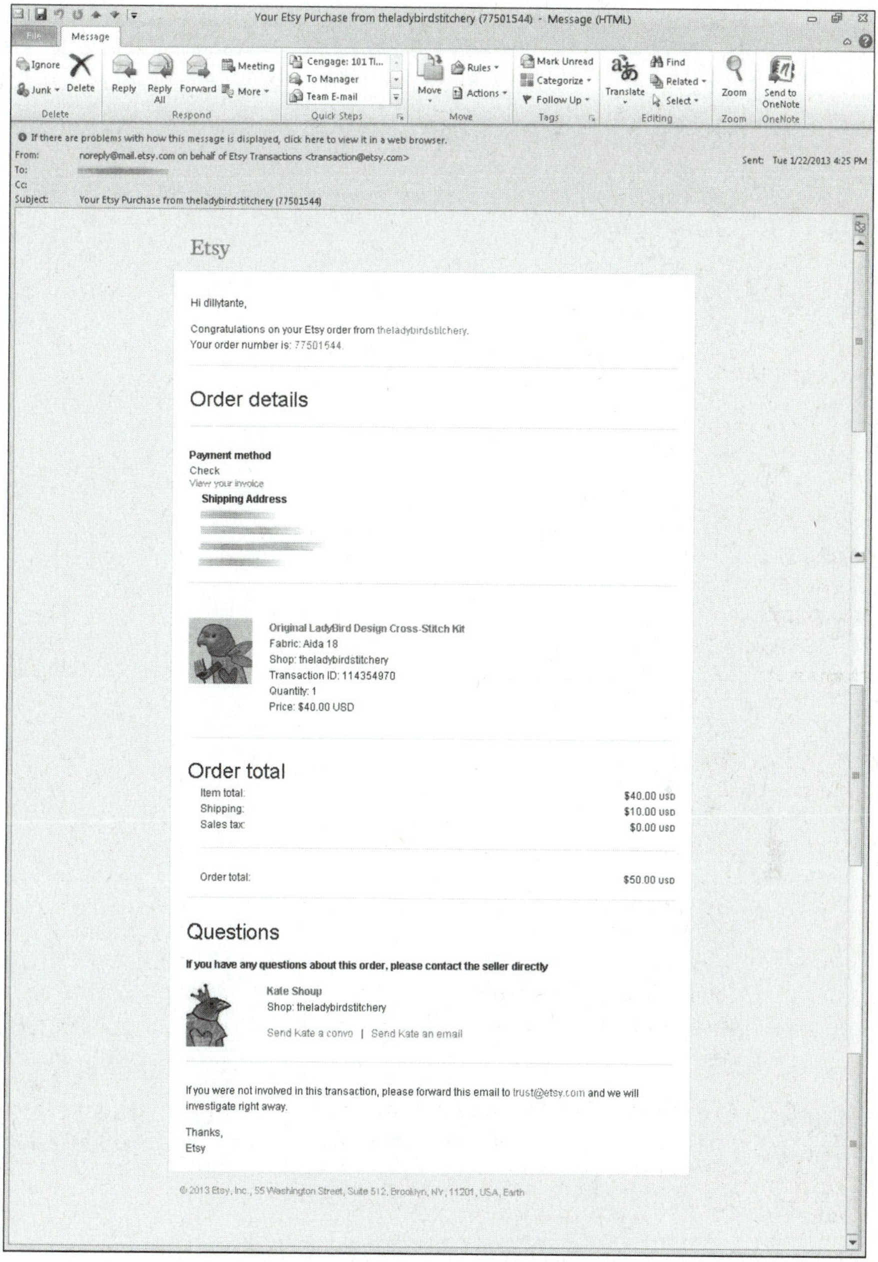

Figure 14-3: Buyers receive invoices automatically.

Sometimes you need to view an invoice for a sale — say, to check the buyer's shipping address. One way to access that invoice is to click the View the Invoice link or the link featuring the order number found at the top of your notification e-mail message (refer to Figure 14-1). Alternatively, log in to your Etsy account and try the following:

1. **Hover your mouse pointer over the Your Shop link along the top of any Etsy page.**

   A list of options appears.

2. **Click the Sold Orders option.**

   The Completed Orders page opens.

3. **Click the Open tab.**

   The Open Orders page appears (refer to Figure 14-2).

4. **Click the listing in the Open Orders page to view it (see Figure 14-4).**

5. **Click the View Invoice link or the Receipt link at the top of the listing page.**

Figure 14-4:
Open the
listing for
the sold
item.

Etsy displays the invoice for the transaction (see Figure 14-5). It contains key info about the transaction — whether the buyer has paid for the item, whether you've shipped the piece, the buyer's shipping address, how much the item cost, and more. It also features a Print Order button (which you can click to print the invoice for your records) and a Print Shipping Label option (if you accept Direct Checkout and are based in the United States).

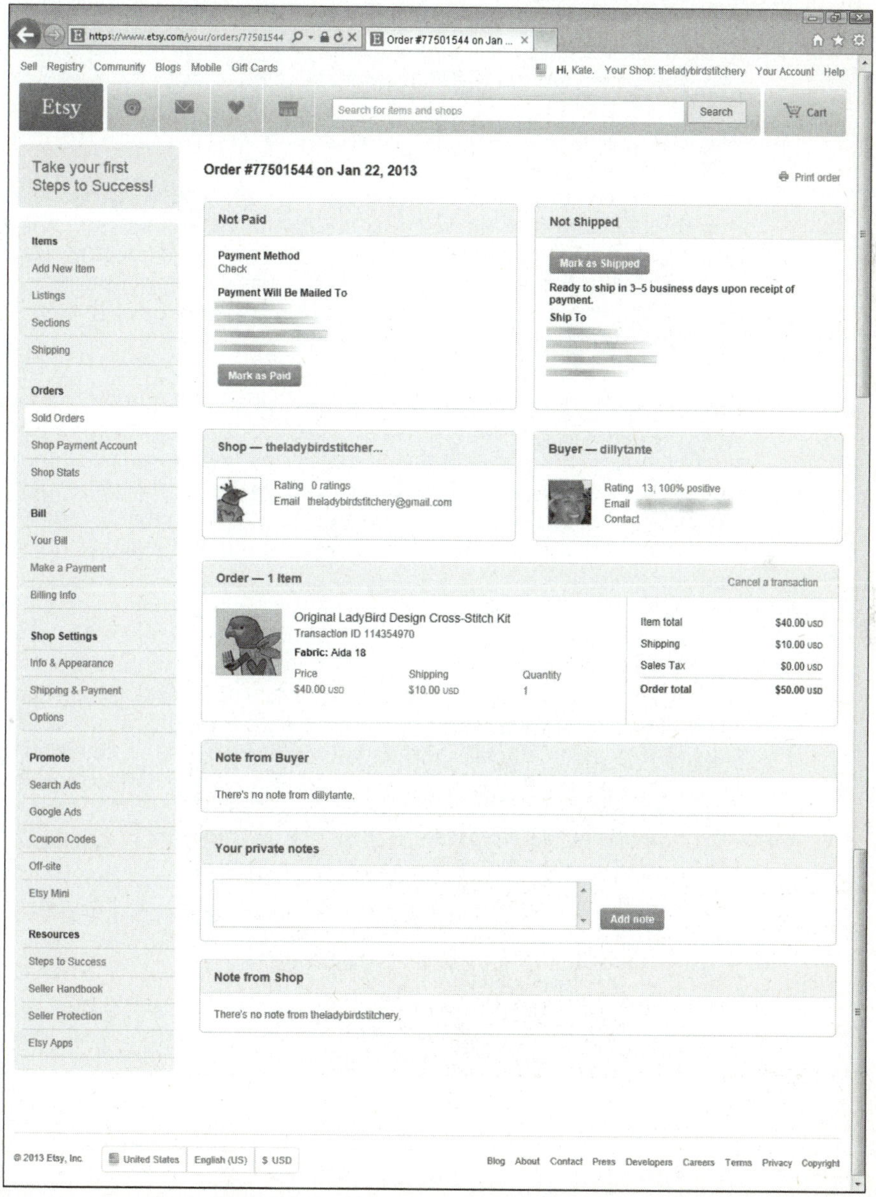

Figure 14-5:
View the invoice.

Show Me the Money: Receiving Payment

As you've probably deduced, exactly how you receive a payment depends on the method of payment used. For example, if the buyer opted to pay by check, you'll receive said check in the mail. Ditto for cashier's checks, money orders, and the like.

Note, however, that there's a Godzilla-size difference between when a check's funds are released to you and when the check actually clears. Make sure that you ship your item only after the check clears; it can take a week or more. Otherwise, you'll be on the hook for those funds if the check bounces. (Note that the same goes for cashier's checks and money orders.)

When you receive a payment via PayPal, you'll receive an e-mail indicating that the payment has been deposited in your PayPal account. Be aware that although your PayPal account is linked to your bank account, they're not one and the same: Dough deposited into your PayPal account doesn't automatically appear in your bank account's balance — you have to transfer the funds manually. For more info, search PayPal's Help files.

If you receive a payment via Etsy's Direct Checkout, and your sales history goes back at least 90 days, Etsy will make your money available to you the next business day. If your sales history does not extend back that far, your money will become available after three days or after you've marked the item as shipped (whichever comes first), although you may have to wait until the following Monday (or, if that Monday is a holiday, the next business day) for your funds to be disbursed.

One more thing: If your buyer paid by check, cashier's check, or money order, and the funds have cleared, you need to do one more thing (apart from shipping the item to your buyer, of course): Mark the item as Paid on Etsy. (This is not necessary if you received payment via Direct Checkout or PayPal.) To do so, click the Mark as Paid button next to the item listing on the Open Orders page's Open tab. Etsy updates the listing to indicate that you received payment (see Figure 14-6).

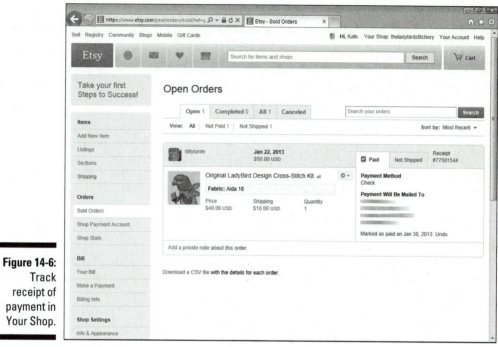

Figure 14-6:
Track
receipt of
payment in
Your Shop.

Chapter 15

The Ship Hits the Fan: Shipping Your Items

In This Chapter

▶ Buying shipping supplies

▶ Packaging your item with care

▶ Finding a shipper (both domestic and international)

▶ Creating a shipping profile

▶ Choosing delivery confirmation and insurance

▶ Printing shipping labels

▶ Closing the order in Etsy

The moment you receive payment for your piece (and, if applicable, the check, cashier's check, or money order has cleared), it's time to begin the difficult process of letting your piece go. As hard as it may be to say goodbye — after all, you slaved over its creation and gave it the best care possible — the time has come to send it on its way. In this chapter, you discover everything you need to know to pack and ship your item to its new happy home.

If you're worried about protecting your privacy during the shipping process, consider obtaining a post office box and using that to send and receive Etsy-related packages. For information, go to https://poboxes.usps.com.

The Right (Packaging) Stuff: Obtaining Shipping Supplies

Imagine a Venn diagram with one circle representing Etsy users and another representing people who love the environment. Odds are, the part where those circles intersect is pretty huge. This duality no doubt explains why so many Etsy sellers prefer to use recycled shipping materials — boxes, bubble wrap, envelopes, packing paper, and the like. Some even go the DIY route, crafting their own mailers and packaging materials from their or others' detritus — for example, running old wrapping paper and magazine sheets through a shredder to create cushioning for fragile items.

Here's another option for no-cost materials: If you mail via the U.S. Postal Service, you can obtain Priority Mail boxes free of charge. Visit the USPS website (www.usps.com) for more info, and see the later section "Stay First Classy: Surveying Shipping Options" for details on Priority Mail and flat rates.

Of course, you can also purchase shipping supplies for your Etsy shop. Even the most devoted recyclers may need to buy some shipping supplies, such as packing tape or the occasional mailer. Whether you seek boxes, bubble wrap, ribbon, or tissue, you can find what you need at these sites:

- ✔ **ULINE:** www.uline.com
- ✔ **Paper Mart:** www.papermart.com
- ✔ **Nashville Wraps:** www.nashvillewraps.com

Needless to say, you can also visit your local office-supply store (think Office Max, Office Depot, Staples, and the like) to stock up on shipping supplies. Note, however, that higher prices may somewhat offset the convenience of shopping for supplies at these bricks-and-mortar retailers.

One more piece of advice: Invest in a postal scale. You'll need it to weigh your packages if you plan to ship from home. Also keep a flexible tape measure on hand, in case your carrier charges by box size instead of weight. (See the section "Stay First Classy: Surveying Shipping Options," later in this chapter, for more information.)

If you have space in your home or studio, set up a shipping station and stock it with all your shipping supplies. Trust us, it'll make the task of packaging your pieces easy-peasy!

Package Deal: Showing Your Love and Care with Packaging

Yes, everyone knows that it's what's on the inside that counts. But that truism doesn't mean that what's on the outside isn't also important. Translation: When shipping your piece to your buyer, be sure to package it with care. In the following sections, we discuss wrapping different sorts of items, using attractive and brand-friendly packaging, and including goodies.

How you package your items says something about you and your Etsy shop. Make sure it doesn't say, "I'm lazy and careless!"

Wrapper's delight: Wrapping any kind of item safely

It goes without saying that you must take steps to ensure that your piece will arrive in one, er, piece. When it enters your buyer's home, it needs to be in excellent shape (think Jillian Michaels). To that end, consider the following guidelines:

- ✔ **Be sure to pack fragile items carefully.** Use cushioning materials such as bubble wrap or shredded paper to prevent breakage, and employ plenty of sturdy packing tape to ensure that your package isn't tattered en route. (We talk about supplies in more detail earlier in this chapter.)

- ✔ **Pack bendable booty — such as art prints and the like — with a firm, flat backing.**

- ✔ **If, like the Wicked Witch of the West, your item is moisture averse, slip it into a sealed plastic bag before sending it on its way.**

Although packaging your items carefully to prevent damage is critical, don't take things too far. Excessive packaging — especially if it doesn't involve recycled materials — is wasteful.

Nice package! Using attractive, brand-friendly packaging

Strive to delight your buyer not only with your piece, but also with your packaging. Don't just toss your lovingly crafted item in an envelope and plop it in the post; instead, develop packaging that, in addition to protecting your item, looks good. You don't have to wrap your packages in expensive gift paper with hand-curled ribbon (although some Etsy sellers do); most buyers are perfectly satisfied with a package that has been carefully and securely wrapped with clean, plain, environmentally friendly paper.

In addition, make sure your packaging reflects your brand. For example, if your brand is frou-frou, your packaging needs to be, too. On the flip side, if your brand is all modern minimalism, you want to ensure that your packaging is similarly under-the-top. Also, invest in stickers or a stamp with your shop's logo for use in your packaging. (You find out more about developing your brand in Chapter 16.)

One way to reflect your brand in your packaging is to use colored tissue paper. For example, if your logo is green and red, you may wrap your items in green and red tissue. If you go this route, be sure to moisture-proof your package by wrapping it in plastic; otherwise, the dye from the paper may bleed onto your piece if the package gets wet in transit.

Goody-goody: Including extras in your parcel

It goes without saying that your package needs to include the item your buyer purchased. Beyond that, you may include any or all of the following:

- ✔ **A handwritten note:** If you want to make your buyer's day, include a handwritten note in your packaging. It doesn't have to be a 40-page opus; just a few lines thanking the buyer for his purchase and wishing him well will do. (Be sure to address him by name — it's so much more personal.) You might also use this opportunity to ask your buyer to leave feedback about you on Etsy.

  Consider investing in special note cards or postcards that reflect your brand — or, better yet, make your own! For example, you may design a note card that includes your shop logo. Alternatively, if you sell art prints, you may design a postcard with one of your best-selling images.

- ✔ **Business cards:** To make sure that your buyer remembers you and your store, slip two business cards into your package — one for your buyer and one for her millionaire best friend.

- ✔ **An invoice:** Unless the package is a gift and it's being sent directly to the recipient, include a printout of the invoice in your package. This is especially important if your buyer lives abroad; it'll keep the package from being held up clearing Customs. To print an invoice, open it as described in Chapter 14 (make sure you've marked the item as paid if the person paid by check or money order); then click the Print Order link (see Figure 15-1) and choose your print settings as normal.

- ✔ **Care instructions:** If the item you're sending requires special care — for example, maybe it needs to be washed by hand — include appropriate instructions in your package.

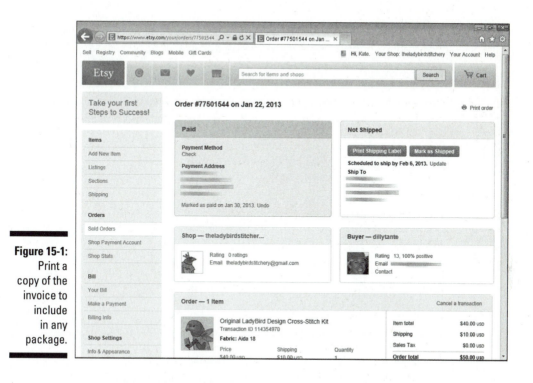

Figure 15-1:
Print a
copy of the
invoice to
include
in any
package.

✔ **A coupon:** Including a coupon — or, more specifically, a coupon code — in your packaging is a great way to generate sales. For help with creating coupon codes, see Chapter 16.

✔ **A freebie:** Some Etsy sellers include freebies in their packaging — small, lightweight items tossed in at no additional cost. The best freebies reflect your brand or your inventory in some way — for example, buttons, bookmarks, stickers, or magnets with your shop logo, or samples of new or favorite products in your line. Another approach is to include freebies that complement the item purchased. For instance, if you specialize in hand-sewn dog collars, you might toss in some Scooby Snacks. Or if you spin yarn, you may include a printout of a simple pattern you designed.

Although some Etsy sellers like to include candy or other treats in their packages, it's not always a great idea. For one thing, some buyers may be diabetic or may suffer from nut allergies, and receiving sweets via post may constitute torture (or death!) for them. For another thing, many buyers live in hot climates, meaning that any candy you send may melt, thereby ruining your piece.

Ship Shop: Choosing a Shipping Carrier

When it comes to shipping carriers, you have loads of options — truth be told, an overwhelming number. To figure out which carrier is right for you, you need to do a bit of legwork. Here are a few places to start:

- ✔ **USPS:** www.usps.com
- ✔ **UPS:** www.ups.com
- ✔ **FedEx:** www.fedex.com
- ✔ **DHL:** www.dhl.com

We're talking domestic shipping in the United States here. For information about shipping internationally, see the later section "Crafters without Borders: Shipping Internationally."

As you research carriers, assess the following:

- ✔ How long they take to deliver
- ✔ What shipping options they offer
- ✔ How much the various shipping options cost
- ✔ Whether such services as insurance and delivery confirmation are included (see the later section "Insure Thing: Insuring Your Parcel" for details)
- ✔ Whether they pick up outgoing packages from your place
- ✔ What they do if a package gets lost

Most Etsy users (at least, ones in the United States) opt for the USPS. That said, FedEx does offer Etsy sellers a lovely price break — up to 26 percent on select FedEx services.

Stay First Classy: Surveying Shipping Options

After you've selected a carrier, you need to give more thought to various shipping options based on speed and price. For example, if you've opted for USPS, you need to decide whether you want to go with First Class or Priority Mail. In general, First Class, which is the less expensive option, is handled in the same way as Priority Mail, but it's put on the truck last — meaning that if the truck is full, the First Class mail has to wait for the next truck, which may affect delivery time. Unless it's a particularly busy time of year (Christmas, we're talking about you) or your packages typically weigh more than 13 ounces each (the First Class cutoff), First Class may suffice for your needs.

You also need to decide whether you're willing to offer expedited shipping — for example, USPS Express Mail for overnight delivery (for an added charge, of course).

If you decide to offer expedited shipping, be sure to indicate in your shop policies (see Chapter 9) and item listing descriptions (see Chapter 12) how buyers can take advantage of that option.

If you've opted to use the USPS, you can use the USPS Postage Price Calculator to determine which shipping option is right for you. Here's how:

1. **Go to** `http://ircalc.usps.com`.

   The Postage Price Calculator page opens.

2. **Click the Select a Destination drop-down list, and choose the country to which you want to ship the item.**

3. **If you've selected the United States, type your zip code in the From Zip Code field; then type the recipient's zip code in the To Zip Code field.**

4. **If you've selected the United States, enter the mailing date and time.**

5. **Note the flat-rate price that applies to your package.**

   To see whether a different option is cheaper, select the shape that best matches that of your package.

6. **If you opt against the flat-rate price by selecting a shape, enter the package's weight in the Pounds and Ounces fields.**

7. **Click Continue.**

   A list of delivery options appears.

8. **To view all delivery options together, click the Display All Options check box.**

Depending on what option you choose, you may be able to purchase and print the postage online, right from the Postage Price Calculator. To find out, click the desired postage option; if a Print Postage button appears in the Product Selected area, it means that you can purchase and print your postage online. (Simply click the Print Postage button to do so.) If not, fret not. You can also print postage right from Etsy, provided your shop supports Direct Checkout.

Flat and rate plus weight: Figuring out which way to go

The USPS offers flat-rate pricing for Priority Mail in addition to weight-based rates. Which option you choose depends on how heavy your item is. If your piece fits in the small flat-rate box or envelope and it weighs more than 1 pound, the flat-rate route is for you. Simply put, the more you can cram into the flat-rate box, the better the deal. If your piece weighs more than 1 pound or requires a medium or large box, run the numbers before you commit to the flat rate. If the item is light or is shipping to a zone near you, the weight-based rate may be better.

Crafters without Borders: Shipping Internationally

Although you can certainly limit your Etsy business to domestic buyers, part of the fun of selling on Etsy is connecting with international customers. First, however, you need to get a feel for the ins and outs of shipping internationally. Keep a few points in mind:

- ✔ **Items shipped to some countries, such as Canada and countries in the European Union, may be subject to duties or taxes.** Make sure that the buyer knows he'll be responsible for these. A good way to do so is to include language to that effect on your shop's Policies page.

- ✔ **If your package contains "potentially dutiable contents" (that's post office speak for items subject to duties or taxes), you need to include a Customs form — period, end of story.** (If you're not sure whether your item is "potentially dutiable," read the next bullet.) To figure out what type of form you need, check with your carrier or go to http://webapps.usps.com/customsforms/helppickaform.htm. Be sure to fill out the form thoroughly, to keep it from being held up at Customs.

- ✔ **Shipping certain items — think food products, plant and animal products, precious jewelry, and so on — is prohibited in some countries.** To find out whether your item is prohibited, check out the Individual Country Listings page on the USPS website (http://pe.usps.com/text/imm/ab_toc.htm). You'll see a list of countries; click the link for the country in question to view a list of restricted and prohibited items. (Note that these prohibitions and restrictions apply regardless of the carrier you use.)

Don't indicate that the item is a gift, even if your buyer asks you to. It's not cricket, and it can get you into trouble. Besides, even gifts may be subject to duties and taxes.

Be sure to warn international customers that you can't be responsible for delays if your package gets stuck in Customs.

If you're just getting started, consider shipping to just a few countries — say, Canada, Mexico, Japan, Australia, and European Union (EU) countries. Then, when you're more comfortable with the procedures involved, you can expand to ship everywhere. Just don't indicate that you're willing to ship anywhere on Earth unless you've done the research to find out how much that will cost!

If you've chosen to ship via USPS, a great place to start is the aforementioned Individual Country Listings page on the USPS website (`http://pe.usps.com/text/imm/ab_toc.htm`). You can also check out the First-Class Mail International Prices page (`www.usps.com/ship/first-class-international.htm`) and the Priority Mail International Prices page (`www.usps.com/ship/priority-mail-international.htm`).

If you find yourself shipping internationally regularly, look into using Endicia (`www.endicia.com`). In addition to enabling you to print labels for domestic packages, Endicia allows you to print international shipping labels that integrate the necessary Customs forms — and with a discount to boot! Plus, Endicia's International Mail Advisor feature helps you navigate the complexity of shipping internationally by spelling out which items are prohibited where, and more.

Ship Happens: Creating a Shipping Profile

Suppose you stock your shop with items of a similar size — say, jewelry, magnets, greeting cards, or stuffed patchwork wiener dogs. In that case, it may behoove you to create a shipping profile. A *shipping profile* is simply a collection of shipping-related settings that you can apply to item listings in one fell swoop instead of entering them one by one.

Before you create a shipping profile, you want to sort out how much it costs to ship your item based on its size, weight, and shipping method. If you plan to ship internationally, you need to get a handle on how much that method will cost as well. For help, contact your shipping provider. Note that you want to factor in any costs associated with packaging your item when calculating your shipping charges.

To create a shipping profile, log in to your Etsy account and follow these steps:

1. **Click the Your Shop link along the top of any Etsy page.**

2. **Click the Shipping & Payment link, under Shop Settings, on the left side of the page.**

The Shipping & Payment page opens, with the Shipping Profiles tab displayed (see Figure 15-2).

3. **Click the Create New Profile button.**

   The Create Shipping Profile page opens (see Figure 15-3).

4. **In the Profile Name field, type a descriptive name for your profile.**

   For example, if the profile is for items in your jewelry line, type **Jewelry**.

5. **Click the Processing Time drop-down list, and specify how long it will take you to process each order.**

6. **Click the Items Ship From drop-down list, and choose your country of residence.**

7. **If you want to set shipping rates on a country-by-country basis, click the Country Specific Shipping drop-down list and choose a country; then click the Add button.**

   The Country Specific Shipping area expands to include a Cost field and a With Another Item field.

8. **Enter the shipping cost for buyers in the selected country in the Cost field and then type the cost for shipping for purchases sent with another item in the With Another Item field.**

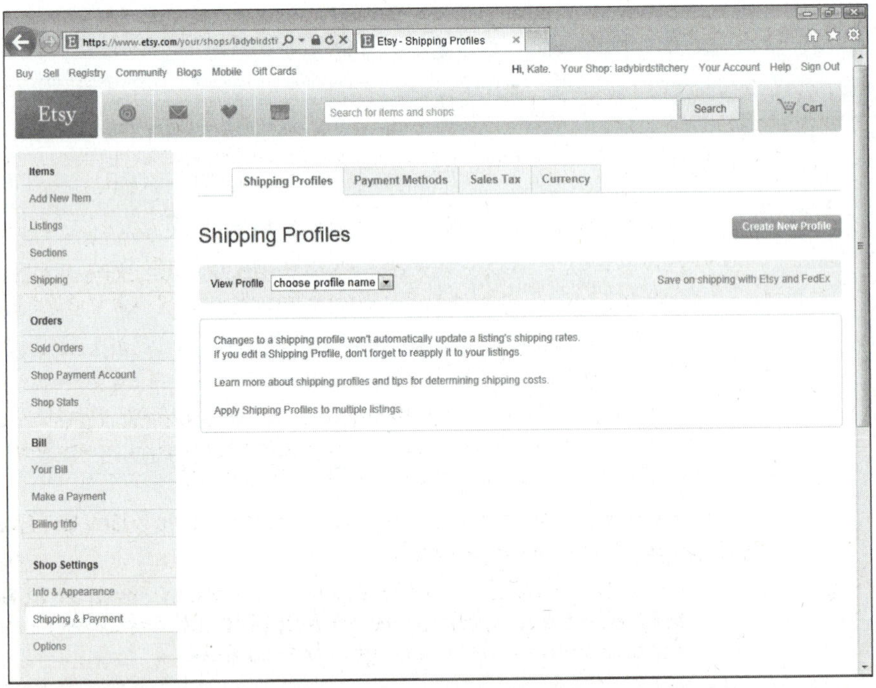

Figure 15-2:
Create a
shipping
profile here.

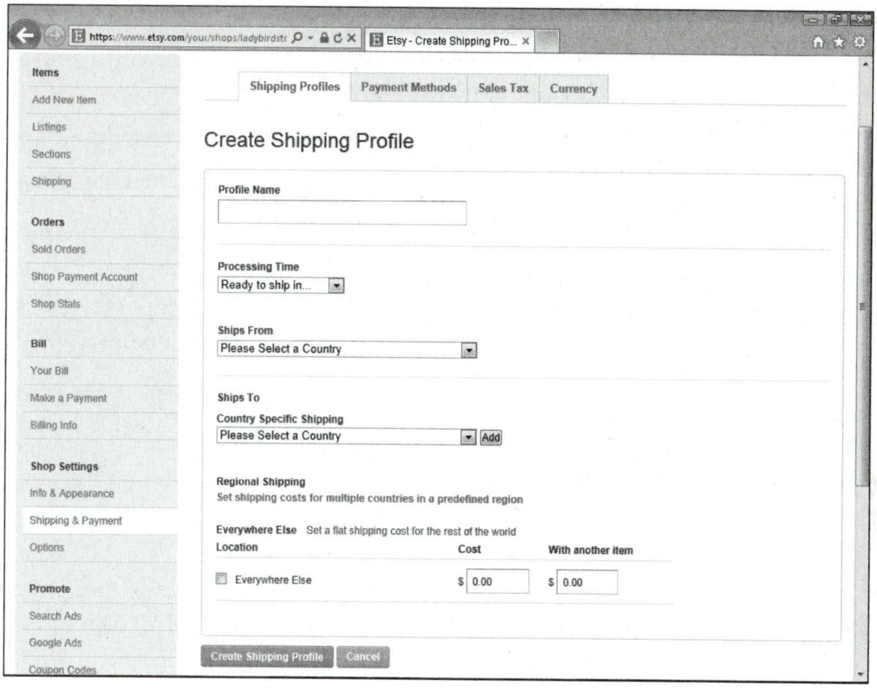

Figure 15-3:
Enter the profile details on this page.

9. **Repeat steps 7 and 8 to add more countries to your shipping profile.**

   Don't forget to add your own country of residence in the Country Specific Shipping area!

10. **To quickly set options for an entire region, such as the EU, click the Set Shipping Costs for Multiple Countries in a Predefined Region link.**

    The Regional Shipping area expands to include a drop-down list.

11. **Click the Regional Shipping drop-down list and choose the region for which you want to set shipping options; then click the Add button.**

    The Regional Shipping area expands further to include a Cost field and a With Another Item field.

12. **Enter the shipping cost for buyers in the selected region in the Cost field, and then type the cost for shipping for purchases sent with another item in the With Another Item field.**

13. **If you're willing to ship anywhere in the world, click the Everywhere Else check box to select it.**

14. **Enter the shipping cost for buyers in all other countries in the Cost field, and then type the cost for shipping for purchases sent with another item in the With Another Item field.**

15. **Click the Create Shipping Profile button.**

    Etsy saves your shipping profile.

If you need to, you can edit your shipping profile. To do so, follow steps 1 and 2 to access the Shipping Profiles tab, click the View Profile drop-down list and choose the desired profile, adjust your settings as needed, and click the Save Changes button.

Insure Thing: Insuring Your Parcel

Remember that movie *Castaway,* with Tom Hanks? He plays a FedEx employee who hitches a ride on a cargo plane stuffed with packages, which crashes, marooning him on a desert island with only a volleyball for company. This storyline just goes to show you that sometimes FedEx planes crash, jettisoning their cargo to the bottom of the sea. If the piece you so lovingly crafted and packaged is onboard, chances are, it won't reach your buyer — unless she's the Little Mermaid.

To ensure that you're covered if your package goes astray, you may want to opt for insurance from your shipping carrier — especially if your item is on the pricey side. (Insuring packages containing less expensive pieces may be prohibitively expensive; you have to decide whether it's worth it to you.) You can also opt for delivery confirmation — it's free with USPS Priority shipping.

Your carrier may not offer insurance for certain items, especially if you're shipping internationally. In that case, you may opt to go with a third-party provider, such as Shipsurance (www.shipsurance.com) or U-PIC (www.u-pic.com).

Print It to Win It: Printing Shipping Labels on Etsy

If you use USPS as your shipping carrier, and you've signed up for Direct Checkout or your shop has been open and active for a certain number of months, you can print your shipping labels right from Etsy. When you print your label from Etsy, delivery confirmation is included automatically; insurance is also available if you want it. You'll be billed for labels on your Etsy bill. (For info on paying your Etsy bill, see Chapter 18.)

To print a shipping label on Etsy, follow these steps:

1. **Click the Your Shop link along the top of any Etsy page.**

   The Your Shop page opens.

2. **Click the Sold Orders link, under Orders, on the left side of the page.**

3. **Click the Open tab.**

   The Open Orders page opens, displaying a list of items that you've sold but not yet shipped.

4. **If necessary, click the Not Shipped tab (see Figure 15-4).**

5. **Click the Print Shipping Label button.**

   A page outlining how this feature works appears.

6. **Click the Continue button.**

   The Confirm Default Ship From Address page appears.

7. **Confirm that the Ship From address is correct (or make changes as needed); then click the Continue button.**

   The Buy Postage page appears (see Figure 15-5).

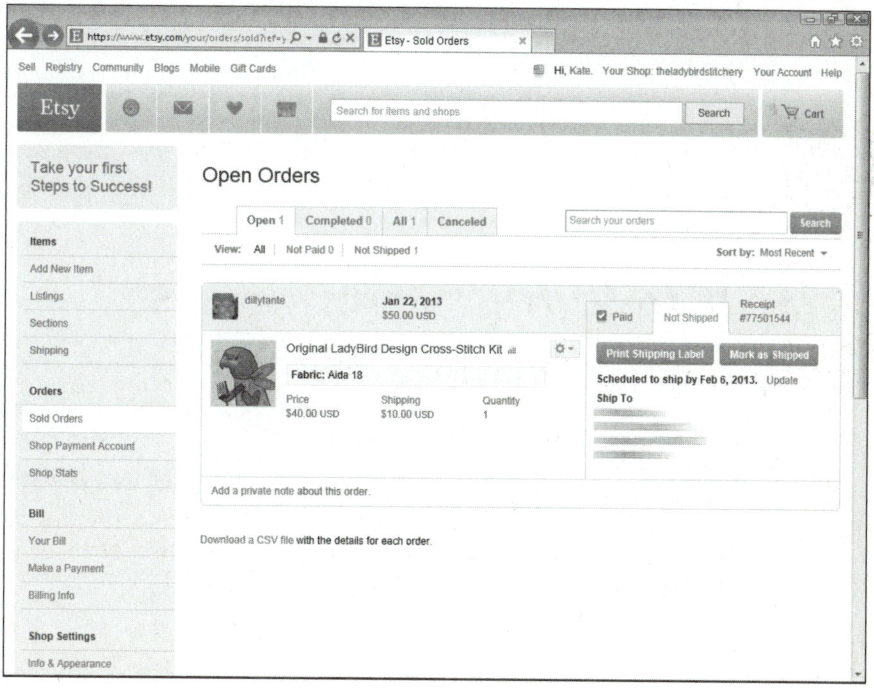

Figure 15-4: Find the item for which you want to print a label on this page.

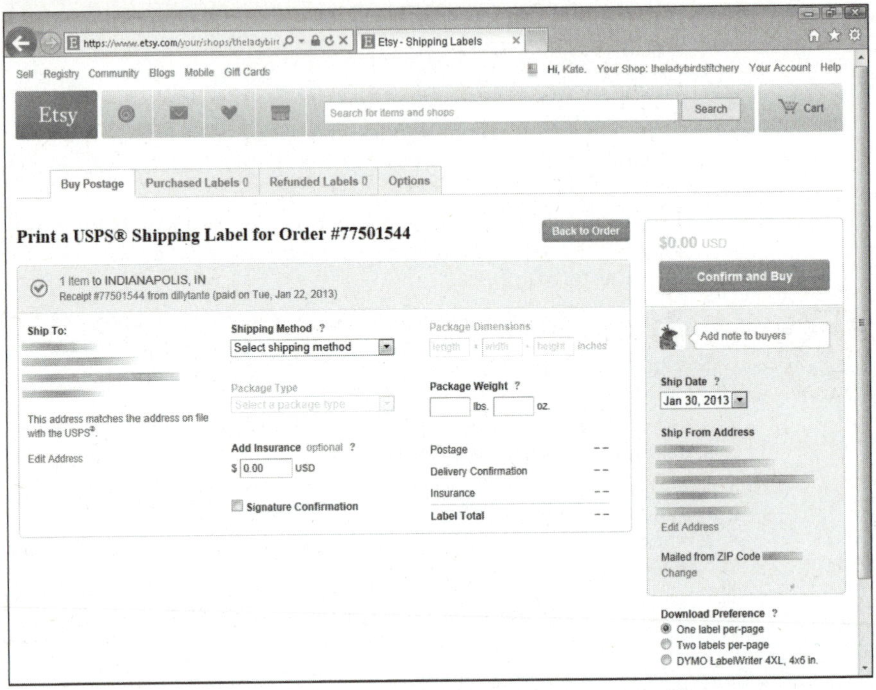

Figure 15-5:
Buy your
postage
here.

8. **Click the Shipping Method drop-down list and choose the desired method — for example, USPS First Class Mail or USPS Priority Mail.**

9. **If prompted, enter the package dimensions.**

10. **If prompted, click the Package Type drop-down list and specify the package type — say, Package/Thick Envelope, Irregular/Unusual Package, or what have you.**

11. **Enter the package weight in the appropriate field.**

12. **Optionally, type a dollar amount indicating the value of the item in the Add Insurance field to insure the package.**

13. **If you want someone to sign for the package, click the Signature Confirmation check box to select it.**

14. **If necessary, click the Ship Date drop-down list and specify the day on which you plan to ship the item.**

15. **Click the Confirm and Buy button.**

Etsy displays a confirmation dialog box, indicating the number of labels purchased and the price.

16. **Click the Buy and Send Notification button.**

    Etsy creates the label and notifies you that it's ready for download.

17. **Click the Download Shipping Labels button.**

    Etsy displays the label as a PDF (see Figure 15-6). Print it as you would any other similar file.

Although you can use regular paper, it's better to use paper with adhesive backing; that way, you don't have to use tape to attach the label to your package.

After Etsy creates your shipping label, it updates the invoice and receipt to show that it has been shipped (see Figure 15-7), essentially closing the order. The item also appears on the Completed Orders tab, which you access by clicking the Completed tab on the Sold Orders page.

Figure 15-6:
Print your
shipping
label.

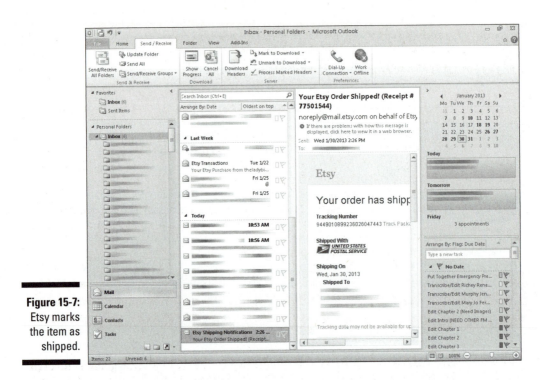

Figure 15-7:
Etsy marks
the item as
shipped.

Be aware: Etsy allots each shop a "shipping label budget." When you reach the limit set by your shop's budget, you'll need to pay your Etsy bill before you're allowed to purchase and print more shipping labels. Each time you pay your Etsy bill, your shop budget will increase.

Etsy also offers a "batch shipping label" feature of sorts. That is, you can purchase and print shipping labels for several orders at once. To do so, follow these steps:

1. **Click the Shipping Labels link in the Orders section of Your Shop.**

2. **On the Buy Postage tab, select the items for which you want to purchase shipping labels and fill in the necessary info for each one.**

3. **Review the order.**

4. **Purchase the labels by clicking the Confirm and Buy button.**

5. **Click the Buy and Send Notification button.**

   Etsy will process your labels and send shipping notifications to your buyers.

6. **Click the Download Shipping Labels button, and print them as normal.**

Deliverance: Sending Your Package on Its Merry Way

After you securely affix your shipping label to your package (if you opted against an adhesive backing, use clear packaging tape, taking care to avoid obscuring the label bar code), you're ready to send it. One option is to request a free carrier pickup from the USPS website (www.usps.com/pickup); alternatively, you can hand it off to your regular carrier, take it to your local post office, or drop it in a collection box.

While we're on the subject of your regular mail carrier: Make it a point to buddy up to yours. That way, if you have any shipping-related questions, your carrier will be happy to answer them!

Marky Mark: Marking the Item As Shipped in Etsy

If for whatever reason you opted out of printing your shipping labels through Etsy — maybe you don't accept Direct Checkout (meaning Etsy's print shipping labels feature isn't currently available to you) or you prefer a different shipping provider over USPS — you'll need to manually mark your item as shipped once you've sent it on its merry way. This essentially closes the order. Follow these steps:

1. **Click the Your Shop link along the top of any Etsy page.**

   The Your Shop page opens.

2. **Click the Sold Orders link, under Orders, on the left side of the page.**

3. **Click the Open tab.**

   The Open Orders page appears.

4. **Click the Mark as Shipped button in the listing for the item you just shipped.**

   Etsy updates the listing to show that it has been shipped (refer to Figure 15-7). The item also appears on the Completed Orders page, which you access by clicking the Completed tab.

An Add Shipping Notification option appears — click it to open a window that enables you to send a message to your buyer, letting him know the package is on its way and informing him of the delivery confirmation number. (This note is optional, but it's a nice way to reconnect with your buyer.) You can even save the text from your note and reuse it for later transactions.

Part IV

All Up in Your Bidness: Handling Business Matters

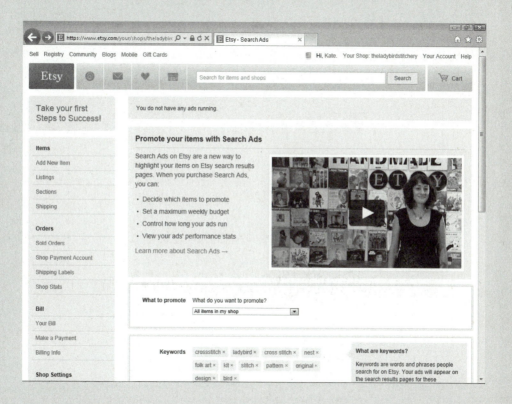

Find out how to collect sales tax, in a free article at www.dummies.com/extras/startinganetsybusiness.

In this part . . .

- ✔ Brand your business like you've always been a brand.
- ✔ Market your business to reach your target customers.
- ✔ Provide unrivaled customer service to keep them coming back for more.
- ✔ Handle financial matters so you can sleep soundly and stress-free.

Chapter 16

High Exposure: Marketing Your Etsy Business

In This Chapter

▶ Defining your brand

▶ Promoting your shop

▶ Publicizing sales

▶ Getting on the Etsy Registry

▶ Building an e-mail list

▶ Engaging in charitable giving on Etsy

Although marketing as a discipline is relatively new, in practice, marketing is as old as Joan Rivers. Indeed, the first marketer was most likely the first Cro-Magnon to convince a fellow knuckle dragger to barter for *his* mastodon-fur cape instead of the one offered one cave over. ("But this mastodon-fur cape 100 percent stench free. Og's not.") Naturally, if you want to evolve your Etsy shop into a thriving enterprise, you need to do the same. This chapter is devoted to the ins and outs of marketing your Etsy business so that it doesn't go the way of the Neanderthal.

Let's be honest: This chapter constitutes a very basic primer on the subject of marketing. If you're serious about your Etsy business, you'll want to study this subject in greater depth. *Small Business Marketing Kit For Dummies,* by Barbara Findlay Schenck (Wiley), is a great jumping-off point!

Brandy, You're a Fine Girl: Building Your Brand

An important part of any business — whether it's a multinational widget-making corporation with more employees than Lichtenstein has citizens, a small mom-and-pop pizzeria that serves the surrounding neighborhood, or your Etsy shop — is its brand.

So, what exactly is a brand? Although many people believe that the word *brand* is synonymous with the word *logo,* it's not. Yes, your logo is part of your brand (more on that in a moment), but the brand itself is a much broader concept. You can think of your *brand* as the image you want to project for your business. Your brand is what you're known for.

Before you begin building your brand, you need to pin down a few key pieces of information:

- ✔ **The brand promise:** Was it Kierkegaard or Dick Van Patten who said, "People don't buy drill bits — they buy holes"? Pinpointing your brand promise means determining what you're *really* selling. What does your brand promise to do? You're not selling handmade aromatherapy candles; you're selling unparalleled relaxation. *That's* your brand promise.

- ✔ **The target market:** You want to have some idea of who's likely to be interested in your product so that you can tailor your brand accordingly. Who is your customer? Is your audience male or female? Young or old? Singleton or smug married? Where does your target market live? How much disposable income does your customer have? What level of education has your target market obtained?

- ✔ **The competition:** In addition to recognizing your target market, you need to identify your competition. Who are they? What do they offer? How are their brands or products similar to yours? How are they different? Do your target markets overlap? This assessment can help you position your own brand in such a way that you gain an advantage.

- ✔ **The brand personality:** Think of your brand as being like a person (preferably not your mother-in-law). Is it quirky? Refined? Silly? Wise? This personality creates an emotional connection with your target market. You convey your brand's personality through visual elements, such as your logo, and through its voice — that is, your tagline (discussed momentarily), your item descriptions (see Chapter 12), your shop announcement (see Chapter 8), your profile page, your about page, and even your Etsy convos (see Chapter 17).

- ✔ **The unique selling proposition (USP):** Every good brand has at least one characteristic that makes it different from everything else on the market. Using the aromatherapy candle example, maybe your candles burn longer than other candles on the market, or smell different, or come in super-pretty jars. Whatever special quality your candles have, that's their USP.

With that information in hand, you're ready to start building your brand. In the following sections, we explain how to create taglines and logos, and we discuss the importance of infusing your brand into everything related to your Etsy shop.

Tag lady: Composing a tagline

Do you recognize the phrase "You deserve a break today"? What about "Just do it," "Don't leave home without it," "The quicker picker-upper," or "Time to make the doughnuts"? If so, then you know the power of a tagline. A *tagline* is a memorable phrase that expresses who your brand is and what it does. It serves as a marketing slogan and reflects the brand it seeks to promote.

Part of building your brand is composing a tagline of your own. As you do, consider that a good tagline

- ✔ **Is short, concise, specific, and, ideally, clever:** The longer the tagline, the more likely people are to lose interest in it.

- ✔ **Speaks to your target market:** If your target market is 20-something hipsters, your tagline shouldn't use language that your grandmother favors.

- ✔ **Reflects your brand's personality:** If your brand is quirky, you don't want a stuffy tagline!

- ✔ **Hints at your brand promise and its USP:** Take the tagline for M&M's, for example: "Melts in your mouth, not in your hands" suggests that M&M's are not only super-tasty, but also not messy.

A great place for your tagline is your shop title or your shop's banner. For help with changing your shop title and banner, refer to Chapter 8.

Loco for logos: Creating a logo

Many people confuse a brand's logo with the brand itself, and it's easy to see why. After all, the logo — along with the tagline — represents the brand. It's critical, then, that the logo (as well as other visual elements, such as the colors and fonts you use in marketing materials like business cards and whatnot) reflect the brand's personality and speak to your audience.

Keep some points in mind as you develop your logo:

- ✔ **Consider your colors.** Different colors evoke different emotions and convey different ideas. For example, if you specialize in custom motorcycle gear, a baby-pink logo may not be the way to go.

- ✔ **Make sure you're sending the right message.** Your logo's visual style communicates something about your brand. For example, if your logo has a minimalist style, it suggests that your brand does, too. Be sure that your logo sends the message you want.

- ✔ **Be original.** Although it's certainly fine to look to other brands and logos for inspiration, don't copy — especially if the logo in question is a competitor's.

If you're not comfortable developing your logo, don't hesitate to get help. If you're on a strict budget, why not ask a friend with an artistic bent for assistance? Alternatively, try bartering with a professional designer.

Consider using your logo as your Etsy avatar. That way, any time you comment in a forum or send a convo, other Etsians see your logo. For help with changing your avatar, refer to Chapter 8.

Integrate expectations: Working your brand into all you do

The key to branding is infusing it in everything you do. Express your brand by using your tagline and logo in your business cards, letterhead, envelopes, postcards, packaging, and other promotional materials. Your brand also needs to permeate your Etsy shop — for example, by appearing in your shop banner and avatar. You can even communicate your brand by using your tagline and logo on a Facebook page and Twitter feed for your Etsy shop. In this way, you increase the chances of your customers noticing *your* brand among the flotsam and jetsam of Etsy.

Poetry in Promotion: Using Etsy Tools to Promote Your Shop

Etsy recognizes the importance of marketing your shop and offers several built-in promotional tools. Specifically, Etsy enables you to generate search ads on Etsy, create coupon codes for your shop, embed an Etsy badge and create a special widget for your blog or other website to advertise your Etsy shop, and promote your shop on social media.

Search party: Using Etsy Search Ads

Fun fact: The word *advertise* derives from the Latin *ad vertere,* meaning "to turn the mind toward." And as anyone who's ever suddenly become ravenously hungry after watching a commercial for pizza can tell you, it works.

Fortunately for you, Etsy makes it easy to advertise your shop. How? By using Etsy Search Ads. An Etsy Search Ad is simply a paid advertising spot that appears at the top of the search results page when prospective buyers enter specific keywords.

To create an Etsy Search Ad, follow these steps:

1. **Click the Your Shop link along the top of any Etsy page.**

   The Your Shop page opens.

2. **Click the Search Ads link under Promote on the left side of the page.**

   The Search Ads page opens, as shown in Figure 16-1.

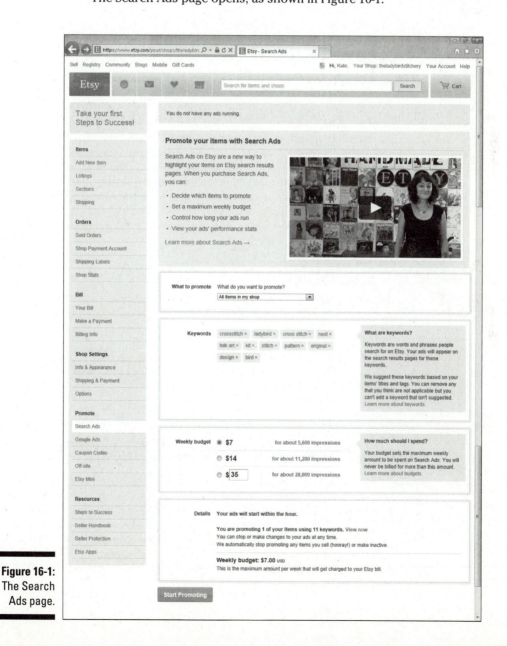

Figure 16-1: The Search Ads page.

3. **Click the What to Promote drop-down list and choose All Items in My Shop, All Items from a Section in My Shop, or Specific Items from My Shop.**

   If you choose All Items from a Section in My Shop or Specific Items from My Shop, you'll be prompted to specify the section or items in question.

   Etsy generates a list of keywords, based on the titles and tags used for the items you want to promote. As you've likely gathered, *keywords* are terms that people enter when searching for items on Etsy.

4. **If any of the keywords does not apply, click its X button to remove it from the list.**

   Note that although you can modify the list by removing keywords, you cannot add keywords to the list.

5. **Indicate how much you want to spend per week on ads.**

   The more you spend, the more impressions you'll receive. (One impression equals one display of your ad.) For example, if you elect to spend $5 per week (the current minimum option), you'll likely garner about 5,600 impressions (although the exact number will vary by keyword). Note that you will only be charged for actual impressions. So, for example, if you receive fewer impressions than expected, you'll be charged less. You will not, however, be charged more if you receive more impressions than expected in one week.

6. **Click the Start Promoting button.**

   Etsy displays the Shop Stats page, where you can see how your ads are faring. (For more information about the Shop Stats page, see Chapter 18.) Don't expect immediate results; it may take as long as an hour for the Search Ad to go into effect.

Once you launch your Search Ad, it will remain in effect until you discontinue it. To do so, click the Stop Your Ads link that appears in the Search Ads page when a Search Ad is running.

Google eyes: A word on Google ads

For the time being, Etsy is doing you a major solid: purchasing Google product listing ads within Google Shopping free of charge for English-language listings that ship to the United States. That means if someone uses Google Shopping to search for a product using keywords that match up with ones used in one of your Etsy listings, that listing may appear as a Google ad along with that person's search results. Enjoy it while it lasts!

Coupon d'état: Creating coupons

Coupons have come a long way since their invention in 1887, when Asa Candler, an early investor in the Coca-Cola Company, devised a plan to distribute millions of coupons for free servings of the now-famous tonic. In fact, these days, coupons are *everywhere,* including on Etsy.

Yes, that's right: You can channel your own inner Asa Candler and offer your Etsy customers discounts on merchandise or free shipping through coupons — or, more specifically, coupon codes. Buyers can then apply these codes to purchases during the checkout process. For example, you may offer a coupon to celebrate your store's anniversary or an upcoming holiday, to reward repeat customers, or to share with your Facebook fans or Twitter followers.

To spread the word about your coupon code, you can simply include the code in the packaging with any items you sell — say, by tucking a business card in with your piece. Alternatively, if you maintain a newsletter, you may want to include a coupon code there to drive sales in your Etsy shop. (You find out more about newsletters later in this chapter.)

To create a coupon code, log in to your Etsy account and follow these steps:

1. **Hover your mouse pointer over the Your Shop link along the top of any Etsy page.**

   A list of options appears.

2. **Click the Coupon Codes option.**

   If you've never created a coupon before, you'll see the Reward Customers with Coupons page, shown in Figure 16-2. Otherwise, you'll see the Coupon Codes page.

3. **Click the Create New Coupon button.**

   The Create New Coupon dialog box opens (see Figure 16-3).

4. **In the Coupon Code field, type the code you want to use for the coupon.**

   Note that this code must contain between 5 and 20 alphanumeric characters (no punctuation), with no spaces.

5. **If you want buyers to receive a coupon automatically upon purchasing an item from your shop, click the Thank You Coupon check box to select it.**

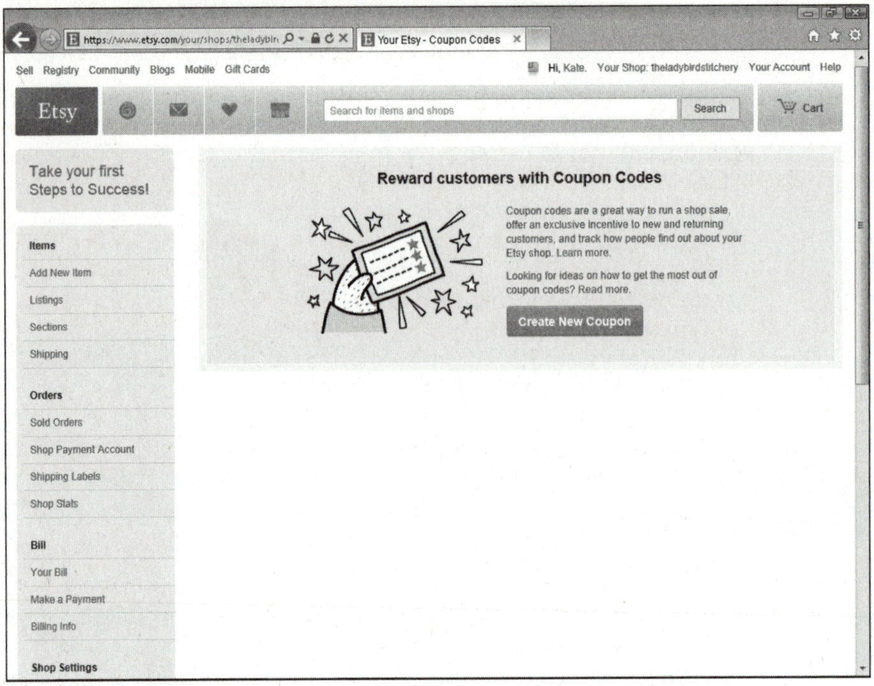

Figure 16-2:
Create a
coupon
code.

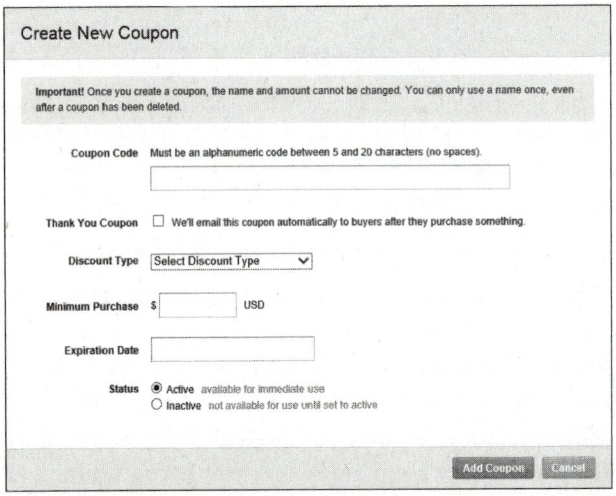

Figure 16-3:
Enter the
coupon
details.

6. **Click the Discount Type drop-down arrow and choose the type of discount you want to offer — Percent Discount or Free Shipping.**

If you choose Percent Discount, type the discount amount in the % Off field. If you choose Free Shipping, optionally check the Only for Domestic Shipping Addresses check box.

When a customer redeems a coupon, Etsy's 3.5 percent transaction fee applies to the discounted price. (Flip to Chapter 1 for more about Etsy fees.)

7. **Optionally, enter a minimum purchase amount.**

   Buyers must spend this amount to be able to apply the coupon.

8. **Optionally, enter an expiration date.**

9. **Click the Active option button to activate the coupon code.**

10. **Click the Add Coupon button.**

    Etsy creates the coupon code and lists it on the Coupon Codes page (see Figure 16-4).

If you want to deactivate a coupon code you can easily do so. Simply click the code's Active link in the screen shown in Figure 16-4. Then, in the dialog box that appears, click the Inactive option button and click Save Changes. Etsy deactivates the code for you. If you want, you can reactivate the code later by clicking the code's Inactive link and clicking Active in the dialog box that appears. You can also simply delete a coupon code by clicking the X button to the right of the code in the Coupon Codes page.

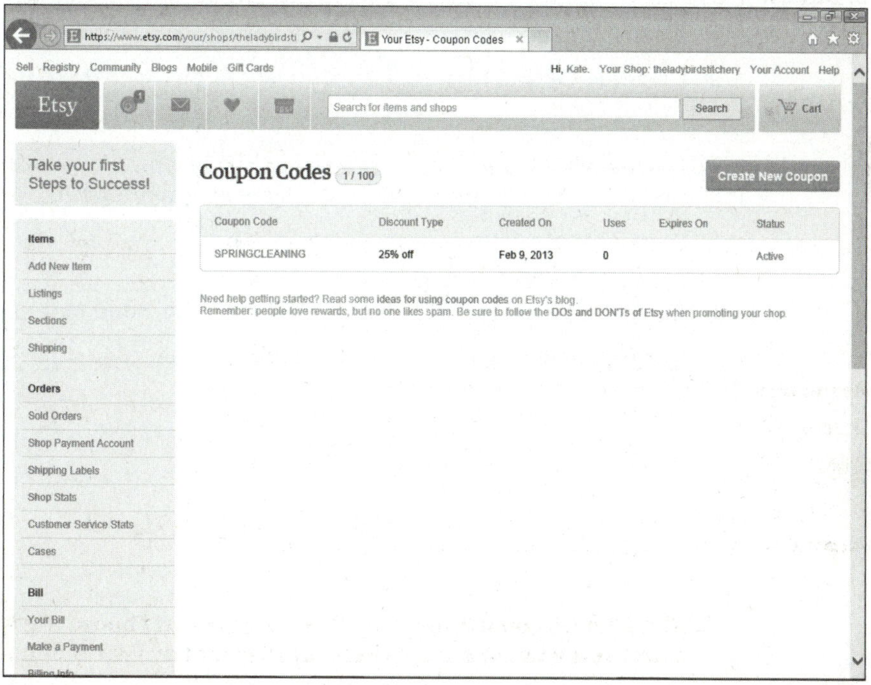

Figure 16-4:
Etsy creates the coupon code.

Badge to the bone: Creating an Etsy shop badge and hosting an Etsy Mini

Do you maintain a blog or some other type of personal website? If so, you can use it to link back to your Etsy shop by displaying an Etsy shop badge, an Etsy Mini, or both.

An *Etsy shop badge* is simply an image, or badge, that you display on your blog or personal website. These badges come in various sizes, including 200 x 200, 500 x 500, 728 x 90, and 160 x 600. When someone clicks the badge, that person is directed to your Etsy shop. In contrast, an *Etsy Mini* is a wee widget that displays items in your Etsy store. People who visit your site can click an item in the Etsy Mini to view it on Etsy. After you install an Etsy Mini on your site, it updates automatically when you list new items.

To add an Etsy shop badge to a blog or website, follow these steps:

1. **Sign into your Etsy shop and your personal website/blog in separate windows or tabs in your browser.**

2. **In the Etsy window, click the Your Shop link along the top of any Etsy page.**

   The Your Shop page opens.

3. **Click the Off-site link, under Promote, on the left side of the page.**

   The Etsy Badges page opens (see Figure 16-5).

4. **Decide which badge you want to add to your blog or website; then, underneath that badge, click the Generate Code link.**

   A dialog box opens, containing the HTML code for the badge you selected, as shown in Figure 16-6.

5. **Select and copy the HTML code, and click the Done button.**

6. **Switch to the browser window containing your blog or website and paste in the code that you copied.**

   Your blog or website updates to include the Etsy Mini (see Figure 16-7).

Figure 16-5:
Choose among a few different sizes of Etsy shop badges.

Figure 16-6:
Select and copy the code you want to use.

Yes, you're right. We skipped a few steps — namely, the ones that cover figuring out how to access your blog or website's code and where in that code to paste the code you just copied. Why? Because those steps vary depending on what kind of site you maintain (a blog or some other type of website). For help, troll the Help files that your site host provided.

Adding an Etsy Mini to your site is just as easy. Follow these steps:

1. **Sign into your Etsy shop and your personal website/blog in separate windows or tabs in your browser.**

2. **In the Etsy window, click the Your Shop link along the top of any Etsy page.**

    The Your Shop page opens.

3. **Click the Etsy Mini link, under Promote, on the left side of the page.**

    The Build Your Own Etsy Mini page opens (see Figure 16-7).

4. **Click the Items from My Shop option button under Items to Show.**

5. **Click the option button for the desired image size — Thumbnail or Gallery — under Choose Image Size.**

Figure 16-7:
Set up your
Etsy Mini.

6. **Under Choose Layout, click the Columns drop-down arrow and select the number of columns you want to display.**

7. **Under Choose Layout, click the Rows drop-down arrow and choose the number of rows you want to display.**

   Etsy displays a preview of the Etsy Mini.

8. **Select the code in the Copy This Code for the JavaScript Version field and copy it.**

9. **Paste the code that you copied into your own website's code.**

   Your web page updates to include the Etsy Mini (see Figure 16-8).

Again, we skipped the steps that cover figuring out how to access your web page's code and where in that code to paste the code you just copied. Those steps differ depending on what kind of site you maintain. For guidance, troll the Help files that your site host provided.

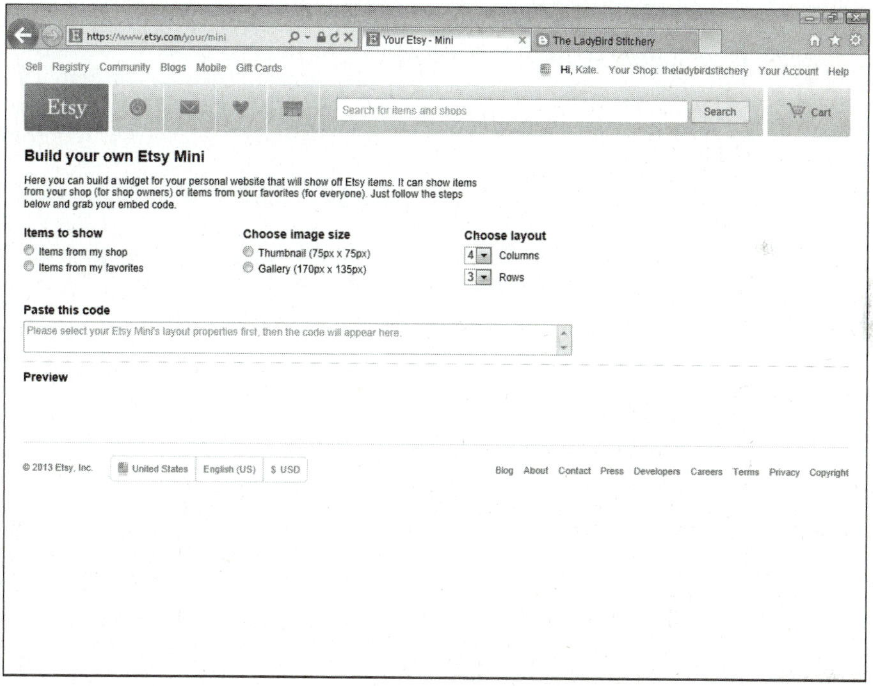

Figure 16-8:
Paste the Etsy Mini code into the HTML in your own web page.

Save Facebook: Promoting your Etsy shop on social media

Everybody knows that social media — most notably, sites like Facebook and Twitter — are great marketing tools. Although large corporations are known to use these platforms, they're particularly great for small businesses, providing significant reach at an excellent price: free.

To help facilitate this, Etsy enables you to link your shop to your Facebook page and Twitter feed. When you do, a Facebook Like button and a Twitter Follow button appear on your shop page, below the banner. People who like your shop can click these buttons to become a fan (Facebook) or a follower (Twitter). In addition, when you list new items, you'll have the opportunity to post info about them on Facebook and/or Twitter during the listing-creation process.

Note that for this to work, you must create a Facebook page for your Etsy shop. Note that we said *page,* not *profile.* Connecting your shop with Facebook works only on Facebook pages designed for businesses, not on the personal profile you probably maintain to keep up with friends. For help with creating a Facebook page, see Facebook's Help info. (It's not a bad idea to create a separate Twitter feed for your shop as well, although this is not required.)

To link your shop to a Facebook page or Twitter feed, follow these steps:

1. **Click the Your Shop link along the top of any Etsy page. (Make sure you're signed out of Facebook.)**

   The Your Shop page opens.

2. **Click the Info & Appearance option under Shop Settings on the left side of the page.**

   The Info & Appearance page opens (see Figure 16-9).

3. **Click the Connect with Facebook link.**

   Etsy prompts you to allow permission to access your page.

4. **Click Allow.**

   As shown in Figure 16-10, if you have multiple Facebook pages, you'll be prompted to specify which one you want to connect to Etsy.

5. **Click your shop's page.**

   Etsy connects your shop to the Facebook page you selected.

Figure 16-9: Link a Facebook page and Twitter account to your Etsy shop.

Figure 16-10: Choose your shop's Facebook page.

To link your shop to a Twitter feed, follow these steps:

1. **Click the Your Shop link along the top of any Etsy page. (Make sure you're signed out of Facebook.)**

   The Your Shop page opens.

2. **Click the Info & Appearance option under Shop Settings on the left side of the page.**

   The Info & Appearance page opens (refer to Figure 16-10).

3. **Click the Connect with Twitter link.**

   Etsy prompts you to allow permission to access your feed.

4. **Click Authorize App.**

5. **Click your shop's feed.**

   Etsy connects your shop to the Twitter feed you selected.

As mentioned, when you connect your Etsy shop to your shop's Facebook page or Twitter feed, you'll be given the option to update both when you publish new item listings, as shown in Figure 16-11.

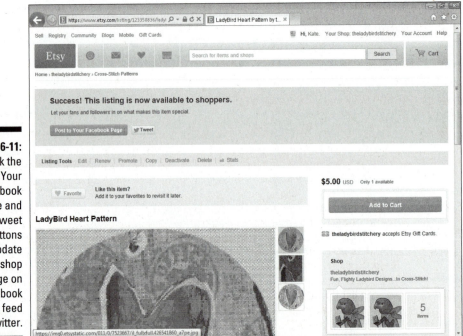

Figure 16-11:
Click the Post to Your Facebook Page and Tweet buttons to update your shop page on Facebook and its feed on Twitter.

Sale sister: Publicizing sales

As we mention in Chapter 10, running the occasional sale can be a great way to draw in customers and move merchandise. When you do run a sale, you'll want to be sure to publicize it using social media — for example, notifying all your Facebook fans and Twitter followers of the sale and providing a direct link to your shop.

In addition to using social media to publicize your sales, consider doing the following:

✔ Talk up your sale in the Etsy community. (For more on the Etsy community, see Chapter 19.)

✔ Share the news on any blogs you maintain.

✔ Upload a special "sale" graphic for your shop banner and/or your avatar. (Refer to Chapter 8 for details on creating shop banners and avatars.)

✔ Post a notice about your sale in your shop announcement. (Refer to Chapter 8 for information on how to create a shop announcement.)

✔ Include the word "SALE!" in your item title and description, and add a SALE tag. (You find out about item titles and descriptions, as well as tags, in Chapter 12.)

Another example of a social media site that you can use to promote your Etsy shop is Pinterest. Pinterest is a virtual pin board, where you can organize and share things you find on the web — including items in your shop. There's a Pin It button on every product listing page, making it easy to pin your items (as well as items from other people's shops) to your pin boards. For more information on "pinning," visit www.pinterest.com.

Go Postal: Sending an E-mail Newsletter

A great way to keep in touch with your customers is to send periodic e-mail newsletters. For example, you may send an e-mail newsletter to announce an upcoming sale, to spread the word about a new product, or to share a coupon.

Who should receive your e-mail newsletter? If your answer is "anyone and everyone who has ever ordered from my Etsy shop," simmer down. The fact is, Etsy considers that behavior spamful, noting in its Terms of Use that "without express consent from the user, you aren't licensed to add any Etsy user to your e-mail or physical mail list." (Check out www.etsy.com/help/article/479 for the complete Terms of Use.) You can, however, add someone's name to your e-mail list if that person gives consent. Naturally, you don't want to convo all your past customers to see if they want a seat on your bandwagon — *that's* a violation of Etsy's Terms of Use, too.

The only way to build your mailing list without honking off Etsy is to simply ask customers if they want to opt in at the same time you e-mail them to thank them for their order and confirm their shipping address (as we explain in Chapter 17).

When it comes to composing and distributing your newsletter, you have a few ways to go:

- ✔ **Use your word-processing software.** Compose your letter, paste it into your e-mail program, enter your customers' addresses, and send it on its way.

- ✔ **Look to an e-mail newsletter service.** As your list grows, you may opt to use an e-mail newsletter service, such as MailChimp (www.mailchimp.com). Not only does MailChimp enable you to manage subscribers and employ different templates to add some visual spice to your newsletter, but you can use it to send up to 12,000 e-mails per month free. Other e-mail newsletter services include Constant Contact (www.constantcontact.com) and Vertical Response (www.verticalresponse.com).

Whatever route you go, make it a point to send your newsletters regularly — say, biweekly, monthly, or quarterly. If you're planning a sale or launching a new product line, you may pepper in a few extra missives.

Chapter 17

You've Been Served: Providing Excellent Customer Service

In This Chapter

▶ Communicating clearly with customers

▶ Shipping packages as fast as you can

▶ Leaving feedback for (and asking for feedback from) your buyers

▶ Handling a bungled transaction

Running your own Etsy shop is a little like being the Wizard of Oz: You preside over your own Emerald City from behind a curtain of sorts, working the wheels and levers of your online craft business while hidden from view.

If you truly want to be a great and powerful Etsy seller, however, you must pull back the curtain and interact with your Ozmites — er, customers. It's not enough to craft gorgeous items and list them in your shop; you must also provide excellent customer service — before, during, and after each sale. In this chapter, we stress the importance of clear communication, prompt shipping, and fast feedback. We also provide guidance on how to gracefully deal with bungled transactions.

Let's Talk: Communicating with a Buyer Before, During, and After a Transaction

Communication is *the* single most critical factor to ensuring the success of your Etsy business. After your fabulous inventory catches your buyers' attention, your prompt and friendly communication — whether it's via e-mail or an

Etsy convo — will keep them coming back for more (not to mention recommending your shop to their friends).

A *convo* — short for "conversation" — is a communication with another member using Etsy's internal messaging system. You can use convos to communicate with any other Etsy member. To access your convos, click the Conversations icon that appears in the Etsy header bar (assuming that you're signed in to the site); the Conversations page appears (see Figure 17-1).

You can also set up Etsy to send you an e-mail anytime you receive a message via convo. Here's how:

1. **Click the Conversations icon.**

   The Conversations page opens.

2. **Click the Notification Preferences link.**

   The E-mails page opens (see Figure 17-2).

Figure 17-1:
Access your
Etsy convos
here.

Figure 17-2:
The E-mails page is where you change various settings related to e-mail.

3. **Click the Someone Sends Me a Convo check box to select it.**

4. **Click the Save Settings button.**

Etsy saves your settings.

When it comes to communicating with buyers, you must strike a balance. Communicate too little, and your buyers may conclude that you don't care about your customers. Communicate too much, and your buyers may perceive you to be a nuisance. So, when exactly do you want to reach out to buyers? And what exactly do you want to say? For guidance, read on.

It's a good idea to set up a separate e-mail address for correspondence on Etsy. That way, you can keep all your business-related messages in one place. Also, set up Etsy to forward convos to your dedicated shop e-mail address.

Questionable behavior: Answering customer questions

Even if you upload five spectacular photos of your item and compose a listing description with enough detail to satisfy Tolstoy himself, prospective buyers will still have questions about your piece. Queries may range from "How big is it?" to "What does it smell like?" to "How fuzzy is it?" to "Um, what is that thing?" to "Can you make this in puce?"

Whatever the question, it's critical that you answer it — and the sooner, the better. Unless you've been stranded on a desert island or you're, say, in labor, try to respond to all questions within 24 hours. Quickly replying to e-mails and convos containing queries from potential buyers does more than just help them determine whether your item is right for them; it reassures them that you're a seller they can count on.

When communicating with customers, keep things simple. Providing too much information may confuse them. Focus on communicating the information that will be most helpful to the customer. For example, if a customer asks how quickly you can put an item in the post, simply respond by telling her, "Tomorrow." Don't say, "Well, I'd do it today, but my dog just ate my cactus, and I have to take her to the vet, so it will have to be tomorrow." TMI.

Mind your manners: Giving thanks

As you may know, Etsy sends you a notification e-mail when someone purchases an item from your Etsy shop. When you receive this e-mail, you should contact the buyer to thank him for his purchase and to confirm that you've received payment for it (assuming that you have). While you're at it, give the buyer some idea of when he can expect to receive the item and invite him to drop you a line if he has any questions. (We provide a sample note covering this and additional info later in this chapter.)

On Etsy, as in life, simple courtesy goes a long way! Saying thank you is key to keeping your customers happy.

You can contact the buyer in one of two ways (the method you choose depends simply on which one you prefer):

- ✔ **E-mail:** As shown in Figure 17-3, Etsy includes the buyer's e-mail address in its notification e-mail. You can also access the buyer's e-mail by hovering your mouse pointer over the Your Shop link found along the top of every Etsy page and choosing Sold Orders; then find the listing for the item in question, click the buyer's name, and click her e-mail address in the list that appears (see Figure 17-4).

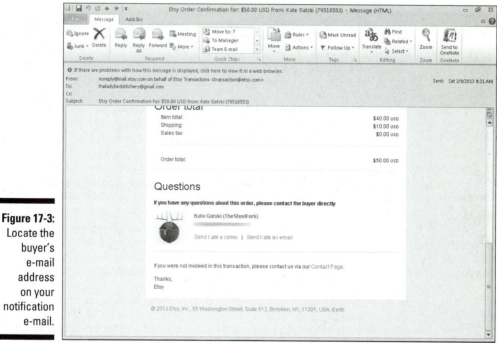

Figure 17-3:
Locate the
buyer's
e-mail
address
on your
notification
e-mail.

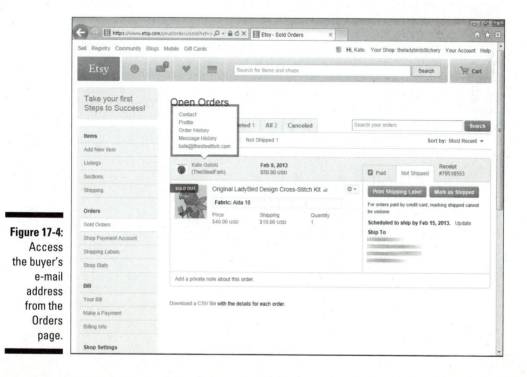

Figure 17-4:
Access
the buyer's
e-mail
address
from the
Orders
page.

✔ **Convo:** You can use Etsy to hold a convo with a buyer (or any other Etsy user) right on the site. To initiate a convo with your buyer, click her name in the Orders page as before, but click Contact in the list that appears (refer to Figure 17-4). When the New Conversation dialog box opens (see Figure 17-5), type your message and click Send.

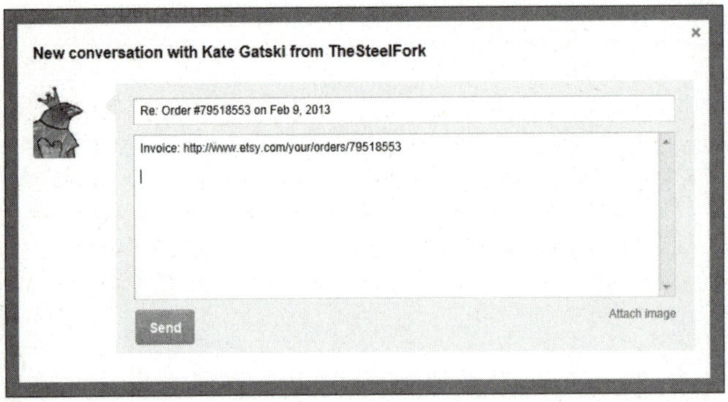

Figure 17-5:
The New Conversation dialog box.

New conversation with Kate Gatski from TheSteelFork ✕

Re: Order #79518553 on Feb 9, 2013

Invoice: http://www.etsy.com/your/orders/79518553

Send   Attach image

To launch an Etsy convo with any other Etsy member (not just someone who has purchased something from your Etsy shop), open that person's Etsy page and click the Contact link under his name. The same box from Figure 17-5 appears.

If you want, you can configure Etsy to include some special text in the transaction notice that buyers receive when they purchase from your shop. For example, you may use this text, which Etsy calls your Message to Buyers, to thank your buyers, to convey your standard shipping practices, to invite them to sign up for your e-mail newsletter, or to share some other useful tidbit. To set up your Message to Buyers, click the Your Shop link that appears along the top of every Etsy page, click the Info & Appearance link under Shop Settings, type your message in the Message to Buyers area, and click the Save Changes button (see Figure 17-6). Note that you don't want to use this auto-generated message in lieu of the one you send yourself; instead, use it as one more point of contact.

Ship happens: Double-checking the shipping address

Know what's a major drag? Placing a perfectly packaged parcel in the post — with the wrong delivery address. To avoid this postal pitfall, double-check with your buyer *before* you ship that the shipping address that appears on the transaction invoice is, indeed, correct. You can do this in your initial convo with the buyer — the one in which you thank him for his purchase. (Check out the later section "Sample shout-out: Covering all the bases in one short, pleasant message" for a sample note.)

Also, make a point to touch base with your buyer after you ship his package, to let him know it's on its way. When you do, be sure to include the name of the shipping company and the package's tracking number (if applicable).

Etsy makes this easy by enabling you to send a message right from the Open Orders page. Simply click the Mark as Shipped button next to the item in question, click the Add Shipping Notification button, and type your note to the buyer in the dialog box that opens. If you like what you wrote, click the Save This Note for My Next Shipping Notification Email check box to select it. Optionally, enter the package's tracking number. Then click the Send Email button.

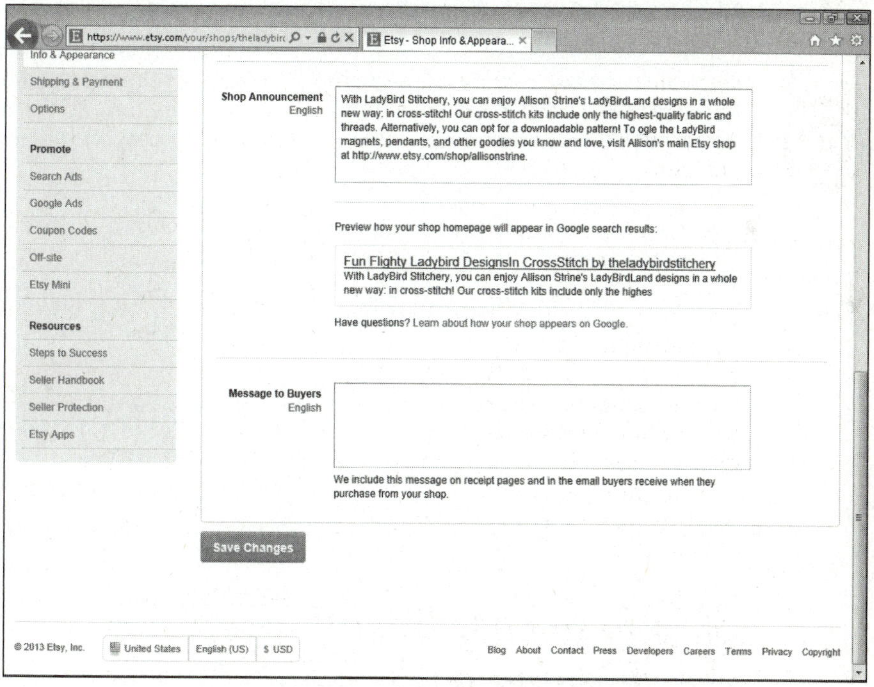

Figure 17-6:
Enter your
Message
to Buyers
here.

Get a clue: Finding out how they found you

In the course of communicating with your buyers, whether it's in your initial convo or later in the process — for example, when you ship the item — ask how they found you. Did the buyer happen upon your store while browsing Etsy? Did she see your work on a blog? Or did an ad pique his interest? This info can help you determine how well your marketing strategy is working — which is critical to the long-term success of your Etsy shop. (Flip to Chapter 16 for the scoop on marketing your Etsy shop.) While you're at it, considering asking buyers if they want to opt into your mailing list (also discussed in Chapter 16).

Lost in translation: Communicating with foreign buyers

Especially if you sell internationally, you must be prepared to correspond with buyers who are not native English speakers. Even if you sell only in the United States, you'll run across the occasional transplant. To ward off misunderstandings when communicating with foreign buyers, keep these points in mind:

- **Keep messages brief and simple.** Using long, complex words and sentences will almost certainly create confusion.

- **Steer clear of slang.** Including nonstandard English is just asking for trouble. At best, your customer may misunderstand you. At worst, you may inadvertently offend her.

- **Avoid abbreviations and jargon.** Spell out what you want to say, using clear, standard language.

Sample shout-out: Covering all the bases in one short, pleasant message

Still a bit stymied over what your initial message needs to contain? Here's a sample missive combining all the elements to cover:

Hi Murgatroyd!

Just a quick note to thank you so much for your purchase. You made me smile!

Payment has been received, and your treats will ship to the following address:

[Insert Address Here]

I'll send you an e-mail when your package is ready to ship.

Also, may I ask where you found my shop — from an ad maybe, or just browsing around Etsy? And while I have you, are you interested in signing up for my monthly newsletter?

Thanks again, and I hope you have a fabulous day!

Kate

Speed Is of the Essence: Shipping It Quickly

If you've ever ordered anything on Etsy — and, let's face it, who hasn't? — you're no doubt familiar with the sweet torture of waiting for that prettily packaged parcel to roost in your mailbox. To keep your buyer from expiring from anticipation, and to improve your chances of getting excellent feedback, be a dear and ship her goodies as soon as is feasibly possible (after she has paid for them and, if applicable, the check, money order, or cashier's check has cleared). Of course, you'll want to double-check her shipping address first (as we explain earlier in this chapter). For more information about shipping options and about packaging your parcel like a pro, refer to Chapter 15.

Feedback Is Good: Leaving Feedback Promptly and Prompting for It

Etsy relies on feedback to facilitate trust among buyers and sellers. At the conclusion of a sale, both the buyer and the seller leave feedback about the transaction. Other Etsy users can then view this feedback to determine whether a particular buyer or seller is aboveboard. You and your buyer have 120 days to leave feedback on your mutual transaction. That's plenty of time to receive payment and for your buyer to receive his item! So, no excuses.

To view another user's feedback score, click the Feedback link on that shop's home page or public profile.

Leaving feedback isn't mandatory. If you opt out, Etsy doesn't send a gaggle of intimidating fellows to your door to harass you. But leaving feedback is a good idea because it helps ensure that buyers feel safe shopping on Etsy — and that's good for everyone. Just remember, any feedback you leave affects your buyer's feedback score — and, by extension, her reputation on the site. Be sure to issue feedback consistently, fairly, and honestly.

You can leave feedback for a buyer as soon as you receive payment, after you ship the package, or when you're certain that the buyer has received the item — whichever you prefer. Here's how:

1. **Hover your mouse pointer over the Your Account link that appears along the top of every page on Etsy and choose Feedback from the list that appears.**

   The Items Awaiting Feedback page appears (see Figure 17-7).

2. **Click the Positive, Neutral, or Negative option button under the transaction you want to rate.**

   Before leaving neutral or negative feedback, see if you can hammer out with the buyer whatever issue is bothering you, via e-mail or a convo. Often, conflicts on Etsy are simply the result of a misunderstanding.

Figure 17-7:
Hover your mouse pointer over Your Account and choose Feedback from the list that appears to access the Items Awaiting Feedback page.

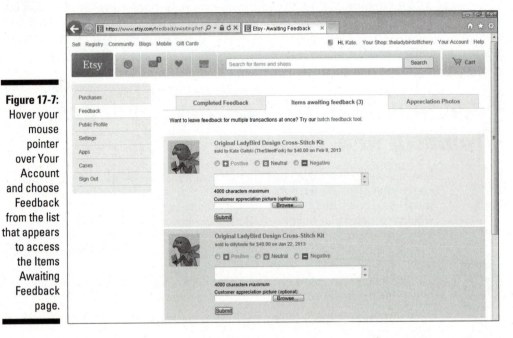

3. **Optionally, type a comment about the transaction or the buyer.**

4. **Click Submit.**

   Etsy posts your feedback on the site.

After the transaction is complete, you can politely ask the buyer to return the favor by leaving feedback for you. Why? Because buyers feel more comfortable purchasing from sellers who have received positive feedback. Keep in mind, though, that leaving feedback is optional. If your buyer opts out of leaving feedback, avoid the temptation to ask her a second time. It's annoying and spammy.

Consider including instructions for leaving feedback in your message — for example, "To leave feedback for me, log in to your account and click the Feedback option in Your Account."

Bungle Fever: Handling a Bungled Transaction and Other Tough Issues

Despite our best efforts, transactions occasionally do go to heck in a handbasket. Payments get lost, parcels get lost, people get angry — it's enough to make you lose your mind, too! To prevent bungle fever–induced insanity, read on.

Hand it over: Prompting a buyer to pay up

Most of the time, buyers pay right away when they purchase from an Etsy shop. In fact, if they opt to use PayPal, they *must* pay right away. But occasionally, you may encounter buyers who take their sweet time when it comes to tendering the Benjamins. If that happens, you must take matters into your own hands by issuing a polite reminder for them to pay up. Not sure what to write? Try something like the following:

Dear Loretta,

Just a quick note to thank you for your purchase. I'm so glad you found some goodies to love!

Whenever you get a chance, please send me your check (the total is $44.50) so that I can put your piece in the mail.

Thanks so much, Loretta! I can't wait until you see your treats. Happy day to you!

Kate

In the end: Opting to Kiss and Make Up

If the result of any mayhem is neutral or negative feedback, fear not. Thanks to an Etsy feature called Kiss and Make Up, buyers and sellers can, er, kiss and make up. To initiate Kiss and Make Up proceedings with a buyer-turned-baddie, go to Your Account, click the Feedback link, click the Completed Feedback tab, and click the red Kiss and Make Up link beneath the befouled feedback entry. Etsy starts a convo between you and the buyer to initiate a change in the feedback rating.

If your buyer fails to respond to your gentle nudge within a reasonable time frame, you may relist the item and cancel the sale. For more information, see the upcoming section "Tropic of cancel: Canceling an order."

If a buyer doesn't pay up, forcing you to cancel the sale and re-list the item, provide feedback on the buyer to that effect. You'll be doing all your Etsy seller brethren a favor.

Lost Etsy: Dealing with lost shipments

"Neither snow nor rain nor heat nor gloom of night," my eye! It's an unfortunate fact that sometimes the postal service and other delivery companies simply fail to deliver. If one of your packages has gone the way of Amelia Earhart, you have a few options:

- ✔ **Ask your buyer to give it a few days.** More often than not, "lost" packages are merely delayed. Shipping times vary depending on destination and time of year. Also, see if he has checked with his neighbor to see whether the package was delivered there instead.

- ✔ **Use the tracking number to locate the package.** If you sprang for Express Mail with the U.S. Postal Service (USPS) or opted for a higher-end carrier, such as UPS or FedEx, you can track the package. Visit your carrier's website for more information. (Flip to Chapter 9 for guidance on setting your shop's shipping policies.)

- ✔ **Report the missing package.** If you sent the package via USPS, you can report it missing. If you're lucky, the USPS will find your package. If not, well, at least you'll have done your part to improve the system. To report a missing package, fill out the form on this web page: https://postalinspectors.uspis.gov/forms/MLNtRcvd.aspx.

If all these efforts fail, you'll unfortunately have to send a replacement item or refund the buyer's money (or, if you're feeling especially customer friendly, both). Yes, it hurts — but it's part of running a legitimate Etsy shop. The exception? If you feel that you're being scammed. Although you can't know for sure whether your buyer is pulling a fast one, checking her feedback rating may give you some insight. If she has received 1,298 glowing reviews, she's probably on the up and up. If, on the other hand, she has garnered multiple negative marks, she may be honesty challenged. Our advice? Trust your gut.

Even if you suspect that you're being taken, refunding a buyer's dough may be worthwhile for the sake of your own feedback rating. It's your call.

One more pointer: If you do refund a buyer's money for an item lost in the mail, you need to cancel the order. That way, you'll at least receive a refund from Etsy for your transaction fee. For help with canceling the order, see the section "Tropic of cancel: Canceling an order."

Case study: Dealing with a reported case

Although Etsy urges buyers and sellers to work through problems related to nondelivery themselves via civilized means such as with convos or e-mails, buyers sometimes feel compelled to report nondelivery cases to Etsy. (Buyers may also launch a case if the item received didn't match its description.) If a buyer launches a case against you, you'll receive an e-mail from Etsy outlining the details of the case and instructions for resolving it. To view details about the case, do the following:

1. **Click the Your Shop link that appears along the top of every Etsy page.**

2. **Click the Cases link under Orders.**

   The Your Cases pages opens.

3. **Click the Cases Reported About Your Shop tab.**

   A page appears with a link to the case.

4. **Click the link to the case.**

   A page containing information about the case appears, as shown in Figure 17-8. (You can also access this page by clicking the Resolve It link that appears at the top of any Etsy page when a case has been launched against your shop or by clicking the Cases link that appears on the left side of the Your Account screen.)

Figure 17-8:
View information about your case.

To resolve your case, you'll need to work directly with your buyer — and you have to start within seven days of the case being launched. Correspondence pertaining to the open case should occur on the case's page. Simply type your message in the Comments box. Note that you can also upload images or photos — say, a scanned image of your delivery confirmation receipt or something similar — directly to the case's page by clicking the Attach Image link under the text box. In the end, you may need to refund the buyer's money. For help, see the next section. When the buyer is satisfied with your actions, she can close the case.

Protective custody: Etsy's Seller Protection program

As we outline in Chapter 6, Etsy offers a Seller Protection program, which guarantees that your account status will remain unaffected if a buyer reports a problem with a transaction with your shop. As a bonus, Etsy's Seller Protection program fully covers items purchased via Etsy's Direct Checkout tool (that is, via credit card or gift card), up to $1,000. So if a good transaction goes bad, you'll be in the clear. To find out whether you're eligible, flip to Chapter 6.

If you're unable to resolve the case, the buyer can send the case to Etsy for review. In addition, Etsy automatically resolves any open, unresolved cases after three weeks. If that happens, Etsy's Trust & Safety team will review the case, at which point you may be contacted for additional information. If the team deems it necessary, they may issue a refund to the buyer using funds from your account (assuming payment was made with Direct Checkout).

Refundsal, Refundsal, give back your fare: Issuing refunds

When it comes to refunds, different sellers have different policies. Some sellers are happy to issue full refunds for any reason, other sellers allow buyers to exchange for other goods in their shop, and still others hold a firm "all sales final" stance.

Whatever position you adopt on this matter, be certain that your shop policies explain it clearly. Flip to Chapter 9 for more about setting up shop policies.

If you do decide to allow refunds, how you process them depends on which payment option your buyer chose. For example, if he sent a check, you'll likely refund his money by sending him a check. If she paid using PayPal, you'll use the site to reimburse her. (For help with using PayPal to reimburse a buyer, visit PayPal's Help Center page. You can find it at www.paypal.com/help.) If the buyer used Direct Checkout or an Etsy gift card, you'll need to follow these steps to refund his money:

1. **Hover your mouse pointer over the Your Shop link that appears along the top of every Etsy page.**

2. **Click Sold Orders in the list of options that appears.**

   The Open Orders pages opens. If you're refunding the money after the item has been shipped, you'll need to click the Completed Orders tab.

3. **Click the Receipt number link on the right side of the listing entry.**

   A page containing information about the order opens (see Figure 17-9).

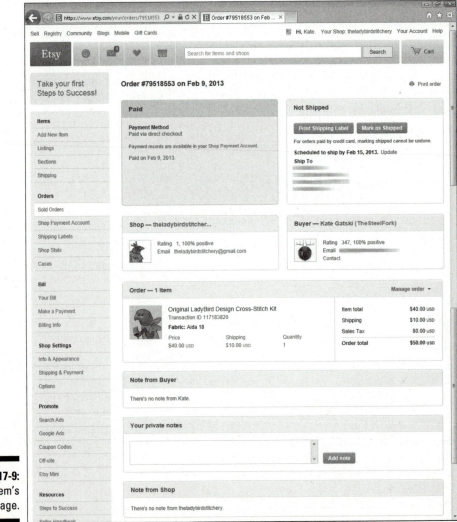

Figure 17-9:
The item's
order page.

4. **Click the Manage Order menu and choose Issue a Refund.**

   The Issue a Refund page, shown in Figure 17-10, opens.

5. **Click the Reason for Issuing a Refund drop-down list and choose the appropriate option from the list.**

6. **Optionally, type a message to your buyer.**

7. **To issue a full refund, click the Issue a Full Refund check box; otherwise, enter the desired amounts in the appropriate fields in the Amount to Refund column.**

8. **Click the Review Refund button.**

   Etsy asks you to confirm the refund.

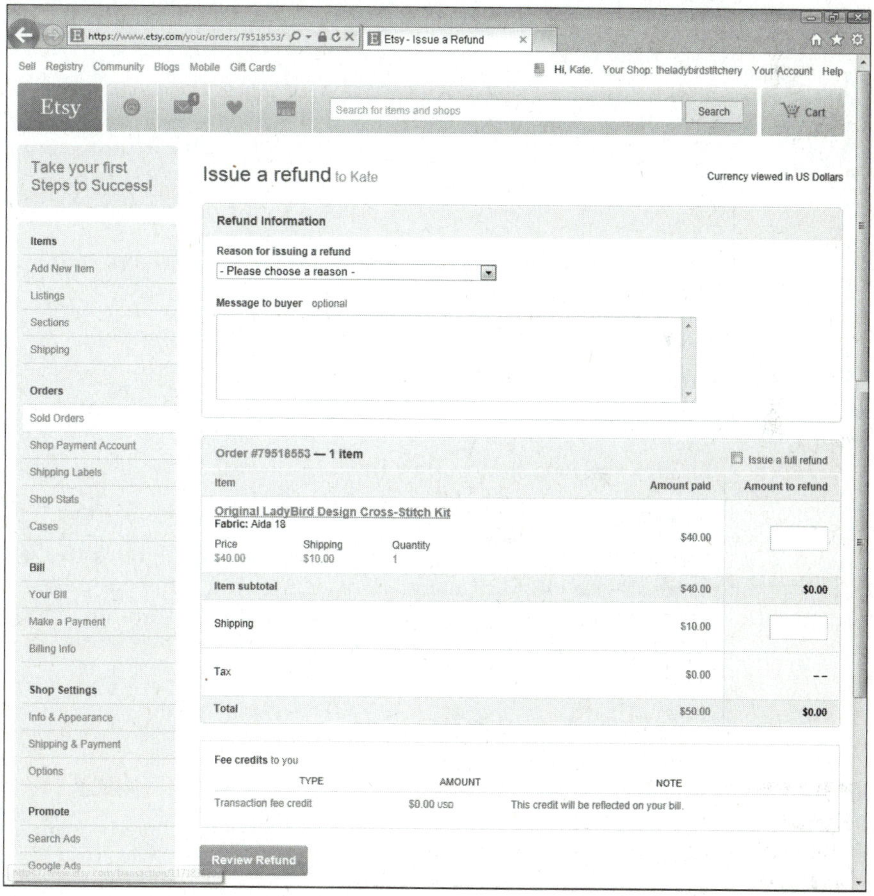

Figure 17-10:
Issue a refund.

9. **Click the Submit button.**

   Etsy refunds the buyer's money. Note that if you've refunded the buyer's money before shipping your item, the refund will be deducted from your pending transaction. For refunds on completed transactions, the amount will be deducted from your available balance or charged to your credit card.

Tropic of cancel: Canceling an order

In certain circumstances, you, as a shop owner, can cancel an order. For example, you may cancel an order if the buyer fails to pay, if both you and the buyer agree to cancel the transaction prior to shipment, if you can't complete the transaction (for example, due to inventory problems), if the item was lost in the mail, or if the buyer returned the item to you. When you cancel an order, Etsy refunds your transaction fee.

If you want to leave feedback for the order, you need to do so *before* canceling it. After an order is canceled, you can't leave feedback for it.

To cancel an order, follow these steps:

1. **Hover your mouse pointer over the Your Shop link that appears along the top of every Etsy page.**

2. **Click Sold Orders in the list of options that appears.**

   The Open Orders pages opens.

3. **If the item has already been shipped, click the All Orders tab.**

4. **Click the Receipt number link on the right side of the listing entry.**

   A page containing information about the order opens (refer to Figure 17-9).

5. **If the item was purchased via Direct Checkout, click the Manage Order menu and choose Cancel Transaction. If a different payment method was used — PayPal, check, money order, or what have you — click the Cancel a Transaction link.**

   The Cancel Transactions page appears (see Figure 17-11).

6. **Click the Reason for Canceling Transaction drop-down list and choose the reason for the cancellation.**

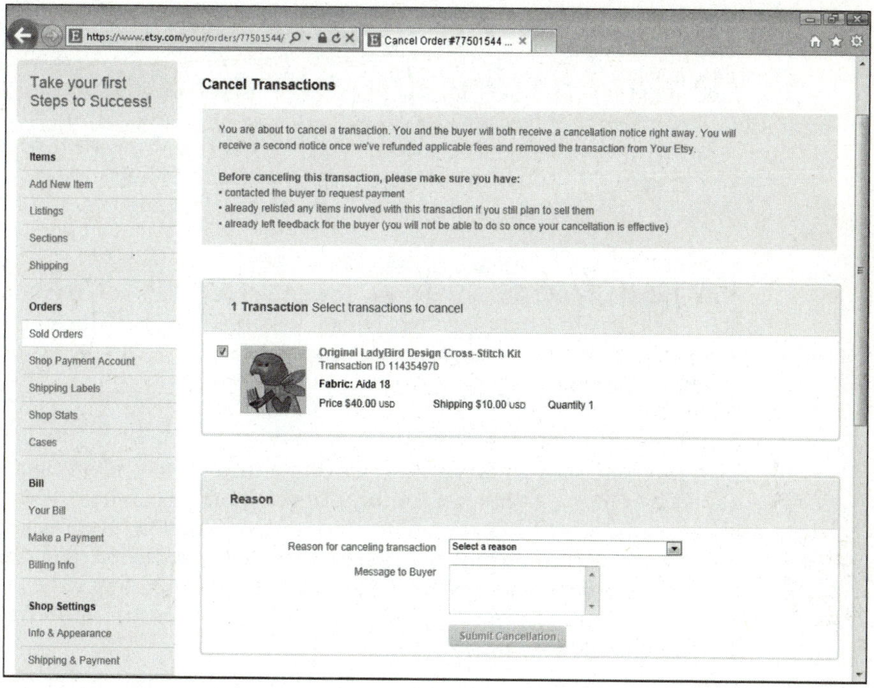

Figure 17-11:
Cancel a
transaction
here.

7. **Answer the questions that appear.**

   The precise questions that appear depend on the reason you select in Step 5.

8. **If you want, type a message for the buyer in the Message to Buyer field.**

9. **Click the Submit Cancellation button.**

After you submit the form, Etsy finalizes the cancellation (it may take up to 48 hours), notifies you and the buyer that the cancellation has occurred, credits your account with any fees associated with the order, and moves details about the transaction to the Canceled tab on your Sold Orders page.

One more thing: Occasionally, you may come across a buyer who requests a cancellation. It's up to you whether you grant her request. If you do, you can follow the same steps outlined here.

The customer is usually right (ish): Dealing with a difficult customer

Honestly, nearly everyone on Etsy is great. For real. But every so often, you're bound to run into someone who, well, *isn't*. Whether the offender is rude, demanding, or simply a pain in the patootie, keep these points in mind:

- ✔ **Polish your policies.** Clear, concise shop policies can go a long way toward heading off problems down the road. Be sure that your shop's policies are as comprehensive as possible. (For guidance on creating your shop's policies, refer to Chapter 9.)

- ✔ **Don't take it personally.** If, after receiving your beautiful baubles, your buyer doesn't appreciate their magnificence, that's on him, not on you.

- ✔ **Be professional.** However tempting it may be to uncork on a difficult buyer, don't — at least, not where that person can hear you. Keep all communications firm, polite, and to the point. Oh, and resist the temptation to air your grievances on the Etsy forums. Everything that you write there is visible to anyone on the Internet — including your mother. Plus, calling out a buyer by name is a violation of the site's policies, which can lead to your expulsion.

- ✔ **Extend the olive branch.** Most buyers aren't evil — really. They just want to feel like you're willing to work with them to achieve a happy, speedy transaction. Kindly communicate to them that you'll do everything possible to make that happen — and then do it.

If you feel that you've done all you reasonably can to rectify a problem with a buyer to no avail, don't be afraid to cut your losses by refunding the buyer's money. Better to get a problem buyer out of your hair than to kill yourself trying to make her happy.

No shirt, no shoes, no service: Refusing service to a buyer

Although Etsy asks that sellers do everything they can to honor a sale, on extremely rare occasions, you may feel that you must refuse service. For example, if you feel that you're being harassed by a buyer, or if a buyer becomes belligerent — or if, say, you're a Hatfield and the buyer is a McCoy — you do have the right to refuse service, no questions asked. You may also refuse service if your gut instinct tells you that the buyer isn't on the up and up — for example, if you sense that he has paid with a stolen credit card or is attempting to commit some other type of fraud.

Refusing service is a rare event, indeed. It's something you want to do only as a last resort.

To refuse service to a buyer, simply use an Etsy convo to politely inform the buyer that you won't be able to send the item she purchased. You don't need to explain yourself; in fact, the less you say, the better. Then take the necessary steps to cancel the sale and refund the buyer's money (as we describe earlier in this chapter).

After you refuse service to a buyer, if that person continues to contact you, you can report the problem to abuse@etsy.com. If Etsy agrees with you that the behavior constitutes harassment, Etsy may suspend the buyer's account.

Chapter 18

Business as Usual: Managing Your Etsy Store

In This Chapter

▶ Settling up with Etsy

▶ Paying taxes and keeping good records

▶ Trying Etsy tools for managing your shop

▶ Choosing a business structure

▶ Running a charitable shop

▶ Going on hiatus

▶ Closing your Etsy shop

*I*f you're a fan of Chinese food, you're probably familiar with the pu-pu platter — you know, the appetizer that features a little bit of everything. This chapter is the literary equivalent. It covers an assortment of topics that relate to managing and growing your Etsy business. They include paying Etsy bills, transferring money from your shop to your bank account, handling taxes and keeping records, running your shop with Etsy tools, and turning your thriving shop into a legitimate business.

Please forgive us: We've tried to cram several books' worth of information into this one wee chapter. We strongly urge you to educate yourself further on all these business matters and more. A good place to start is *Small Business For Dummies,* 4th Edition, by Eric Tyson and Jim Schell (Wiley). Also try *Home-Based Business For Dummies,* 3rd Edition, by Paul Edwards, Sarah Edwards, and Peter Economy (Wiley).

I'm Just a Bill: Paying Your Etsy Bill

You're not the only baby who needs a new pair of shoes; the folks at Etsy have their own financial obligations. As we mention in Chapter 1, Etsy stays afloat by charging sellers a listing fee (currently, 20¢) for each item listed on the site. In addition, Etsy collects a commission from the seller for each item sold — currently, 3.5 percent of the total price of the item (not counting shipping), as well as fees for shipping labels and search ads. These fees are assessed at the end of each month. Etsy lets you know when it's time to pay up by sending you a billing statement via e-mail.

To pay your bill, log in to your Etsy account and follow these steps:

1. **Click the link in the billing statement that Etsy sent via e-mail to open the Your Bill page on Etsy.**

   You can also access the Your Bill page, shown in Figure 18-1, by hovering your mouse pointer over the Your Shop link that appears along the top of every Etsy page and clicking the Your Bill option in the list that appears.

2. **Click the Make a Payment Now button.**

   The Make a Payment page opens (see Figure 18-2).

3. **Under Amount to Pay, indicate whether you want to pay your entire Etsy bill, the portion that's due at this time, or some amount in between.**

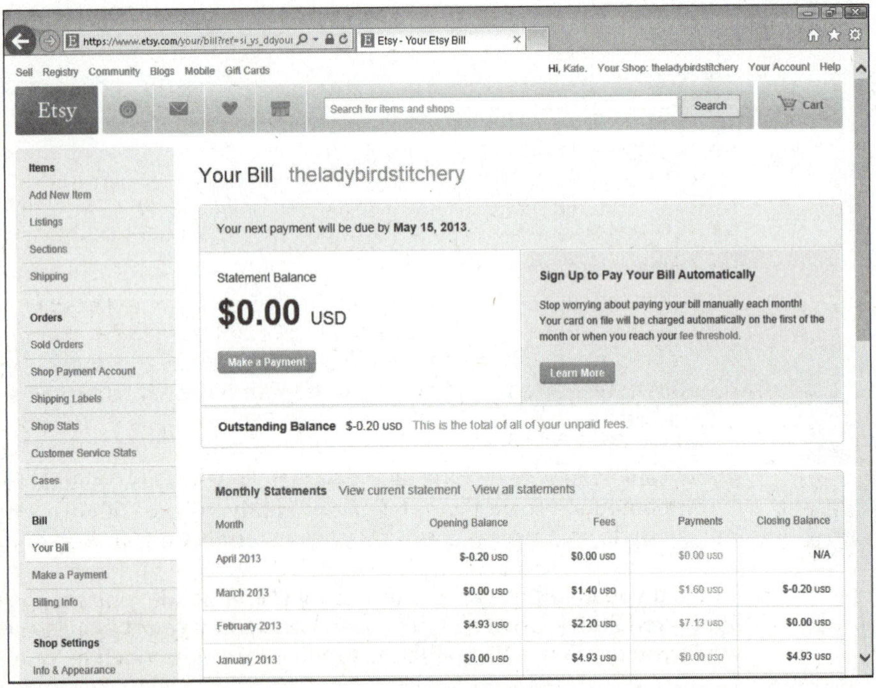

Figure 18-1:
View your
Etsy bill.

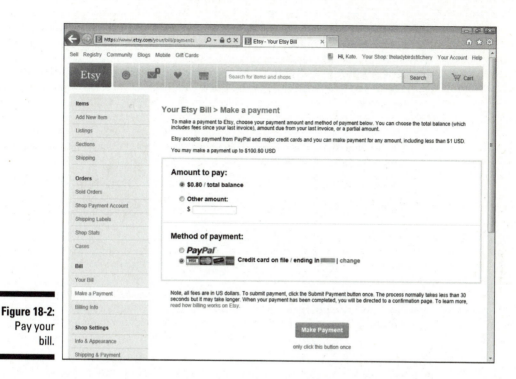

Figure 18-2:
Pay your
bill.

4. **Under Method of Payment, choose PayPal or the credit card that you have on file with Etsy.**

5. **Click the Make Payment button.**

   If you opted to pay with a credit card, you'll see a screen that thanks you for your payment, with a link that you can click to return to your Etsy bill.

   If you opted to pay with PayPal, Etsy directs you to the PayPal site (www.paypal.com), where you're prompted to log in. After you do so, review the payment information. Assuming that it's correct, click the Continue button. PayPal processes your payment and directs you back to Etsy.

If you want to remain in good standing with Etsy, it's crucial that you pay the current amount due on your Etsy bill promptly, by the 15th of each month. If you fail to do so, Etsy can suspend or even terminate your Etsy account.

Worried you might forget to pay your bill? Fret not. If your shop is based in the United States, you can enroll with Etsy to pay your bill automatically. When you do, Etsy will charge the credit card you put on file for all outstanding fees on the first of every month or when it reaches a calculated fee threshold. To set up automatic bill pay, follow these steps:

1. **Hover your mouse pointer over the Your Shop link that appears along the top of every Etsy page and click the Your Bill option in the list that appears.**

   The Your Bill page opens (refer to Figure 18-1).

2. **In the Sign Up to Pay Your Bill Automatically section, click the Learn More button.**

   The Enroll to Pay Your Bill Automatically page opens (see Figure 18-3).

3. **Select the credit card you want to use for billing (or add a new one if needed).**

4. **Click the Validate Your Card to Enroll button.**

   Etsy signs you up for its automatic bill-pay service.

If you change your mind and decide you'd rather pay your bills manually, just click the Looking to Turn Off Automatic Bill Payment link at the bottom of the Your Bill page. Etsy asks you to confirm your action; click the Turn Off Automatic Bill Pay button to confirm.

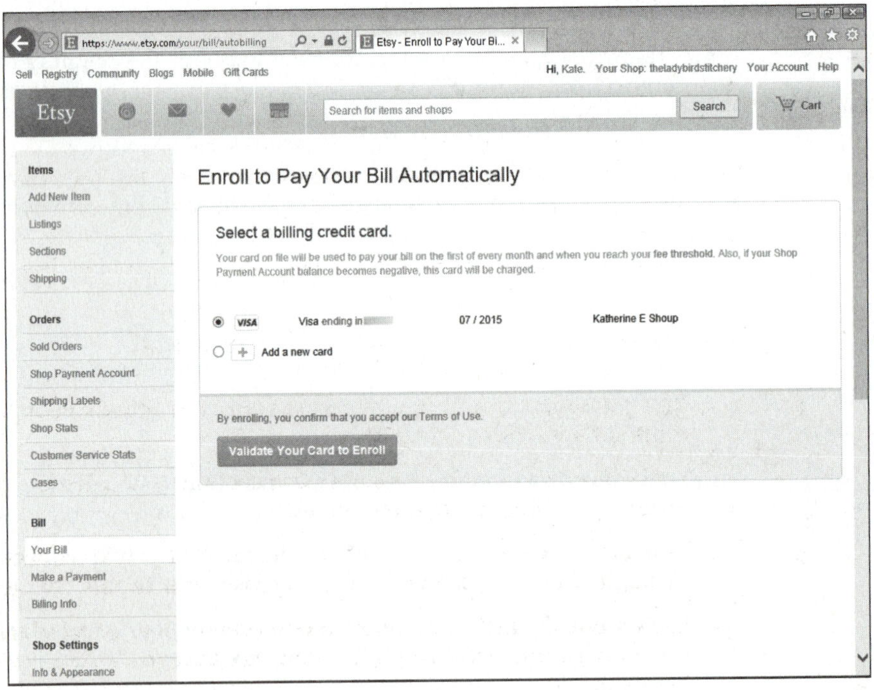

Figure 18-3:
Enrolling in Etsy's automatic bill-pay service.

Taxing Matters: Appeasing Uncle Sam

A world with no taxes would be lovely indeed — except for the fact that it would also be a world with no roads, public school teachers, or firefighters. Indeed, without taxes, there would be no Internet — and, by extension, no Etsy! After all, taxes bankrolled the U.S. government's Advanced Research Projects Agency (ARPA), which, in 1969, created the network that would eventually become the Internet. (Thanks, Al Gore!) To make sure you're square with Uncle Sam, read on.

We're not licensed accountants or lawyers, nor do we play them on TV. To be absolutely certain that you're in compliance with local and federal tax laws, seek the advice of these experts.

To tax or not to tax: Collecting sales tax

Odds are, you need to collect sales tax at least some of the time, unless you live in Alaska, Delaware, Montana, New Hampshire, or Oregon, five states that don't impose a statewide sales tax. You also may not need to collect sales tax if you use your Etsy shop to sell prescription drugs (not recommended); agricultural products, such as seeds; food; or products for resale. So, when *do* you need to collect sales tax?

Here's the short answer: You must collect sales tax — sometimes called a *franchise tax,* a *transaction privilege tax,* or a *use tax,* among other aliases — on most goods and some services delivered to a customer who lives in a U.S. state where your business maintains a physical presence, such as a store, office, or employee. So, for example, if you run your Etsy shop from your fifth-floor walkup in Brooklyn, and someone from the state of New York buys something from your shop, you need to hit that person with sales tax. But if your buyer lives in Cali, you're both off the hook (unless your shop is a collective and your partner lives in Long Beach).

In general terms, the sales tax process works like this:

1. **You get a sales tax ID number from your state (check your state government's website for details).**

2. **Each time you conduct a taxable transaction, you calculate the tax owed and collect it from the buyer.**

3. **You keep excellent records about the tax that you've collected through your Etsy business (as we advise later in this chapter).**

4. **Each month, quarter, or year (depending on your level of sales), you file a tax return and submit the sales tax that you've collected to your state.**

5. **You stay out of jail.**

So, how much sales tax do you need to collect? Aye, there's the rub. Sales tax rates vary widely from state to state. Plus, some cities, counties, and jurisdictions impose sales tax above and beyond the state rate. To make sure that your Etsy shop complies, you absolutely want to research your local laws and maybe even consult a fancy-pants accountant or attorney for guidance.

Here's the good news: You can set up your Etsy shop to calculate and collect sales tax automatically. That way, when a shopper from your neck of the woods ponies up for one of your items, she's charged the appropriate tax automatically. It's like magic! For help with setting up your shop to collect sales tax, refer to Chapter 9.

The sales tax ID number that you obtain from your state entitles you to buy supplies and other items for your Etsy business wholesale — which is typically at least half off the retail price. Holy bonus, Batman!

Drawn and quartered: Paying quarterly income tax

If you run your business as a sole proprietorship (covered later in this chapter) and you live in the United States, you have the distinct pleasure of paying income taxes not once, not twice, not three times, but *four times* per year — on April 15, June 15, September 15, and January 15 (unless any of those days falls on a weekend or holiday, in which case you must pay up on the next business day).

Paying these quarterly taxes is a breeze. You can download the necessary form (called a 1040-ES) from the IRS's website, here: www.irs.gov/pub/irs-pdf/f1040es.pdf. You need to download a similar form from your state government's site. Then fill out the forms, cut your checks, and send them to the appropriate office. (Check the form for details.)

Alternatively, you can pay your taxes online using the Electronic Federal Tax Payment System (EFTPS): www.eftps.gov/eftps. (***Note:*** EFTPS is for federal taxes only; check with your state to see what resources are available for paying your state taxes online.)

Figuring out how much you owe is a little more involved. One approach is to simply look at your prior-year tax return, figure out how much you paid in taxes, divide that number by four, and send that amount for each quarterly installment — but that strategy won't do if you expect your income to be vastly different. Our advice? Don't listen to us. Seek the guidance of a qualified accountant.

1099 bottles of beer on the wall: Filing your 1099-K

If your sales are high enough — that is, you receive more than 200 orders and gross more than $20,000 by the end of the year — Etsy is required by federal law to file a 1099-K form on your behalf with the IRS and to send you a copy so you'll have it when you file your taxes. (If you don't make those numbers, Etsy won't file a 1099-K.)

For all this to work, Etsy needs your taxpayer ID. To provide it, click the Your Account link that appears along the top of any Etsy page. Then click the Settings button. On the Taxpayer ID tab, click the Employer Identification Number (EIN) or Social Security Number option button, enter your taxpayer ID, and click the Submit button. When prompted, click Yes to confirm that the number you entered is correct.

Write this off: Determining tax deductions

If your Etsy shop is a proper business (rather than a hobby) and it's set up as a sole proprietorship (one of the arrangements we discuss later in this chapter), you're free to deduct shop-related expenses from your taxable income. Here are a few examples (again, for a complete list, hit up a qualified accountant):

- ✔ **Cost of goods sold (COGS):** This category is the cost of the materials that you purchased to craft your inventory. For example, if you make jewelry, your COGS may include the price that you paid for beads, thread, findings, and so on. The COGS may also include what you shelled out for your pretty packaging and your shipping costs.

- ✔ **Equipment:** Did you buy a kiln to fire the ceramic bowls that you list in your Etsy shop? Or a laptop to help run your Etsy business? Or a printer to print invoices for your Etsy customers? If so, you can deduct the cost of these items from your taxable income.

- ✔ **Selling expenses:** These expenses include Etsy fees, PayPal fees, banking fees — even phone calls related to your business.

- ✔ **Advertising fees:** Say you printed some snazzy business cards for your Etsy shop. These costs and other marketing expenses are fair game. (Chapter 16 provides a general introduction to marketing tasks.)

- ✔ **Office expenses:** These purchases include pens and pencils, paper, letterhead, printer supplies, and the like.

- ✔ **Mileage:** Do you regularly drive to your local craft store to stock up on supplies for your Etsy shop? Or to the post office, to ship items to Etsy buyers? If so, you can deduct your mileage for those outings; the current rate, as of this writing, is 56.5¢ per mile. Any tolls or parking fees that you incur en route are also deductible.

✔ **Home office:** If you use a portion of your home to run your Etsy shop — maybe you devote a special room to crafting the pieces that you sell or handling administrative tasks — you can claim a home-office deduction. If you rent studio space, you can deduct that area instead.

✔ **Legal or professional services:** If you follow our advice and hire an accountant, you can deduct her fee. Ditto for any fees associated with other professionals who serve your business — attorneys, graphic designers, and the like.

If you forked over more than $600 to a particular person for services rendered — for example, your attorney or graphic designer — you must send that person a 1099 form. Ask your tax consultant for more information.

If your Etsy shop earns a profit — that is, its gross income is higher than the deductions that you claim for it — in any three of five consecutive years, it's officially a "for-profit" business in the eyes of the IRS. That status means you're free to deduct away! Otherwise, the IRS places severe limitations on what expenses you can deduct. Put another way: Don't deduct the supplies that merely feed your craft addiction but don't support a business. The IRS will notice if your deductions dwarf your income. Avoid waving the proverbial red flag by ensuring a reasonable balance!

Recording Artist: Keeping Accurate Records

Yes, we know. Record-keeping is for squares. But if you want to avoid getting sideways with the IRS — not to mention stay on top of your business — you'll want to be scrupulous about your record-keeping, however tedious it may be. Keep careful track of all your sales and expenses. And keep all receipts — even the little ones. All those road tolls and parking fees add up! You'll also want to hang on to invoices, bank statements, and any other financial-type documents that cross your desk.

It's smart to put all this information in one place. An accordion file is a good way to go; it enables you to separate your receipts and other documents by month or by category. Another approach is to use a digital solution, such as QuickBooks (http://quickbooks.intuit.com), Outright (www.outright.com), or even a simple Microsoft Excel spreadsheet; all three are great for keeping track of your sales and expenses.

Separation anxiety: Separating your personal and business finances

Especially if you plan to grow your Etsy business into a full-time operation, do yourself a favor: Open a business bank account for your Etsy shop, preferably with a credit or debit card. Then use that account to handle all expenses related to your Etsy shop. At tax time, you won't have to cull your business transactions from your personal ones to report your business expenses. Plus, if you ever need to verify your income — say, if you're taking out a loan to make a major purchase — you'll be able to provide the lending authority with everything it needs. Depending on your location, you may need to show your business license to open a business account with your bank. (You find out more about business licenses later in this chapter.)

To make it easier for you to manage your shop, Etsy enables you to download sales data in comma-separated value (CSV) form and save it on your hard drive. You can then view this data by opening the CSV file in a spreadsheet program such as Excel. To download this data, follow these steps:

1. **Hover your mouse pointer over the Your Shop link that appears along the top of every Etsy page and choose Sold Orders from the list that appears.**

   The Open Orders page appears.

2. **Click the Download a CSV File link at the bottom of the page to initiate the download.**

   The Download Shop Data screen appears.

3. **To download a CSV containing all listings currently for sale, click the Download CSV button under Currently for Sale Listings and follow the onscreen prompts to save the file to your hard drive. (The steps differ by operating system.)**

   To download a CSV with order information, click the CSV Type drop-down list and choose Order Item, Order, or Direct Checkout Payments; select the desired month and year; click Download CSV; and follow the onscreen prompts.

You can also download your monthly Etsy bill in CSV format. Hover your mouse pointer over the Your Shop link that appears along the top of every Etsy page and choose Your Bill from the list that appears. On the Your Etsy Bill page, click the desired month; then click the Download This Entire

Monthly Statement as a CSV File link at the bottom of the page that appears and follow the onscreen prompts.

You'll also want to keep an eye on your inventory as part of your record-keeping so that you don't run low. One approach may be "one out, one in" — that is, as soon as you sell an item, you make and list a new one.

Need a little help on the record-keeping side? Check out Stitch Labs. This tool helps you manage everything from inventory, orders, and expenses to contacts and statistics, all in one place. It will even renew sold items for you on Etsy! (Sadly, however, it will not fetch your coffee.) For more info, visit www. stitchlabs.com.

Don't Be a Tool: Using Etsy Tools to Manage Your Shop

Anthropologists used to say that tool use differentiated humans from other animals — until a few observant researchers spotted chimpanzees modifying sticks and using them to fish termites from holes in the ground. Tool use does, however, differentiate the serious Etsy sellers from other shop owners on the site — specifically, the use of Etsy tools to manage a shop. This section covers a few of Etsy's more popular termite-fisher-outers.

We need those numbers, stat! Viewing Shop Stats

Ever wonder how many people have visited your Etsy shop? Or what keywords they used to find an item in your store? Or what page they were on before they landed on your doorstep? (This last one is helpful for determining whether that ad you placed on that blog is actually directing readers to your Etsy shop like it's supposed to.) Thanks to Etsy Shop Stats, you can find out. You can also use Etsy's Shop Stats tool to assess your sales activity at a glance. This tool offers you a great way to quickly digest whether sales in your shop are up, down, or steady. To access the tool, follow these steps:

1. **Hover your mouse pointer over the Your Shop button that appears along the top of every Etsy page and click Shop Stats in the menu that appears.**

   The Shop Stats page opens.

2. **Click the Stats For drop-down list and choose the desired time period — for example, Last 7 Days, Last 12 Months, or what have you (see Figure 18-4).**

Figure 18-4:
Checking your shop sales stats is a cinch.

As you can see, this screen boasts a plethora of information, in text and graph form:

- ✔ **The number of views:** This helps you gauge how well the tags and key-words in your title are working for you.

- ✔ **The number of people who have favorited your shop:** This helps you determine how well your brand is working for you — that is, whether your entire shop is so compelling that someone would want to favorite it.

- ✔ **The number of orders received:** This can help you track order fluctua-tions — by day, by week, and by month — which is useful in planning. With this information, you know when your high and low cycles are, so you can plan for them (for example, ordering supplies before they get critically low).

- ✔ **The amount of revenue generated:** This can help you determine how well you're meeting your income goals.

- ✔ **Sources of shop traffic:** This offers a gauge of how well your marketing efforts are working. With this info, you can figure out whether you need to focus more on getting found within Etsy — for example, by springing for Etsy Search ads — becoming more active on Pinterest, or what have you.

- ✔ **Sources of shop traffic from within Etsy:** Use this info to determine how well you're represented on Etsy. You may discover that you need to put a bit more emphasis on improving your results with Etsy Search or other Etsy tools.

- ✔ **Keywords used on Etsy, Google, and other search sites to find your shop:** This is a great place to find new keywords to use in your product titles and descriptions, not to mention find new tags for your items.

- ✔ **Specific shop pages viewed and listing favorites:** Both of these are a gauge of which items in your shop are the most popular. You can use this to inform new designs.

The Shop Stats page can also help you gauge the success of any Etsy Search Ads you may have running, including the amount spent on Search Ads, the number of impressions your ad has received, the number of times your list-ing page was viewed from your ad, the number of times your items have been favorited from an ad, the number of orders resulting from ads, and the rev-enue generated from ads.

Oh, one more thing: You may notice a Web Analytics tab in the Options page, which you access by clicking Options in the Shop Settings section of Your Shop. This is for shop owners with a Google Analytics account. We don't go into that here, because Etsy's Shop Stats are pretty effective on their own. But if you're interested in Google Analytics, read this Etsy Help article: www. etsy.com/help/article/230.

Statistically speaking: Viewing Customer Service Stats

In addition to viewing Shop Stats, you can view Customer Service Stats, Doing so will help you get a handle on areas where your customer-service skills excel — and which areas need a little work. To access your Customer Service stats, hover your mouse pointer over the Your Shop button that appears along the top of every Etsy page and click Customer Service Stats in the menu that appears.

These stats, which are based on the last 60 calendar days of your shop's activity, cover the following:

- ✔ **Response time to buyer conversations:** Etsy suggests that you respond to any convos initiated by buyers from your listings, your shop, a purchases page, or a receipt page within one business day. This stat indicates whether, on average, you meet this benchmark.

- ✔ **Providing processing times:** This stat reflects the percentage of active listings in your shop for which processing times have been set. Setting a processing time helps to manage your buyers' expectations when it comes to how long it will take you to ship their items. You can set a processing time when you create or edit a listing, or by clicking the Provide Processing Times link on the Customer Service Stats page.

- ✔ **Meeting processing times:** Of course, it's not enough to set a processing time. You must also to meet it. This stat reflects whether, on average, you ship within one day of the processing times you set.

- ✔ **Marking items as shipped:** Marking items as shipped helps you to keep track of whether you're meeting your processing times; it also lets buyers know their goodies are on the way. This stat indicates how frequently you mark items as shipped, measured as a percentage. (Note that if you use Etsy to print shipping labels, items are marked as shipped automatically.)

- ✔ **Providing tracking information:** Etsy is a fan of providing tracking numbers for buyers to help keep them informed and to help you avoid being hit with a non-delivery case. Using this stat, you can gauge how frequently you offer this service, in percentage form.

An app a day: Using Etsy apps to run your store

Need some extra help running your Etsy shop? Try installing some Etsy applications, or *apps,* for short. Apps are available to handle all manner of jobs: minimizing the hassle of international shipping (ATS International Shipping), managing your inventory (RunInventory), handling taxes (TaxTime), renewing listings (Clockbot), and more.

Third-party vendors develop most apps. That's a techy way of saying that although you can access the apps from Etsy's website, for the most part, Etsy didn't build them. And *that's* a polite way of saying that if you have a problem with an app, don't bug Etsy about it; bug the company that actually *made* the app.

You can find out what apps are available by browsing the App Gallery. To access it, click the Your Shop link that appears along the top of any Etsy page. Then, on the left side of the page, under Resources, click the Etsy Apps link. Finally, to view shop-related apps, click the Shop Tools link on the left side of the page (see Figure 18-5).

To find out more about an app, click the app's link. To download it, click the Visit website button that appears on the app's page (see Figure 18-6) and follow the onscreen instructions. (We'd walk you through the process, but the precise steps vary by app.)

Figure 18-5: The Etsy App Gallery.

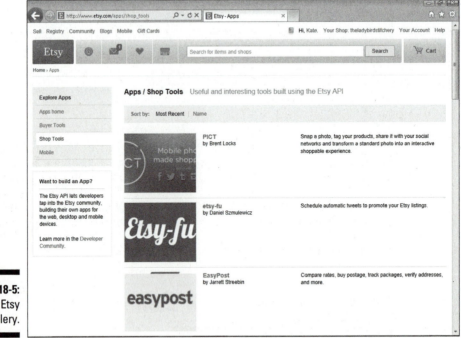

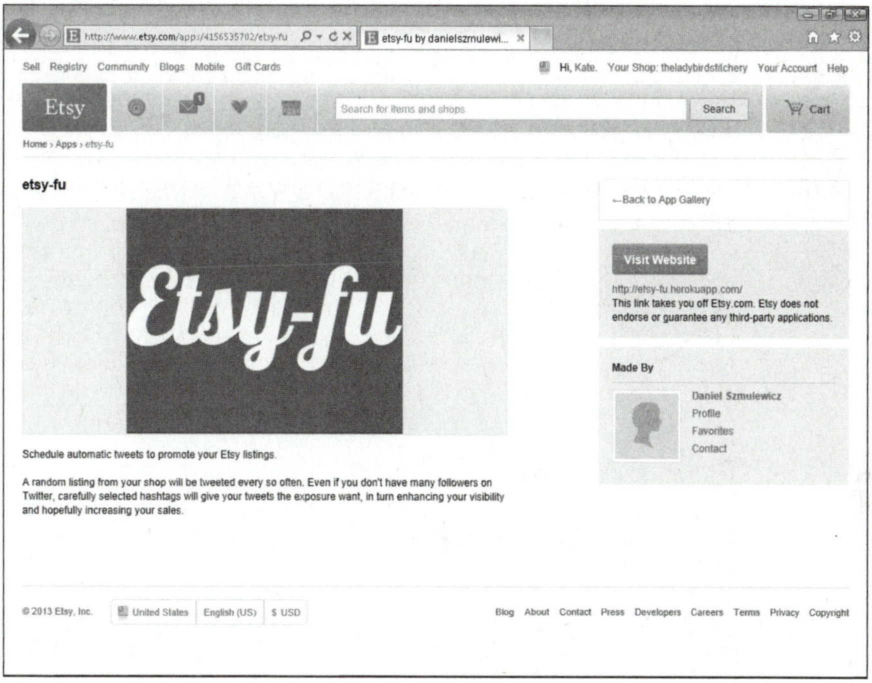

Figure 18-6:
Download
an Etsy app.

Too Legit to Quit: Making Your Business Legit

If you're starting your Etsy shop as a hobby, you probably haven't given much thought to the structure of your Etsy business. It's just you, making stuff and putting it up for sale on Etsy. But if your Etsy shop has grown into a full-time operation — or if you want it to — you'll need to consider what business structure is best for you. The structure that you choose affects both your personal liability if your business is sued and the taxes you have to pay.

You have a few main options:

- ✔ Sole proprietorship
- ✔ General partnership
- ✔ Limited liability company (LLC)
- ✔ Corporation

So how do you decide what type of business structure is right for you? That's an excellent question — and one that you want to direct to a lawyer or accountant. Also, be sure to seek the help of a lawyer or accountant when it comes to actually setting up your company, because the precise steps for doing so differ depending on where you live.

Depending on your location, you may be required to obtain a business license to operate your Etsy shop in an aboveboard manner. You may also need a business license to open a business checking account. For information about business license requirements in your area, visit `www.sba.gov/local resources`.

O sole mio: Understanding sole proprietorships

If you're just starting out with your Etsy business, odds are, you're running a sole proprietorship sort of by default. That is, you own your business out-right and you're solely responsible for all decisions and debts that pertain to it. This type of business is by far the easiest to start, but it's also the riskiest type to run. Why? Because you're held personally accountable if something goes wrong. For example, if someone using your product becomes sick or injured, that person could sue you, personally, placing your assets (and any assets that you hold jointly with a spouse) at risk. You're also personally accountable for any debt that the business assumes.

Grab your partner, do-sell-do! Getting a handle on partnerships

A general partnership consists of two or more co-owners. Typically, the parties in a general partnership split the profits from the business equally, although that's not always the case. For example, if you and your friend go into business together, but you invest more in startup costs, you may agree to a different split of the profits — say, 60/40. General partnerships are simi-lar to sole proprietorships, in that you and your partner(s) are personally responsible for any debt that the business incurs.

In addition to general partnerships, limited partnerships exist. In that case, one partner contributes funds and shares in profits but assumes no role in the workings of the company.

Collective soul: Checking out Etsy collectives

On Etsy, a shop run by multiple peeps is called a *collective.* A collective may consist of two or more friends or, say, members of a particular Etsy team. A collective may be a collaboration, in which you and your partner combine skills to make and list items in your Etsy shop — for example, you spin yarn, and your partner knits it into scarves. Alternatively, you may set up a collective so that you and your partner can make your own pieces but sell them from the same storefront. Yet another type of collective is one in which you act as the artist but a partner handles shop-management tasks, such as listing or shipping items.

If you go the collective route, you need to know a few rules:

✔ The About page for the collective's shop must list each person in the collective, each person's role in the shop, and each person's relationship to other members of the collective.

✔ The person who creates the Etsy account for the collective is responsible for all account-related activities, including paying the account's Etsy bill. That is, Etsy can't split responsibility for the bill (or other transactions) between partners. This person is also responsible for any action taken under the banner of that account in the Etsy forums and teams.

✔ If you and your partner have a falling-out about the account, Etsy can't mediate your dispute.

Although running your Etsy shop with a partner can be a great way to grow your business on the double, it can also double your headaches. Be sure to weigh the benefits of running your shop in tandem with someone else (an extra set of hands to build your inventory and an extra set of gray matter to bounce ideas off) with the drawbacks (profit sharing and potential conflicts). Choosing your partner carefully goes a long way toward minimizing problems. Although it may be tempting to leap into a collective with a friend or family member, be aware that doing so may strain the relationship. Be absolutely certain that you and your prospective partner share the same vision and work ethic, and that your relationship is strong enough to endure any bumps along the way.

LLC Cool J: Looking at limited liability companies

A popular choice for many business owners, a limited liability company (LLC) is a sort of hybrid between a partnership and a corporation (see the following section). It's a popular choice for business owners because an LLC not only limits your liability for business debt, but also allows you to choose whether you want to be treated as a partnership or as a corporation, depending on which has the lower tax burden.

Go corporate: Considering corporations

A corporation is a legal entity all its own, separate from its founders (you), managers, and employees, and owned by its shareholders (again, you, along with anyone else you decide to bring into the fold). Operating as a corporation means, among other things, that your personal assets are protected in case the company is sued.

Two types of corporations exist: C-corporations and S-corporations. Although C-corporations provide the most financial protection to shareholders and offer other advantages, many small businesses go the S-corporation route because they're cheaper to start and easier to maintain.

To avoid running afoul of the IRS, speak to your accountant in detail about how to deal with profits if you opt to form a corporation.

Sweet Charity: Handling Charitable Giving

Some kindly Etsy sellers use their shops as fundraising vehicles — for example, donating proceeds from certain listings to a particular charity or even devoting an entire shop to a cause. However, due to the fact that fundraising is subject to many laws, and also that the occasional bad apple may confuse "charity" with "larceny," Etsy has established strict policies on charitable listings and shops. Members who fail to comply are subject to suspension of account privileges and/or termination (of their account, not their corporeal existence).

Here are the high points of Etsy's policies on charitable giving:

✔ All charitable fundraising that occurs on Etsy must comply with applicable laws.

✔ Any seller who promotes the fact that that his Etsy shop engages in charitable fundraising on behalf of a recognized tax-deductible charitable organization must receive appropriate consent from the charitable organization.

✔ The seller must include clear information about the charitable organization in question, as well as donation details, in the listing and/or other public area of the shop.

✔ No fair generating listings solely to solicit donations. All listings must be for a tangible item available for sale.

✔ Sending unsolicited donation requests to other Etsy users via convos or in the forums is verboten.

The Artist Is Out: Switching to Vacation Mode

Although many people don't take nearly enough vacations, it's a well-known fact that they're as good for you as Brussels sprouts. Vacations do more than help you rest and relieve stress; they promote creativity — which is pretty important when the success of your Etsy shop depends a great deal on your ability to be creative!

Of course, the key to getting the most out of any vacation is being able to put aside your work while you're away. Fortunately, Etsy enables you to put your Etsy shop in vacation mode. When your shop is in vacation mode, your listings aren't visible to anyone who visits your shop. In addition, you can add a special vacation mode notice, to appear along the top of your shop page. Anyone who attempts to convo you receives an auto reply containing the text that you specify.

It's not a bad idea to put your shop in vacation mode a day or two before you leave. That way, you have time to handle all your orders before you depart. You may also leave your shop in vacation mode for a day or two after you get back so that you can ease into things.

You don't have to actually be "on vacation" to put your shop in vacation mode. You can use this feature any time you need a break from your Etsy shop.

To put your shop in vacation mode, follow these steps:

1. **Click the Your Shop button that appears along the top of every Etsy page.**

2. **Under Shop Settings on the left side of the page, click the Options link.**

3. **Click the Vacation Mode tab.**

   The Vacation Mode page opens (see Figure 18-7).

4. **Click the On Your Shop Is On Vacation option button under Vacation Mode.**

5. **Type the desired text — how long you'll be away, when you'll be back, and so on — in the Vacation Announcement field.**

   This text replaces your shop announcement.

6. **In the Conversation Auto-Reply field, type the message that you want prospective customers to receive if they convo you while you're away.**

7. **Click the Save button.**

   Etsy puts your shop in vacation mode.

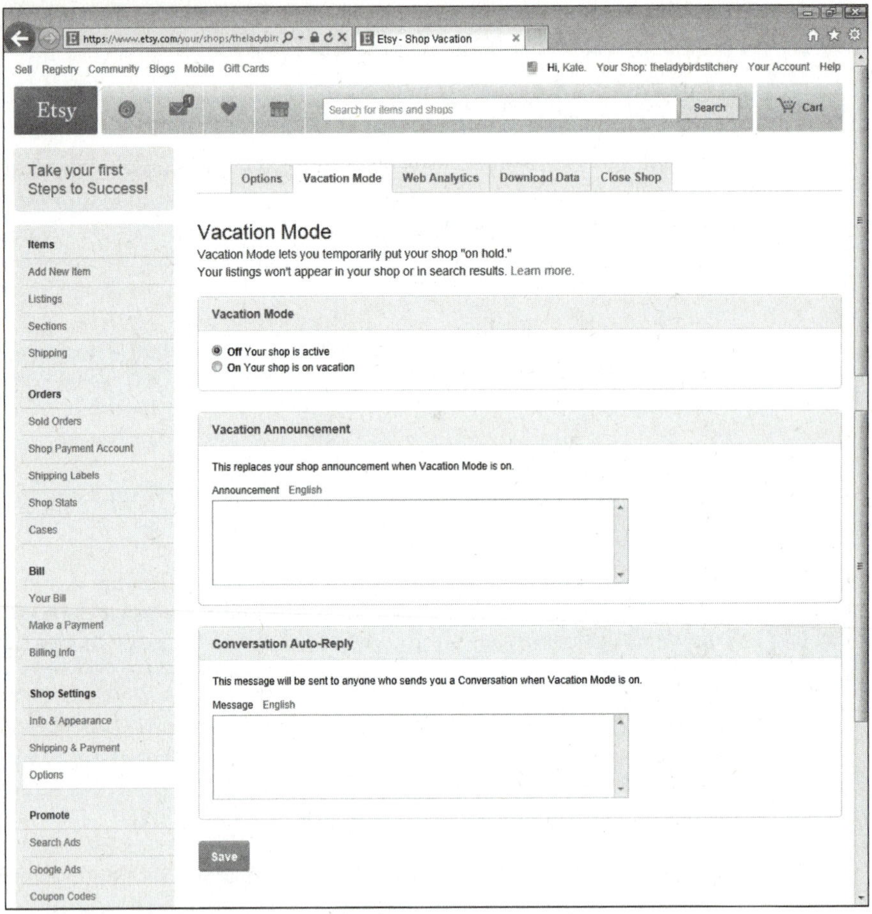

Figure 18-7:
Put your
shop in
vacation
mode any
time you
need a
break.

 It doesn't hurt to add a special "on vacation" shop banner to your shop anytime you put it in vacation mode. For help with swapping out your shop banner, refer to Chapter 8.

Hanging It Up: Closing Your Etsy Shop

If — God forbid — you decide that running an Etsy shop just isn't for you, you can close your Etsy shop (assuming you've closed all unresolved cases and paid any overdue fees). When you close your shop, your shop and listings will no longer appear on Etsy. If someone tries to view your shop, she will be redirected to your profile. Anyone who attempts to view a listing from your shop will see a "Page Not Found" error.

To close your shop, follow these steps:

1. **Click the Your Shop button that appears along the top of every Etsy page.**

2. **Under Shop Settings on the left side of the page, click the Options link.**

3. **Click the Close Shop tab.**

   The Close Your Shop page opens (see Figure 18-8).

4. **Click the Close Shop button.**

   Etsy prompts you to confirm the closure.

5. **Click the Close Shop button again.**

   Etsy closes your shop. (Note that it may take 30 minutes or so for your request to be processed.) Your Etsy account will now be for buying only.

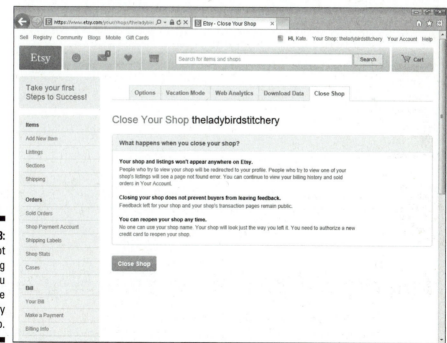

Figure 18-8:
Things not working out? You can close your Etsy shop.

If — hallelujah! — you later change your mind and want to reopen your shop, you can easily do so. Simply hover your mouse button over the Your Account link found along the top of every Etsy page and choose Re-open Shop. Etsy will prompt you to re-enter your billing info and will re-validate your credit card before re-opening your shop. (Again, it may be a half-hour or so before your request is processed.)

Part V

Commune System: Exploring the Etsy Community

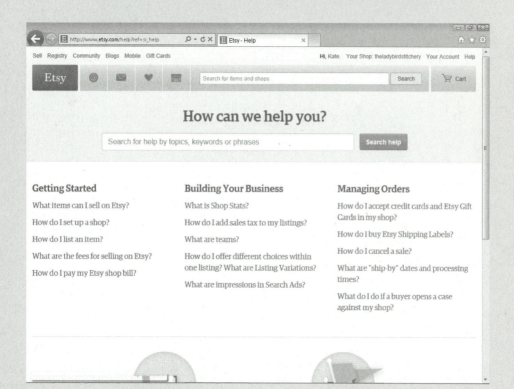

Find out what the Etsy Blog has to offer at www.dummies.com/extras/startinganetsybusiness.

In this part . . .

✔ Join the Etsy community and learn from and laugh with your fellow Etsians.

✔ Keep up with Etsy news so you're up to date on all the latest features.

✔ Show your love for other Etsy sellers and build up some good karma.

✔ Find out how to get help from Etsy when things go wrong.

Chapter 19

Community Building: Joining the Etsy Community

. . . .

In This Chapter

▶ Reaching out on forums

▶ Exploring Etsy teams

▶ Chatting with other Etsy members

▶ Learning in Etsy's Virtual Labs

▶ Minding your manners in the Etsy community

. . . .

Anyone who has spent more than 30 seconds on Etsy knows that it's a bang-up place to buy and sell gorgeous handmade and vintage pieces. But Etsy is more than just an amazing online marketplace; it's also a vibrant community of interesting, creative people. On Etsy, connections are created, friendships are formed, love matches are made, and lives are enriched. In this chapter, you discover how you can participate in this lively Etsy community.

Talk amongst Yourselves: Using Etsy Forums

The *Merriam-Webster Dictionary* defines *forum* as "a public meeting place for open discussion," derived from the marketplaces and public places found in ancient Roman cities across that great empire. Similarly, Etsy's forums serve as meeting places for Etsy members. In essence, Etsy forums are public message boards where members can discuss all manner of topics.

Etsy supports five main forums:

- ✔ **Announcements:** This forum is reserved for Etsy staff, for posting site-related announcements. Check this forum for news about upcoming site changes.

- ✔ **Site Help:** If you have general questions about how to use Etsy, questions about site features, or queries related to site policy, this forum is for you. Odds are, someone in the Etsy community or on the Etsy staff can — and will — answer your question!

- ✔ **Business Topics:** Are you looking for shop-related advice — for example, help running and marketing your Etsy shop, assistance with payment-related issues, info about shipping, or advice on navigating the ups and downs of running a small business? If so, visit the Business Topics forum.

- ✔ **Ideas:** Did you wake up at 3 a.m. with an idea that could revolutionize Etsy? Then post it in the Ideas forum. It acts like a suggestion box of sorts. You can also use this forum to discuss changes to the site or offer site-related constructive criticism.

- ✔ **Bugs:** If you come across some part of the site that's not working as intended, check the Bugs forum to see if anyone else has experienced the same glitch. If not, use the forum to report it.

In the following sections, we explain how to access these Etsy forums, view and respond to threads, and start your own thread.

None of Etsy's forums is meant to serve as a complaint desk. If you need to air a grievance, e-mail it to community@etsy.com.

Forum letter: Accessing Etsy forums

To participate on an Etsy forum, follow these steps:

1. **Click the Community link along the top of any Etsy page.**

   The Community page opens (see Figure 19-1).

2. **Click the Forums link on the left side of the page.**

   The Forums page opens (see Figure 19-2).

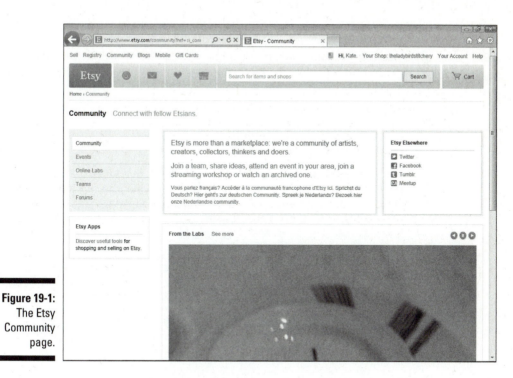

Figure 19-1:
The Etsy
Community
page.

3. **Click the title of the forum that you want to visit.**

   The forum page opens.

Postess with the mostess: Viewing and responding to posts in a thread

Notice that posts in any Etsy forum are divided into threads (Figure 19-3 shows threads in the Business Topics forum). You can view and respond to any thread you want. Here's how:

1. **Click a thread that interests you.**

   A page opens, showing the post that started the thread, along with any responses to that post (see Figure 19-4).

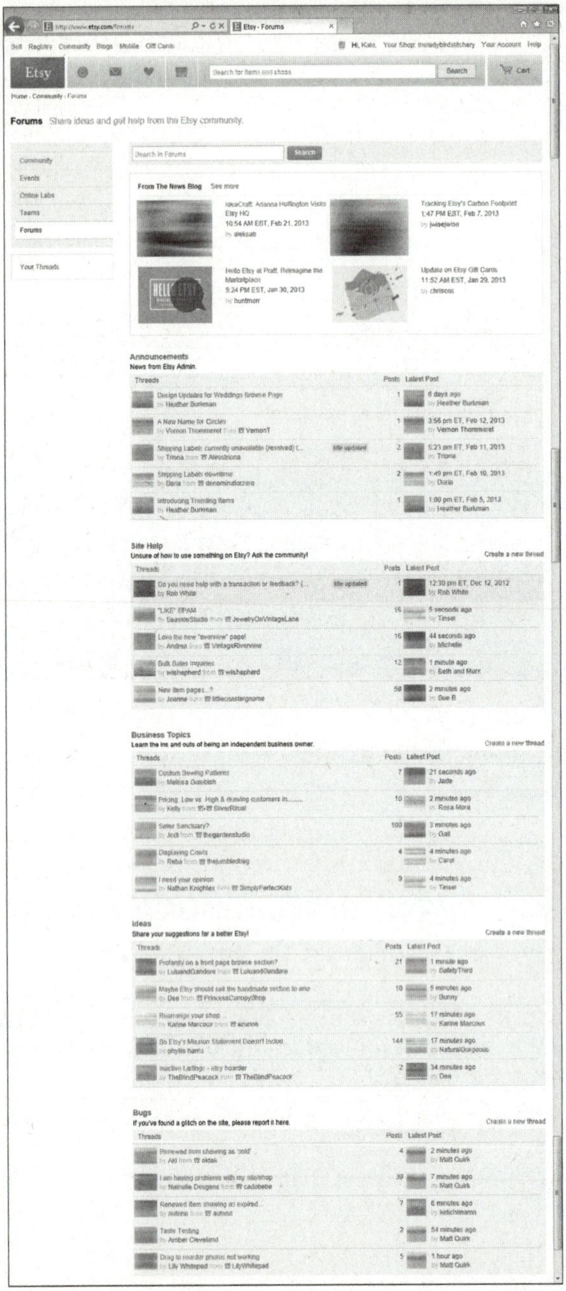

Figure 19-2: Etsy's forums are a great resource.

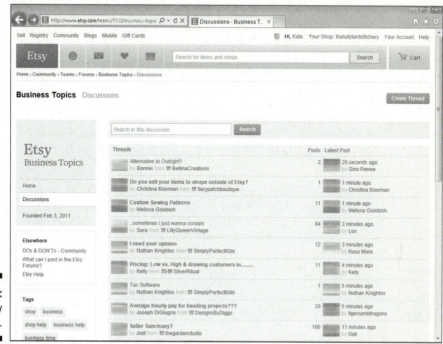

Figure 19-3:
An Etsy
forum.

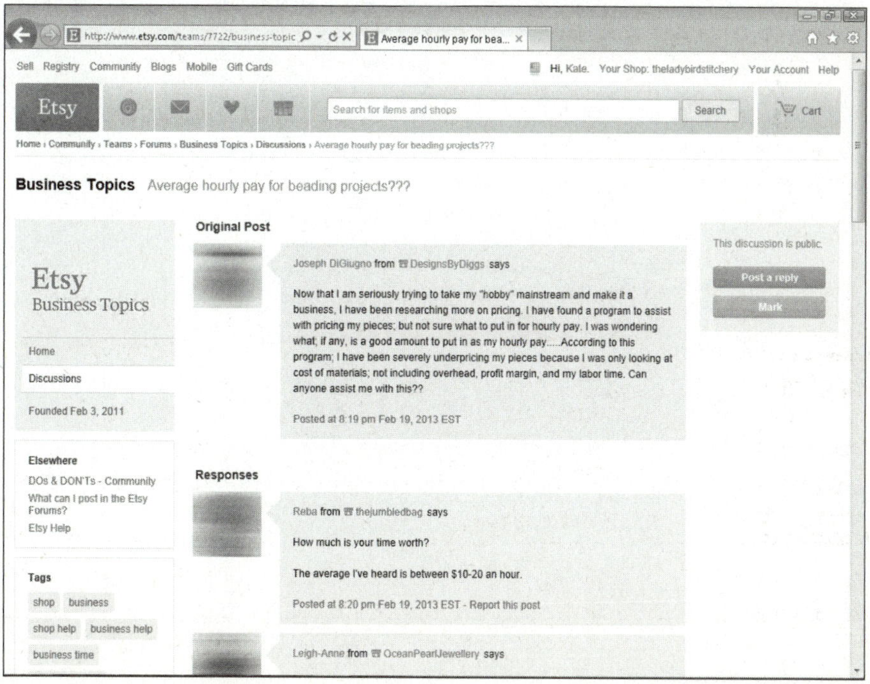

Figure 19-4:
An Etsy
thread.

2. **To respond to a post, either click the Post a Reply button at the top of the page or scroll down to the bottom of the page.**

   The Post a Reply box appears (see Figure 19-5).

3. **Type your reply and then click Post a Reply.**

   Your post appears at the end of the list of replies.

To view threads in which you've posted a reply, click the Your Threads link on the left side of any forum screen, click the Threads You've Posted In tab, and click the thread that you want to view (see Figure 19-6).

If you find a thread that's particularly interesting, you can mark it. That way, you can easily keep track of new posts in that thread. To mark a thread, open the thread and click the Mark button (refer to Figure 19-4). To view threads that you've marked, click the Your Threads link on the left side of any forum screen, click the Marked Threads tab, and click the thread that you want to view.

Before you reply to a thread in an Etsy forum or start a new thread of your own (see the next section), be sure that your post doesn't violate Etsy etiquette (which we discuss later in this chapter).

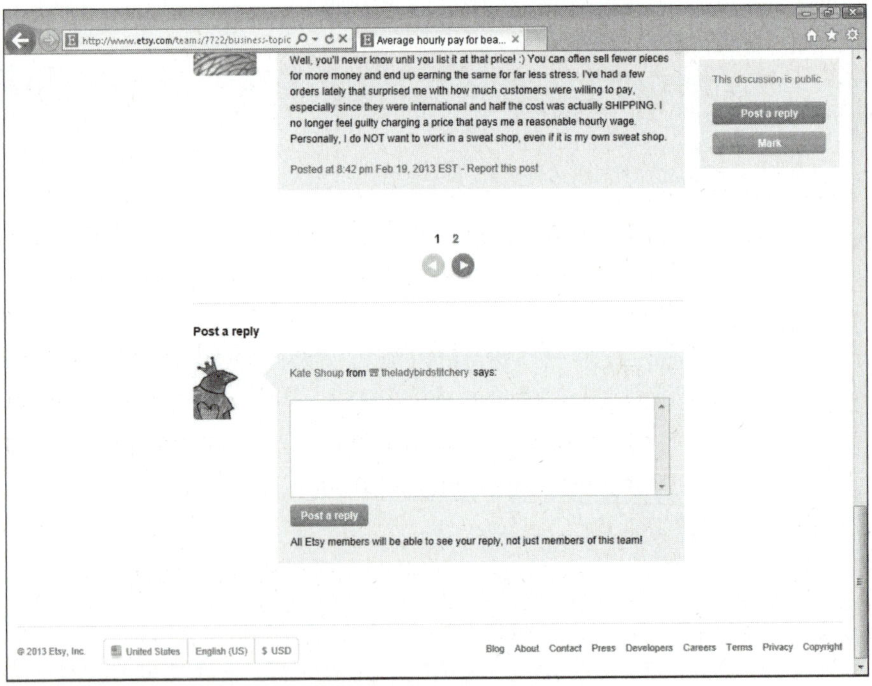

Figure 19-5:
Reply to a
post.

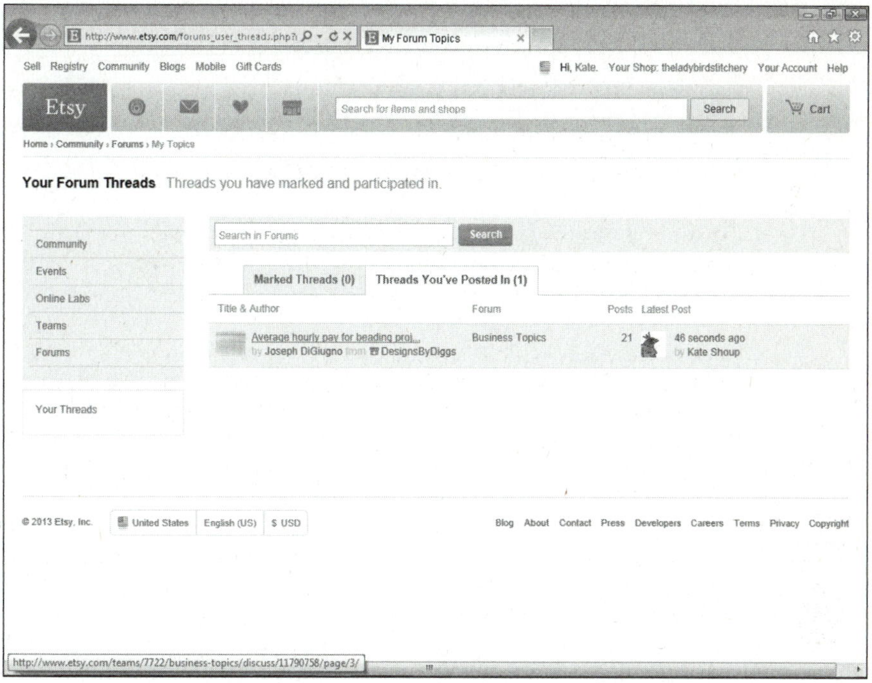

Figure 19-6:
View your
forum
threads.

Thread Zeppelin: Starting a new thread

In addition to responding to posts in threads that others have started, you can start your own new thread. Here's the drill:

1. **Click the title of the forum in which you want to create a new thread.**

2. **Click the Create Thread button in the upper-right corner of the forum page.**

   The Create a New Thread page opens (see Figure 19-7).

3. **Type a descriptive, relevant title for your thread in the Title field.**

   For best results, type your whole question into the Title field (if it fits).

4. **Type your post in the Post field.**

5. **Click the Create Topic button.**

   Etsy creates a new thread, with your post at the top.

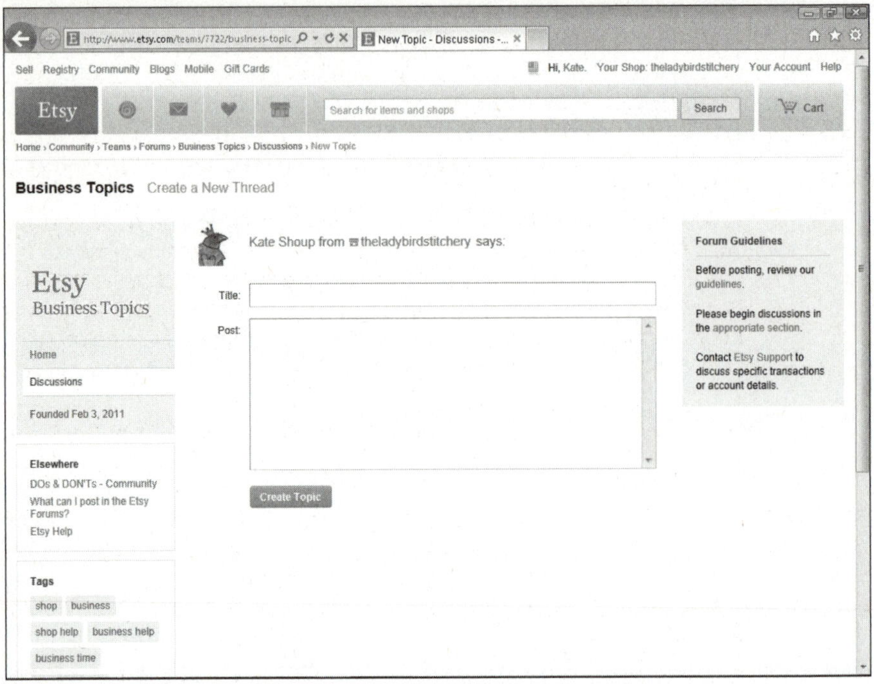

Figure 19-7:
Create a
new thread
in a forum.

When you start a new thread, be sure to start it in the correct forum. For example, don't start a thread asking for advice about your Etsy shop in, say, the Site Help forum. That discussion belongs in the Business Topics forum. Be aware that if you do start a thread in the wrong forum, Etsy may move it to the appropriate forum without notice.

Before you start a new thread, try searching for existing threads that cover your topic of interest. To do so, open the main Forums page, type a relevant keyword or phrase in the Search field in the header bar, and click the Search button. Etsy searches existing forum threads for the keyword or phrase that you entered and displays a list of matches.

Go Team! Exploring Etsy Teams

Etsy's forums are splendid — if your area of interest is announcements, site help, business topics, ideas, or bugs. But what if you're itching to explore some other topic? Say, product photography, quilting, Bauhaus style, or even a charitable cause? Or maybe you just want to connect with other Etsy members in your geographic area. In that case, Etsy's teams are for you.

Etsy teams act a lot like Etsy forums. People start discussion threads, and others add their two cents. The difference? With teams, you must join to participate. Although non–team members may be able to view posts in a team — when team members start new threads, they specify whether those threads are public (visible to anyone on Etsy) or private (visible to team members only) — they can't respond to those posts or start new threads of their own.

In addition, each Etsy team has its own captain (usually the person who started the team), who may appoint other members as "leaders." The team captain and team leaders are responsible for administering the team — that is, approving membership applications (some teams are open to any and all Etsy members; others require that you apply), moderating the team's discussion forum, and so on.

In the following sections, we show you how to search for a team, join a team, and start your own team.

Finders, keepers: Searching for an Etsy team

Literally thousands of Etsy teams exist, so you can surely find one for you. For example, you could join a team based on the type of items you sell, your particular interests, or your geographic location. To find a team, log in to your Etsy account and follow these steps:

1. **Click the Community link along the top of any Etsy page.**

   The Community page opens (refer to Figure 19-1).

2. **Click the Teams link on the left side of the page.**

   The Teams page opens (see Figure 19-8).

3. **Type a keyword in the Search box and click the Search button.**

   Etsy searches teams for the keyword that you entered and displays a list of matches (see Figure 19-9). You can sort your matches by Relevancy, Most Recent, and Least Recent by clicking the appropriate link at the top of the list.

4. **Click a team in the list of matches to learn more about it.**

   The team's page opens (see Figure 19-10). The team's page includes information about the team and who's eligible to join; a Discussions area, which lists recent threads (click the Discussions link to view more); and a sampling of team members (refer to Figure 19-10).

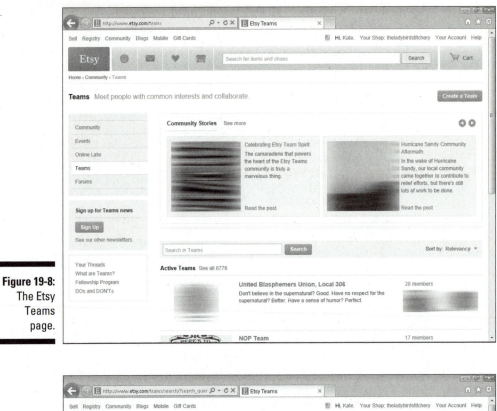

Figure 19-8:
The Etsy
Teams
page.

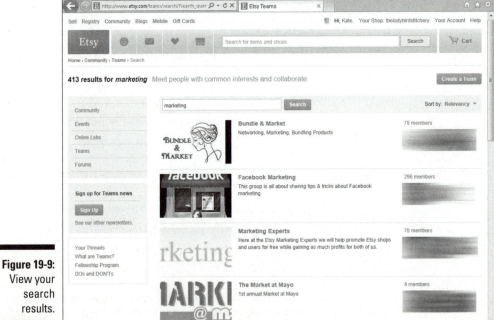

Figure 19-9:
View your
search
results.

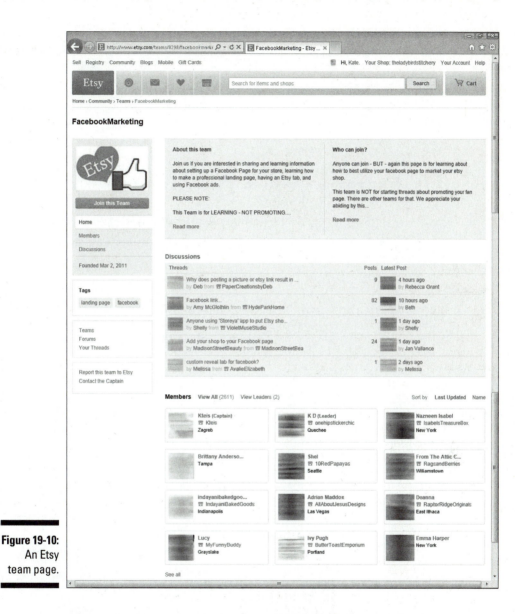

Figure 19-10:
An Etsy
team page.

Sign me up! Joining an Etsy team

As mentioned, some teams are open to any and all Etsy members. Others are moderated, meaning that they limit their membership based on certain criteria.

To join a team that's open to all, simply click the Join This Team button that appears in the top-left corner of the team's page (refer to Figure 19-10). Then, when prompted, click Join This Team again. A welcome message appears at the top of the team page, and your avatar appears in the list of team members. The team that you joined also appears near the top of your main Teams page (see Figure 19-11).

Joining a team that restricts membership, called a *moderated team,* is a bit more involved. Instead of simply clicking a button, you must apply for membership, which sometimes means jumping through a few hoops. To join a moderated team, follow these steps:

1. **Click the Apply to Team button in the top-left corner of the team's page (see Figure 19-12).**

   An Apply to Team dialog box appears (see Figure 19-13).

2. **Read the information in the dialog box and answer any questions in the field at the bottom.**

3. **Click the Apply to Team button to apply.**

Assuming that you meet the membership criteria, as determined by the team captain and laid out in the team charter, you'll likely be accepted — although the team leadership may deny membership at its discretion. Either way, after the team makes a decision, it'll notify you via e-mail.

When you become a member of a team, you can view and respond to posts in existing threads and create new threads, as described earlier in this chapter.

You can also opt to subscribe to team digest e-mails, which contain a summary of the team's most recent discussion activity. That way, you can keep track of the team's goings-on without having to log in to Etsy first. To subscribe to a team's digest e-mail, simply click the Subscribe to Email Digest link on the left side of the team's main page once you become a member. Then, when prompted, click the Subscribe button. (You'll have to do this for each team individually.) To unsubscribe, simply click the Unsubscribe from Digest link that appears on the team's main page when you subscribe.

Start me up: Starting your own Etsy team

If you don't find a team that meets your needs, you can start one of your own. For example, you may want to start a team for other Etsy members who share your passion for your medium, who live in your geographic area, who are devoted to a particular style of design, who share similar goals with their Etsy shops, or what have you. Note that when you create a team, you automatically become its captain, so administrative duties fall to you (unless you delegate them to other members).

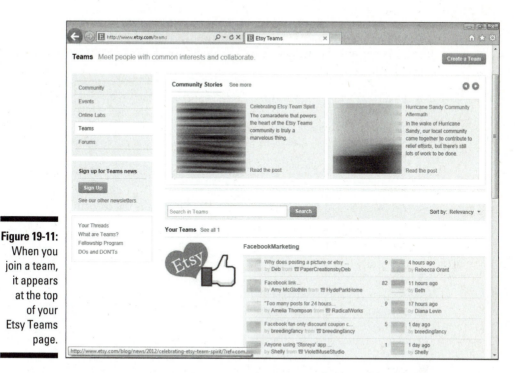

http://www.etsy.com/blog/news/2012/celebrating-etsy-team-spirit/?ref=com...

Figure 19-11:
When you join a team, it appears at the top of your Etsy Teams page.

Figure 19-12:
Click the Apply to Team button.

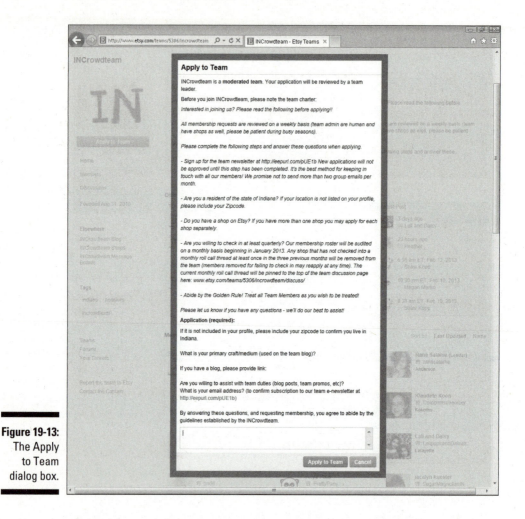

Figure 19-13:
The Apply
to Team
dialog box.

To create a team, click the Create a Team button in the top-right corner of the main Etsy Teams page (refer to Figure 19-8). Etsy prompts you to enter the team details (see Figure 19-14):

✔ The name and team type

✔ A short description and (optionally) a long description

✔ Rules about team access and (optionally) who can join

✔ Application questions (if needed)

✔ The team's logo

✔ Tags to describe your shop (check out the sidebar "Tag, you're it! Tagging your Etsy team" for details on tags)

✔ Related links (for example, you may include a link to your own personal website or to some other relevant page online)

After you fill in the requested information, click Create Team.

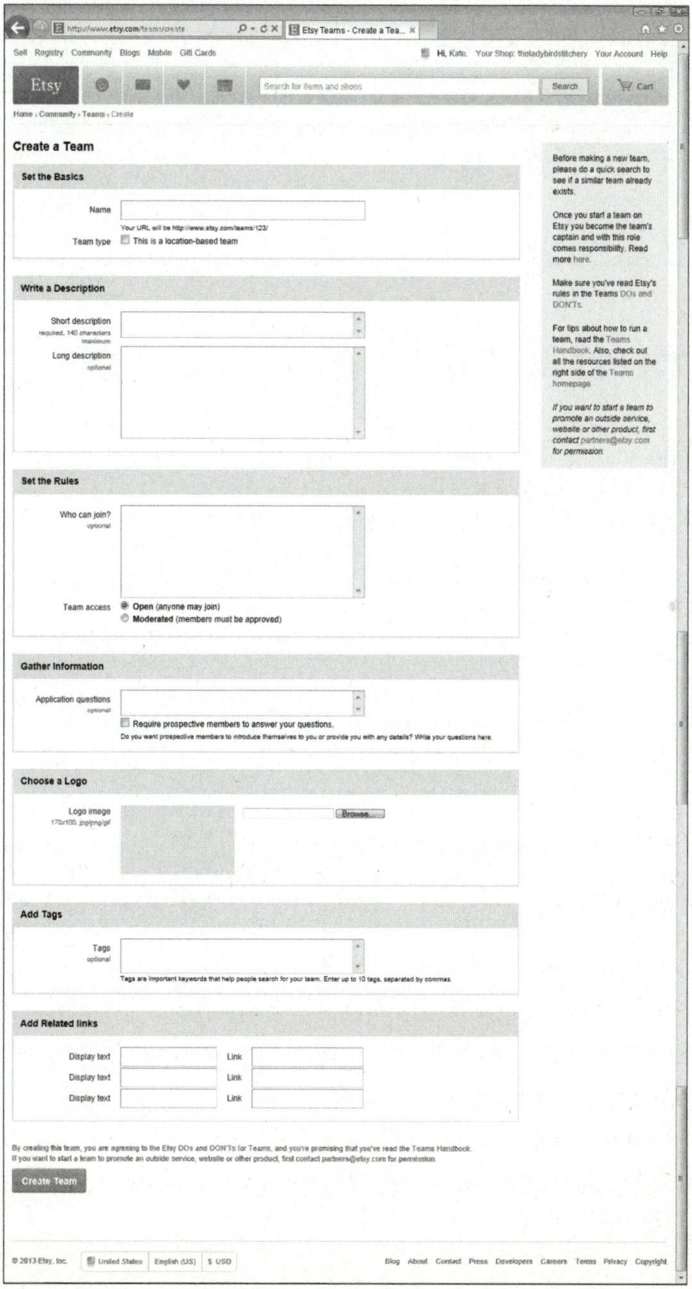

Figure 19-14:
Create a
new team.

Tag, you're it! Tagging your Etsy team

When you create your team, you're prompted to enter tags that describe it — for example, where your team is based, the focus of your team, and so on. These tags act a lot like the tags that you add to your item listings (see Chapter 12): When someone searching for a team enters keywords that match your tags, your team appears among the matches.

Note that the tags you enter to describe your Etsy team are different from what Etsy calls *team tags*. A team tag is a tag that team members use to tag their item listings, to identify themselves and their listing as being affiliated with a particular Etsy team. These tags must be unique terms — say, your team's name — and must contain the word *team* in them. When you create a team, you can establish a team tag for it, noting it in the team's description.

Lab Partner: Exploring Etsy's Online Labs

Etsy's Community section features a special page with Online Labs — essentially, videos in which Etsy staffers and members share vital info such as crafting how-to's, seller tips, and other educational tidbits. To access these Online Labs, open the main Etsy Community page (refer to Figure 19-1); then click the Online Labs link on the left side of the page. The Online Labs page opens. On this page, you can view existing Online Labs in the video library and see upcoming events. These events are largely informational in nature. Most are about selling on Etsy, but some cover craft how to's or other topics. They may be in various formats, such as a presentation held at Etsy HQ or a conversation between an Etsy Admin and an "expert" in a particular topic or between Etsy Admin and shop owners. In general, these events are a great way to further your Etsy education!

To view an existing Online Lab video, click one of the several categories that appears under the Video Library heading. These vary depending on what events have gone down but might include Etsy Success, Etsy How-To, Etsy Code as Craft, Hello Etsy, Etsy Teams, and more. Then click a video you want to watch. Etsy plays back the video in the main Online Labs window.

To participate in an Online Labs event, simply visit the Online Labs page at the event's scheduled time. (Upcoming events are listed on the Online Labs page, as well as on the Events page, discussed in the next section.) Online Labs events are interactive, meaning you can ask questions by typing them in the box below the streaming video. You can also use the box on the right side of the screen to chat with other participants.

Although you're not required to do so, you can RSVP to upcoming events. When you do (by clicking the event's RSVP Now button), Etsy will send you an e-mail reminder about the event 15 minutes before it starts.

Event Horizon: Staying Apprised of Etsy Events

Etsy does more than host virtual gatherings; it also organizes real-world events, such as craft- and business-related gatherings at its Brooklyn-based offices. It also hosts and/or sponsors craft- and business-related summits at various locations worldwide. To stay apprised of Etsy events, click the Events link on the Community page; the Events page opens (see Figure 19-15). (Note that in addition to listing real-world events, this page lists Online Labs events.) To see information about an event listed on the Events page, simply click its Learn More button (see Figure 19-16).

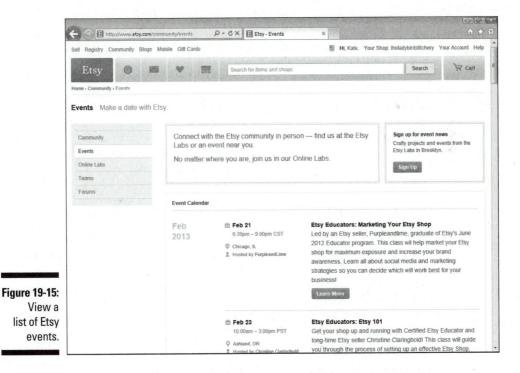

Figure 19-15:
View a list of Etsy events.

Figure 19-16:
Click an
event to find
out more
about it.

Miss Manners: Respecting Community Etiquette

When it comes to interacting with the Etsy community — for example, in the forums or within a team — some important ground rules apply. Etsy's DOs & DON'Ts spell out these rules in detail (see www.etsy.com/help/article/483). If you violate any of these rules, Etsy may take action, ranging from removing your post or closing your thread to booting you from the site entirely.

Chief among these rules is this: For Pete's sake, *be nice*. It should go without saying that you need to treat all Etsy members with respect, but we're saying it anyway, just so there's no confusion. Also, never knowingly harass, insult, abuse, or otherwise dog another site user. Finally, don't "call out" an Etsy member, shop, or item — that is, discuss him, her, or it in a negative manner. (Duh.)

Beyond that, keep a few other points in mind as you mingle in the Etsy community (for a complete list, check out the aforementioned DOs & DON'Ts page):

- ✔ **Don't post angry.** Yes, discussions in Etsy's community spaces sometimes get testy. After all, the Etsy community consists of millions of passionate, creative types. But if you find yourself getting your dander up, step away from the keyboard. In the history of the world, no good ever came from firing off a message in anger! Besides, if you do, you'll likely violate the aforementioned "Be nice" rule.

- ✔ **Stay on topic.** Sure, tangents happen. But if the tangent intensifies to such a degree that it threatens to smother the main discussion, others interested in the "real" topic can't find the info they need. If you find yourself part of a discussion that's gone off the rails, consider starting a new thread to handle that tangential issue.

- ✔ **Protect your privacy.** Don't share private information of any type, such as your (or someone else's) e-mail address, phone number, address, or what have you, on Etsy's public spaces. Also, put the kibosh on public discussions about specific transactions or feedback that you've received. For help on those issues, contact Etsy support (support@ etsy.com).

- ✔ **Don't solicit.** Even if you're raising money for the best, most important charity on the planet, Etsy members are prohibited from trolling for donations or engaging in other types of fundraising on the Etsy teams and forums. Similarly, spamming Etsy teams and forums — that is, posting unsolicited advertisements — is prohibited.

Chapter 20

OMG, Did You Hear? Keeping Up with Etsy News

In This Chapter

▶ Checking out the Etsy Blog

▶ Subscribing to Etsy e-mails

▶ Following Etsy via social media

▶ Joining Etsy Prototypes

As big and active as Etsy is, staying abreast of all its goings-on can be as challenging as solving a Rubik's Cube during a blackout. Fortunately, Etsy maintains several news sources to help members stay on top of Etsy-related info, including a blog, multiple e-mail newsletters, and various social media pages. You can also stay on Etsy's cutting edge by joining Prototypes, which are special projects run by Etsy admin that explore using Etsy in different ways. In this chapter, you discover all the ways you can keep up with Etsy news.

All the News That's Fit to Print: Exploring Etsy Blogs

Maybe you're looking for tips to improve your Etsy shop. Or perhaps you want to explore a new craft medium. Or maybe you want a glimpse into the lives of other Etsy sellers. In any case, Etsy's blogs are for you. These blogs (there are various editions: Etsy Blog, Etsy News Blog, and Seller Handbook, plus international editions) act like community newspapers of sorts, serving up loads of fresh content daily. There's also a special Etsy Weddings Blog.

To access Etsy's blogs, simply hover your mouse pointer over the Blogs link that appears in the upper-left corner of any Etsy page; then click the blog you want to visit from the list that appears. Figure 20-1 shows the Etsy Blog.

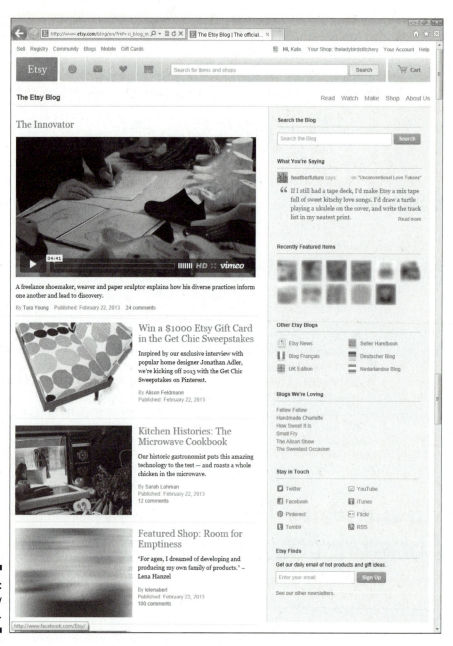

Figure 20-1:
The Etsy
Blog.

Etsy has organized its main blog, the Etsy Blog, into several handy sections to help you find the info you need. Simply click a section's link along the top of the main blog page to access that section. These sections include the following:

- ✔ **Read:** Click this link for quick access to written pieces on the Etsy Blog.

- ✔ **Watch:** The Etsy Blog doesn't just feature the written word. It also boasts video content, including visual how-to's, profiles of Etsy sellers, and more. To access this content, click the Watch link.

- ✔ **Make:** Looking to master a new crafty skill? Check out Make section, with links to loads of how-to articles and videos.

- ✔ **Shop:** This section is where you can track down Etsy's Featured Sellers, chosen by Etsy administrators. You can also read other regular segments, such as "Fresh Shops," "Editor's Picks," "Short Stories" (devoted to sharing the stories behind extraordinary pieces found or created by Etsy sellers), and more.

- ✔ **Editions:** For quick access to other editions of the Etsy Blog, such as the Etsy News Blog, Seller Handbook, or any of the international editions (discussed momentarily), click this link.

- ✔ **About Us:** Want to meet the magicians behind the curtain? Check out the About section of the Etsy Blog. In addition to spelling out the Etsy Blog's mission statement, the About section reveals the Etsy staffers behind the blog's content and includes an area where you can pitch your own story ideas.

As mentioned, Etsy also hosts blogs for members in other countries — namely, Blog Francais, UK Edition, Deutscher Blog, and Nederlandse Blog. To access these, click the appropriate link under Other Etsy Blogs on the right side of any Etsy blog page. Alternatively, access them by clicking the Editions link along the top of any blog post. (Note that these alterna-lingual blogs are not accessible from the Etsy Weddings blog, only from the Etsy Blog, the Etsy News Blog, and Seller Handbook.)

To read an article or view a video in any of Etsy's blogs, simply click the article title. Etsy opens the article in its own page, as shown in Figure 20-2.

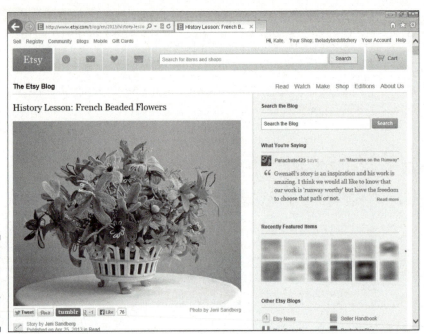

Figure 20-2:
Read an
article on
the Etsy
Blog.

To search for an article in any of Etsy's blogs (except for Etsy Weddings, which, mysteriously, does not support search), follow these easy steps:

1. **Type your keyword in the Search the Blog box in the upper-right corner of the blog's main page.**

2. **Click the Search button.**

   Etsy displays a list of blog articles containing the keyword you typed.

3. **Click an article title to view it.**

In addition to reading the articles on Etsy's blogs, make it a point to peruse the comments left by Etsy members. These comments are often as enlightening as the article itself. If you have something to add, don't hesitate to weigh in; just scroll to the bottom of the comments, type your two cents in the Add Your Comment box, and click the Add Your Comment button.

If you have an idea for an article for the Etsy Blog, why not pitch it? Although the Etsy Blog is written primarily by various Etsy staffers, members of the Etsy community sometimes contribute. To pitch your idea, click the About Us link on the Etsy Blog to open the About Us page. Type your e-mail address in the field provided; then type your story idea, optionally including an image to pique Etsy's interest. Finally, click the Submit button. If Etsy likes your idea, it'll let you know!

Mail Bonding: Signing Up for Etsy E-mail Newsletters

If you've ever felt overwhelmed by the sheer number of fantastic items on Etsy, or wished you could employ a personal shopper to sift through them for you, or if you just feel adrift on the Etsy sea, you'll want to sign up for Etsy e-mail newsletters. When you do, you'll receive handy messages featuring all manner of kicky items, right in your e-mail inbox (see Figure 20-3). Click any entry in an Etsy e-mail to launch Etsy in your web browser and view the associated item listing.

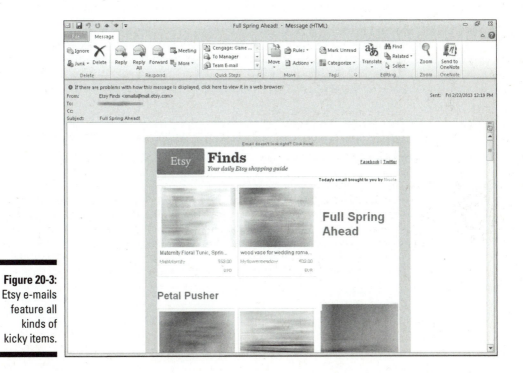

Figure 20-3: Etsy e-mails feature all kinds of kicky items.

In the following sections, we describe the kinds of e-mail newsletters that are available and explain how to sign up to receive them.

Red-letter day: Sifting through different types of e-mail newsletters

You can choose to subscribe to any or all of the following Etsy e-mail newsletters:

- **Etsy Finds:** This daily e-mail is chock-full of clever goodies from a variety of Etsy sellers.

- **Etsy Gifts:** This e-mail, sent seasonally, is stuffed with gift ideas for everyone on your list.

- **Etsy Fashion:** If fashion's your bag, you'll enjoy tracking fashion trends on Etsy with this biweekly e-mail newsletter.

- **Etsy Weddings:** Sure, all weddings are special. But let's face it, weddings featuring handmade or vintage items are even more special. If you're in the midst of planning your own nuptials or you craft items that are made just for brides, grooms, or other members of the bridal party, this weekly e-mail newsletter is for you.

- **Etsy Dudes:** Yes, it's true, Etsy members are overwhelmingly female. But when you're talking about a community as large as Etsy, you'll still find thousands of guys around. If you have a Y chromosome (or buy presents for someone who does), you'll love this weekly e-mail newsletter geared toward dudes.

- **Etsy Teams:** The Etsy Teams e-mail, sent once a week, broadcasts team-related news (see Chapter 19 for more about teams).

- **Etsy Success:** For tips from top sellers, subscribe to the Etsy Success e-mail, sent biweekly.

- **Etsy Labs:** Do you live in or near Brooklyn, New York, where Etsy's offices are located? If so, you'll want to sign up for the weekly Etsy Labs e-mail newsletter, which includes a schedule of events at Etsy Labs. A community workspace of sorts, Etsy Labs plays host to various events. To make sure that out-of-towners aren't left out, Etsy broadcasts some of these events in the Online Labs, which we discuss in Chapter 19.

In addition to the e-mail newsletters listed here, Etsy sends newsletters in French, German, and Dutch, as well as ones for crafting communities in the United Kingdom, Australia and New Zealand, and Canada.

Subscription prescription: Subscribing to e-mail newsletters

To sign up for Etsy e-mail newsletters, follow these steps:

1. **On any Etsy Blog page, scroll down until you see the Etsy Finds field on the right. Alternatively, on Etsy's main page, scroll down until you see the Daily Finds Email field on the left. Then click the See Our Other Newsletters link.**

   The Etsy E-mails page opens (see Figure 20-4). Notice that in addition to enabling you to choose what newsletters you want to subscribe to, you can perform other e-mail–related actions, such as indicating what types of e-mail notifications you want to receive from Etsy.

2. **Click the check box next to each newsletter to which you want to subscribe.**

3. **Click the Save Settings button.**

   Etsy signs you up to receive the newsletters you selected.

If you decide that you no longer want to receive a newsletter, simply click the blue Unsubscribe link that appears along the bottom of any Etsy newsletter. Alternatively, manage your subscriptions by returning to the page shown in Figure 20-4 and unchecking the check boxes next to the newsletters to which you want to unsubscribe.

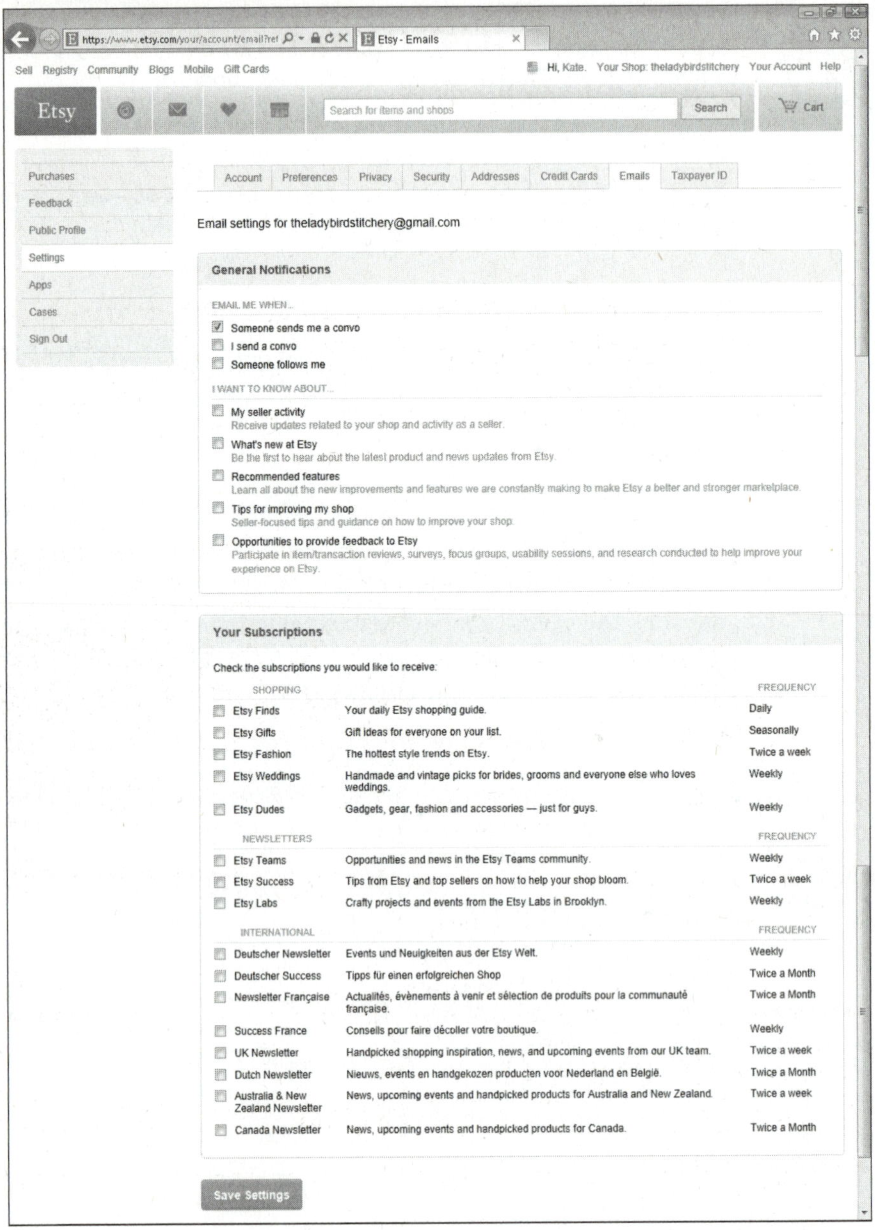

Figure 20-4:
Sign up for
Etsy e-mail
newsletters
here.

Social Skills: Staying in Touch Using Social Media

If you're like one billion or so other people, you maintain a Facebook account. Not surprisingly, Etsy does, too! If you're on Facebook — or you use Twitter, Pinterest, Tumblr, YouTube, iTunes, Flickr, or RSS — you can stay on top of Etsy's goings-on even when you're not on Etsy.

To connect with these other sites, simply scroll down to the Stay in Touch section of any blog page (except for pages in the Etsy Weddings blog, which don't feature this section) and click the desired site. When you do, you'll be taken to Etsy's presence on the site in question, which you can "like," "follow," or otherwise sign up for. Figure 20-5 shows Etsy's Twitter account.

Figure 20-5: "Follow" Etsy on Twitter.

Proto Baggins: Joining Etsy Prototypes

Want to be on the cutting edge on Etsy? Then look into Prototypes. Prototypes are projects run by Etsy Admin that explore different ways of using Etsy. The idea behind Prototypes is to gather data and observe how people use the tools offered in the Prototype. Figure 20-6 shows the Prototypes page, which you access by clicking the Prototypes link under More Ways to Shop on Etsy's home page.

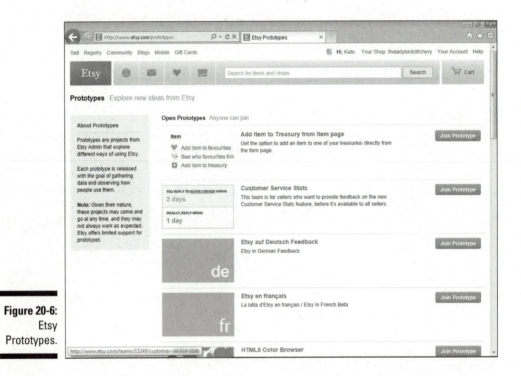

Figure 20-6:
Etsy
Prototypes.

To participate in an Etsy Prototype, you must join it. To do so, click the Join Prototype button next to the Prototype on the main Etsy Prototypes page. You'll be prompted to confirm your choice; click Join Prototype again. Note that when you join a Prototype, you're automatically added to a team dedicated to that Prototype. This enables you to discuss the Prototype and interact with Etsy Admin.

Be warned: Because of their experimental nature, some Prototypes don't work as planned. Don't panic — it's not like anything will explode. It's just that some Prototypes end up being somewhat of a bust, in which case they may be discontinued by Etsy. On the plus side, if a Prototype works exceptionally well, it may be incorporated into the larger Etsy site — in which case, you'll have the advantage of already knowing how to use it!

Chapter 21

A Love-Love Relationship: Showing Your Love for Other Etsy Sellers

· ·

In This Chapter

▶ Flagging your favorite items and shops

▶ Following others on Etsy

▶ Creating a Treasury

· ·

How do we love Etsy? In lots of different ways, actually. One way you can love Etsy is to heart the items and stores you adore — that is, mark them as favorites. Another is to follow Etsy sellers so that you stay apprised of their goings-on. Yet another is to create a Treasury to showcase your favorite goodies. This chapter is devoted to all the ways you can love — and be loved on — Etsy.

Heart and Sold: Hearting on Etsy

If you've spent any time at all on Etsy, you've no doubt run across a bazillion pieces and shops that you positively adore. Fortunately, Etsy enables you to keep track of all these gorgeous goodies by "hearting" them. When you heart an item or shop on Etsy, you essentially flag it as a favorite. You can view all these hearted must-haves from one easy-to-access page. In addition, others who visit your Etsy profile can see what items and shops you've hearted.

Why heart an item? Lots of reasons. For example:

- ✔ You may heart an item that you're dying to buy but that will have to wait until payday.

- ✔ You could heart your favorite supplier's shop so that the next time you need to stock up, you'll be able to find it more easily.

- ✔ You might heart an item or shop simply to let another Etsy seller know that you appreciate her work.

In the following sections, we explain how to heart items and shops and view them in a handy list. We also note how to keep your hearted items and shops private.

A piece of my heart: Hearting items and shops

Hearting an item is simple. First, make sure you're signed in to your Etsy account (see Chapter 2 for details). Then click the Favorite button on the right side of the item's listing page (see Figure 21-1). Etsy adds the item to your list of favorites. The hearted item also appears in your Etsy Activity Feed (more on that later in this chapter).

As an aside, you can also click the Tweet button in the item listing to share the item on Twitter, the Pin It button to pin it on Pinterest, or the Like button to post it on Facebook.

Hearting an Etsy shop is just as easy: Simply click the Add to Favorites link along the left side of the shop's main page, or click Add Shop to Favorites on the right side of any of the shop's listing pages.

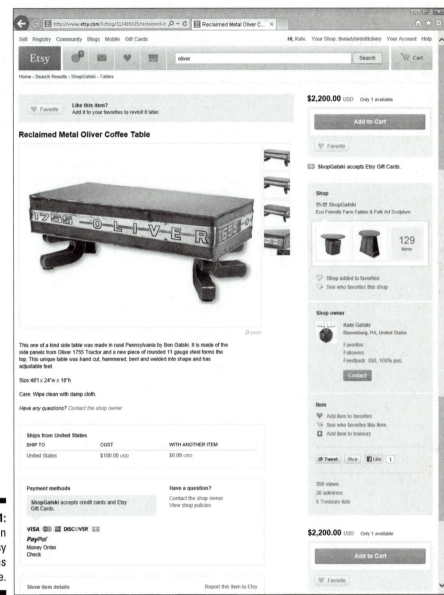

Figure 21-1:
Heart an
item on Etsy
to mark it as
a favorite.

Turn on your heart light: Viewing hearted items and shops

To view items and shops that you've hearted, click the Favorites button (the one with a heart on it, of course!) in the header bar that appears along the top of every Etsy page. Your Favorites page opens, with hearted items displayed by default, as shown in Figure 21-2. (If hearted items don't show up, click the Items tab to reveal them.) To view shops you've hearted, click the Shops tab.

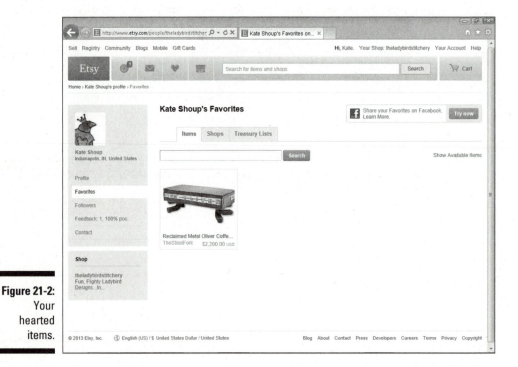

Figure 21-2:
Your
hearted
items.

To remove a hearted item or shop from your list, place your mouse pointer over the item or shop on your Favorites page and click the X that appears.

Over time, you may collect so many favorites that finding them in your list is hard. To help you, Etsy includes a handy-dandy Search field on the Items tab (refer to Figure 21-2). Simply type a relevant keyword, click the Search button, and — *voilà!* — Etsy displays items you've hearted that match your criteria.

A private matter: Being a secret admirer

Normally, when you heart an item or shop, it's visible to anyone who clicks the Favorites link in your Etsy profile. Similarly, if someone visits an Etsy shop or views an item listing, he can see which Etsy members have hearted that shop or item by clicking the See Who Favorites This Shop link or the See Who Favorites This Item link, respectively. (You can see these links in Figure 21-1.)

If you prefer to keep your favorites private — maybe you're a secret agent or a ninja, or perhaps you're just shy — you can easily do so. Here's how to become a secret admirer (after you log in to your Etsy account):

1. **Click the Your Account link that appears along the top of any Etsy page.**

   The Your Account page opens.

2. **Click the Settings link on the left side of the Your Account page.**

3. **Click the Privacy tab (see Figure 21-3).**

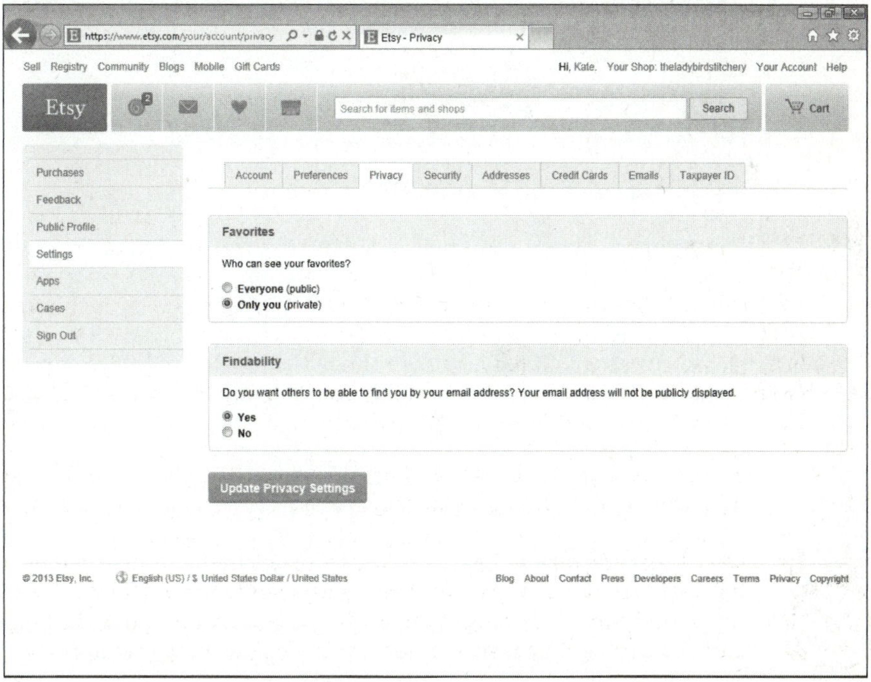

Figure 21-3: Keep your favorites to yourself.

4. **Click the Only You option button under Favorites.**

5. **Click the Update Privacy Settings button.**

   Etsy updates your settings.

Follow Me! Following Others on Etsy

Yes, Etsy's raison d'être is to serve as a marketplace for artisans. But as you find out in Chapters 19 and 20, Etsy also supports a vast and vibrant community of fascinating individuals.

To help you build your own place in this larger Etsy community and generally share the love, Etsy enables you to follow other Etsy members — say, family members on the site, friends who run their own Etsy shops, or other Etsy members you admire. When you follow someone, you can stay on top of that person's activity on Etsy. For example, if a person you follow posts a Treasury, you'll know. (If you're curious, we discuss Treasuries later in this chapter.) You'll also know if someone you follow hearts an Etsy store, item, or Treasury, or starts following someone else. We explain everything you need to know about following in the upcoming sections.

Where you lead, I will follow: Following another Etsy member

Following someone on Etsy is a cinch. To do so, first make sure that you're signed in to your Etsy account. Then open the person's profile page by clicking the link with the person's username that appears in the Shop Owner section of her Etsy shop or by clicking her username on any item listing page. Next, click the Follow button on the left side of the person's profile page, as shown in Figure 21-4. When you follow someone, Etsy notifies that person via e-mail, by default.

A great way to find people to follow is to use Etsy's Find Your Friends feature. With Find Your Friends, you can search your Facebook, Gmail, Yahoo! Mail, or AOL Mail accounts to locate people in your address book who are also on Etsy. To use Find Your Friends, follow these steps:

1. **Click the Activity button in the header bar (the one next to the Etsy button) to view your Activity Feed (more on that later in this chapter).**

2. **Click the Find Your Friends button.**

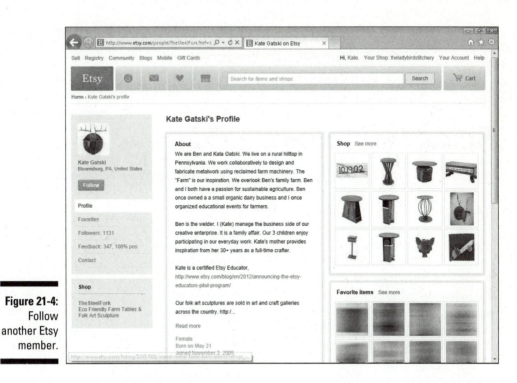

Figure 21-4:
Follow another Etsy member.

3. **Click the appropriate tab (Facebook, Google, Yahoo!, or AOL), click Find Friends on X (where X is Facebook, Google, Yahoo!, or AOL), and follow the onscreen prompts.**

Of course, if you don't use any of these services, you can always use Etsy's Search feature to search for your friends by name.

Circle up: Viewing your Etsy "circle"

To view your Etsy "circle" — that is, the members you're following, as well as any who are following you — make sure that you're logged in to your account. Then follow these steps:

1. **Open your Etsy profile page by clicking your username in the upper-right corner of any Etsy screen.**

2. **Click the Followers link on the left side of the screen to open your Followers page.**

3. **Click the Following tab (see Figure 21-5).**

Figure 21-5:
View your
Etsy circle.

To stop following someone on Etsy, click his entry on the Following tab to open his profile page. Next, hover your mouse pointer over the Following notification and click the X that appears. Etsy prompts you to confirm the removal; click Yes.

Interested in finding out who's following you? You're in luck. By default, Etsy notifies you via e-mail any time someone follows you. (If you don't want to be notified, click the Your Account link that appears along the top of every Etsy page, click the Settings link on the left side of the page, click the Emails tab, uncheck the Someone Follows Me check box, and click the Save Settings button.) In addition, you can view a list of people who have followed you by clicking the Followers tab on the Followers page (you can see this tab in Figure 21-5). Note that just because someone has followed you doesn't mean you'll see her info in your activity feed (discussed in the next section). You must follow her for that to happen.

If you've gone the secret-admirer route with your favorites (as we describe earlier in this chapter), anyone who follows you isn't able to see items and stores you've hearted. Otherwise, this info is visible for all to see.

Active ingredient: Checking your activity feed

To keep abreast of goings-on among the people you follow on Etsy — for example, who in your circle has increased her own circle by following new members — you can check your activity feed.

To view your activity feed, click the Activity button (the one with a spiral shape on it) in the header bar that appears along the top of every Etsy page. As shown in Figure 21-6, your activity feed will open.

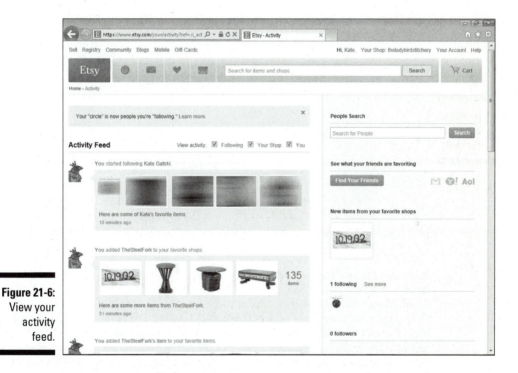

Figure 21-6:
View your activity feed.

As you can see, your activity feed contains two tabs: Following and Your Shop. At the top of the Following tab you'll see new items in your favorite shops. The Following tab also shows when someone you follow has hearted an item, shop, or Treasury; when someone you follow has created a new Treasury; and when someone you follow has started following another member. The Your Shop tab shows when someone has hearted your shop or an item in it, when someone has made a purchase from you, when someone leaves feedback for you, and when someone adds one of your items to a Treasury list.

Treasure Island: Creating a Treasury

A great way to spread the love on Etsy is to create a Treasury. A Treasury is a collection of as many as 16 Etsy listings. These listings may be your favorite things or maybe items that relate to a particular theme (say, bunnies or boats or the color blue). You can then share this list with the larger Etsy community on the Treasuries page. If your Treasury is super-beautiful and interesting, it may land on the site's main page — a major karmic boost for you!

It's considered bad form to include your own items in a Treasury. The idea is to call attention to others. Also, limit your list to one item per shop.

Creating a Treasury is easy. After logging in and gathering the items you want to highlight, follow these steps:

1. **Click the Treasury link under Ways to Shop, on the main Etsy page.**

   The Treasury page, shown in Figure 21-7, opens.

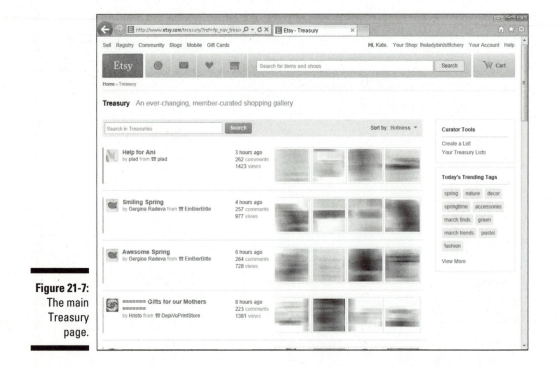

Figure 21-7:
The main
Treasury
page.

2. **Click the Create a List link in the upper-right corner of the Treasury page.**

   The Create a List page, shown in Figure 21-8, opens.

3. **Type a catchy title for your list in the Title field.**

4. **Type a snappy description of your list in the List field.**

5. **Under Privacy, click the Everyone option button to share the Treasury with everyone.**

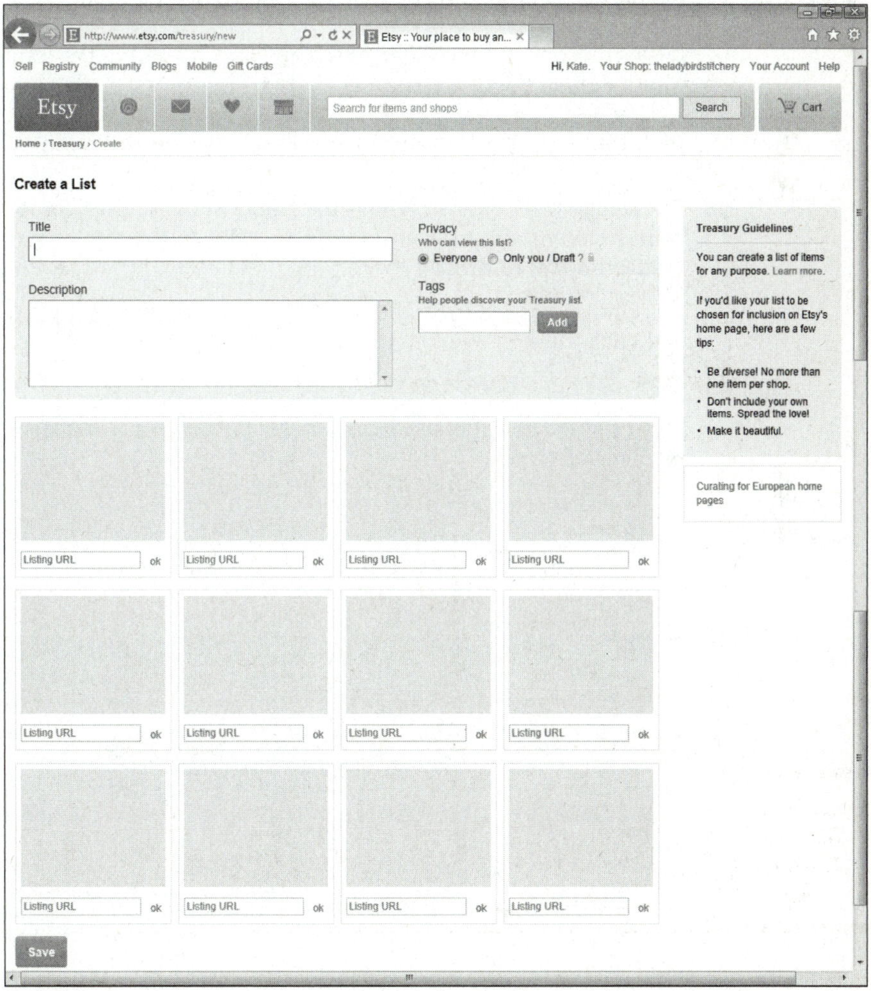

Figure 21-8:
Use this
page to
create your
Treasury.

6. **To help people find your Treasury, type tags in the Tags field, clicking Add after each tag.**

   Flip to Chapter 12 for an introduction to tags.

7. **Open the listing page for the first item you want to add to your Treasury, select the page's URL in your browser's address bar, and copy it.**

8. **Click in the first Listing URL box in the Create a List page, paste the link you copied, and click OK. Alternatively, click the Add Item to Treasury link on the listing page (located on the right side of the listing, in the Item section).**

   A photo of the item appears in the box.

9. **Repeat Steps 7 and 8 to add the remaining items that you selected to your list.**

   You can include as many as 16.

10. **To change the order in which the items appear, click an item you want to move, drag it to the desired order in the list, and release your mouse button to drop it there.**

    To remove an item from the list, hover your mouse pointer over the item and click the Remove link that appears.

11. **Click the Save button to save your list.**

    Etsy creates your list and cites you as its "curator." Etsy also adds it to the Treasury page.

Chapter 22

Help! Getting It When You Need It

. . . .

In This Chapter

▶ Searching for Help topics on your own

▶ Using Etsy FAQs

▶ Receiving personalized answers to your questions

. . . .

*Y*es, Etsy is super-easy to use. But that doesn't mean you won't ever need a little help. Fortunately, Etsy maintains copious resources to help members find answers to all their burning questions. (Well, answers to their burning questions about using Etsy, anyway.) In this chapter, you discover all the ways you can get help on Etsy.

Search and Rescue: Searching for Help on Etsy

Given the proclivity of Etsy users for DIY, it's no surprise that the site offers tools for finding help on your own. Perhaps the easiest of these is the Search Help tool, which enables you to search the site's Help information for the answers you need by entering a keyword or phrase.

To use the Search Help tool, follow these steps:

1. **Click the Help link that appears along the top of any Etsy page.**

   The Help page opens (see Figure 22-1).

2. **Type a keyword or phrase in the Search Help field at the top of the page.**

3. **Click the Search Help button.**

   Etsy displays a list of articles, or answers, that match your criteria (see Figure 22-2).

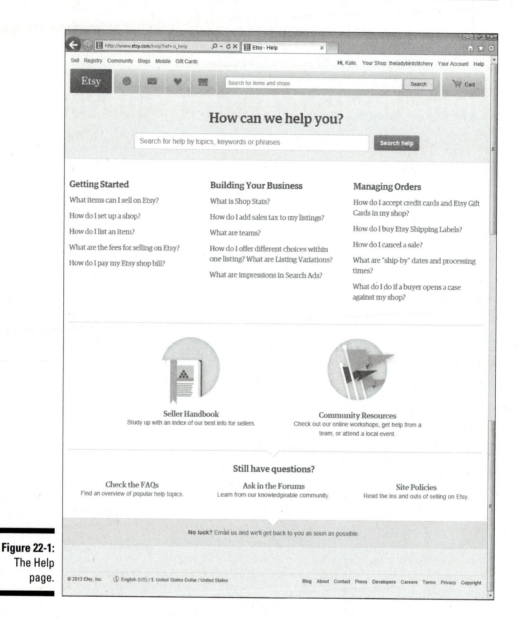

Figure 22-1:
The Help
page.

4. **Click an answer link.**

    Etsy displays the answer (see Figure 22-3).

Etsy displays links to other answers related to the one you just read at the bottom of the Help article. Simply click a link to view it.

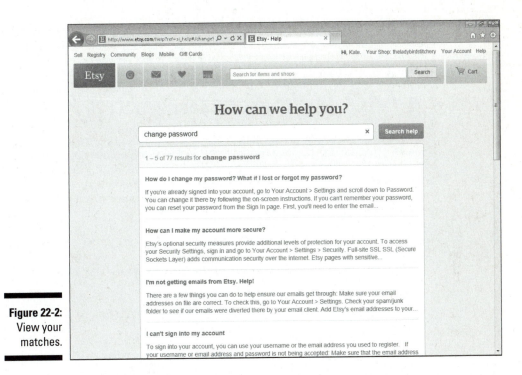

Figure 22-2:
View your
matches.

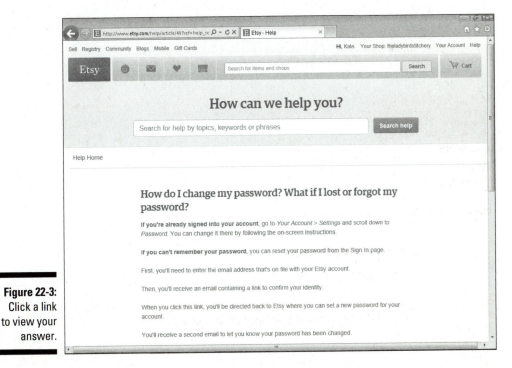

Figure 22-3:
Click a link
to view your
answer.

TIP

If your search efforts fail to yield useful results — for example, Etsy returns too many matches — try the search techniques in Chapter 5.

That's a FAQ Jack: Accessing Etsy FAQs

With as many members as Etsy has, odds are, you're not the first person in the history of the site to have thought of the question you need answered. In fact, certain questions — How do I purchase an item on Etsy? How do I set up my shop? How do I list an item? — get asked a *lot*. For this reason, Etsy has compiled FAQs (that is, a list of frequently asked questions and their answers) for your perusal.

To access the Etsy FAQs, follow these steps:

1. **Click the Help link that appears along the top of any Etsy page.**

   The Help page opens (refer to Figure 22-1).

2. **Click the Check the FAQs link at the bottom of the Help page.**

   A list of categories appears, as shown in Figure 22-4.

3. **Click a category.**

   A list of questions and topics appears, as shown in Figure 22-5.

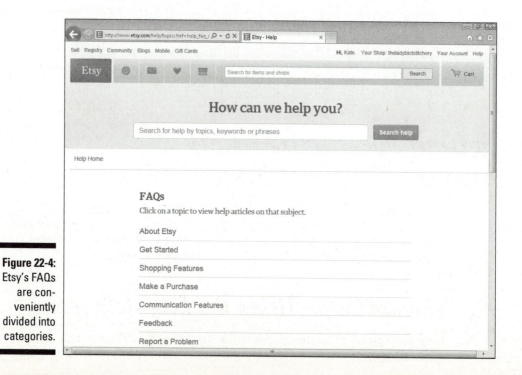

Figure 22-4: Etsy's FAQs are conveniently divided into categories.

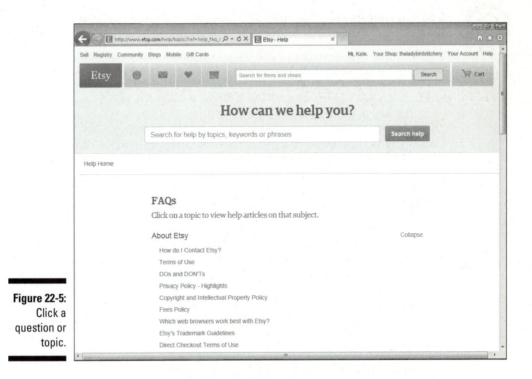

Figure 22-5:
Click a
question or
topic.

4. **Scroll through the list to find a question that you want to answer or a topic you want to explore.**

5. **Click a question or topic in the list.**

   Etsy displays an article pertaining to that topic or question (refer to Figure 22-4).

Getting Personalized Help from the People at Etsy

Sometimes you simply want to be able to ask a question and have it answered by an actual *person*. Fortunately, Etsy can accommodate you! You can use Etsy's Help forum to get help from other Etsy users. If that doesn't work, you can e-mail Etsy Support to find the answers you need.

Forum letter: Using the Etsy Help forum

As we explain in Chapter 19, Etsy's forums serve as public message boards where members can discuss all manner of topics — including help.

Specifically, Etsy's Site Help forum, shown in Figure 22-6, is a great resource if you have general questions about how to use Etsy, questions about site features, or questions related to site policy. Odds are, someone in the Etsy community or on the Etsy staff can — and will — answer your question!

You can access the Site Help forum directly from Etsy's Help page. Simply click the Ask in the Forums link at the bottom of the main Help page. Alternatively, hover your mouse pointer over the Community link that appears along the top of every Etsy page, click Forums, and click the Site Help forum to view it. For info on using the forum, refer to Chapter 19.

Life support: Contacting Etsy Support

Suppose that you have a problem with your account. Or maybe you need help with a transaction. In either case, you can send a message to Etsy Support right from the Help page. You can also send a message to Etsy Support to notify that group of a problem on the site. Here's how:

1. **While logged in to your Etsy account, click the Help link that appears along the top of any Etsy page.**

   The Help page opens (refer to Figure 22-1).

2. **Click the Email Us link at the bottom of the page.**

   The Email Etsy Support page opens, as shown in Figure 22-7.

3. **Click the Select a Topic drop-down arrow and select a category.**

   Choices include categories that pertain to account settings, setting up your shop, seller tools, listings, payment methods, troubleshooting, Direct Checkout, and more.

   Etsy displays a list of articles that may help to answer your question (see Figure 22-8). Click one to read it. Otherwise, continue to the next step.

4. **Type a subject for your message in the Subject field.**

5. **In the Message field, type your message.**

6. **Optionally, you can attach a file; to do so, click the Choose a File button, and then locate and select the file that you want to attach.**

   For example, if you're experiencing a problem with your shop page, you might capture a screen shot of the page and attach that image file to your message.

7. **Click Submit.**

   Etsy notifies you that your question has been submitted (see Figure 22-9); it also sends you a confirmation e-mail to that effect.

   When it has your answer, Etsy sends it to you via e-mail. You can reply to the person who sent the e-mail if you have further questions.

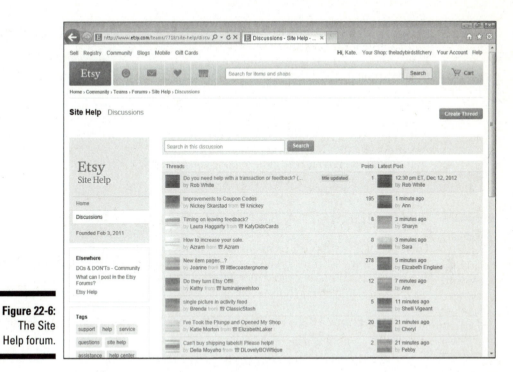

Figure 22-6:
The Site
Help forum.

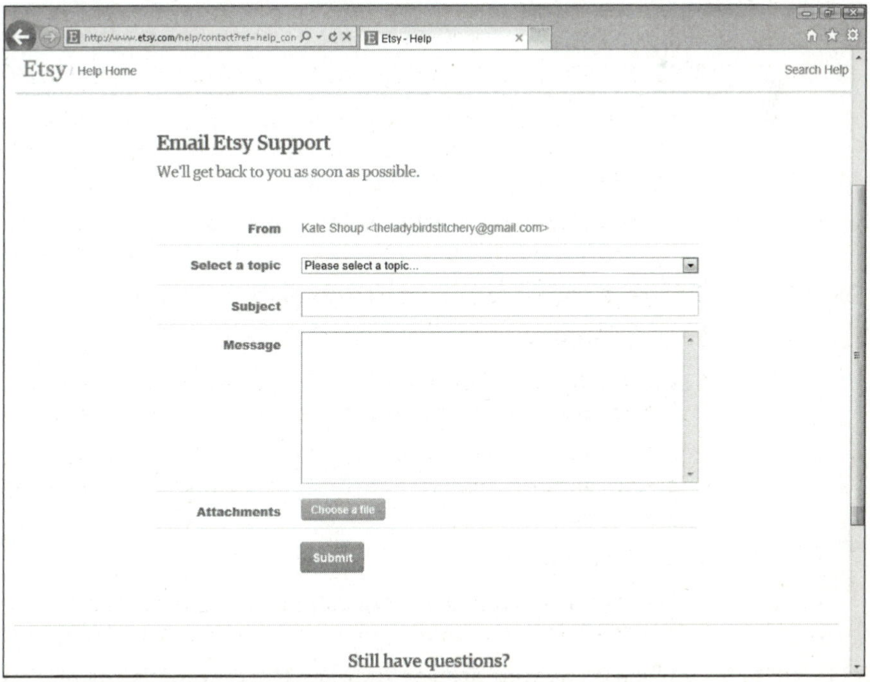

Figure 22-7:
The Email
Etsy Support
page.

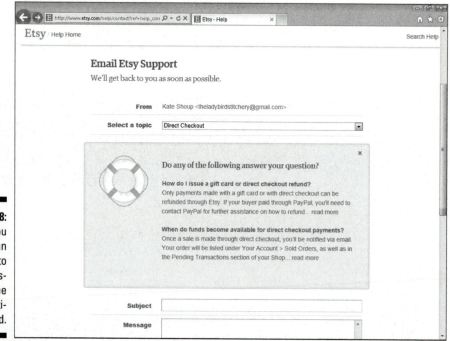

Figure 22-8:
See if you can find an answer to your question in one of the articles listed.

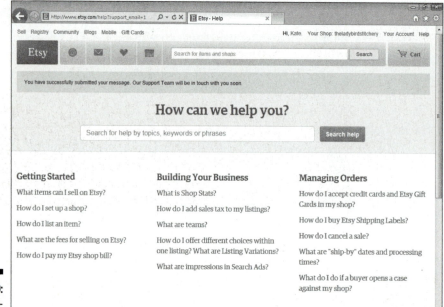

Figure 22-9:
Your message is sent.

Part VI
The Part of Tens

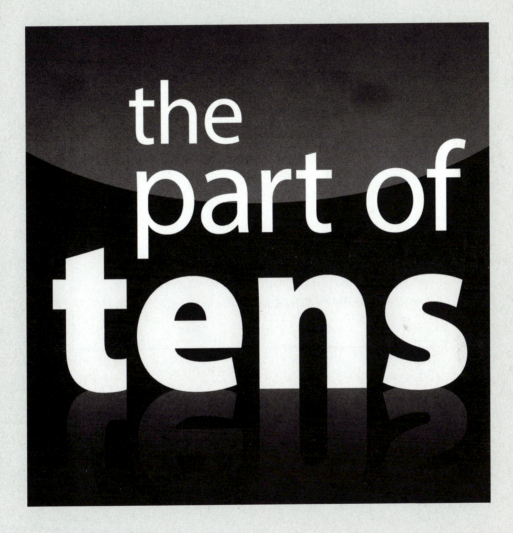

For ten tips for saving money and time as an Etsy shop owner, head to www.dummies.com/extras/startinganetsybusiness.

In this part . . .

- ✔ Find ten tips that'll help you be the best Etsy seller you can be.
- ✔ Find ways to make money doing what you love and boost your happiness quotient.
- ✔ Figure out how to draw people to your shop to make sales.
- ✔ See how to market your wares online and off so your business succeeds.

Chapter 23

Ten Terrific Tips for Etsy Sellers

In This Chapter

▶ Getting (and staying) organized

▶ Serving customers and networking

▶ Loving what you do

Running an Etsy shop — even if it's just a hobby — is no small undertaking. Organization is critical, as is offering top-notch customer service. Here's the place where we offer a neat, concise roll call of ten terrific tips for Etsy sellers. Drumroll, please!

Have a Place for Everything

Nothing is as frustrating as trying to find just the right bead, button, ribbon, or supply when you have 11 orders breathing down your neck. Do yourself a favor: Get organized! Figure out the best way to store all your supplies, both for your craft and for your business. First, sort all your supplies by type or color. Then stash everything in a place where you can easily find it.

In our experience, clear boxes with labels are the only way to go.

Save Time with Twosies

We've wasted too much time looking for the scissors, and then tracking down the tape, and then wondering where the heck that marker went. Save yourself a ton of time and aggravation by buying many, *many* multiples of oft-used supplies.

Our advice? Head to a discount store and knock yourself out. Get a dozen pairs of scissors, a zillion rolls of tape, and lots of whatever else you need. Live a little!

Organize Your Paperwork

Even if it's just a shoe box, have a place to stick all your business-related receipts, whether they're for crafting tools, packaging supplies, or what have you. Then have *another* place for your other paperwork — invoices, bank statements, and such. Tax time is tough enough without having to sort through all that stuff at the eleventh hour! (Flip to Chapter 18 for more details on handling paperwork and other business-related issues.)

Use What You Discover from Other Shops

Before you start selling on Etsy, buy a handful of items from a handful of sellers. Pay attention to the way each seller communicates with you, the packaging he uses, how long it takes for her to ship to you, and so on. What are other sellers doing right? Where can they improve? Then put what you learn to work in your own Etsy shop.

Offer Service with a Smile

No, your online customers can't see you. But that doesn't mean you can cop an attitude with them. In fact, even though you're "out of sight," your lousy outlook will ooze into everything you do.

On Etsy, it's all about customer service! Offering service with a smile is a good way to ensure that you get a smile in return. (Check out Chapter 17 for more customer service tips.)

Network, Network, Network

Networking is a wonderful way to grow your Etsy business. Whether you're interacting with others in the Etsy community (see Part V) or just going about your day in the real world, make it a point to connect with people. Ask questions. Coax those you meet to share their stories. Offer to help others. Engage in the kinds of behaviors that let people know who you are; what you're about; and, eventually, what you do. (Chapter 16 has plenty of guidelines to get you started.)

Keep a Blog

If you're serious about your Etsy shop, consider starting a blog. A blog can serve as an excellent marketing tool to help you grow your customer base. Blogging is a great way to share tips and ideas, and you can even run contests and giveaways. Plus, a blog is easier to maintain than a newsletter, and you can add to it any time.

Popular blog-hosting sites include Blogger (www.blogger.com), Tumblr (www.tumblr.com), TypePad (www.typepad.com), and WordPress (www.wordpress.com).

Learn to Say No

As an Etsy seller, you'll almost certainly be inundated with requests for freebies, donations, and discounts. You know what? It's perfectly okay to say no to some or even all of these requests. Pick and choose. Say yes to the requests that make you feel good and that are good for your business; to everything else, say no.

Never Give In

Take a lesson from the great British Prime Minister Winston Churchill: "Never give in. Never give in. Never, never, never, never." Although Churchill uttered those words in an attempt to galvanize the British against their Axis foes, they apply equally to Etsy sellers — with a spin: If you have an original idea for a product that you love, never stop pushing yourself. Never stop developing and finessing and improving and learning and changing and working hard. Never, never, never, *never*.

Have Fun!

You're not out to change the world here, one beaded necklace at a time. Selling your work on Etsy should be fun! Do your best to maintain perspective. Chortle on the inside when a customer requests a gum-wrapper purse made entirely of Clark's Teaberry wrappers, and enjoy yourself!

Chapter 24

Ten Strategies for Marketing Your Etsy Shop

In This Chapter

▶ Bringing folks to your Etsy shop (and keeping them there)

▶ Using technology to your advantage

▶ Marketing your wares in the real world

Marketing is the key to any successful business, your Etsy shop included. Here, we offer ten tips you need to know to successfully market your Etsy shop (flip to Chapter 16 for even more guidance).

Offer Tiered Pricing

If all you had to offer were $25 gumball machines, you'd really be limiting your customer base. By offering a $5 item as well as a $100 item, you open your shop to buyers with different-sized pocketbooks. With so-called "tiered pricing," you can include big-ticket items to make your shop seem more exciting, while at the same time offering goodies for entry-level shoppers so they can test the waters of your shop, so to speak.

Understand That Giving Begets Giving

Helping someone by giving her more than she asked for makes that person want to return the favor. Build trust and develop relationships with your customers by offering something for nothing, whether it's advice on your blog or a gift with a purchase.

But don't go the cheap route — it may actually work against you by turning off customers. Make sure that you offer only good-quality stuff.

Provide a Guarantee

No doubt about it, you can engender a lot of trust by offering to replace or refund an item if the customer isn't happy for any reason. Buying online can be a scary proposition; you can break down a barrier by letting shoppers know that you're willing to work with them. We guarantee it!

Consider a Loyalty Program

A loyalty program or frequent-customer card can be a great way to bring back return customers. Your loyalty program may offer prizes, future discounts, and other incentives designed to keep customers doing repeat business with you.

As you develop your loyalty program, don't forget your branding. Design customer cards that reflect your shop's color, logo, design, and feel.

Impose a Deadline

Research shows that procrastination is the leading factor in delaying doing things. Overcome the customer's natural tendency to put things off by offering a sale with a deadline. Add a sense of urgency to your marketing message, and customers will respond.

Create a Great E-mail Signature

Most e-mail programs enable you to create an *e-mail signature* — a bit of text or an image that appears at the bottom of every e-mail message that you send. Take advantage of this feature! Creating an e-mail signature gives you a chance to share your contact info and reinforce your branding.

Your e-mail signature is the last thing the person reading your message will see — you want it to reflect your personality!

Connect with Social Media

It's really easy to get so caught up in sharing our own stories online that we forget to listen to others. Instead of using Facebook and Twitter as one big opportunity for you to advertise your wares, use them to reach out to others. Read and comment on others' posts. Congratulate a fellow seller on his successful sale or cheer up a Twitter buddy who's down in the dumps. It's karma, baby!

Make Google Your Best Friend

With this newfangled interweb thingy, you can find the answer to literally any question you have (including marketing questions). Don't be afraid to turn to Google as you grow your Etsy shop! You'll find everything from tips on developing a logo to the best marketing strategy for your craft business.

Use Your Items in the Real World

One of the simplest ways to promote your work is to use or wear your pieces in everyday life, and to always have a business card handy. That way, when Aunt Sarah compliments you on your beautiful feathered and bedazzled bracelet, you can hand her your business card and tell her where to get one of her very own (and one for Uncle Frank, too).

Help Your Community

Get your craft business some publicity by doing something to benefit your community. For example, create a special breast cancer awareness necklace to honor a neighbor, or hold a special sale to help someone in the area. Make sure you let the local paper know what you're up to!

Index

• A •

About page, 106–111
accessing
　Etsy Blogs, 313
　Etsy forums, 294–295
　FAQs, 338–339
　optional account features, 73
　Your Account, 39–40
"accidental" background, 146
account
　about, 11–12
　accessing, 39–40
　confirming your, 18–21
　options, 40–44
　revising settings, 42–43
　setting up, 18–21
activity feed, checking, 331
Activity link (header bar), 30
adding
　About page, 106–111
　banners, 89–92
　Etsy Minis to your site, 240–241
　Etsy shop badges to blogs/websites,
　　238–240
　items to cart, 54–56
　occasion for listings, 183
　recipient for listings, 183
　selling information for listings, 184–185
　shop titles/announcements, 92–94
　style for listings, 183
　variations of listings, 180–181
Additional Policies and FAQs section
　　(Policies page), 122–123
adjusting
　color, 161–162
　exposure, 161–162
　passwords, 69–70

privacy settings, 67–68
　Your Shop settings, 48–49
Adobe Photoshop (website), 90
advertising. *See also* marketing
　on Etsy, 66
　fees for, 275
　Google, 234
analytics, 280
Announcements forum, 294
answering customer questions, 249–250
aperture, 144
aperture-priority mode, 143
API Terms of Use web page, 23
App Gallery, 282
apps
　App Gallery, 282
　ATS International Shipping, 281
　for business management, 281–283
　Clockbot, 282
　EtsyText, 201
　RunInventory, 282
　TaxTime, 282
　tracking, 43–44
ATS International Shipping app, 281
authentication, two-factor, 72
autofocus, 142–143
avatar, 104
avoiding scams, 70–71

• B •

backgrounds, for photographs, 145–146
banners
　adding, 89–92
　defined, 14
　uploading, 90–92
bill, viewing your, 47–48
Billing Policy web page, 23

bio, writing your, 112–114
Blogger (website), 347
blogs
  about, 347
  adding Etsy shop badges to, 238–240
  Etsy Blogs, 3, 16, 313–317
  reading recent posts, 36–37
Blogs link (home page), 27–28
brand, building your, 229–232
brand personality, 230
brand promise, 230
browsing Etsy, 31
Bugs forum, 294
bundling, 136
business cards, 212
business finances, separating from
      personal finances, 277
business management
  about, 269
  business structure, 283–286
  charitable giving, 114, 286
  closing your shop, 288–290
  paying your Etsy bill, 269–272
  recordkeeping, 276–278, 346
  separating personal and business
      finances, 277
  taxes, 272–276
  tools for, 278–283
  vacation mode, 287–288
business matters, 15–16
business model, of Etsy, 7–8
business structure, 283–286
Business Topics forum, 294
buyers and buying. _See also_ customers
  communicating with buyers, 247–255
  filing complaints against sellers, 62–64
  foreign buyers, 254
  leaving feedback, 60–62
  prompting buyers for payment, 257–258
  reasons for buying, 51–52
  refusing service to buyers, 266–267
  reporting issues, 75–76
  response time to buyers, 281
  Search tool, 52–54
  transaction details, 54–60

• C •

cameras, choosing, 142–144
canceling orders, 264–265
care instructions, 212
cart, adding items to, 54–56
Cart link (header bar), 29
cashier's check, 70–71
Categories page, 33
C-corporations, 286
changing
  color, 161–162
  exposure, 161–162
  passwords, 69–70
  privacy settings, 67–68
  Your Shop settings, 48–49
charitable giving, 114, 286
check
  paying via, 59
  setting up payment options, 97
checking
  activity feed, 331
  feedback, 41
checking out, 57–59
choosing
  avatars, 104
  cameras, 142–144
  keywords, 170–173
  passwords, 68–70
  shipping carriers, 214
  shop name, 88–89
"circle," viewing your, 329–330
Clockbot app, 282
closing Etsy shops, 288–290
closing the deal
  about, 199
  finding out you have a sale, 199–201
  managing invoices, 202–205
  receiving payment, 206–207
  tracking sales, 201–202
COGS (cost of goods sold), 275
collectives, 285
color, 161–162
Colors page, 34
comma-separated value (CSV) form,
      277–278

communicating with buyers, 247–255
community, 351
community (Etsy)
  about, 16, 66
  etiquette, 310–311
  Etsy forums, 293–300
  Etsy Teams, 300–308
  events, 309–310
  networking, 346
  Online Labs, 308–309
Community link (home page), 27
competition, 133–135, 230
composing
  e-mail signature, 350
  photographs, 154–158
  taglines, 231
confirming your account, 18–21
Constant Contact (website), 246
contacting Etsy Support, 340–342
Conversations link (header bar), 30
Conversations section, 66
convo, 248–249, 252
copying listings, 191
Copyright & IP web page, 23
corporations, 286
cost of goods sold (COGS), 275
cost of materials, calculating, 128
coupons, 213, 235–237
creating
  coupons, 235–237
  Etsy Search Ads, 233–234
  Etsy shop badges, 238–241
  logos, 231–232
  Treasuries, 332–334
credit card
  paying via, 57–58
  setting up for making payment of fees on,
    101–102
  setting up payment options, 97
cropping photographs, 163–164
CSV (comma-separated value) form,
  277–278
customer service
  about, 247
  communicating with buyers, 247–255

feedback, 255–257
  importance of, 346
  managing bungled transactions, 257–267
  managing difficult customers, 266
  Seller Protection program, 261
Customer Service Stats, viewing, 281
customers. *See also* buyers and buying
  answering questions from, 249–250
  thanking, 250–252
Customs form, 216

• D •

Daily Finds Email, 32
deactivating listings, 195–196
deadlines, imposing, 350
deductions, tax, 275–276
depth of field, 144, 159
descriptions and titles
  about, 165–170, 182–183
  composing, 169–170
  driving traffic with search engine
    optimization, 170–176
  proofreading, 176
determining tax deductions, 275–276
DHL (website), 214
Digital Photography for Dummies (King), 141
Direct Checkout, 23, 97, 206
direct sunlight, 151–153
disclaimer, 114
displaying
  activity feed, 331
  Customer Service Stats, 281
  Etsy bill, 47–48
  feedback scores, 255
  hearted items and shops, 326
  home page, 25–27
  posts in Etsy forums, 295–299
  public profile, 41–42
  Recently Listed Items section, 37
  reported cases, 44
  Shop Stats, 278–280
  your "circle," 329–330
DOs & DON'Ts page, 22, 65–66, 79, 116, 310
downloading sales data, 277–278

• E •

Economy, Peter (author)
  Home-Based Business For Dummies,
    3rd Edition, 269
editing
  listings, 188–190
  photographs, 160–164
  shop settings, 114
Edwards, Paul (author)
  Home-Based Business For Dummies,
    3rd Edition, 269
Edwards, Sarah (author)
  Home-Based Business For Dummies,
    3rd Edition, 269
EFTPS (Electronic Federal Tax Payment
    System), 274
e-mail newsletter
  about, 245–246
  contacting buyers via, 250–251
  signing up for, 317–320
e-mail signature, 350
enabling
  Rearrange Your Shop feature, 196–197
  vacation mode, 287–288
equipment, deductions for, 275
etiquette, community, 310–311
Etsy. *See also specific topics*
  advertising on, 66
  browsing, 31
  business matters, 15–16
  business model, 7–8
  community. *See* community (Etsy)
  home page. *See* home page
  purpose of, 7–8
  registering with, 9
  safety. *See* safety and privacy
  searching what's for the sale, 13
  selling process, 15
  signing in, 23–24
  storefront. *See* storefront
  website, 1, 23
  Your Account, 11–12
  Your Shop, 11–12

Etsy Apps
  App Gallery, 282
  ATS International Shipping, 281
  for business management, 281–283
  Clockbot, 282
  EtsyText, 201
  RunInventory, 282
  TaxTime, 282
  tracking, 43–44
Etsy bills, paying, 269–272
Etsy Blogs, 3, 16, 313–317
Etsy Dudes newsletter, 318
Etsy events, 309–310
Etsy Fashion newsletter, 318
Etsy Finds newsletter, 318
Etsy forums, 293–300, 339–340
Etsy Gifts newsletter, 318
Etsy Help forum, 339–340
Etsy Labs newsletter, 318
Etsy link (header bar), 29
Etsy Mini, 238–241
Etsy Mobile, 37–38
Etsy News Blog, 16
Etsy Prototypes, joining, 322
Etsy Search Ads, 232–234, 280
Etsy shop badges, creating, 238–241
Etsy Shop Stats, 173
Etsy shops. *See also* Your Shop
  closing, 288–290
  featuring items in, 198
Etsy Success newsletter, 318
Etsy Support, 75–76, 340–342
Etsy teams, 300–308
Etsy Teams newsletter, 318
Etsy Weddings Blog, 16
Etsy Weddings newsletter, 318
EtsyText app, 201
evaluating
  pricing, 133–137
  target market, 135
events, 309–310
exchanges and returns, 119
expired listing, renewing, 194
exposure, 144, 161–162
extras, 212–213, 349

• F •

Facebook, linking your shop to, 242–243
FAQs, accessing, 338–339
Favorites link (header bar), 30
featured shop, 36
FedEx (website), 214
feedback
  about, 255–257
  checking, 41
  leaving, 60–62
Feedback section, 66
fees, for advertising, 275
Fees web page, 23
filing complaints against sellers, 62–64
Find Your Friends feature, 328–329
First-Class Mail, 217
flagging feature, 66
flat-rate pricing, 216
focus, for photographs, 158–159
following, 328–331
foreign buyers, communicating with, 254
forums, 293–300, 339–340
franchise tax, 273–274
freebies, 213, 349
full-site SSL, 72

• G •

getting started, 86–89
gift card, paying via, 57–58
Gift Cards link (home page), 28
Gift Cards page, 33–34
Gift Cards Terms of Use web page, 23
GIMP (website), 90
"golden hours," 151
Google, 351
Google Analytics, 280
Google Shopping, 234
grammatical errors, 176
guarantees, providing, 350
guarding your privacy, 66–70

• H •

handling
  bungled transactions, 257–267
  difficult customers, 266
  invoices, 202–205
  item listings, 46
  lost shipments, 258–259
  reported cases, 259–261
  sold items, 46–47
  your business. *See* business management
handmade items, selling, 80–81
Handpicked Items section, 31–32
handwritten notes, 212
header bar, 29–30
hearting, 323–328
help
  FAQs, 338–339
  personalized, 339–342
  searching for, 335–338
Help files (website), 16
Help link (home page), 28
home office, deductions for, 276
home page
  about, 25
  browsing, 31
  Daily Finds Email, 32
  Etsy Mobile, 37–38
  featured shop, 36
  Handpicked Items section, 31–32
  header bar, 29–30
  navigating, 9–11
  reading recent blog posts, 36–37
  "top of the page" links, 27–29
  viewing, 25–27
  viewing Recently Listed Items section, 37
  ways to shop, 33–35
Home-Based Business For Dummies,
    3rd Edition (Edwards, Edwards,
    and Economy), 269

• I •

icons, explained, 2
Ideas forum, 294
image-editing software, 160–164
images
  about, 141–142
  adjusting exposure and color, 161–162
  backgrounds for, 145–146
  cameras, 142–144
  composition of, 154–158
  cropping, 163–164
  editing, 160–164
  focus, 158–159
  lighting, 151–154
  live models, 149–150
  props for, 147–149
  quantity of, 159–160
  reflectors, 153–154
  rule of thirds, 157–158
  styling, 144–150
  uploading for listings, 181–182
  watermarking, 164
in-bound links, 171
insurance, for shipping, 220
international shipping, 216–217
Internet resources
  Adobe Photoshop, 90
  Blogger, 347
  Constant Contact, 246
  DHL, 214
  DOs & DON'Ts page, 79, 116, 310
  EFTPS (Electronic Federal Tax Payment
    System), 274
  Etsy, 1, 23
  Etsy Blog, 3, 16
  Etsy News Blog, 16
  Etsy Weddings Blog, 16
  EtsyText app, 201
  FedEx, 214
  GIMP, 90
  Help files, 16
  IRS, 274
  MailChimp, 246
  Nashville Wraps, 210
  Paper Mart, 210
  PayPal Help Center, 261
  Picasa, 90, 160
  Pinterest, 245
  QuickBooks, 276
  Seller Handbook, 3, 16
  Shipsurance, 220
  Small Business Administration, 284
  Stitch Labs, 278
  Terms of Use, 116
  Tumblr, 347
  TypePad, 347
  ULINE, 210
  U-PIC, 220
  UPS, 214
  USPS, 210, 214, 216, 217, 225, 258
  Vertical Response, 246
  WordPress, 347
invoices
  including in package, 212, 213
  managing, 202–205
IRS (website), 274
ISO, 144
issuing refunds, 261–264

• J •

joining
  Etsy Prototypes, 322
  Etsy teams, 303–304

• K •

Kalin, Rob (Etsy founder), 8
keywords, choosing, 170–173
King, Julie Adair (author)
  Digital Photography for Dummies, 141
Kiss and Make Up feature, 258

• L •

labels, shipping, 220–224
labor costs, calculating, 128–130
launching Etsy convo's, 252
leaving feedback, 60–62
legal services, deductions for, 276
light box, 154

light tent, 154

lighting, for photographs, 151–154

limited liability company (LLC), 285

links

  in-bound, 171

  "top of the page," 27–29

listings

  about, 177

  adding recipient, occasion, and style, 183

  adding selling information, 184–185

  adding variations, 180–181

  copying, 191

  deactivating, 195–196

  describing items, 182–183

  editing, 188–190

  filling in item information, 180

  managing, 46

  moving, 197–198

  for new items, 177–188

  process for, 178–179

  reactivating, 195–196

  rearranging Etsy shop, 196–198

  renewing, 191–194

  reviewing, 185–188

  tagging items, 184

  uploading images, 181–182

live models, for photographs, 149–150

LLC (limited liability company), 285

login history, 72

logos, creating, 231–232

love

  creating a Treasury, 332–334

  following, 328–331

  hearting, 323–328

lowering prices, 135–136

loyalty programs, 350

• M •

macro setting, 142

MailChimp (website), 246

mailing list, 254

managing

  bungled transactions, 257–267

  difficult customers, 266

invoices, 202–205

item listings, 46

lost shipments, 258–259

  reported cases, 259–261

  sold items, 46–47

  your business. *See* business management

manual mode, 143

Market Research Tool, 134

marketing

  building brand, 229–232

  creating coupons, 235–237

  e-mail newsletter, 245–246

  Google Shopping, 234

  logos, 231–232

  promoting your shop, 232–245

  publicizing sales, 245

  on social media, 242–245

  strategies for, 349–351

  taglines, 231

Marketplace Criteria section, 66

Marketplace Integrity Trust & Safety
  Team, 84

marking items as shipped, 225, 281

mature items, selling, 83

Membership section, 65

metadata, 175

mileage, deductions for, 275–276

Mobile link (home page), 28

money order

  about, 70–71

  paying via, 59

  setting up payment options, 97

monitoring

  Etsy apps, 43–44

  information, 281

  purchases, 40

  sales, 201–202

moving listings, 197–198

• N •

Nashville Wraps (website), 210

natural light, 151

navigating home page, 9–11

networking, 346

news
about, 313
blogs, 313–317
e-mail newsletters, 317–320
Prototypes, 322
social media, 321
newsletter, e-mail, 245–246

• O •

occasion, adding for listings, 183
office expenses, 275
Online Labs, 308–309
options (Your Account), 40–44
orders
canceling, 264–265
submitting, 59–60
organizing
importance of, 345
paperwork, 346
overhead, calculating, 130

• P •

packaging, 210–213
pages
About, 106–111
API Terms of Use, 23
Billing Policy, 23
Categories, 33
Colors, 34
Copyright & IP, 23
DOs & DON'Ts, 22, 65–66, 79, 116, 310
Fees, 23
Gift Cards, 33–34
Gift Cards Terms of Use, 23
People Search, 35
Policies, 123–125
Privacy, 22
Shop Local, 35
Trademark Guidelines, 23
Treasury, 34
Paint, 160
Paper Mart (website), 210
paperwork, organizing, 346

partnerships, 284
passwords, 13–14, 68–70
paying
Etsy bills, 269–272
quarterly income tax, 274
via check, 59
via credit card, 57–58
via gift card, 57–58
via money order, 59
via PayPal, 58–59
Payment section (Policies page), 121–122
payment-related policies, 116–118
payments
prompting buyers for, 257–258
receiving, 206–207
setting up options, 96–100
PayPal
about, 206
paying with, 58–59
setting up payment options, 97
PayPal Help Center (website), 261
People Search page, 35
personal check, setting up payment
options, 97
personal finances, separating from
business finances, 277
personality, brand, 230
photographs
about, 141–142
adjusting exposure and color, 161–162
backgrounds for, 145–146
cameras, 142–144
composition of, 154–158
cropping, 163–164
editing, 160–164
focus, 158–159
lighting, 151–154
live models, 149–150
props for, 147–149
quantity of, 159–160
reflectors, 153–154
rule of thirds, 157–158
styling, 144–150
uploading for listings, 181–182
watermarking, 164
Photoshop (Adobe), 90

Picasa (website), 90, 160
pictures
  about, 141–142
  adjusting exposure and color, 161–162
  backgrounds for, 145–146
  cameras, 142–144
  composition of, 154–158
  cropping, 163–164
  editing, 160–164
  focus, 158–159
  lighting, 151–154
  live models, 149–150
  props for, 147–149
  quantity of, 159–160
  reflectors, 153–154
  rule of thirds, 157–158
  styling, 144–150
  uploading for listings, 181–182
  watermarking, 164
Pinterest (website), 245
policies
  about, 115
  exchanges, 119
  fairness of, 116
  page setup, 120–125
  payment-related, 116–118
  returns, 119
  shipping, 118–119
  simplicity of, 116
Policies page, populating, 123–125
populating Policies page, 123–125
preferences, payment, 98–100
press clippings, 114
pricing
  about, 127
  of competition, 133–135
  evaluating, 133–137
  flat-rate, 216
  formulas for, 128–133
  lowering prices, 135–136
  raising prices, 136–137
  retail, 131–132
  for sales, 138
  tiered, 349
  vintage items, 137–138
  wholesale, 131–132

printing shipping labels, 220–224
Priority Mail, 216, 217
privacy and safety
  about, 13–14
  avoiding scams, 70–71
  changing settings, 67–68
  DOs & DON'Ts page, 65–66
  guarding privacy, 66–70
  optional account features, 72–73
  in public places, 71–72
Privacy Policy, 67
Privacy web page, 22
processing times, 281
product info, 114
products. *See* photographs
professional services, deductions for, 276
profile, shipping, 217–220
prohibited items, 82–83
promise, brand, 230
promoting your shop, 49, 232–245
proofreading, 176
props, for photographs, 147–149
Prototypes, 35, 44, 322
public profile
  setting up, 102–105
  viewing, 41–42
publicizing sales, 245
purchases, tracking, 40
purpose, of Etsy, 7–8

• *Q* •

quarterly income tax, paying, 274
QuickBooks (website), 276

• *R* •

raising prices, 136–137
reactivating listings, 195–196
reading recent blog posts, 36–37
Rearrange Your Shop feature, enabling,
    196–197
rearranging Etsy shop, 196–198
receiving payment, 206–207
Recently Listed Items section, viewing, 37

recipient, adding for listings, 183
recordkeeping, 276–278, 346
reflective surfaces, 145
reflectors, for photographs, 153–154
refunds, 261–264
Refunds and Exchanges section (Policies page), 122
refusing service, 266–267
Register link (header bar), 29
registered users, becoming, 17–23
registering with Etsy, 9
Registry link (home page), 27
Remember icon, 2
renaming sections, 95
renewing listings, 191–194
reported cases
  managing, 259–261
  viewing, 44
reporting issues to Etsy, 75–76
requesting custom items, 60
resolving cases, 260–261
responding to posts in Etsy forums, 295–299
response time, 281
retail pricing, 131–132
returns and exchanges, 119
reviewing listings, 185–188
revising account settings, 42–43
rule of thirds, 157–158
RunInventory app, 282

• **S** •

safety and privacy
  about, 13–14
  avoiding scams, 70–71
  changing settings, 67–68
  DOs & DON'Ts page, 65–66
  guarding privacy, 66–70
  optional account features, 72–73
  in public places, 71–72
sales
  pricing for, 138
  publicizing, 245
  tracking, 201–202
sales data, downloading, 277–278

sales tax, collecting, 273–274
sales tax ID number, 274
SBA (Small Business Administration), 284
scale, conveying, 147
scams, 14, 70–71
Schell, Jim (author)
  Small Business Marketing For Dummies, 4th Edition, 269
Schenck, Barbara Findlay (author)
  Small Business Marketing Kit For Dummies, 229
S-corporations, 286
seamless background, 146
search engine optimization (SEO), 170–176
Search Help tool, 335–338
Search tool, 13, 52–54
searching
  Etsy blogs, 316
  for Etsy teams, 301–303
  for help, 335–338
secret admirers, 327–328
sections
  Additional Policies and FAQs (Policies page), 122–123
  Conversations, 66
  Feedback, 66
  Handpicked Items, 31–32
  Marketplace Criteria, 66
  Membership, 65
  Payment (Policies page), 121–122
  Recently Listed Items, 37
  Refunds and Exchanges (Policies page), 122
  renaming, 95
  Shipping (Policies page), 122
  Transactions, 66
  Welcome (Policies page), 120–121
Secure Sockets Layer (SSL), 72
selecting
  avatars, 104
  cameras, 142–144
  keywords, 170–173
  passwords, 68–70
  shipping carriers, 214
  shop name, 88–89

Sell link (home page), 27
Seller Handbook (website), 3, 16
Seller Protection program, 73–74, 261
sellers and selling. *See also* closing the
        deal; listings; storefront
    about, 79
    on Etsy, 15
    filing complaints against, 62–64
    handmade items, 80–81
    services, 83
    supplies, 81–82
    tips for, 345–347
    vintage items, 81
    what you can sell, 80–82
    what's not allowed, 82–83
selling expenses, 275
SEO (search engine optimization), 170–176
services, selling, 83
settings
    editing shop, 114
    privacy, 67–68
    revising account, 42–43
    Your Shop, 44–49
setup
    account, 18–21
    credit card for making payments, 101–102
    payment options, 96–100
    Policies page, 120–125
    public profile, 102–105
    storefront sections, 95–96
shipping
    about, 209, 225
    choosing carriers, 214
    double-checking addresses, 252–253
    insurance, 220
    internationally, 216–217
    managing lost shipments, 258–259
    marking items as shipped, 225, 281
    options, 214–216
    packaging, 210–213
    printing labels, 220–224
    profile for, 217–220
    speed of, 255
    supplies, 209–210
    tracking information, 281

shipping policies, 118–119
shipping profile, 185
Shipping section (Policies page), 122
Shipsurance (website), 220
shop
    about, 11–12, 44–45
    changing settings, 48–49
    choosing your name, 88–89
    handling sold items, 46–47
    managing item listings, 46
    promoting, 49
    viewing Etsy bill, 47–48
Shop link (header bar), 30
Shop Local page, 35
Shop Stats, viewing, 278–280
shop titles/announcements, adding, 92–94
shout-outs, 254–255
shutter speed, 144
Sign In link (header bar), 29
signing in, 23–24
signing up
    becoming a registered user, 17–23
    for Daily Finds Email, 32
    for e-mail newsletters, 317–320
Site Help forum, 294
Small Business Administration (SBA), 284
Small Business Marketing For Dummies, 4th
        Edition (Tyson and Schell), 269
Small Business Marketing Kit For Dummies
        (Schenck), 229
social media
    about, 351
    promoting your Etsy shop on, 242–245
    using for news, 321
software, image-editing, 160–164
sold items, managing, 46–47
sole proprietorships, 284
specifying payment preferences, 98–100
spelling errors, 176
SSL (Secure Sockets Layer), 72
starting
    an Etsy team, 304–307
    threads in Etsy forums, 299–300
Stitch Labs (website), 278

storefront
about, 14–15, 85–86
adding an About page, 106–111
adding banners, 89–92
adding shop titles/announcements, 92–94
choosing an avatar, 104
editing shop settings, 114
getting started, 86–89
setting up credit card for paying fees,
101–102
setting up payment options, 96–100
setting up public profile, 102–105
setting up sections, 95–96
writing your bio, 112–114
structure, business, 283–286
style, adding for listings, 183
styling photographs, 144–150
submitting orders, 59–60
subscribing to e-mail newsletters, 319–320
sunlight, direct, 151–153
supplies
buying, 345
selling, 81–82
shipping, 209–210

• T •

tagging
an Etsy team, 308
items, 184
tagline, 231
tags, 175–176
target market, 135, 230
tax calculator, 116
taxes
about, 273
collecting sales tax, 273–274
determining deductions, 275–276
quarterly income tax, 274
1099-K, 275
TaxTime app, 282
team tags, 308
teams, 300–308
Technical Stuff icon, 2
1099-K, filing, 275
Terms of Use, 21–23, 116

thanking customers, 250–252
third-party vendors, 282
tiered pricing, 349
"times 2," 130–131
Tip icon, 2
titles and descriptions
about, 165–170, 182–183
composing, 169–170
driving traffic with search engine
optimization, 170–176
proofreading, 176
tools
for business management, 278–283
for promoting your shop, 232–245
"top of the page" links, on home page,
27–29
tracking
Etsy apps, 43–44
information, 281
purchases, 40
sales, 201–202
Trademark Guidelines web page, 23
traffic, driving with search engine
optimization, 170–176
transaction privilege tax, 273–274
transactions
about, 54
adding items to cart, 54–56
checking out, 57–59
submitting orders, 59–60
Transactions section, 66
Treasuries, creating, 332–334
Treasury page, 34
Tumblr (website), 347
Twitter, linking your shop to, 244–245
two-factor authentication, 72
TypePad (website), 347
Tyson, Eric (author)
Small Business Marketing For Dummies,
4th Edition, 269

• U •

ULINE (website), 210
unique selling proposition (USP), 230
upcycling, 80

U-PIC (website), 220
uploading
  banners, 90–92
  images for listings, 181–182
UPS (website), 214
use tax, 273–274
USP (unique selling proposition), 230
USPS (website), 210, 214, 216, 217, 225, 258
USPS Postage Price Calculator, 215

• V •

vacation mode, 287–288
Vertical Response (website), 246
viewing
  activity feed, 331
  Customer Service Stats, 281
  Etsy bill, 47–48
  feedback scores, 255
  hearted items and shops, 326
  home page, 25–27
  posts in Etsy forums, 295–299
  public profile, 41–42
  Recently Listed Items section, 37
  reported cases, 44
  Shop Stats, 278–280
  your "circle," 329–330
vintage items, 81, 137–138

• W •

Warning icon, 2
watermarking photographs, 164
web pages
  About, 106–111
  API Terms of Use, 23
  Billing Policy, 23
  Categories, 33
  Colors, 34
  Copyright & IP, 23
  DOs & DON'Ts, 22, 65–66, 79, 116, 310
  Fees, 23
  Gift Cards, 33–34
  Gift Cards Terms of Use, 23
  People Search, 35
  Policies, 123–125

  Privacy, 22
  Shop Local, 35
  Trademark Guidelines, 23
  Treasury, 34
websites
  adding Etsy shop badges to, 238–240
  Adobe Photoshop, 90
  Blogger, 347
  Constant Contact, 246
  DHL, 214
  DOs & DON'Ts page, 79, 116, 310
  EFTPS (Electronic Federal Tax Payment
    System), 274
  Etsy, 1, 23
  Etsy Blog, 3, 16
  Etsy News Blog, 16
  Etsy Weddings Blog, 16
  EtsyText app, 201
  FedEx, 214
  GIMP, 90
  Help files, 16
  IRS, 274
  MailChimp, 246
  Nashville Wraps, 210
  Paper Mart, 210
  PayPal Help Center, 261
  Picasa, 90, 160
  Pinterest, 245
  QuickBooks, 276
  Seller Handbook, 3, 16
  Shipsurance, 220
  Small Business Administration, 284
  Stitch Labs, 278
  Terms of Use, 116
  Tumblr, 347
  TypePad, 347
  ULINE, 210
  U-PIC, 220
  UPS, 214
  USPS, 210, 214, 216, 217, 225, 258
  Vertical Response, 246
  WordPress, 347
Welcome section (Policies page), 120–121
white balance setting, 143
wholesale pricing, 131–132
WordPress (website), 347
writing your bio, 112–114

• **Y** •

Your Account
  about, 11–12
  accessing, 39–40
  confirming your, 18–21
  options, 40–44
  revising settings, 42–43
  setting up, 18–21

Your Shop
  about, 11–12, 44–45
  changing settings, 48–49
  choosing your name, 88–89
  handling sold items, 46–47
  managing item listings, 46
  promoting, 49
  viewing Etsy bill, 47–48

About the Authors

Kate Gatski: Kate is a handmade entrepreneur. She and her husband Ben make sculpture and furniture full-time in their rural shop. Their business, Gatski Metal, is celebrating its tenth year. They enjoy working with a growing group of fantastic customers via their Etsy shop at www.etsy.com/shop/shopgatski. Kate is also a handmade educator and consultant, helping others establish and grow their own successful enterprises. Her recipe is revealed in a self-published e-book called *All Craft: A Recipe to Make It Pay.* Kate was born into craft; raised by a full-time rag-rug weaver, she has hidden behind many a craft show booth. Kate is mother to three children who keep her from going all crafts, all the time. She finds peace in the kitchen and the woods.

Kate Shoup: During the course of her career, Kate Shoup has authored more than 25 books, including *Not Your Mama's Beading, Not Your Mama's Stitching,* and *Rubbish: Reuse Your Refuse* (all published by Wiley), and has edited scores more. Kate also co-wrote a feature-length screenplay (and starred in the ensuing film) and worked as the Sports Editor for *NUVO Newsweekly.* When not writing, Kate, an IndyCar fanatic, loves to ski (she was once nationally ranked), read, craft, and ride her motorcycle. She also plays a mean game of 9-ball. Kate lives in Indianapolis with her lovely boyfriend, her brilliant daughter, and their dog.

Allison Strine: By day, Allison Strine is a happy artist who takes unreasonable joy in her Etsy shop feedback comments. She is also the author of *LadyBirdLand!* (StoryPeople Press), a colorful book that brings her irrepressible creations to vibrant reality. At night, Allison is a not-very-good cook; wife to a right-brained hunk (or is it the left? — the one that's all about math and not really about art); and tucker-inner of two perfectly behaved, well-groomed children. Allison writes in the third person and hawks her wares at www.etsy.com/shop/allisonstrine.

Dedication

Kate Gatski: To all of you — crafters, artists, makers, designers — who quietly labor away, creating something beautiful to share with the world. May this make some part of your efforts a little easier.

Kate Shoup: For Heidi, as always.

Authors' Acknowledgments

Kate Gatski: Thanks foremost to my brilliant co-authors. It was a snap, thanks to both of you! Thank you to Elizabeth Kuball for her steadfast work and to Lindsay Lefevere for making the process simple and smooth. Thanks to Ben for playing with the kids while I typed away; and to Ivan, Hazel, and Evelyn, who are eager "to do Etsy" now, too. You're my inspiration!

Kate Shoup: The publication of any book is an enormous undertaking, and this one was no exception! Thanks go first to my excellent co-author, Kate Gatski, who — figuratively, at least — pried more than one razor blade from my fingers. Thanks also go to Allison Strine, whose work on the first edition of this book was second to none. Thanks, too, to Lindsay Lefevere for giving us the opportunity to tackle this exciting project, and to Elizabeth Kuball for her dedication and patience in guiding this project from start to finish. Thanks to technical editor Caroline Colom Vasquez, who skillfully checked each step and offered valuable input along the way. Thanks to the Composition Services team at John Wiley & Sons, Inc., for their able efforts. Thanks to the Etsy sellers and talented photographers who graciously allowed us to feature their gorgeous photographs. Finally, thanks to Etsy itself for enabling craftspeople the world over to make a living by selling their work online.

On a personal note, many thanks and much love to my beautiful and brilliant daughter, Heidi Welsh; to my incredible parents, Barb and Steve Shoup; to my wonderful sister, Jenny Shoup; to my brother-in-law, Jim Plant; to my nephew, Jake Plant; and to *mon ti lapin,* Francois Dubois. I love you all so much, it chokes me up sometimes.

Publisher's Acknowledgments

Executive Editor: Lindsay Sandman Lefevere

Project Editor: Elizabeth Kuball

Copy Editor: Elizabeth Kuball

Technical Editor: Caroline Colom Vasquez

Project Coordinator: Patrick Redmond

Cover Image: © iStockphoto.com/artvea

Math & Science

Algebra I For Dummies,
2nd Edition
978-0-470-55964-2

Anatomy and Physiology
For Dummies,
2nd Edition
978-0-470-92326-9

Astronomy For Dummies,
3rd Edition
978-1-118-37697-3

Biology For Dummies,
2nd Edition
978-0-470-59875-7

Chemistry For Dummies,
2nd Edition
978-1-1180-0730-3

Pre-Algebra Essentials
For Dummies
978-0-470-61838-7

Microsoft Office

Excel 2013 For Dummies
978-1-118-51012-4

Office 2013 All-in-One
For Dummies
978-1-118-51636-2

PowerPoint 2013
For Dummies
978-1-118-50253-2

Word 2013 For Dummies
978-1-118-49123-2

Music

Blues Harmonica
For Dummies
978-1-118-25269-7

Guitar For Dummies,
3rd Edition
978-1-118-11554-1

iPod & iTunes
For Dummies,
10th Edition
978-1-118-50864-0

Programming

Android Application
Development For
Dummies, 2nd Edition
978-1-118-38710-8

iOS 6 Application
Development For Dummies
978-1-118-50880-0

Java For Dummies,
5th Edition
978-0-470-37173-2

Religion & Inspiration

The Bible For Dummies
978-0-7645-5296-0

Buddhism For Dummies,
2nd Edition
978-1-118-02379-2

Catholicism For Dummies,
2nd Edition
978-1-118-07778-8

Self-Help & Relationships

Bipolar Disorder
For Dummies,
2nd Edition
978-1-118-33882-7

Meditation For Dummies,
3rd Edition
978-1-118-29144-3

Seniors

Computers For Seniors
For Dummies,
3rd Edition
978-1-118-11553-4

iPad For Seniors
For Dummies,
5th Edition
978-1-118-49708-1

Social Security
For Dummies
978-1-118-20573-0

Smartphones & Tablets

Android Phones
For Dummies
978-1-118-16952-0

Kindle Fire HD
For Dummies
978-1-118-42223-6

NOOK HD For Dummies,
Portable Edition
978-1-118-39498-4

Surface For Dummies
978-1-118-49634-3

Test Prep

ACT For Dummies,
5th Edition
978-1-118-01259-8

ASVAB For Dummies,
3rd Edition
978-0-470-63760-9

GRE For Dummies,
7th Edition
978-0-470-88921-3

Officer Candidate Tests,
For Dummies
978-0-470-59876-4

Physician's Assistant Exam
For Dummies
978-1-118-11556-5

Series 7 Exam
For Dummies
978-0-470-09932-2

Windows 8

Windows 8 For Dummies
978-1-118-13461-0

Windows 8 For Dummies,
Book + DVD Bundle
978-1-118-27167-4

Windows 8 All-in-One
For Dummies
978-1-118-11920-4

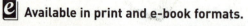 **Available in print and e-book formats.**